THE JOURNALS OF THOMAS HUBBARD HOBBS

THOMAS HUBBARD HOBBS
PORTRAIT BY JOHN ANTROBUS, 1856
Courtesy Elizabeth Hobbs Higgins Estate

THE JOURNALS OF THOMAS HUBBARD HOBBS

A CONTEMPORARY RECORD
OF AN ARISTOCRAT FROM ATHENS, ALABAMA
WRITTEN BETWEEN 1840,
WHEN THE DIARIST WAS FOURTEEN YEARS OLD,
AND 1862, WHEN HE DIED SERVING
THE CONFEDERATE STATES OF AMERICA

EDITED, WITH NOTES AND INDEX, BY

Faye Acton Axford

THE UNIVERSITY OF ALABAMA PRESS

Library of Congress Cataloging in Publication Data

Hobbs, Thomas Hubbard, 1826–1862.
The Journals of Thomas Hubbard Hobbs.

Includes index.
1. Athens, Ala.—Social life and customs.
2. Southern States—Social life and customs—
1775–1865. 3. Hobbs, Thomas Hubbard, 1826–1862.
I. Axford, Faye Acton. II. Title.
F334.A8H62 976.1'98'050924 74–2819
0-8173-1289-7 (pbk: alk. paper)

MANUFACTURED IN THE UNITED STATES OF AMERICA

CONTENTS

FOREWORD

The Journals of Thomas Hubbard Hobbs are more than an autobiographical record; they are a comprehensive description of the social life and customs of a region that has been largely overlooked by social historians. The Journals reveal Hobbs in relation to all the major institutions: home, school, church, and state. Hence the work discloses, in a fascinating way, the richness of life as lived by a leading citizen of Athens, Alabama, in the mid 1800s.

However, the descriptions and observations are not limited to the one region. Today we are filled with awe in contemplating the travels of Hobbs and his friends and relatives. These journeys were made by train, riverboat, stagecoach, and horseback in all kinds of weather. There are accounts of trips to various towns outside of Alabama, including Chattanooga, Knoxville, Memphis, Atlanta, Richmond, Charlottesville, Petersburg, Baltimore, Washington, Philadelphia, Buffalo, Albany, and Brooklyn. From Virginia, the wartime Journal entries relate the experiences of the officer and his men who undergo long marches and dreary encampments, who anxiously wait for news of battles or their own destination, and who hear of casualties that include friends.

The Journals deserve careful consideration on several counts. The writer himself is a Southern gentleman of great stature who merits our interest; the social conditions in the period leading up to the Civil War are important for an understanding of the conflict and reasons for it; the numerous references to other historic figures in their relationships with Thomas Hobbs give the work a unity with the total history of the period and area.

Hobb's own interests in agriculture, music, poetry, politics, and the development of the resources of Alabama fill the pages of his Journals with information intriguing to the reader. The Journals are further enriched by the annotations of Mrs. Axford, who has supplied additional information about people and places mentioned by Hobbs. The result is not only an intimate narrative of the life of a Southern gentleman—a family man of tender sensibilities—but also a reference volume filled with information about historic places and prominent families of Alabama and elsewhere in the South.

SIDNEY E. SANDRIDGE
President
Athens College

PREFACE

The January night in a small Alabama town was enclosed in quietness, and the scratching of a quill pen was the only audible sound in the room. Suddenly there was a noise from outside. The young gentleman listened, then recorded in his journal, "Half past eleven—stage horn blowing." It was indeed the eleventh hour for a way of life in a state so recently weaned from its frontier clumsiness. Now it was spoon-fed from a cup of politics, poetry, dueling pistols, protracted camp-meetings, and involuntary servitude.

More than chronological years separate our twentieth-century existence from the world of the young diarist that night in 1847. Innumerable revolutions have shattered the placidness of mid nineteenth-century thought and pattern. The progressive diarist foresaw a few of these changes, and recorded them in the course of his life span; but he did not witness their far-reaching effects.

Young Thomas began his diary in 1840 with these words: "Thomas Hubbard Hobbs was born on the 19th of April, 1826. He never made the pilgrimage to Mecca, never invented perpetual motion, nor found out why the magnet points to the north. But he was contented to keep within its proper limits . . ." In his own evolutionary process from student to husband and father, and from legislative service to that of raising and directing his own military company, he was ever aware of the axiom penned in his youthful diary: "Learning is an acquisition, it is neither nature's endowment, nor the teacher's gift." There is interest and insight into the gradual change of thought patterns as the diarist expands agrarian horizons through exposure to the urban centers of the northeast. Here America reveled in the Romantic Age, symbolized in such buildings as the Catskill Mountain House and the St. Nicholas Hotel.

There is humor revealed in the pages, providing glimpses into nineteenth-century urbanity and provincialism. "Old Mr. Collin Hobbs asked me yesterday if land warrants would not become valueless if Congress should pass the 'Bedstead Law.' He meant, as I found out, the *Homestead Law,* now being discussed in Congress."

Thomas Hobbs' indefatigable efforts in the state legislature, were in support of a railroad from Decatur to Elyton, which led eventually to the building of Birmingham. He made countless speeches on behalf of free school development in the state, and he introduced the bill providing for an institution for the deaf, dumb, and blind. As a novice legislator, he had presented a bill calling for the opening of legislative sessions with prayer. Soon after the bill had passed in the house, the senate also adopted the practice.

The diaries, depicting events of state, national, and international importance, form a continuity and content rarely found, a fact recognized and appreciated by the distinguished historian of Virginia, Douglas Southall Freeman. The original diaries are now in the possession of The University of Alabama, where they were placed in the spring of 1973 by the descendants of Thomas Hobbs.

The editor has selected the Journal text included within this volume. Ellipses indicate omissions within the Journal entries but not at the beginning or end of an entry. In rare instances only has the punctuation been changed for the purpose of clarity. The later Journals are filled with newspaper clippings that Hobbs attached at various dates, making these Journals serve also as scrapbooks. It has not been possible here to reproduce all such clippings, although some articles are retained. Included with the diary text are explanatory notes and identifications, which are intended as aids to the amateur historian and casual reader. Typographer's marks (*, **, †, §) are used to relate these notes and identifications to the particular statements in the diary text whenever the relation might not be entirely obvious.

INTRODUCTION

Aristocratic holders of worn Virginia lands joined in the vast exodus to Limestone County, Alabama, in the first decades of the nineteenth century. They bought large tracts of the newly ceded lands, and engraved their personalities into the homes they built. Occasionally those of the planter class erected houses reminiscent of the finest in the Old Dominion; while others were content to remain in their log houses, with random additions necessitated by growing families and preeminence within the community. Some of the county's wealthiest citizens lived in such a manner, including among others, Nicholas Davis, James Hurt Gamble, and Major Thomas Maclin.

Major Maclin, maternal grandfather of Thomas Hubbard Hobbs, had inherited a spirit of service to his native Brunswick County, Virginia. His ancestor, William Maclin, sat on the bench as a King's Justice upon the formation of Brunswick in 1732. William and John Maclin, brothers, served as vestrymen of St. Andrew's Parish, which incorporated that area. Major Thomas Maclin represented Brunswick in both houses of the Virginia legislature prior to the War of 1812.

When Major Maclin pitted his thoroughbreds in Limestone County against those of Nicholas Davis, Samuel Ragland, Nathaniel Terry, and others, he was carrying forward a long-established tradition. Recorded evidence shows that horses from the Maclin stables raced against those from such well-known Virginia plantations as Mt. Airy, Mt. Vernon, and Westover.

Thomas and Julia Edmonds Maclin had nine children in Brunswick County. Julia died after the birth of their last child in 1818, and although several of the children made the move to Limestone with Major Maclin, only two were living in 1840—Rebecca Maclin Hobbs, and Dr. Benjamin Maclin.

Soon after Rebecca's graduation from a Philadelphia finishing school, she was married to Ira Hobbs. Their families had been friends long before that portion of Brunswick County in which the Hobbs lived was incorporated in Greensville in 1795. Hubbard Hobbs, a Revolutionary soldier, and his wife Martha Meredith, raised a large family before Hubbard's death in 1817. Martha came to Alabama with the family around 1820. The oldest son, John, settled in Madison County where he owned extensive acreage, including the Tennessee River island that still bears his name. Dr. David Hobbs, his brother, Ira, and several sisters were among those who settled Limestone lands near Major Maclin.

Realizing the need for educational and social advantages afforded by Athens life, Ira and Rebecca Hobbs purchased lots in 1836, and built a large home on Marion Street. There was much more space than was needed for Ira, Rebecca, and their only child, Thomas. They were thus fulfilling a sense of obligation which they felt to the community, for there were always visiting ministers to be housed and students to be boarded. Since there were no dormitory facilities at the female institute where Rebecca served as principal, the Hobbs family joined other leading citizens in providing for nonresident students attending both the male and female academies in Athens.

In the 1840s Athens was known as the most moral town in Alabama. Although stocks and pillories were still in evidence on the courthouse green in 1840, they were seldom used and were removed soon after. The hanging tree at the foot of the courthouse hill served as a grim deterrent to crime, though executions were rare.

The most powerful influence in the small town was of the Protestant persuasion. Three denominations, Methodist, Baptist, and Presbyterian, had met in the Union Church until 1836, when the Methodists built their own house of worship. The dedication of the Presbyterian Church in 1852 comes within the scope of the diaries.

Rebecca Maclin Hobbs was considered the mother of the local Methodist Church, having taught school and sold her jewelry (with the exception of one gold watch), to pay off an original deficit in the building fund. It was largely through Rebecca's efforts, while serving as principal of the female academy, that the Methodist Church was persuaded to elevate the academy to collegiate status. Rebecca's family deeded the land upon which the college was built, and Dr. Benjamin Maclin is credited with having been the largest single contributor to the building fund. This building, Founders Hall, was erected with the aid of others, notably the Malone and Coleman families.

Ira Hobbs, a carpenter at heart, supervised work on the building's interior, which still serves as a focal point for college and community activities. Weddings are held in its chapel, and receptions in the parlor, where hang portraits of Major Thomas and Dr. Benjamin Maclin, Ira and Thomas Hobbs, John Nicholas, and Dr. Stith Malone. Rebecca's portrait is in the school Library, which is in a wing added to the original structure.

THE JOURNALS OF THOMAS HUBBARD HOBBS

THOMAS MACLIN, GRANDFATHER OF THOMAS
DATE AND ARTIST UNKNOWN
Courtesy Maclin H. Frierson, Athens, Alabama

ATHENS, ALABAMA 1840-1841

November 2, 1840. The young ladies of the Female Academy visited us at the Institute today, viz., Misses Abernathy, Bass, Binford, and Keyes. . . . I was honored tonight with the presence of Miss Jane Keyes, who was very interesting in conversation.

The Female Academy, forerunner of Athens College, was at this time under the leadership of the Rev. Simpson Shepherd. Sarah Catharine Abernathy was the daughter of Jesse and Sarah Bailey Abernathy and stepdaughter of David Blackburn. Maria, Octavia, and Harriet Bass were daughters of Thomas, proprietor of the Bass Hotel, which stood on the southeast corner of the courthouse square in Athens. This hotel stood on the site of an early trading post established for Indian trade by 1810. Lucy Binford was the daughter of Addison, one of the county's wealthiest and most progressive planters. Lucy married Dr. Thomas Brandon, of a prominent Huntsville family, in 1842. Jane and Martha Keyes were daughters of George, and granddaughters of Revolutionary Captain John Wade Keyes, for whom the local DAR chapter is named. The Keyes family remained close to Thomas Hobbs throughout his life. Jane later married General John Rather, and Martha married Judge Henry C. Jones. Chancellor Wade Keyes, assistant attorney general for the Confederacy; Dr. John Washington, and George Presley ("Pres") Keyes were brothers of Jane and Martha, and close friends of Thomas.—Limestone County Records.

November 4th, 1840. Heard a political speech from Dr. Spottswood and a Mr. Sykes from Decatur.

Dr. John Spottswood (or Spotswood) was the first druggist in Athens. He later moved to Huntsville, and is listed in the 1859 directory as being located at #15, Commercial Row, south side of the square. Here he sold, among other items, surgeons' instruments and supplies, paints, oils, spices, Landreth's garden seed, and almanacs. James Turner Sykes, president of the Decatur branch of the State Bank, represented Morgan County in the legislature in 1828.—McClellan, 24.

7th. Tonight I composed 3 pieces of poetry, an acrostic on my name, the speech of the Scythian ambassador to Alexander, and a piece to Scott, who was nodding before me; commenced reading Shakespeare, at the

Two Gentle[*men*] *of Verona.* Pa bought me a cassinet coat from Messrs. Hine and Brother.† . . . The acrostic:

The God, who made us all
Heaven, Earth and Creature, too,
Omniscient, omnipresent, wise,
Made *all* things good;
And stubborn man looks on,
Sees all, and then denies his being.

How poor, how rich, how august, Man!

How complicate, how wonderful, is he!
Of all God's creatures, wisest, best
Best not in form alone
But best in faculty of reason
Surest and strongest faculty of all.

†Roswell and William Anson Hine owned a mercantile and real estate business on the south side of the square. Roswell, 1811–1878, married Mary, daughter of John Petway and Sally Hobbs Malone, and had one daughter, Betty. After Mary's death in 1841, Roswell and Betty lived for a time with the Hobbs family. Betty then finished school in Philadelphia and married Dr. Nicholas Davis Richardson, son of William and Ann Davis Richardson. During the Civil War, Roswell Hine buried a sum of gold in the cellar of this store, and then evacuated the city while it was under siege. The store was burned, but the gold remained hidden, and it was the means by which Roswell purchased the William Richardson home for Betty and her husband. William Anson Hine, 1822–1894, married Leticia Sloss, daughter of Joseph, and lived in the home on Jefferson Street now owned by Dr. and Mrs. D. J. Wilson.—Pat Jones, "The Richardson Home," May 19, 1935; Hine Family Papers.

November 8, 1840. Went to Sunday School, and with Leonidas McCracken,* examined the geological formation of the earth, and also some of the objections to the Mosaic account, where Mr. E. H. English (our teacher)** gave us three arguments against the doctrine that the earth is eternal which are these: I. If the earth is eternal, the same causes which exist now, have existed ever since the earth existed. Philosophers tell us there exists under the surface of the earth, fires, which continually consume the internal parts of the earth, and that in some places on the globe, there is nothing but shell, the portions underneath being consumed by these fires. Now if the earth existed from eternity, these fires also existed, and would have consumed this world by the present time. II. If the earth existed eternally, man must have existed also, because the earth could not have created him, for we know that it has not the power to create, neither could he have formed himself, (for the thing created is always less than the creator) and to say that he is greater than himself is absurd, thus we see if the earth is eternal, man is also, and if man were eternal, the population of the world would be a great [deal] larger. III. We see in the various functions of nature (germination, the formation of rain, etc.) a design, and we know that the earth cannot design; therefore, we conclude that there must be a designor [*sic*], who existed eternally. We, therefore conclude that if Moses is true in this account, on which all the others depend, he must be right in the rest; for logically, when we lay down a number of propositions, depending on each other, and no one of them can be disproven, the rest are considered true also. Went to church at 11 o'clock, and heard a sermon . . . another at night . . . by Geo. W. Kelso.

*"Mac was the quintessence of eccentricity; his wife one of the best women of the world. . . . Their son, Leonidas, was a sprightly, intelligent boy. He was raised in a drug store and afterwards was a physician. He was exceedingly neat in his person."—Tanner, July 28, 1876.

**Elbert H. English represented Limestone County in the 1839 legislature. In 1840 he married Julia Agnes Fisher, daughter of Jacob, and moved shortly after to Little Rock, Arkansas, where he practiced law and rose to the position of chief justice of the supreme court in that state. Patriarch of the English family in Limestone County was Captain James English, listed in the 1820 census as having nine in his family, with eleven slaves. He settled near Swan Creek, south of Athens, at English's Springs, which was one of three locations contending for the county seat in 1818. Cambridge, some four miles east of Athens, and Athens were the other contenders. Athens is said to have won by two votes only.—McClellan , 3; Brewer, 324.

November 9, 1840. Went to Mr. Stanley and had my coat cut. I there measured and found that I was 4 feet 9 inches high. I did not go to school today, because it was the presidential election, and Mr. Fraser wished to come in, and vote; therefore a great many people in town, and a good deal of excitement. I went down to the sale of the property of Mrs. Mary Lane, where I bought two books, Cowper's *Task* and Whelpley's *Compend of History.*

The presidential campaign of William Henry Harrison and John Tyler was the most exciting, perhaps, in American politics until that time. It was the first in which large political meetings and processions were held. The number of powerful Whigs in north Alabama had swayed many votes to the "Tippecanoe and Tyler, too" camp. A close personal friend of John Tyler, General Jesse Winston Garth, lived in Morgan County. Other strong Whigs in the area were Captain Nicholas Davis and Judge Arthur Hopkins.—Owen, III, 641.

10th. Read six pages in Cowper's *Task.* I am much pleased with it, his language is plain and beautiful, his style elegant.
11th. Went to church and heard a sermon from the Rev. Joshua Boucher.

The Reverend Joshua Boucher, 1782–1845, came to Madison County from Kentucky in 1808. He was the first minister in the Limestone Circuit, organized in 1818, and the first minister of the Methodist Church in Athens. So that the good reverend would lose no time in his preaching endeavors, he is said to have been buried standing up in the old Athens Cemetery on East Washington Street! There is no written evidence, however, to substantiate this allegation.—Lazenby, 69, 70.

November 13, 1840. Went to school today, but did not stay the whole of the morning, because the boys came home to see the circus, which came up this morning; they had a cameleopard which was 17 feet high,* and an [*sic*] gazelle: but I did not go, because ma and pa were not willing. Mr. Thos. Maddin (our presiding elder) came down this evening, and our first quarterly meeting will commence tomorrow; we all fasted today in accordance with the rules of our church.** I received a cat today for the purpose of procuring its skeleton, which I shall do in a short time. Read a few pages in Comstock, and the IX Psalm.

*This animal might have been the same one that in Montgomery during December, 1840, was billed as the first living giraffe to be exhibited in the United States.—Blue, 90.

**Thomas Maddin came to Alabama in 1819 as the second pastor of the Cataco Circuit, composed of Cataco (later Morgan) and Lawrence counties. A trustee of the Athens Female Institute, he remained active in the ministry over sixty years. Maddin had three distinguished sons: Dr. Thomas, Jr., (classmate and close friend of Hobbs) who was a professor of medicine at the University of Nashville (later Peabody) for fifty years; Dr. John, who practiced with his brother; and Ferdinand Maddin, an educator.—Lazenby, 73, 1063; McGregor, 53.

November 18, 1840. Read one of *Alexander's Weekly Messengers* to-night, where I found that the population of Mobile is 12,700.
November 21st, 1840. I arose this morning some time before sunrise, and copied some of Cowper's beauties. . . . There are great rejoicings in town to-night, the Whigs being victorious so far as heard from, have illuminated the Court-house, and their own houses. They with the rabble, are hallooing and whooping, and firing, as if, an important victory

had been won, over our most inveterate enemy. How it pains me, thus to see our citizens, thus rejoicing at their brothers' defeat! May I never be so carried by party principles, as to forget the rules of *decency* and *order*.

The *Southern Advocate*, a Whig newspaper in Huntsville, of December 10, 1840, praised the Whigs for their fine conduct in the election.

22nd. I went to Sunday School, and examined the creation of light. But how did we have light before the creation of the sun? The matter of which light is composed pervaded universal nature, and thereby we had light; but on the fourth day, God gathered the light into one place, or in other words made the sun; and the revolution of the earth caused night and day.

28th. Made a toothbrush of hickory bark for one of the ladies, and this evening played "cat" on the square with Hon. E. H. English and Mr. R. Shepherd.

"One-eyed-cat," forerunner of baseball, was still being widely played, for the "great American game" had made its debut in Cooperstown only in the previous year.

December 8, 1840. I received a beautiful butterfly, from Miss Lucy L. Binford, for which I give [*sic*] her both [hands. In place of the word, Hobbs sketched two small hands.]

9th. I read . . . in the *Edinburg*[*h*] *Review*.

11th. I went to the examination today and came off pretty well. There were a good many people present, as many as our house would well hold. Today Thornton was hung in Huntsville.

"A man by the name of White was murdered and robbed about four miles from town on the Brown's Ferry Road; . . . The robbers were followed, one captured just going off the far end of the old bridge at Nashville, and the other in Franklin, Ky., and were brought back by Col. H. H. Higgins, were tried, found guilty and one of them was executed here and the other in Huntsville: their names were Thornton."—Tanner, July 7, 1876.

11th. I returned from Grandpa's today,* after having spent my vacation of one month down there. I went to school to Mr. Fraser and there were but 4 of us present, but in the evening we were augmented by 3 others, making in all seven.** Tonight I heard a phrenologist, by the name of Worster, lecture; he has a good many followers, and some few opposers.† He examined the heads of Major Higgins, and John Tanner,§ and told their characters tolerably well.

*Major Thomas Maclin lived on his plantation, Slopeside, in the Quid Nunc area, between Swan Creek and the Tennessee River. Calhoun Community College is now on a portion of the Hobbs plantation, as well as the General Motors steering plant now being erected. It was at Slopeside that Tom would make his home after marriage.

**John Fraser, 1801–1882, was born in Petersburg, Virginia. He married Martha A. Wyche, 1807–1882, a cousin of Tom Hobbs from Brunswick County, Virginia. John Fraser continued to prepare young gentlemen for college in his Classical Institute until a few years before his death.

†The ancient science of phrenology had been revived by Dr. Francis Gall around 1800, and his popularity still abounded on the American interior, as evidenced in the debate held in Athens on January 21st, 1841, when William Keyes selected Dr. Gall as the greatest man in history.

§Major Hiram Higgins, 1802–1874, apparently promoted to brigadier general during the Civil War, was born in Mt. Sterling, Kentucky. He married Elizabeth Elliott, sister of Rev. James Elliott, in 1828. The 1850 census of Limestone lists four children: Mary Lane, Samuel, Hiram, and Nancy. Major Higgins is credited with the design and building of the Athens Courthouse of 1834, and subsequent ones in Moulton, Alabama, and Pontotoc, Mississippi. He designed Founders Hall for the Athens Female Institute, built in 1843, and in 1845 altered the Beaty-Mason home on Beaty Street, the columns of which are similar in design to those of Founders Hall. John Tanner, to whom we are indebted for having written a history of Athens, was the son of Samuel, 1787–1874. Samuel, born in South Hampton County, Virginia, was a merchant and the first mayor of Athens. John was also mayor for several terms, and in 1888 was the Vice-Presidential candidate on the Prohibition ticket.—Owen, IV, 1643; Mason Scrapbooks, Vol. I.

January 12, 1841. I went to school, as usual, and recited my lessons tolerably well. Today Thomas Wood came to board with us, and to go to school, which makes our number eight. I anticipate great pleasure this session, from my associations, and from learning, which is the fountainhead of happiness.

13th. We were increased by 3 today, which makes our number eleven. My studies this session are Latin, Graeca Majora, Algebra, Geometry, Reading, Writing and Spelling. This evening I cut some wood, and found it fine exercise.

January 15th, 1841. I went to the Juvenile Debating Society; we reorganized it, and received all those who were willing to join us in the acquirement of useful knowledge.

17th. This evening at 3 o'clock, a Temperance meeting was held, and we had an address from Mr. Richard Shepherd, a very good one, too.

18th. I went to school. . . . when I arrived there, I found that the boys had gone down to a pond near by, to skate, or rather, slide. We had fine fun.

20th. I found today that Sir Issac Newton supposes "that if the world were compressed so that there would be no pores in it, it would be no larger than a cubic inch."

21st. I went down to prayers, which were at seven. I learned today that the tune of "Yankee Doodle" was made by a doctor in the British army, in ridicule of the Americans in 1755. I went up tonight to hear Mr. Kelso teach some boys stenography.

22nd. I went to the debate tonight, and we debated the question, Who was the greatest man that ever lived? I took [George] Washington; William Keyes,* Dr. Gall; John W. Keyes, LaFayette; Laertes Keyes, Alexander the Great. The president decided in favor of Washington. I had my hair trimmed today.

*William and Laertes Keyes were sons of Washington Keyes, twin brother of George Keyes. Washington Keyes was an early merchant in Mooresville. For an interesting account of the Keyes family, see Pat Jones, *The Story of Mooresville,* 13–14.

January 25th, 1841. I saw the following piece in the *South-Western Christian Advocate,* "The largest library in the world is said to be the one in the British Museum. It contains more than half a million of printed books, and a hundred and twenty thousand manuscripts. . . . The number of newspapers in England is about 240, and the annual average number of convictions for murder is 13 or 14. The number of papers in Spain a few years ago was *one,* & the number of convictions for murder was upwards of 1200. "A little learning is a dangerous thing."

31st. I found it raining this morning when I arose, and it has continued all day; so we've had no preaching, nor Sunday School. I spent the day in reading, and teaching the Negroes to read. I intend to give them a testament, as soon as I can obtain one, with large print.

Although a law had been passed in 1832 forbidding the teaching of slaves to read because of the flood of abolitionist literature, this law was not strictly observed by progressive masters. The Hobbs and Maclin families were noted for their efforts in the educational and spiritual enlightenment of their slaves. The first Negro church in the area, Fraser's Chapel, was built after the Civil War through the donation of land and money by Dr. Benjamin Maclin, the uncle of Thomas Hobbs.—Mason Scrapboks, Vol. II.

February 5th, 1841. Today, Mr. Fraser gave me, & my classmate Samuel Matthews, the subject for our next essay, viz., A well spent youth.

Samuel Matthews was the son of Luke and Judith Peete Matthews, of Cotton Hill plantation on the township road leading from Brown's Ferry to Huntsville. Luke bought the land at the Huntsville Land Sales of 1818, and built a commodious house there around 1830, possibly in anticipation of the sixteen children he would have by Judith, and his second wife, Lucy Ann Spotswood.—Pat Jones, "The Rowe Home," June 23, 1935.

8th. Benjamin Allen came to board with us today.

Benjamin Allen, 1829–1855, was the son of the Reverend James Wilburn Allen, 1801–1858, a Methodist minister. Allen opposed Hobbs in the legislative campaign of 1855, but died before the election.

15th. Shall I go to school today? Yes, I beleive I will go, and see what I can learn. So away I go jogging along through wood and field to the sacred grounds of the Classical Institute, to hear the instructions which drop from the mouth of Mr. John Fraser, Professor of ancient languages, Natural Philosophy, etc.

16th. I went to a meeting of the Juvenile Musical society which held its first meeting tonight, we conducted it only tolerably well: we played several tunes together.

February 17th, 1841. Recited over 100 lines of Latin, and made a finish of the 10th book of the *Aeneid.* I am much pleased with the poetry and likewise the style of Virgil.

20th. I spent the day in roving about in search of curiosities; etc. I found six different kinds of moss on one old stump, which I brought home and placed in a safe place.

22nd. I did not go to school today, on account of the celebration of Washington's birthday. . . . The Philomathic Society, of which I am a member, celebrated it by 3 speeches, delivered by Robert C. Brickell,* Leonidas McCracken, & Mr. E. H. English, our president. . . . We met at Mr. Bass' hotel at 10, and marched to the Court-House, headed by suitable music, under command of Col^{n} E. J. Jones.**

*Robert Coman Brickell, 1824–1900, became recognized as one of the great legal minds of the country. This son of Richard and Margaret Coman Brickell assumed manhood at an early age, as the oldest of six fatherless children. Richard Brickell was the first state printer, published the first newspaper in Franklin (now Colbert) County, the *Franklin Enquirer*, in 1824, and was editing the *Athens Athenian* at the time of his death. Robert Brickell studied law under Judge Daniel Coleman, went into practice with Luke Pryor, and later moved to Huntsville to become a partner in the firm of Walker, Cabiness, and Brickell. He later became chief justice of the Alabama supreme court.—Owen, III, 214.

**Egbert J. Jones, 1820–1861, practiced law in Athens after graduating from the University of Virginia Law School. In 1844–45 he represented Limestone County in the legislature, and raised a company of men for service in the Mexican War the following year. The diaries record several events in Col. Jones' life, including an account of his death following the Battle of First Manassas.—Owen, III, 928.

February 23, 1841. I borrowed a Hedge's *Logic* from L. McCracken, from which I learned that "logic is to direct the intellectual powers in the investigation of truth, and the communication of it to others. . . ."
26th. I took a music lesson from Miss Shepherd, who has undertaken to teach Thomas Wood and myself the notes of the flute. . . . I can fill the plate tolerably well now; Pa will send for one for me when Hine & Bro. go on after goods, which will be in a short time.

Mary Shepherd, daughter of Rev. Simpson Shepherd, assisted her father at the Female Academy.

March 1, 1841. This is court week, and court has been called; there is one criminal case, of a certain Lowe, who moved his trial from Lawrence County.
March 3, 1841. I did not go to school this morning, in expectation of the criminal trial. I went to prayer meeting to-night, where I heard an exhortation from Mr. DeWoody; . . . and had several prayers from Mr. Hilliard, Nelson and others.

Samuel DeWoody, one of the charter members of the Methodist Church in Athens, was one of the trustees to whom George Malone deeded the land upon which the Cambridge Camp Ground was established in 1832. At one time Samuel owned the old stagecoach inn in Mooresville. The DeWoody family later moved to Iuka, Mississippi.—Tanner, July 7, 1876; Pat Jones, *Mooresville,* 13.

Judge Frederick Nelson came to Limestone in 1817. One of his sons, Frederick, Jr., was killed in the Mexican War; other sons, Tom, Stephen, S. O., and Owen became successful businessmen, Owen being one of the founders of Sheffield, Alabama.—Owen, IV, 1271.

12th. I found two wild silk-worms in the woods near the Institute, which I brought home and secured until they shall hatch.
April 1, 1841. I went to school as early as usual, and played a game of shinny or bandy. Finished the 11th book of the *Aeneid;* also finished Mair's *Introduction to Latin Syntax.* I am reading Comstock's *Physiology,* which I borrowed from L. McCracken; I am very much pleased with it.
May 16, 17, 18, 19, 1841. This time is distinguished for the falling of the "honey dew." This is a certain kind of thick dew, sticky, and very sweet, hence its name. I examined, but could discover no difference in

the weather, clouds, or state of the atmosphere. I was told by an old man that it falls about once every 15 years, and has fallen several times in his life.

SLOPESIDE, THE HOBBS PLANTATION EIGHT MILES SOUTH OF ATHENS
Courtesy Robert Womack, from original drawing by Thomas Hobbs, Hobbs Family Papers

LA GRANGE COLLEGE, ALABAMA 1844-1845

Although Thomas Hobbs did not resume his regular diary recording until 1844, he became a student of La Grange College in 1842, as evidenced by the various debate topics recorded in July of that year. A few of these titles indicate the issues at the time: "Should Capital Punishment be Inflicted for Any Crime?," "Should Slavery Be Tolerated?," "Should foreigners Be Allowed to Vote?" "Should the United States Assist Ireland if She Were to Revolt?"

It was on January 30, 1830, that the youthful president, Robert Paine, welcomed the first students to La Grange, first college in Alabama, and second Methodist college west of the Alleghenies. Sixteen years later, while Thomas Hobbs was a student, Robert Paine became a bishop in the Methodist Church. He was a man of wit and humor, a man who "did not interfere with the innocent hilarity of youth," as Rev. Richard Rivers wrote of him. No better accolade could be paid the character of Robert Paine than the story of the carriage ride. Having learned that some mischievous students planned to take his carriage to the foot of La Grange Mountain on a given night, Dr. Paine secreted himself in the carriage and closed the curtains. The boys came, rolled the carriage out of the carriage house and stole down the mountain, stopping to rest at intervals. At one of these times, Dr. Paine pulled back the curtains, thanked them for the ride, and suggested that they return to the school. The boys expected severe reprimands, but the sagacious educator forgot to mention the incident to the faculty!

In 1844 the faculty consisted of Dr. Henry Tutwiler, Dr. Carlos G. Smith, and Joseph Towler. Dr. Tutwiler was recipient of the first Master of Arts degree conferred by the University of Virginia. After teaching chemistry and math at La Grange for seven years, he established the famed Green Springs School in Greene (in what is now Hale) County, Alabama, and in 1866 discovered the "New Star," although he was never given proper credit for it. Among his children was Julia Strudwick Tutwiler, one of the state's most prominent women. Dr. Carlos Smith, professor of Ancient and Modern Languages, served later as president of The University of Alabama. Joseph Towler, tutor of the freshman class, practiced medicine in Columbia, Tennessee, after leaving La Grange.

Before a student could enter the college, he was required to translate four books of Caesar's *Gallic Wars,* six books of Virgil's *Aeneid,* Jacob's or Felton's *Greek Reader,* and one book of Xenophon's *Anabasis.*

Tuition and servant's attendance amounted to $26 a session in 1845, with board and laundry being an additional $10 a month. The first session began in July, and the second late in January.

July 4th, 1844. This is the sixty-eight anniversary of American Independence. It is celebrated throughout the United States by . . . bonfires, and other manifestations of public joy and gratitude. . . . We have no celebration here today, and it is the dryest "fourth" that I have ever seen. . . . I neglected at the close of last session to secure a room, and I am compelled to be here. . . . The Senior Class, of which I am a member . . . will be studying Natural Philosophy, Chemistry, Agricultural Chemistry, Astronomy, Mental Philosophy, Political Economy, Terence's Plays, and a Greek play. . . . G. Presley Keyes [and I] are both boarding with Professor Tutwiler, together with . . . Coe, Smith, and Mason.

Jesse Coe, Jr., was the son of one of the original trustees of La Grange College. Jesse, Sr., is listed in the Limestone County census of 1820 as the head of a family of five, with forty slaves, an unusual number in Alabama at that time. Wyndham Mason, apparently called "Wynn," later moved to Nashville and became a prominent citizen there.—Tanner, July 21, 1876.

7th. Saturday night is the time for the meeting of the LaFayette Literary Society, of which I have the honor to be a member. . . . We debated the policy of annexing Texas, and the decision was in favour of the affirmative.

9th. Recited this morning . . . Greek, a part of one of the dialogues of Socrates, just before his death. . . . I am reading Prescott's *Mexico,* and am really astonished at the civilization, yea, refinement, of the Indian tribes when first visited by Cortes.

July 22nd, 1844. Since writing last I have taken a jaunt to Florence, in company with six of my school fellows. There was a barbecue at a spring near that place, and so we chartered a waggon . . . and about twelve miles brought us to the bridge.* This bridge across the Tennessee is about a half a mile long, supported by six stone piers. We saw about the middle of it where it had been struck by lightning some time since. A small, trifling steamboat, called the *Muscle,* came up while we were there. There is, near the bank of [the] river, a circular mound, near 40 or 50 feet high, supposed to have been raised by the Indians, but for what purpose, no one can tell.** . . . [At the barbecue] we found Senator Terry speaking . . . hurling invectives against the other (Whig) Party.† While we were eating . . . a small cannon was fired . . . 26 times in honor of the U. S. and once for Texas. Saw Gen. George S. Houston,§ who has just returned from Congress.

*This bridge was built by the Florence Bridge Company in 1840. It originally had eight spans, but two of the piers had been destroyed by a cyclone. The bridge was burned in 1862 by Confederate cavalrymen under Colonel Helm, and an eyewitness described the steel on the burning bridge as "curling up like red ribbon."—Douglas, taped interview; Leftwich, 80–81.

**This mound is the largest in the Tennessee Valley, 43 feet in height, and having a diameter of 145 by 94 feet at the summit. It was obviously used as a ceremonial mound.—Tennessee Valley Historical Society, 33.

†Senator Nathaniel Terry had served four times as president of the senate while representing Limestone County between 1837 and 1844. He was defeated in this gubernatorial campaign by another Limestone Countian, Joshua Martin. Terry moved to Texas soon after this election.—William Garrett, 168.

§With the exception of one term, George Smith Houston, 1811–1879, served in Congress from 1841 until the secession of Alabama, and it was he who presented the formal withdrawal to the Speaker of the House on that occasion. Houston served as chairman of the Military Affairs, Ways and Means, and Judiciary committees in Congress. He was first married to Mary Beaty, 1815–1856, daughter of Robert, a founder of Athens. After Mary's death, he married Ellen, daughter of James Irvine, prominent lawyer of Florence.—Owen, III, 848.

July 23rd, 1844. Recited in [Political Economy] to Mr. Paine, or I should say Dr. Paine, for the title of D. D. was lately appended to his name . . . by the Wesleyan University.

29th. Slept on a pallet on the floor, leaving the entire bed to Pres, who was quite sick . . . all day yesterday . . . he has recovered tho' now, and ready to destroy as many watermelons as ever. . . . Last evening . . . Jesse Coe laid down after dinner, as most college boys do on Sunday evening, to enjoy a nap. While he was going to sleep, two of the boys went into the garret above his room . . . for the purpose of having some sport. Another party in the meantime collected around the sleeper for the purpose of burning him with "cotton fleas." Just at this moment one of the party above, by a false step, broke the plaster of Jesse's room. The noise of the fall, of course, awakened him, and as he arose, those standing around him ran off for fear of detection. Jesse, being startled by the noise of the falling plastering, and noticing . . . his companions all running away fast, concluded that there was an earthquake, and accordingly, he took to his heels and scampered downstairs, far surpassing . . . his pleased companions, nor did he stop running until he reached the lowest story.

July 31st, 1844. Professor T. . . . gave me a small piece of zinc and some copper wire, with which Pierce and I succeeded in electrifying a grasshopper's legs . . . made many experiments with this simple apparatus.

August 5th. Mr. L. Garrett,* who is a candidate for Major-General, sent up three waggons for the students to go down and vote for him. The waggons were filled . . . and started for Tuscumbia. The students marched boldly to the polls, many of us to vote for the first time . . . hereafter the candidates for military offices may not disregard me.** Several Germans went down with us and seemed to think that the welfare of the whole country depended solely on their votes! Poor fellows, where they were born they have no such privilege. . . . I confidently believe that these poor foreigners would have ridden forty miles to exercise the power which every American lad trifles with.

*Lewis Garrett was successful in his candidacy. Saunders refers to "General" Lewis Garrett, of Huntsville and Tuscumbia, who married Sarah Hubbel, became wealthy, and bought a plantation on the Arkansas River.—Saunders, 54.

**Apparently, the only requisite for voting in militia elections was to get there. The German laborers were on La Grange Mountain as a result of the Immigration Societies, which had been organized in the 1840s to bring in white laborers.

August 9th, 1844. Recited Terence to Professor Smith. During the recitation one of the class fell asleep, and commenced snoring. . . . Even [Professor Smith's] gravity could not withstand this shock, he was forced to laugh, and dismissed the class, rather than wake him up. . . . Have finished Prescott's *Mexico,* and have taken out *Don Juan.* Like the poetry very much, but think a better subject might have been selected.

11th. We had an interesting debate last night on the question, "Should Foreign Immigration be Prohibited?" I was on the negative side, although I am in favor of the other. . . . Our side gained the question.

This entry is the first diary reference to the immigration laws that led to the development of the "Know-Nothing" Party of the 1850s.

August 24th, 1844. Was up last night . . . with the dead body of Mr. A. C. Harland, a tailor of this place. He died . . . just before we (Duke, Pierce, Taylor & Maddin)* arrived at his house. . . . Several of the young ladies of the hill were sitting up with her [his sick wife]. We behaved very cheerfully, considering the occasion. . . . his body was buried . . . in the public burying ground, which is situated in a shady, retired, high hill. Most of the graves are dug in the solid sand-rock.**

*William Duke was probably a son of William H. Duke, listed as a justice of the peace in Franklin County in 1820. The others are John G. Pierce, R. V. Taylor, who became a minister, and Thomas Maddin, noted previously as professor of medicine at the University of Nashville.—McGregor, 20, 53.

**The sandstone base at La Grange cemetery possibly accounts for its deplorable condition at the present time (1975). Prominent residents of the mountain and the wide valley below are buried here: Maddins, Kings, Napiers, Kumpes, and others. The broken stone of La Grange College's third president, Dr. J. W. Hardy, is almost obscured by undergrowth. The most impressive monument here, and perhaps in Alabama, is the massive tomb of Abraham Ricks. It was hauled from Tuscumbia landing in 1852, utilizing sixteen oxen and three days' time for the distance of less than ten miles.

25th. We debated the question: "Ought the poor to be supported by law?" There was, of course, great dispute as to what constitutes a poor man. The decision was given in favor of the affirmative. I was on the other side and the question [was] gained by an admission I unluckily made, that such laws *were* beneficial in England.

August 27th, 1844. Our chemistry lesson today embraced the subject of the compounds of Nitrogen and Oxygen. Of these the protoxide is most remarkable. It is commonly known as Exhilerating Gas, from its effects, when inhaled. After evening prayers, we went down to see it tried upon some of the Students. It had various effects upon them. The first, T[urner] Saunders, was pugnacious, and pursued his running antagonist. The second, [James] Lowe, said he was the "greatest speaker alive," and would give them a speech upon Texas, but he turned pugnacious also, and knocked a fellow student down flat. The last one, M[att] Clay, took atmospheric air, and chased our tailor, half dead, to his shop!

Turner Saunders, 1829–1882, was the first son of the Reverend Turner Saunders and his second wife, Henrietta Weeden Millwater, and a half brother of James Edmonds Saunders, author of *Early Settlers in Alabama.* In 1852 Turner Saunders married Marie Victoria McRae at St. Andrew's Episcopal Church in Prairieville, Alabama. Victoria was the direct descendant of the Duke of Athol, and granddaughter of Frederic Ravesies, whose family had been among the wealthiest on Santo Domingo Island before the uprising there. Frederic's mother and sister were murdered during the insurrection, and Frederic and his father escaped to Philadelphia. Frederic soon became director of the bank of Philadelphia. After the death of his first wife, Mary Roan, Frederic Ravesies married the widow of one of Napoleon's favorite generals, Davide, and they were associated with the Vine and Olive Colony in Alabama. Portraits of the Ravesies hang in Sturdivant Hall in Selma, and pictures are included in *Alabama Portraits Prior to 1870,* 289.—Winston Smith, 78.

Matt Clay was the son of Matthew, who came to Alabama in 1816 with Judge Arthur F. Hopkins and other prominent north Alabamians. The Clays, relatives of the Kentucky Clays, owned a large plantation in Lawrence County. Matt married Mary Harrison, close relative of the President, and of the Hampton family of South Carolina.—Saunders, 270, 271.

September 1st, 1844. Preaching today by the Rev. Turner Saunders. . . . The old gentleman gave us an excellent discourse. . . . Wrote home today by Major Kennerly.

Rev. Turner Saunders, 1782–1854, born in Brunswick County, Virginia, and a relative of the Maclin family, came to Lawrence County around 1818. The house that he built around 1821 stands just north of Town Creek, one of the most architectually interesting in the state. Rev. Saunders was president of the first Board of Trustees for La Grange. His stepdaughter, Mary Eliza, was the wife of Robert Paine. The two families moved later to Aberdeen, Mississippi, where Turner Saunders built another house of extant beauty, Lauri Mundi.—Robert Gamble.

Major James Kennerly was postmaster at La Grange.

September 3rd, 1844. We have taken up the study of the hydrostatic press, which is the most powerful of all machines, for by its instrumentality a child may break bars of iron which would sustain thousands of pounds.

6th. The birthday of LaFayette has come. Raise your huzzas, fire your cannon, light your illuminations! . . . We formed a procession and marched to the church, where we heard an excellent oration from our representative, W. D. S. Cook. . . . at night the fun came on. . . . the rooms and the Debating Halls were illuminated, which was beautiful—then two balloons . . . we tried to raise, but were unsuccessful—as none of us had ever attempted such a thing before. They were both burned as they started up—then came the fire balls, some of the largest and brightest I ever saw. Then a procession was formed, each man bearing a lighted candle. . . . we paraded about the village in grand style. In the meantime, some one fired an old, useless stable, and we collected around this and enjoyed ourselves.

8th. This is Pres' birthday—which he did not recollect until sitting at the supper table—he was made fifteen today, the age at which the Roman youth left school, but Pres on the contrary (oh, how unclassical!) is just commencing his collegiate course.

September 10th, 1844. Henry Malone and Junius Pulliam arrived here from Limestone last night. . . . Poor Henry! He reached home just in time to see his mother expire. I sincerely pity any man who is deprived of the tender treatment, and affectionate smiles of his mother. Long,

I pray God, may that time be when I can say that I sympathize with such a one.

Henry Booth, 1825–1868, son of George and Sally Malone, graduated from the medical school in Charleston, served as surgeon of the 4th Alabama Infantry, and lived for many years in Cincinnati, where he died unmarried. His father, George, had settled east of Athens, at Cambridge, around 1818, and built a large brick home, which burned in 1954. He gave the land for the Cambridge Camp Ground where many Methodists, including Tom Hobbs and John B. McFerrin, were converted to the faith. Among other children in this family were John Nicholas, state senator and judge, Louisa, Sarah, and James C. For several years Henry Malone kept a diary, and portions have been copied by a member of his family, Mrs. Nancy Malone Johnson, and are on file at the Athens Public Library.

19th. Have visited in Athens and home. . . . Last Saturday Judge Henry C. Jones and I left La Grange in his buggy.* . . . There are 15 interesting (and some of them beautiful, too) young ladies [at home] such as would take the eye of any youth of eighteen.**

*"The eloquent advocate" was the way in which James E. Saunders described this portly man. Willis Brewer spoke of him as "fluent and effective, and vehement in utterance." Henry Cox Jones was born in Franklin County in 1821, graduated from La Grange, and read law under Judge Daniel Coleman in Athens. Without soliciting for the office, he was elected judge of the county court of Franklin in 1841, and subsequently served in both houses of the state legislature.—Brewer, 304.

**Young ladies attending the Female Institute in Athens from other localities boarded with prominent citizens of the town. Even in those days of putting several people in one room, fifteen boarders were a prodigious number.

October 2nd, 1844. Last Saturday commenced our protracted meeting here. . . . last night at least one dozen went to be prayed for. . . . [James] Lowe seems determined to get religion, let it cost what it will.

8th. Most of the mourners prefer the silent grove to any other place, and so the professors of religion go with them there and pray and sing.

12th. Went down to Tuscumbia today to vote again. . . . We voted for J. K. Ferguson for Colonel, by the by, he paid $40 for about the same number of votes, which I consider very dear.

October 14th, 1844. This is the day appointed to the marriage of Judge H. C. Jones and Miss M. S. Keyes, to which my chum [Pres] has gone. The Judge is to be envied, for he has now the heart, and by this time, the hand of one of the sweetest girls that ever blessed a husband. . . . I have no doubt but my love for her approximates to the sincerest affection of her brother. How often have we romped and frolicked in the paternal mansion, aye, more, how often have kissed and embraced each other — whenever I returned home from college.

26th. Mrs. Tutwiler (heaven bless her) sent a servant around to wake us up. . . . Hughes has left for Conference, and so will Dr. [Paine] today . . . so we will be rid of reciting to him for the rest of the session — he will, however, return in time to examine us. . . . Last night we debated whether slavery was justifiable or not. I was on the affirmative, Cook and Maddin on the other . . . we gained the decision. Yesterday Prof. Tutwiler and I tried to raise a balloon which I had made of tissue paper — but we could not succeed, it being too porous.

November 5th. Tonight some of the students went to see the "ninth wonder of the world," as the owner calls it — that is a wild man, said to be a native of Borneo. It goes on all fours — can speak English very well. Most of those who saw it think it nothing but a deformed child.

6th. We were all on tiptoe to see the menagerie . . . exhibited here today. About nine o'clock we discovered two moving masses about two or three miles off in the valley, which we at once knew to be the elephants — soon the long train of carriages appeared in sight. As soon as they reached the top of the hill, the elephants were geared up, and attached to the music wagon. . . . We first looked at the animals — there were a lion and two lionesses, a tiger, two or three leopards, three hyenas, a quagga, and a lama [*sic*].

January 19th, 1845. The vacation is over, another session is begun. . . . I remained in town [Athens] until the young ladies left, and to Grandpa's to hunt.

22nd. A few nights since my watch was stolen from the nail over the mantel piece where it was hanging. I heard the thief when he came in — but I concluded from the noise which he made among the bucket, dipper and pan, that it was one of my fellow students, seeking for water. . . . I heard him take hold of my watch. . . . I bolted at him . . . but . . . he escaped. . . . could find no trace of him, as it was raining, we could not track him. . . . Recited before breakfast to Professor Smith in the *Oedipus Rex* of Sophocles.

25th. Mr. Tutwiler gave me two pamphlets, the remaining numbers of "Martin Chuzzlewit," by Charles Dickens, which I delivered to the Librarian of our Society. In this work I have heard that Boz brings his hero over to America, for the sole purpose of lashing us. This he did in his "American Notes," to which a countrywoman of ours has lately retorted quite severely.

26th. Actually did shave . . . for almost twelve months have I scraped the downy cheek. . . . One of our circuit preachers [Mr. Smith W. Moore] preached a plain, practical sermon today. An excellent trait in his sermon was its brevity, for it was only 30 minutes long. . . . Got a catalog of Yale College . . . 559 students, of which freshmen, 115.

The Reverend Smith W. Moore served on the faculty of the Tennessee Conference Female Institute (Athens College) and in 1852 became president of that institution. In 1853 he was elected to the chair of mental and moral philosophy at La Grange, and served as president of the college in 1853, until the election of Dr. Richard Rivers to this position. "He was a man of many accomplishments, a poet, prose writer and preacher of ability," wrote Mary Norman Moore in *History of Athens College.*

January 28th, 1845. I am reading Lester's *Condition and Fate of England,* where he relates the oppressions of the Irishmen, as also their many attempts to throw off the yoke.

30th. Before the union of the two countries, Ireland had comparatively no national debt, but now she groans under a very heavy one. In 1842, says Lester, a petition for redress and reform was carried into the House of Commons upon the shoulders of six men; it was signed by 3,500,000 names — such was its size that it was impossible for it to be carried in at the door, whole. . . . Yet, notwithstanding its size, it was rejected without a reading. . . . Played at backgammon, and beat Pierce & Pres both.

February 1st. I was engaged with others of a *special committee,* in *taking up the carpet* of LaFayette Hall. . . . scattered straw on the floor and then put it down again. . . . We had a fine debate on the question whether woman's mind is as capable of improvement as man's. Felton and I advocated the negative, while Cook and Maddin showed their gallantry on the affirmative. Our side gained the decision. . . . B. W. Maclin and J. L. Coman were elected honorary members of the Society.

James Lindley Coman, son of Dr. Joshua and Jane Lindley Coman, and grandson of Dr. Jacob Lindley, founder of Ohio University, was born in Athens. He became a prominent lawyer.—Owen, III, 383.

February 9th, 1845. Last night . . . I concluded to visit some of the ladies of the mountain; therefore Taliaferro & myself . . . went to President Paine's, where we found Miss Glover, Miss Caledonia Oliver and Miss Maria Oliver. . . . The young ladies, being divided as to politics, had a hot discussion of some of the leading points, after we had some music on the guitar, and then the fortunes of some of the ladies were tried.

David Taliaferro, son of Major Benjamin and Martha Watkins Taliaferro, became a brilliant lawyer. He was a grandson of General Benjamin Taliaferro, who served as president of the Virginia senate, was a member of the U. S. Congress, and a judge of the Superior court.—Saunders, 251.

Maria and Caledonia Oliver were daughters of John and Ruth Weeden Oliver. Maria married Dr. Stirling (or Sterling) Paine in 1847, and Caledonia married Thomas Clay, brother of Matthew, in 1845.—Saunders, 423.

February 11th, 1845. Last night I cut up some rare "shines" in the way of somnambulism.

13th. I read a part of one of James' novels, entitled *The Gypsy,* with which I am very much pleased. . . . James has an excellent style, and then he lugs in so many wise remarks upon human nature and so many moral suggestions—that one may derive a benefit from his novels. . . . went serenading tonight with Taliaferro and Turner Saunders. We were preceded by a company with tinpans drum and Jews harps, so our music sounded better from the contrast. Neither company got anything to eat.

George Payne Rainsford James, 1799–1860, English novelist, wrote *The Gypsy* in 1835.

15th. Yesterday being St. Valentine's Day, the office was crowded with documents named after this saint. There was one for me . . . confined by a ribbon instead of a seal, containing some arborvitae and a crocus flower, accompanied by these consolatory words, "May you be happy." I am, of course, very grateful to my unknown friend.

19th. Professor T., having prepared a good deal of this [exhilerating] gas, promised to give some the opportunity of taking it. . . . he brought the gas from the laboratory in a bladder. The first one who took it, Lowe, danced and commenced speaking. Another stood still. Mason exclaimed as soon as the bladder was withdrawn, "High low Jack & the game," then taking off his cap, threw it violently to the ground. . . . B. DeGraffenried seized a fellow by the hair, but was shaken from his hold, and fell on the ground. Pres . . . seemed desirous of giving every one a good stout slap.

B. DeGraffenried was probably a son of Abram Maury and Maria White DeGraffenried, a direct descendant of Baron Christopher DeGraffenried, and closely related to Matthew Fontaine Maury. Abram was the first justice of the peace in Lawrence County; the first sermon preached in the county was in his home, and he planted the first orchard in the area. He later opened a tavern on La Grange Mountain, which was on the route of the old Byler Road, one of the earliest public roads in the state.—Saunders, 310.

February 21st, 1845. Professor Smith . . . told us . . . he proposes to begin [French] as soon as we have finished the play of Sophocles. . . . About a year ago Professor Tutwiler offered to teach me. . . . Mrs. T. joined our class, and so we made considerable progress. We read two books of *Telemachus* and some in the *Henriade,* an epic poem by Voltaire.

22nd. Celebration of Washington's Birthday. . . . In due time our badges were put on, and the procession formed. I wore two badges, that of the LaFayette Society and of the Kuklos Adelphon. . . . The procession today displayed a variety of badges — there was the ribbon and rose of the LaFayette Soc., the blue sash of the Dialectical Soc., the silver pendant of the Kuklos Adelphon, the gold breast pin of the Coenochresian, the star and ribbon of the Philomathic, and lastly, the banner of the Baldheaded Buzzards. This latter company is of late origin, and their object is unknown (perhaps to themselves). On their banner (which was of red flannel!) was represented a buzzard in the act of carrying off a dead hog! On the other side was a large Jews' harp, with which instrument this company sometimes serenades the citizens. At night tho', there was a frolic . . . transparencies . . . turpentine balls. . . . One [of these fiery balls] lodged on the College. Munson and myself ran up and succeeded in extinguishing it, tho' the shingles were on fire.

February 26th, 1845. For the past two days John W. Keyes has been with us, on his way to Athens, returning from Louisville, where he has been to attend the medical lectures. . . . I think he bids fair to make an excellent physician.

John Washington Keyes became renowned both as a physician and dentist. After serving as a surgeon of the 17th Alabama Infantry Regiment, CSA, during the Civil War, he moved with the Gunter colony to Brazil. There he was dentist to Emperor Dom Pedro. John Keyes married Julia Louisa Hentz, daughter of Nicholas Marcellus and Caroline Lee Whiting Hentz, founders of the Locust Dell Academy in Florence, Alabama. Dr. Hentz was a well-known artist and entomologist. Both Mrs. Hentz and her daughter, Julia, were accomplished poets. Two of Julia's poems were included in William Gilmore Simms' anthology, *War Poetry in the South,* printed in 1866.—Benjamin Williams, 248.

March 4th, 1845. This is a great day in Washington City today. Mr. James K. Polk is inaugurated President of the United States of America. . . . It has been raining hard nearly all day long, but it did not prevent some persons here from going to a great inauguration ball in Tuscumbia.

So successful was this ball, held at the Franklin House in Tuscumbia, that it was suspended until the evening of the 6th. James K. Polk had many friends and relatives in the area. An aunt of his, Mrs. Naomi Knox Leetch, lived in Moulton; and Polk's wife, Sarah Childress, had a nephew who married a Gilchrist, of Courtland. The *North Alabamian* in Tuscumbia carried an account of the ball on March 14, 1845.—Douglass, *My Southern Families,* 93; Saunders, 110.

8th. Received a letter from William Richardson,* relative to the Band which we expect to invite over to our Commencement Day. . . . Also received the *New York Mirror,* edited by N. P. Willis and Geo. Morris,** which I regard as one of the most trifling papers now in existence, considering the reputation which its editors have. . . . commenced reading Prescott's *Ferdinand and Isabella,* which work has tended vastly to raise the literary reputation of our country. Prescott is blind, and his daughter acts as his amanuensis. Professor T. shocked me powerfully . . . with his new magneto-electrical machine.

*William Richardson, 1825–1852, was the son of John M. Richardson, who was born in Sullivan County, Tennessee in 1795, and died in 1856, having outlived a number of his children, as evidenced in the diaries. According to John Tanner, John Richardson lived on the site of the present Trinity School. He was a "quiet, unpretending man; he died and was buried here; he had a family of noble sons and lovely and accomplished daughters. Aunt Polly, his companion, was all goodness of heart and sincerity of purpose."

**Nathaniel Parker Willis was conceded to be the most successful journalist of his time, largely through publication of his articles, "Pencillings by the Way." In 1845 he merged his *American Monthly* magazine with that of George Pope Morris, the *New York Mirror.*

March 12th, 1845. Ate three boiled eggs and drank two cups of most excellent coffee, which comfort Mrs. Tutwiler understands the art of decocting as well as any one I ever met with. . . . Dr. Paine . . . informed us that lead ore was found in this neighbourhood of great purity, yielding 95 per cent and that, if it could be found in sufficient quantities, he thought a lead manufactory would be profitable here.

14th. It is reported here that the annexation of Texas has at last taken place; the democrats are all rejoicing at this measure. The addition of 500,000 square miles to our territory is certainly no small affair. Texas is about 5 times as large as England proper. This extent of fertile land, together with Iowa and Florida, which have just been admitted into the Union, are great additions to our confederacy. A bill has passed Congress, it is said, to reduce the postage wonderfully. There are but two prices for single letters — if carried over 300 miles, the price is 10 cents; if under that distance, 5 cents. I am not a zealous advocate for this law . . . for I do not think that the Post Office Department will now support itself, and consequently funds must be drawn from the already exhausted Treasury to supply the deficiency. . . . By the new bill letters are charged by their weight, one half ounce being the weight of a single letter.

March 16, 1845. Judge Jones passed thro' this place on his return from Athens, and brought me an engraving of the Institute there. . . . took a stroll to Paradise, visited Maddin . . . supper with Prof. Smith.

"Northeast of the college spring about 200 yards is what was called 'Paradise Hill.' Here were three offices, two rooms each," which were used for bedrooms.—McGregor, 4.

20th. Recited before breakfast to Prof. Smith in the Greek play, also at 11 in Astronomy to Prof. Tutwiler. Here I learned that eclipses of the sun happen more frequently than those of the moon, yet the latter seem to occur oftener. . . . A most remarkable solar eclipse took place in June, 1806 — and the next total solar eclipse will be on the 7th of August, 1869.

March 22nd, 1845. We debated whether the late annexation of Texas would [benefit] the North or the South more. I spoke in favor of the South, but, as I had little help, we lost it. I was fined 12½ cents for disorder.

25th. For several days past I have been trying to fix some electro-typing apparatus, but have hitherto failed, because Prof. T., in giving me directions, left out an important part. The apparatus is very simple. . . . If properly managed, the model will soon become coated to any thickness whatever, and the coating may be removed by heating the model, and will be an exact copy of it even to the finest mark.

28th. Felton and I took a long stroll over the mountains. I picked up some specimens of rocks — for instance — a pudding stone — a rock containing iron — several kinds of flint and several arrowheads. These latter we found abundantly in a large level field near this place which was cleared by the Indians, it is said — perhaps it was a battlefield — else why so many, many arrowheads in this particular place?

30th. Dr. Paine preached the funeral of Miss Frierson today, a beautiful young lady, whose parents reside here. . . . Yesterday I went on a geological excursion to "Toe-Nail," a spur of this mountain, and found some of the finest scenery I ever witnessed. . . . there are large masses of the rock which have been detached by some mighty force, and which have slid off some distance from their former place, assuming a variety of shapes and positions.

April 1st, 1845. All Fools Day has again come, and has been celebrated with proper exercises. . . . none of the morning classes recited except ours, and there were but half of us there, at which Prof. Smith was considerably perturbed. About breakfast time the doors of the chapel were barricaded — and the windows fastened down, so that it was with difficulty that Prof. T. opened them, and this was unnecessary, for no one came when the bell rang. At 11 our class again recited, notwithstanding some wished to quiz Prof. T. These faltered at first, but seeing some resolute, they all went down at last. Some also deserted from Dr. P. at 4, but he bore it very well & at the end of the recitation he remarked, "Give my respects to those militia and tell them that they can't stand the tug like the regulars."

9th. Today I returned from Athens, to which place I started on last Thursday. Judge Jones offered me his horse as far as Decatur, to which place he was going on the car. So I walked to Leighton, and there got the horse and started about 8 o'clock. My charger was an excellent one, though skittish, and paced along so rapidly that I arrived at Courtland before the car, though we traveled the same road the greater part of the way.* I reached Grandpa's that night, without my baggage, tho', for this went on to Huntsville by the stage, as it was not taken off the car. The next day Grandpa and I went up to town, and broke in unexpectedly upon the "home folks," who had just sent the carriage to Brown's Ferry for Jessie Coe and me. . . . I bought some clothes for Commencement, and left that city, for the last time as a student of La Grange (perhaps!).

*The condition of Alabama's first railroad, and second east of the Alleghenies, was quite poor at this time, and Hobbs' statement would indicate that the car was not able to follow the tracks all the way. The Tennessee Company bought the road in 1846, and it served as the basis for the track of the Memphis and Charleston Railroad, built around 1850.

April 11th, 1845. At dinner today we had several of our board of Trustees, who have a meeting today. Majr. Fenner, Dr. Shackelford and Mr. Harris dined with us, and an excellent meal had we. They related some excellent anecdotes of some of our soldiers in the revolutionary and last war — one of whom was knocked down for playing "Yankee Doodle" while a prisoner.

Robert Fenner, from Halifax, North Carolina, married Lucy Saunders, of Lawrence County, Alabama. Two of their sons served with the Courtland

"Red Rovers." One was massacred, and the other escaped by having been sent out on a reconnoitering party before the massacre by Santa Anna's men at Goliad. Dr. Jack Shackelford, 1790–1857, organized the "Red Rovers" in 1836, all of whom were killed except Dr. Shackelford and three other doctors—spared to treat the Mexican soldiers—and those in the reconnoitering party. Dr. Shackelford's son, Fortunatus, was among those killed. Mr. Harris was probably John Hunter Harris, 1800–1866, who was the son of Norfleete and Mary Hunter Harris. His home, just north of Courtland, was one of the finest in the Tennessee Valley, until destroyed recently by time and decay.—Saunders, 269, 322, 500.

April 13th, 1845. After breakfast T. Maddin proposed that we go to Leighton to preaching, as we have no service here today. . . . we were an hour and a half walking about 5 miles. . . . we found the church so much crowded that we could scarcely obtain seats. Dr. Paine preached nearly two hours. . . . We were invited to Mr. Gurley's to dinner and had to walk another mile to reach his house. . . . I wore a pair of tight shoes and suffered considerably from the walk.

Davis and Patience Bland Gurley lived on a plantation one mile west of Leighton. Their three sons (Edward, James Henry, and Davis Robert) were all students at La Grange.—McGregor, 62.

17th. Mr. Tutwiler showed me the invoice of our books, which are coming on soon. There are 90 volumes, cost 130 dollars. . . . I presided [at the meeting of the Society], as I was elected president while I was at home. . . . I fined Felton and Banks for not taking off their hats.

William Banks, of Courtland, became a physician. He was a brother-in-law of J. J. Ormond, chief justice of the Alabama supreme court, and the uncle-in-law of the supreme court justice, H. M. Somerville. From this family came the prominent Birmingham attorney, Ormond Somerville.—Saunders, 268, 269.

April 19th, 1845. The nineteenth day of April, 1826, gave me birth, as I am informed, and so this is the eighteenth anniversary of it. One might with great propriety remark the swift flight of time, as well as the increasing responsibilities of life I may be said to be just entering. In a few more years I shall be legally considered a man, but whether I shall be qualified to discharge the duties of an intelligent, a moral citizen, will of course, depend upon my actions. I have enjoyed excellent advantages—from my earliest infancy have I been at school. The earliest sound which I can remember was the ringing of a small bell, for school to commence. This school was taught by Ma, and composed of the children of the neighborhood. In this school I was, of course, early placed, and since that time I have not been longer than 5 months out of school at any one time. My moral training has been equally as good as my mental. I have pious parents, strict Methodists, who have ever endeavored to lead me in virtue's paths, both by precept and example; and I hope I have not been unmindful of their teachings. I expect at some future date to study law, but how and where I have not yet determined. Perhaps, if circumstances will permit, I will spend some time at Yale College. . . . I incidentally informed Mrs. Tutwiler (the dear Mrs. T.) that this was my birthday, and she said that "if she had known it sooner she would have honored me with a better dessert." However, she had a fine plum pudding made and sent up to my room after supper. . . . In the evening assisted Prof. T. to inflate a small balloon with hydrogen gas. It went up beautifully to the heighth of 30 or 40 feet, when the weight of the string prevented its further ascent.

23rd. This evening the Senior Class was invited to tea at Dr. Paine's, and thither we all repaired. . . . found a large assembly of ladies. . . . we had a good handed supper and afterwards refreshments in abundance; among other things a plate of iced hearts, called the "lottery of hearts," each one of these had the name of one of the company upon it, and are drawn by the company. I drew Miss Catherine Kennerly, a second effort brought me Miss Lawson, and . . . a third with the name of Maria L. Oliver.

Thursday, May 1st, 1845. There is a bookseller here at this time, the immortal Billings, who has a good, large wagon full of books, some excellent and recent works amongst them. I bought of him three of Punch's works — his *Punchiana, Medical Student,* and *Bowl of Punch.* They are all amusing, especially the latter, which is composed of the odds and ends of Punch's wit. He is particularly severe upon Pennsylvania on account of her repudiation.

Repudiation, the refusal to pay interest on debts incurred in promoting internal improvements, was adopted by several states, following the panic of 1837. Illinois, Indiana, Pennsylvania, Maryland, Mississippi, Michigan, and Louisiana adopted this policy. All of these states, except for Michigan, Mississippi, and Louisiana, eventually paid.

May 3, 1845. We had a fine bowl of strawberries for dinner today. . . . Carried my speech down to be corrected . . . hope Prof. T. will point out all the errors.

7th. Took a stroll in the evening up to the old Academy where some of the boys were playing nine pins.* I joined them, I found it a more difficult game than I had anticipated. Hence I was not present for supper, but made my appearance soon afterwards and ate with the children — no uninteresting company.**

*The old Academy was either the old building for the LaFayette Female Academy, abandoned in 1830, or the school "of high grade for boys," which was taught at La Grange by Edward Dromgoole Sims before the establishment of the college.—McGregor, 12.

**One wonders what Julia Tutwiler was like at the age of four.

9th. Yesterday I had the pleasure of witnessing an astronomical phenomenon; this was the transit of Mercury. It has been predicted for a long time by the knowing ones, and the exact fulfillment of their calculations is another bright triumph of science. . . . Prof. T. sent for me to come down to his laboratory. . . . I found him gazing fixedly at the sun thro' his telescope. Prof. T. said that as the observations of two persons were much apter to be correct than of one alone he wished me to assist him. He gave me a piece of coloured glass, and directed me to watch on the western edge of the sun, and the moment I saw a notch in it to inform him. . . . At 32 minutes [after 10] . . . he saw it . . . the shadow of Mercury on the sun's disc seemed to me about the size of an ordinary buckshot, to others it seemed larger, and to some, not larger than a mustard seed. . . . It . . . passed off precisely at 5 P.M. It is said that Galileo on his deathbed regretted never having seen this planet, and we have this day enjoyed, by means of his wonderful invention, a sight he was unable to behold.

May 10th, 1845. The Senior Class met at an early hour in the morning to read over together their forthcoming speeches. It occupied about 4 hours, and some of us read rapidly, too. We found a great sameness in the classical allusions, almost every one referring to the flourishing or wasting cities of Greece and Rome.

15th. Received rumour of a war with Mexico by today's mail, do not believe them.

17th. Went down this evening to assist Prof. T. in putting his compound blowpipe into operation. This instrument has not been put up since I have been here, so I was anxious to witness some instances of its great heat. Pierce and I were to keep the funnels full of water, and to regulate the back set of stop cocks, while Prof. T. held the substance to be fused, and managed the front stop cocks. We were all busy, for there is considerable danger in the affair if the instrument is not strictly watched. At first the jet of oxygen was so strong as to put out the inflamed hydrogen, but we soon learned to regulate this, and finally succeeded in melting an old steel file, none of these operations required more than a few seconds.

May 19th, 1845. Henry Malone returned from his brother's wedding, and brought some cake, news, and so forth.

Evidently this entry refers to the marriage of John Nicholas Malone to Mary Lucy Kernachan, although Owen, IV, 1150, gives his marriage date as 1844.

21st. Mr. Paine . . . is expected home about the last of this week; by the last news the Convention was progressing finely, and bade fair to come to a speedy and quiet issue, in a short time. Report says there will certainly be a division of the Church, and however much it may be disliked, it is thought to be the best course that could be pursued.

This historic convention of the Methodist Church was held in Louisville, Kentucky, at which time, "after nearly three weeks of prayerful consideration, it was voted to organize the Southern Conference into the Methodist Church, South." The controversy had boiled since 1844, when, at the General Conference in New York, several members bitterly attacked the Georgia bishop, James Osgood Andrew, for being a slaveowner. At that time Robert Paine had read Bishop Andrew's statement to the assembly, asserting that he had never bought a slave, but had inherited them.—Lazenby, 266.

23rd. I arose to prayers and recited before breakfast to Prof. Smith, at which time we ended our review of the Greek play, *Oedipus Tyrannus,* of Sophocles. By the by, I notice in the papers that they are acting over three old plays . . . at the North. The chorus is introduced and sings and dances as it did when the play was first performed.

May 27th, 1845. Dr. Paine has returned at last from Louisville. The Convention decided on a separation of the Church. They appointed another meeting on the adjustment of affairs to take place on May next. He purchased some fine curtains for the LaFayette Society — they were a part of a set which cost 800 dollars, and we give 70 for these we get. . . . We had a meeting of the Society this morning and appointed a committee to put them up, ready to show them off at the coming, or rather, present, Examination.

29th. Met Prof. Tutwiler at 8 in Optics, on the subject of Vision. . . . I learned among other interesting things, that the chrystalline lens of the eye, sometimes become . . . coated, and the operation of modern surgery called the couching for cataract, consists in the removal of this lens entirely from the eye. This is indeed a bold stroke of surgery, and yet it is frequently performed.

31st. Yesterday afternoon the long expected Examination commenced.

The preparatory class were first brought up. . . . Heard that Pa, Ma, and my cousin-aunt, Mrs. Maclin will be here on next Monday.* The Athens Band comes on Wednesday to play for our Class on Commencement. . . . Had an exhibition of the magic lantern tonight, saw some astronomical pictures amongst the rest.

*The "cousin-aunt" Anna Eliza Hobbs, daughter of Tom's uncle, John, and Keziah Fennell Hobbs, married Dr. Benjamin Maclin in 1838. She was only five years older than Tom.—Hobbs Family Papers.

Sunday, June 1st, 1845. Took breakfast with a Rev. Hopkins,** one of the visiting Committee from the Alabama Conference. . . . Mrs. Clark and her daughter, Martha (the remarkable), took dinner with us today. I have often heard my Grandfather speak of this old lady, they lived in the same neighbourhood in Virginia, she told me that she had often had my mother on her lap when a small girl.

**Rev. Nathan Hopkins, as a member of the Alabama Conference, was the first pastor of the Tabernacle Camp Ground, located on the state line, near Columbus, Mississippi. This camp ground has long been a favorite with many Methodists. Among the most prominent was the Waights G. Henry family. Dr. Waights Henry, Jr., president of La Grange College in Georgia, was licensed to preach at the Tabernacle Camp Ground meeting in 1928, the 100th anniversary of its founding.—Lazenby, 1083.

5th. This was a great day at La Grange College, not only because it was her regular Commencement Day, but because in addition to this, the largest class was graduated today which they have ever had. It was a fine day, too, perhaps a little too bright, considering the exercises were to take place under an arbor, it being supposed that the Church would not be sufficiently large to accommodate the visitors. There were 12 speakers, 8 before dinner, and four afterward, which together with the excellent music performed by the Athens Brass Band . . . caused the day to pass pleasantly away.† We had a good valedictory address by Joseph P. Billups,§ after which the degree was conferred by Dr. Robert Paine. . . . I felt very peculiar emotions as the sheepskin was handed me; for the first time the thought struck me that I was now to be considered a *man*, and that hereafter I must act as if I considered myself as such, and yet I feel as boyish as I did five years ago, hence it will be by constraint that I play the man. At night we had a large Commencement Party. . . . I had the pleasure of seeing there some of my female aquaintances from Athens . . . knowing that they were amongst the very first in point of "recommendables," such as wit and beauty. On the next day I went to Tuscumbia for the purpose of re-announcing my watch, which was stolen at the beginning of the session. It was carried to the silver-smith in that place for repair, he recognized it and retained it.

†"On a June Commencement in 1845, the music was furnished by a brass band. . . . one visitor wrote: 'The day was beautiful, the concourse very large, the music (performed by the celebrated Athens Brass Band) delightful, and the speaking such as fully sustained the high reputation of the graduates of this institution.' "—Posey, 15.

§Joseph Billups was the son of Col. Thomas and Sarah Moore Billups, members of one of Mississippi's most prominent families. Joseph was described by Saunders as "kind, genial, and quite a humorist, died unmarried, and greatly lamented."—Saunders, 368.

DR. BENJAMIN MACLIN, UNCLE OF THOMAS
PORTRAIT BY JOHN ANTROBUS, 1856
Photo by John Axford, courtesy Athens College

IRA E. HOBBS, FATHER OF THOMAS
PORTRAIT BY JOHN ANTROBUS, 1856
By permission of the National Society of the Colonial Dames of America in the State of Alabama,
ALABAMA PORTRAITS PRIOR TO 1870, *1969*

Rebecca Maclin Hobbs, mother of Thomas
portrait by John Antrobus, 1856
Photo by John Axford, courtesy Athens College

ANN ELIZA HOBBS MACLIN, AUNT OF THOMAS
PORTRAIT BY JOHN ANTROBUS, 1856
Photo by John Axford, courtesy J. E. Horton, Greenbrier, Alabama

PHILADELPHIA, PENNSYLVANIA 1846

In November, 1845, Thomas Hobbs went to Philadelphia, accompanied by Professors Tutwiler and Smith, to enter Hoffman's Law Institution, founded by David Hoffman, 1784–1854, the author of *Course of Legal Study,* and one of the founders of the law school at the University of Maryland. In 1843 Hoffman left Maryland and moved to Philadelphia, home of his wife, Mary McKean, whose grandfather, Thomas, was a signer of the Declaration of Independence, and served several times as governor of Pennsylvania. Hoffman was undoubtedly an estimable professor, but was seldom on the scene to lecture, as noted in the diaries.

In 1846 Philadelphia contained some 95,000 inhabitants, whose varied interests found expression in the theater, musical societies, art museums, educational and social reforms, and in foremost business transactions for the nation. Both Greek and Gothic Revival architecture previewed on the American scene in this city, and the finest buildings in the nation were represented here in the designs of Latrobe, Strickland, Mills, Walter, LeBruni, etc.

For all of its urbanity, this city was more closely associated with the agrarian South than any other American city. A large number of the southern young people were educated here. Large numbers of north Alabama merchants traveled here at least once a year to replenish their supplies.

Thursday, January 1st, 1846. I am now snugly fixed in my new room at No. 303 Hech Street, just opposite my former boarding house, kept by Mrs. Warren. The principal cause of my change was the slothfulness of the servants. . . . In this house all the servants . . . seem waiting to do your commands, and voluntarily perform many acts of neatness and kindness. . . . I pay $3.50 per week for board, fuel and lights. Bought today this [diary] and another notebook, also some needles and thread. . . . 75, 50, 7 . . . oysters 12½.

2nd. Rose half-past seven, some slight improvement, and after breakfast went down to Hoffman's Law Institution for the purpose of entering it, did not find him in— some of the students entertained me for a short time, and offered me the books which are generally read first. Saw Mr. H [offman] in the evening, he goes to Wash. City tomorrow to argue a case involving $50,000.

4th. I went out to church on North Fourth Street and heard Dr. Durbin on the institution of the sacrament. . . . The church was much crowded. . . . I contributed 2 cents to the collection . . . gave 5 cents to the collection for the poor.

Dr. John Price Durbin had previously served as president of Dickinson College, and as Chaplain of the United States Senate.—Maag, March 25, 1971.

6th. Spent half a cent for an apple, which was the only expense I have had today, growing more temperate, surely. . . . forgot to state that I had bought a vial of Jackson's Pectoral Syrup for 31¼ cts.

January 7, 1846. I called for the books I purchased at auction on last night. . . . *Amazonian Republic*, 8 cts.; 2 vols. *Glory & Shame of England*, 65 cts.; Homer's *Odyssey,* 78 cts.; and 3 vols. *Ferdinand and Isabella,* 4.55. . . . Bought tonight . . . Milton, 85 cts.; Cowper, bound to match, 80 cts.; and an Italian Testament, 37½. . . . Am getting quite a little library, in number now 23 vols.

8th. Twenty guns were fired early this morning in honor of the ever glorious eighth [the anniversary of the Battle of New Orleans].

10th. I finished Hoffman's *Legal Outlines.* . . . visited Barret's Gymnasium, for the purpose of examining it. . . . think I shall become a subscriber, so that I may take an hour's exercise every day. Spent a cent for an apple, and at night bought a morning gown, or wrapper, for which I paid $3.00.

12th. Commenced another Rutherford's *Institutes.* Mr. Hoffman not yet returned. . . . very unexpectedly met W. O. Clack,* an old schoolmate, he is now a student of Yale College, and is here for the purpose of being cured of stammering by Dr. Comstock. Went out tonight to see a fire, but it was put out before we arrived.

*There were undoubtedly members of the Clack family in Alabama, but the principal connection of the Clack family with that of Tom Hobbs was in Brunswick County, Virginia. Here, in 1754, William Maclin married Sally Clack, daughter of James, who in 1740 had bought 2500 acres of Brunswick land from the Mumford family.—Douglass, *My Southern Families,* 160; Saunders, 385.

January 14th, 1846. I weighed myself today—weight 119 pounds, height 5 feet, 8¾. I wish to know if I grow any from my exercising there. . . . Called on Messrs. Taylor & Paulding and received a check for $100 on the Bank of North America. . . . wrote to John Keyes tonight, and went to the ice-cream shop and had 3 plates, 18¾ [cents].

15th. Mims is now rooming with me. . . . I went to a concert tonight, heard two brass bands play together and separately, also some good singing, and some horrid screeching.

17th. I went this evening to the University to see the students take exhilarating gas (protoxide of nitrogen). They performed divers wonderful & funny feats, admittance 12½ cents, ran to a fire tonight, but was disappointed.

18th. Saw a fire tonight, for the first time. . . . It was on the wharf between Chestnut and Walnut. I left it still burning away finely, and altho' there were many fire-engines there, they seemed to accomplish but little. They were hindered by the frozen water of the hose.

19th. Mims and I walked to the place where the fire occurred. . . . Only two houses were destroyed, but these were large commission houses, and were two or three stories high. I was engaged all the forenoon in having my upper bicuspids on both sides plugged. . . . paid $4.00 for the job. . . . also paid 35 cents for some alterations in a shirt and neckerchief. The work was done by the Union Benevolent Association. I gave a cent for a *Ledger,* in order to see the list of advertised letters.

January 20th, 1846. Went to Grigg and Elliott's and purchased Rycroft's Course of Reading, a most useful work to the student. . . . called at Tryon's establishment and saw a variety of guns, some rifles he is making for the U. S. Army. They are percussion locks and look like a musket, the stock is of plain, solid walnut. . . . Went to the Theatre tonight to hear and see Murdoch, the great orator and actor. I saw him, but was rather disappointed.

James Edward Murdoch had gained fame by playing opposite Fanny Kemble for some time. He had recently returned to the stage after a period of retirement. During the Civil War Murdoch devoted his time to the entertainment of wounded soldiers, and later taught elocution in Cincinnati.

21st. Went to the Walnut and saw Mr. Murdoch and Mrs. Wallach [Wallack] in *Much Ado & School for Scandal.* I think the latter hard to beat. I'm done with theatre now.

The Walnut Street Theatre, established in 1809, is the oldest theater in continuous use in America. Although the Chestnut Street Theatre is older, it has not been in continual operation.—Burt, 451.

January 22nd, 1846. A deep snow is still on the ground, and the pavements are so slippery that one cannot easily walk without india-rubber shoes. . . . I find my strength and agility are improving.

23rd. Everything now is covered with a glassy coat of sleet, and the wires of the telegraph are bent under the weight of ice upon them.* . . .

Took a sleigh ride with Brunson. The air resounds with bells, there is one continual merry jingle, jingle. They say they do not often have such good sleighing. . . . Paid for my ride 6½, and for ice-cream, which I got at Miss 'Til's, 6¼.

*This is the first mention of the telegraph, which made its debut in May, 1844.

24th. Finished the first volume of Rutherford's *Institutes.* Mr. H. has not yet returned. . . . went to examine a large lot of English books which are to be sold at auction soon. Some of them are said to have been in the library of His Highness, the Duke of Sussex. There are some valuable works amongst them, but they are generally very old books, many of them are two centuries old. I received a *Chronicle* from home, but no letter. I paid postage of 1½ cents. . . . also bought an apple for a cent.

26th. Got a letter which had been two weeks coming, delayed doubtless by the snow on the railroad tracks. . . . 95 pupils at the Institute. . . . Bought a description of the telegraph.

January 27th, 1846. The books at the auction brought very good prices. . . . They were bought principally by the public libraries of the city. An illustrated Shakespeare sold for $10, and was bought by Dr. Goddard. . . . There are some fine engravings to be sold tomorrow evening, some of Bonaparte's battles.

28th. Got at last my volume of Scott's works, which has been at the binders for nearly two weeks. However, I should not complain, as it is most beautifully bound. Turkey morocco back and corners. . . . Finished a letter to Prof. Tutwiler.

29th. Went to hear a lecture from Gen. Lewis Cass. . . . he said some good things, but he said nothing well, as I thought his delivery was not good. He gave a glowing account of the burial of the remains of Napoleon, which he witnessed while Minister to France.

Lewis Cass, 1782–1866, had served as Governor of Michigan Territory, and by negotiating treaties with the Indians wrested the lands which formed the nucleus of Michigan, Indiana, Ohio, Illinois, and Wisconsin. Cass served as Secretary of War in Jackson's cabinet, and was minister to France in 1839. In 1846 Cass was serving in the U.S. Senate, speaking in opposition to the Wilmot Proviso.

30th. At the gymnasium today I performed several feats which I could not do in the beginning. . . . Attended Lord's auction of books. . . . bought Rowley's *Poems,* which are the literary cheat of Chatterton,

price 62½ cents. I also bought, on the way to the room, a cocoa-nut, for which I gave 6½ cents, or, as it is called here, a fip-and-a-bit.
February 1st, 1846. Went out tonight to hear and see the celebrated Gough, the great champion of Temperance, and he is a champion indeed. Altho' unlearned, he speaks naturally, and whoever does this, always speaks well.

John Bartholomew Gough, born in England in 1817, knew well the hazards of intemperance from experience. He became one of the most popular lecturers of the nineteenth century.

3rd. Bought two excellent engravings, the "Return from Elba," and the "Battle of Waterloo." Gave $1.50 for them, which is cheap enough. Went tonight to see a taking of laughing gas. I had no idea of taking it myself when I went, but concluded I would try its effects on me, as I never took it. I cannot describe the sensation. I remember crying out "Hurrah for North Alabama! God save North Alabama! Hurrah for Texas, Oregon, and California!" I ran and tried how high I could kick on the wall. I was conscious of what I was about, but could not do otherwise, if the world depended on it.

The anesthetic possibilities of "laughing gas" (nitrous oxide) were recognized by Sir Humphrey Davey in 1800, but the medical benefits of this or other anesthetics were still not generally known in 1846.

February 8th, 1846. Went to Dr. Durbin's church. . . . not a vacant seat in the house. . . . I went down to Christ Church, on 2nd St., one of the oldest churches in the place. The King's arms were once upon it, but during the Revolutionary War, someone went up and pulled them down. I heard a cold, lifeless sermon from somebody in robes.
9th. Got two letters, one from Ma and one from Henry Malone. . . . Attended two lectures and commenced reading Blackstone. I am reading Tucker's edition, which is better adapted to American readers than most others.
10th. On the way [to the Post Office] I saw it placarded about on the street that the resolutions to give the notice to England in regard to Oregon, had passed the House by a very large majority.

"Fifty-four-forty-or-fight," the 1844 campaign slogan, was being shouted anew. England demanded that the boundary for the Oregon Territory be set at the fifty-fourth parallel. A compromise was reached under Polk's administration, fixing the boundary at the forty-ninth parallel, which is the present boundary.

12th. I went out this morning to the High School to witness the commencement exercises, and just such a crowd I never wish to be in again.

Central High School, Philadelphia's first and only high school for several years, and one of the nation's first, was chartered in 1836.—American Guide Series, *Philadelphia,* 176.

February 13th, 1846. I attended a lecture this morning on the Roman Civil Law, which Mr. Hoffman considers of great importance to the modern student, altho' it is generally held in great contempt by them. After lecture Mr. H. caught several of us smoking in his rooms, in violation of his laws, but we talked him into a good humour, and that avoided a reprimand.

14th. I was lying stretched on three chairs around the stove reading Blackstone . . . when our servant girl . . . brought me a letter handed her by the carrier. This was somewhat unexpected, but it is what I have been endeavoring to accomplish for some time past. I shall now get letters as soon as they arrive, without the trouble of attending the office, and at the additional expense of only two cents per letter.

16th. This significant appendage I have learned tonight from a most interesting tale . . . *Picciola.* I recollect having heard Mrs. Tutwiler speak of this tale whilst I was with her, and I am now reading it on that account. The hero, an imprisoned French noble, wrote upon his wall, with charcoal, this atheistical sentiment, "Chance, tho' blind, is the sole author of the creation." Afterwards, wavering as to this opinion he added, "Perhaps." . . . Tonight I bought 2 cents worth of sugar to eat with snow. Snow is 5 inches deep.

February 18th, 1846. Came round by Messrs. Taylor & Paulding's in order that I might leave my card, so that Mr. Sloss may find me out when he comes.* I there got a letter from William Richardson, which was sent to me in their care. . . . I went out tonight to hear and see Mrs. Lucretia Mott lecture on Temperance, as I have never seen a female stand in the public pulpit.** She spoke fluently, but is undoubtedly a fanatic and she considers the Temperance & Anti-Slavery reformations as closley united. Paid for this 10 cents to be applied to the poor.

*James Withers Sloss, 1820–1890, came to Athens from Mooresville in 1843, and soon became the most successful merchant in that place. He was the son of Joseph Sloss, the Mooresville tailor who taught Andrew Johnson how to make the Prince Albert coat. J. W. Sloss, as president of the Tennessee and Alabama Central Railroad, had opportunity to study the mineral resources in the central part of the state. It was he who had the tenacity to work with a small crew of men, and after many failures, succeeded in producing iron from the Alabama coke, thus ensuring the future of the little town of

Birmingham. Here Sloss built the Sloss-Sheffield furnaces, which have now been designated a National Landmark.—Owen, IV, 1572–73; Tanner, July 7, 1876.

**Lucretia Coffin Mott, a Quaker minister, was one of the earliest advocates for women's rights.

20th. Today we got very important news from England, viz., the repeal of the corn laws, and a pacific feeling in regard to Oregon. I sent Drs. Sowell & Maclin a paper containing the late news.† Finished 1st vol. of Blackstone. Am getting frugal, for instance — 0.

†"His name would have honored any medical institution in the country," wrote John Tanner of Dr. James F. Sowell. Dr. Sowell, born in Virginia in 1814, married Elizabeth Hobbs, daughter of Dr. David Hobbs. Sowell read medicine under Dr. Hobbs, and later accepted a professorship in the medical school in St. Louis.

February 21st, 1846. We concluded to adjourn to a funeral of a naval officer. . . [saw] one of the city soup-houses, where this article is given out to the poor. Truly a sad-looking company was assembled there for the reception of their soup. They were mostly Negroes.

22nd. Mr. Sloss surprised me by stopping in today, the surprise was very agreeable, he brought me the Daguerrotype likenesses of my parents and a host of letters.

23rd. I had made up my mind to see the movements of the military, who are to be out in honor of yesterday, which could not be thus celebrated. . . . I also had the good fortune to meet Mr. Hine and Cousin David Malone.§ . . . went down to Congress Hall tonight, and we had a very social Southern chat. Mr. Sloss was also with us. . . . Paid out 8 cents for something to eat during the day. How liberal I'm getting since Mr. Sloss came!

§David was the son of John Petway and Sally Hobbs Malone, and brother of Mary Malone Hine.

February 24th, 1846. Met Cousin D[avid] this evening, and with Andrew O'Dell and John Tanner, who are here buying goods, I went down after supper and we all went to the Walnut to see Booth. I was greatly disappointed, he can't act at all. Mr. Wallack is much better, and Mrs. Wallack is not to be beaten.

Junius Brutus Booth, 1796–1852, was the intemperate father of Edwin, only 13 at the time, and of John Wilkes Booth, 7.

Mr. Wallack is probably John Wallack, who is the only one of that famous family listed as having married an actress, a Miss Turpin.—Stephen and Lee, XX, 574–76.

25th. Cousin D. and I went to the University to see a great surgical operation. . . . the patient was brought in, having an immense tumour on the side of head and neck, which was equally as large as his head. . . . Dr. Gibson . . . gave us to understand that it was the greatest operation which we would ever see, perhaps. . . . went out tonight and heard Leopold De Meyer perform on the piano, slightly in advance of anything I ever struck!

Leopold De Meyer was a nineteenth-century Victor Borge. "He would sit at the piano, then decide he did not like its location, and would have it pushed around, meanwhile making speeches to the audience. Sometimes he played with his thumbs, sometimes with the fists and elbows. Audiences loved it!" It was reported that Steinway paid De Meyer $15,000 to demonstrate their instrument.—Schonberg, 179.

February 26th, 1846. Went to the Arch Street Theatre tonight to see Burton, who stands with the English at the head of the list of our comedians. I saw him in the *Broken Heart,* and . . . especially in the Drunken scene, I never saw anything to equal it.

27th. We went to see the Mint this morning. They were coining half-eagles. . . . went down to the bay and looked at the shipping. I bought a number of the London *Punch,* and sent it to John Keyes.

28th. Snowing. . . . remained in my room and wrote a letter on a candle sheet, to Cousin Eliza.

March 1. Still snowing. . . . now six or eight inches deep, which is the deepest snow I ever saw.

3rd. Went to Jones' hotel and found my friends in. Cousin D. and I went to see some books to be sold tonight, and then continued our walk to the Delaware, which we found very much obstructed by ice. . . . We went to the Navy Yard, and saw . . . the carriage upon which the *Peacemaker* was, when it bursted [*sic*]. Also, the great gun which was made to match that, it is called the *Oregon.*

4th. Called for Cousin D., and we went to the Museum of the University. . . . Called at Lord's rooms and got my books, bought last night, viz., Bocaccio's *Decameron* (75); D'Aubigne's *Reformation* (98); Bentham on *Legislation* (45), *Diary* of Marryatt (17); *Crescent and Cross* (70); and *Visit to Northern Europe* (55). . . . Attended the commencement of the Pennsylvania School of Medicine. No. of graduates—36.

March 6, 1846. I spent the morning . . . buying presents for the children at Aunt's. . . . Wrote to Aunt in the evening, which I shall send per Cousin David, who as well as Mr. Hine, will leave for Boston tomorrow morning, and they will take Claverack in the route back to this place.

Cornelia van Wyck Hobbs (Aunt) was the widow of Tom's uncle, Hubbard. Cornelia, born in Claverack, Columbia County, New York, in 1807, married Hubbard in New York in 1825. Hubbard was appointed a midshipman in the U. S. Navy in 1815, and continued to serve in the Navy throughout his life, except for a few years after his marriage. At that time the couple came to Alabama, and a section of the Hobbs land was named the "New York Quarter" in honor of Cornelia. Hubbard and Ira Hobbs established one of the first cotton mills in the state at Fulton, on Swan Creek, around 1829. Twins were born to them in 1832 while they were still residents of Alabama, but in 1834 a son, Thomas Maclin, was born in Claverack. Two years later Hubbard died while serving on the *Brandywine,* and was buried in the Protestant Burial Grounds in Valparaiso, Chile. Cornelia died in 1850, and her children moved west.—Hobbs Family Papers.

March 7th, 1846. Read some in Capt. Marryatt's *Diary,* he says Mr. Jefferson was one of the most unprincipled men that ever existed.

Captain Frederick Marryatt, born in London in 1792, entered the British Navy at the age of 14. He became known for his sea stories, notably *Midshipman Easy,* published in 1836. He then toured the United States and Canada, gathering an assortment of biased opinions which he incorporated into *A Diary in America.* His review of N. P. Willis' *Pencilings by the Way* so angered Willis that he challenged Marryatt to a duel. The two exchanged shots, but neither was wounded.

9th. Continued my letter to Pa. . . . also wrote to R. H. Rivers, in regard to the cost of diplomas, both of these letters I sent by Mr. J. W. Sloss, who left for Athens this afternoon, as well as Mr. Vasser.

Richard W. Vasser "was one of the earliest settlers in town and a more useful man never lived here. He was a man of the highest sense of honor, and thought it a disgrace to any man not to pay an honest debt. . . . He possessed more influence perhaps than any man in Limestone County, and could elect any man to office he might desire," said John Tanner of him. Born in Amelia County, Virginia, in 1800, Richard Vasser came with his family to Limestone in 1819. While clerking for the merchants, Lane and Barnes, he saved enough money to buy his first store in partnership with Judge Daniel Coleman. It was the first of many shrewd investments which were to earn for him the title of "merchant prince," with interests in three states. Two of his sons died during the Civil War, and Mr. Vasser also died, while refugeeing in Georgia in 1864. He was buried in the old Athens Cemetery, next to the beautiful home of the Vassers, which still stands on the corner of Washington and Beaty Streets.—Tanner, July 28, 1876; Pat Jones, "The Vasser Home," June 9, 1935.

March 11, 1846. Mr. Wm. Allen and a Mr. Gray, from Mooresville, called upon me and left two letters, one from Ma and another from Henry Malone. . . . I called on them tonight and found Major Townshend [*sic*] with them, sat an hour, and on my way home bought some ground peas.

William Tynes Allen, 1819–1866, was the son of Benjamin and Mary Wilburn Allen. In 1843 he married Louisa Massie in Giles County, Tennessee. Major Brice Townsend, 1818–1884, married Willie C. Featherstone, whose brother, John, succeeded Thomas Hobbs in command of Company F, 9th Alabama Infantry, C.S.A. The generosity of Brice Townsend was recorded by John Tanner on July 7, 1876. Tanner's father had suffered such a reversal in finances that he had been forced to sell all his possessions. He was given financial assistance by Brice Townsend and Cyrus Arledge.

March 13, 1846. Went out tonight and bought two nos. of the *Paul Pry* for the benefit of J.W.K. and H.B.M.

This newspaper was probably the one published by that "aggressive, intolerant, outspoken, suspicious, meddlesome, non-conforming but patriotic, and fascinating woman," Anne Royall, one of the nation's first woman journalists. *Paul Pry* and its successor, *The Huntress,* were published from 1831 until Mrs. Royall's death in 1854. This pioneer newspaperwoman came to the Alabama Territory in 1817, and her accounts of the early life in the area are invaluable to the historian.—Royall, 10.

14th. Went to Congress Hall after supper, and sat . . . with my friends and Mr. Peebles, of Mooresville.

Either John T. or Robert Peebles, who had a brick store in Mooresville. This building was converted into a residence in 1936 by L. B. and Emily Peebles Leftwich.

17th. After breakfast walked down to the bay, and went on board of the *Saranak,* a beautiful packet which has just arrived from Liverpool. The fare across the ocean in this ship is $80, and she sometimes makes the trip in 18 days, tho' she was out 50 the last. Continued my walk to the Exchange,* and saw the Magnetic Telegraph at work. . . . Bought a number of the *Dollar* newspaper and sent it to Wm. Richardson.

*The Stock Exchange, designed by William Strickland, is one of the best examples of Greek Revival buildings in America.

March 18th, 1846. Brunson, Mims and I . . . went to the Post Office, and thence to the wharf where we hired a boat and took an excursion. We boarded the slaver *Pons,* which was lying at a dock in Southwark, saw nothing peculiar on deck, and we were not permitted to go into the hold, where the 900 slaves were confined. . . . Visited some rolling mills.

The importation of slaves was illegal at this time, therefore the *Pons* was engaged in illicit operations. It was seized shortly thereafter.

19th. Mr. DeWoody called on me this morning, direct from Athens. He brought a letter from my parents, inclosing [*sic*] Dr. Franklin's code for the division of his time, which certainly is a very good one. . . . Brunson, Mims and I went to an exhibition of the deaf and dumb this evening, which was very interesting.

Philadelphia led the nation in its number of charitable institutions. Interest in these reforms formed the basis for Hobbs' later attempts in his native state.

20th. Beautiful day. . . . took a stroll down to the river, and noticed the business and commerce there. A steamboat had just arrived from N. Jersey, crowded with market people and their produce. The bow was taken up with live calves, sheep, etc., while the whole deck was covered with potatoes, turnips, eggs, fowls, vegetables. . . . spent the night writing an article for the *Chronicle.*

March 23rd, 1846. We all took an omnibus for Girard College,* which is visited by all who come to the city. . . . We examined, and of course, greatly admired the buildings. . . . Thence we walked over to Fairmount,** and looked at the machinery, falls, etc.

*"God's instructions for building the ark were as nothing" in compaison with Stephen Girard's plans for his school. America's first multimillionaire left over five million dollars for the establishment of a school for poor white males, with strict limitations as to age, race, and native habitat of the applicants. The college, completed in 1846, was the design of Thomas Walter, architect of the wing additions to the U. S. Capitol. It was considered the finest Greek Revival building in America.—Burt, 229.

**The Fairmount Waterworks were the result of Benjamin Latrobe's design for the Philadelphia Waterworks in 1800. The Fairmount Park Aquarium was later housed in the Greek Revival buildings of the old waterworks, and a gala bicentennial celebration is planned for the park in 1976.—American Guide Series, *Pennsylvania,* 288.

24th. We . . . went to the Musical Fund Hall to the commencement of the Jefferson Medical College — there were 106 graduates. Bought a copy of the *National Police Gazette.*

The Musical Fund Hall, designed by William Strickland, was built on Locust and Eighth streets in 1824. It was the center of all the important concerts, operas, and public meetings until the Academy of Music was built in 1857.—Burt, 462.

March 28th, 1846. Mims, Horner and I went to the prison at Moyamensing, having obtained a ticket yesterday evening. We were admitted on presenting this, and shown thru by an officer, who took some pains to show us thru. The cells were very neat and ventilated, and warmed when necessary. They had books, pictures, and some of the prisoners had employed their spare hours in making toys, etc. We saw the women's department, and heard one raving. . . . Took a warm bath. (25)

29th. I presented my certificate, and was received [into the church]. Several others joined, amongst them was a converted Jew, named Israel Lazurus.

30th. Heard while at breakfast that a letter was advertised for me, and immediately went for it, paid postage (14). It was from Prof. Tutwiler.

April 1st. All Fool's Day has again come forward to cause merriment and fun.

2nd. Dropped into the court-room as I was returning [from the Institute] and heard part of a trial for libel. Hays vs. an Alabama quack, who had put out a pill and a book. Dr. Hays had reviewed the book severely, and this was the cause of the action. In the afternoon, went with a party of ladies and gentlemen . . . to the Asylum for the Deaf and Dumb. We there witnessed the manner of teaching, of conveying abstract ideas, etc. Saw the girls and boys at work, the former weaving, the latter shoemaking.

April 3rd, 1846. Attended the commencement of the University of Pennsylvania, (i.e.) the Medical Department. They conferred the degree upon 168 young men.

8th. Mr. Hoffman has ceased his lectures. Played draughts with Hagerty, and beat him.

10th. This week . . . I have received 5 letters and 3 newspapers, and my postage has amounted to 66 cents. . . . After dinner I went with some friends rowing on the Schuykill, we went up as far as Laurel Hill Cemetery. . . . admired mostly the one [monument] of Com. Hull.

11th. Bought a *Ledger* containing an account of the capture of the slaver *Pons.* Sent it to H. B. M. and the *Chronicle.* . . . Tonight Mims, my roommate, left for the South, via Pittsburgh and the Ohio River. . . . bought . . . the *Columbiad,* by Joel Barlow. The best epic our country has produced.

Joel Barlow, fired with the revolutionary spirit, first published the "Vision of Columbus" in 1787, and it was reprinted in Paris in 1793. The long poem "had a far-reaching effect upon the political harmony of mankind," declared Van Wyck Brooks.

April 16th, 1846. I received a letter today from Mrs. Tutwiler rather unexpectedly. . . . No news except that Prof. Tutwiler had sent in his resignation to the board. I fear for the prosperity of the college when three of the faculty will leave at once.* Walked down Chestnut to the Post Office, & saw it stuck up on the corners that Mr. Slidell has returned from Mexico,** and that the Texan & Mexican armies had encamped in sight of each other on different sides of the river.

*Dr. Paine (who assumed his duties as bishop in 1846), Professor Tutwiler, and Professor Smith were the faculty members who left. Although Dr. Paine was ably replaced by Dr. Richard Wadsworth, the school began its decline from this time.

**When John Slidell was appointed minister to Mexico in 1845, the Mexicans refused to receive him, and the Mexican War began soon after. He was the diplomat who was involved in the *Trent* affair during the Civil War.

19th. This is the anniversary of my birthday, this day makes me twenty years old. . . . heard a sermon from one McFerrin, whom I at first thought was John B., but learned afterwards was his brother. . . . real Southern backwoods sermon, and seemed to open the eyes of some of the congregation.

John B. McFerrin, author of the *History of the Tennessee Conference,* was licensed to preach at the Cambridge Camp Ground.

April 20th, 1846. Went upon the steeple of the State House while I was waiting for the session of the court. . . . Attended Hollick's trial in the criminal court, he was indicted for the publication of obscene book and pictures; but he was acquitted on the ground that the book was published in N. Y., and hence not punishable here.

21st. The postman brought me a letter and a paper from H. B. Malone. The paper contained a piece I wrote for it . . . giving an account of the early settlement of Phila., etc.

23rd. Finished the 3rd volume of Blackstone; one more & I shall be thro' with it.

28th. Spent several hours this morning in visiting engraving establishments to have some diplomas struck for Rev. Rivers.

29th. Commenced another article for the *Chronicle.* This one is to be about the old Independence Hall, etc.

30th. Put three soft eggs into the mammoth cave of my mouth, which has some fine stalactites in it, by the way, some of them "water worn."

May 1st. Had to be called up to breakfast, and when I looked out of the parlor window I noticed most of the horses which passed were rigged

out in flowers and branches, & then I was first reminded that it was the first of May.
2nd. After dinner went to see Sterling Paine at his boarding house. Clack and I sat some time with him, and we talked of old times, etc. They called for me after supper to go with them to the Arch Theatre, and altho' I would have preferred not, yet I consented. Saw *Romeo and Juliet* & *Tom Crinker's Leg,* both badly done.
May 3rd, 1846. Took a walk with Mr. Burr and talked with him about Jackson, marriage & slavery. To the first and last he was much opposed, but rather inclined towards the second.
11th. When I got into the streets I found them thronged, and great excitement prevailed on account of the report of actual hostility commenced with Mexico. . . . Heard today that Drs. Paine & Capers were elected bishops.

Dr. William Capers, of South Carolina, and Dr. Robert Paine were elected at the first conference of the Methodist Episcopal Church, South, at Petersburg, Virginia.

12th. Went out this morning to attend to the deportation of the diplomas. Paid all charges, had them packed in a cigar-box and sent by one of the express lines to Petersburg to Rev. F. G. Ferguson.

Rev. Frederick Guthrie Ferguson was born in Spartanburg, South Carolina, in 1809. He was one of the first trustees of the Institute at Athens, and one of the professors there. This was the year of the first graduating class of the Institute.—Lazenby, 1064; Mary Norman Moore, 10.

13th. My mind was somewhat agitated about the summons of war; I can scarcely realize that this is possible, until [I] remember that my own state has been called on to furnish her quota of men, and that some of her sons have actually gone forth on the call. Today I attended a meeting of the citizens called by the Mayor to deliberate on our present affairs. It was the largest concourse I ever beheld, [it] was held in Independence Square.
May 14th, 1846. Went to the office and mailed a *Ledger* containing an account of the meeting of yesterday to Drs. S. & M. . . . news of the passage of the bill for raising 50,000 volunteers, and appropriating $10,000,000 for the expenses.
15th. Attended the trial of some negroes in the District Court for mutiny. The Captain of the vessel was examined: the testimony is clear against some of them & they will doubtless hang. They have David

Paul Brown in their defense, and he is esteemed one of the best criminal lawyers of the city.
18th. The *Ledger* contained quite a eulogium on Alabama for her promptness in sending volunteers to Texas. It said that the Ala. troops would be the first in the field.
19th. News reached the city today that Matamoras had been burnt by the American forces, but this is doubted by many.

No word of burning was mentioned in a letter from General Zachary Taylor, written on May 9th, and printed in the Huntsville *Southern Advocate,* in which he reports a complete victory over the Mexican camp, and a peaceable possession of the city. The only restriction placed upon the citizens was the curtailment of liquor sales. Gaining Matamoras gave the United States control of central Mexico.

May 20th, 1846. Tonight Ashley & I went to an anti-slavery meeting of a part of the Presbyterian Church. It was very dull — on our return bought some candy.
22nd. I went to court and heard the celebrated criminal lawyer, David Paul Brown, speak in the defense of the mutineers. From what I heard I must certainly concur in his great fame — he used no notes, and yet he kept the relative positions of those five men, during their various transactions, perfectly clear and distinct.
23rd. The jury brought in a verdict against three of the mutineers today, and acquitted three. Ashley and I went to buy some gaiter shoes, found some, gave $4.00. . . . bought a pair of half-hose.
26th. Read 30 pages of law this morning in Walker's *Introduction.* . . . had some strawberry ice-cream tonight.
27th. After breakfast the carrier brought me a letter from Mr. D. P. Davis, of Reading, who formerly was a fellow-student here. He wishes me to accompany him to New York and West Point about the middle of next month. . . . In the afternoon I read some, slept a few minutes and went to French for the last time.
May 28th, 1846. Wrote to Davis tonight in reply to his of yesterday — promised to meet him in New York. At the auction tonight I bought Gibbon's *Autobiography* (.45), and a good book called the *Jews' Letters to Voltaire.*
29th. I got another letter from home this morning; it gave an account of the very great excitement among the people concerning the war, also of the raising of a company of ninety-six, to volunteer when necessary. It also suggests that I should return home next fall, fearing that another winter would be too severe for my constitution.

31st. Today, instead of going to my own church, I concluded to attend a Catholic cathedral. I did so, & as this was one of their holy days, I was fortunate in selecting it. The bishop was present, with a scarlet robe with a long train, and when he was arrayed before us, in his golden-worked garments and pontifical cap he looked like the high-priest of mummery. . . . Went to our own church tonight, and hear[d] a very queer sermon from a Presbyterian.
June 1st. Seemed that in the time of Blackstone, there were 160 crimes punishable by death, by the law of Ohio there is *1.* In the afternoon commenced a letter to Pa, in regard to remaining here, money, etc. . . . did not finish it, as I am writing it with due consideration, it will probably determine my stay in Phila. Walked in the Square & gave a little girl a cent.
June 3rd, 1846. Got a catalogue of his Institute from Rev. R. H. Rivers. . . . Finished the letter to J. W. Keyes in regard to attending his wedding.
5th. Went to the Institute. . . . finished the chapter on Chancery Proceedings, and I think it the most interesting portion of the law I have yet read. . . . Heard today that our troops have occupied Matamoras, and without a gun being fired.
6th. Finished Walker's *Introduction to American Law,* a book I admire and think very useful to the student — it is designed as a book between Blackstone and American Law in detail. . . . Ashley and I took a lunch prepared by the kindness of our landlady, and then set out for Burlington on the steamboat *Sun.* We bought some cigars, & puffed away agreeably on the way. We went the distance (25 miles) in about an hour & a half, and paid for it *13* cents. . . . walked about in Burlington, bought some confectionery and enjoyed the luxury of lying on the green grass and walking on *the ground.*
7th. Went to class-meeting, which is a favorite means of grace with me.
9th. The postman brought me two *Chronicles* from H. B. Malone. One gives an account of the presentation of a flag to the Limestone volunteers by Miss Maria Bass. Went to the Institute and read some of Kent, commenced with the municipal law, having read the other part of Vol. I with Judge Coleman.

Daniel Coleman, 1801–1857, was the son of Daniel and Martha Cocke Coleman, of Concord, Caroline County, Virginia; and nephew of General Hartwell Cocke, of Bremo, Fluvanna County. The Coleman family made notable contributions to Virginia's legal and educational institutions. In 1819 Daniel Coleman came to Mooresville, and was made circuit judge of Limestone County at the age of 19, through the influence of Captain Nicholas Davis. Coleman refused to run for governor when he was pressed to do so, but reluctantly agreed to serve on the state supreme court for a time, and served briefly as chief justice. Among the prominent lawyers who studied under Judge Coleman were: R. C. Brickell, Luke Pryor, William B. Wood, Henry C. Jones, Wade Keyes, and Nicholas Davis, Jr.—Owen, III, 373.

June 10th, 1846. Finished the first volume of Kent. . . . On my way home I indulged in the following expenses — a silk hat (3.00), a vest (mersailles, 2.50), a figured cambric handkerchief (.75), a neckerchief (.37).

11th. Had rhubarb pies for dessert, which are not slow eating. . . . the President and Gen. Scott are getting up a little private warfare because the Gen. did not take command of the Army on the Rio Grande when *requested* by the Pres. . . . bought . . . a pocket diary to keep matters straight when I go to New York (3).

13th. Well! I have disposed of a little of my small change today, *sure.* I have been buying since breakfast. . . . two books for a present to Mrs. van Wyck (1.00), and a carpet bag (2.50), a pair of suspenders (1.50), also two Bibles for Tom & Virginia (3.25).

June 14th, 1846. I went to church and heard an excellent sermon from a blind preacher, Milburn, who was, or is, a chaplain to Congress.

William Henry Milburn, the "blind preacher," 1823–1903, suffered the loss of his eyesight at the age of five. He became an itinerant Methodist minister in 1843, and held charges in Mobile and Montgomery, Alabama. Two years later he was elected Chaplain of the U. S. House of Representatives, and later of the Senate.

15th. I was sorry to learn yesterday that . . . I shall have to travel most of the way in the night.

16th. Porterage to boat (.25), fare to New York (4.00), boat hand (5), and a coach to the Astor House (25).* . . . Met my friend, Davis, at breakfast. . . . took our seats in the omnibus and saw the *Great Western* Steamship. . . . did not come up to my expectation. Went to Niblo's Garden and saw the Ravel Family.**

*Even Capt. Marryatt defended Americanism, in opposition to the continentalized American, James Fenimore Cooper, when Marryatt wrote, "The bill of fare of . . . the Astor House is printed every day. I have one on me . . . to prove that the eating is not as bad in America as described by Mr. Cooper."—Thomas, 33-34.

**Niblo's Garden, at Broadway and Prince streets, was one of several enterprises of William Niblo.—Robotti, 516.

17th. Left the Astor House early for West Point. Paid my bill (3.50) . . . Going up the Hudson, we sat on deck and enjoyed its delightful scenery, when I ascended this river before it was night, and I saw not its far famed beauties. West Point is undoubtedly the prettiest place I ever saw, the ascent is rugged; but the top is a large plain, in the center of which stand the buildings of the Military Academy. I saw the cadets in only a few movements as it was vacation, but at night we had some fine fire works, and some of the best military music I ever heard.

June 18th, 1846. At two o'clock today we took the boat for Hudson, leaving with regret this lovely place. . . . I made arrangements with the driver to take me to Claverack immediately. This he did, I drove to Aunt's house and got out. . . . I found all well, and a niece of Aunt, Miss Weaver, with her.

19th. Spent the day in the company of my friends, and talking of good old times long gone past.

21st. Went to the village church [the Dutch Reformed], which is very plain, but venerated for its age. It was built in 1767, which date is known by its being painted in large characters on the side of the building. It has a fine situation on the top of a hill in a nice grove.

24th. We intended to have gone to the Catskill Mountain House, but the weather was so cool that we sat by fire, with great pleasure, so we abandoned our trip.

"A glowing page in the history of American Romanticism," was the Catskill Mountain House, built high in the Catskills in 1840, a gleaming white landmark that could be seen for miles. This building was the first and finest of resort hotels, beloved by artists and writers of the period. It stood for over 120 years, and was demolished in 1963.—Van Zandt, 27.

June 25th, 1846. Went out to Stockbridge, a village in Massachusetts, near which Aunt has placed Tom at school. . . . We went on a poor railroad to this village (1.00) and to dinner there at a miserable inn (25). . . . Left Aunt's for Hudson, to continue my trip to Boston.

26th. Arrived in Albany about day-break, went to a hotel and took breakfast. Found a note for me from Davis. He had gone to Boston, and wished me to follow him thither. . . . I ran down to the wharf and just got on board in time. . . . Fare to Boston(5.00). . . . Paid porterage to the Tremont House.

The Tremont House was *the* Boston hotel for many years. An interesting description of early 19th century dining there can be found in Linscott's *State of Mind,* 165.

27th. We went out to Cambridge and called on our friend . . . Alfred Davis. He showed me Harvard University, the Law School, etc. It is a venerable place, and presents a grand old appearance.

28th. We visited several of the churches, one almost opposite the hotel, called King's Chapel, in which there is a statue of Charles 2nd, the building having been erected during his reign. . . . We walked out after dinner to see the short sleeves and dresses of the Boston ladies, they have nice little feet, and ankles, and round arms, so they dress so as to show off these parts.

June 29th, 1846. Today we went to the celebrated Bunker Hill monument. . . . to Cambridge. . . . to Mt. Auburn. . . . we continued our ride (on horseback) to the gardens of Caleb Cushing.

Caleb Cushing had only recently returned to the United States from China, where as ambassador from the United States, he had negotiated the treaty of Wang Huja, by which five Chinese ports were opened for trade.

30th. We took the cars and proceeded to Lowell (.65), where we saw the factories, the gals and many doings too numerous to mention. There are many gals and many spindles, and, of course, from these two there must be much noise.

July 1st, 1846. Left Boston early this morning, paid bill at Tremont House (10.09). . . . Arrived in New York late at night and went to the Pearl St. House.

3rd. Shinkle and myself went to Harlem by the cars, and then to the large reservoir of Croton Water, whence we *walked* to the High Bridge, being misinformed as to the distance.* Boys are already beginning to fire crackers in honour of the coming 4th July, tho' we have a prospect of a poor day. I visited the Picture Gallery (.25) and saw Titian's "Venus," did not admire it much.

*It was quite a walk! The Croton Distributing Reservior was located on Fifth Avenue, between 40th and 42nd streets, and the High Bridge over the Harlem River is at West 174th Street. The Bridge, connecting Manhattan to the Bronx, carried water from the Croton Reservior to Manhattan. Croton Reservoir was opened in 1842, but the High Bridge was not completed until 1848. The masonry arches were a favorite subject for artists, and Edgar Allen Poe spent much time here.

July 6th, 1846. Again safe at home!

7th. I did nothing memorable today, except to make arrangements for going on a fishing excursion in a few days to the Delaware Water Gap. Had Paine and Woodruff to see me, they are of the party.

The gap formed by the Delaware River as it runs through the Blue Mountains, about 80 miles north of Philadelphia, is an area of indescribable beauty.

9th. Started about 5 A.M. . . . engaged a conveyance to take us to Water Gap.
12th. We learned here that there was no fishing at this place, but that about ten miles up the river among the mountains we would find sport. . . . We went over a bad road, to an inn called Henryville, after the name of the only inhabitant.

There is a village of Henryville northeast of the Water Gap at the present time, which can be reached by State Highway 447.

July 14th, 1846. Our landlord's name is James Henry, and has called the place after himself—he is a plain, simple, but very accommodating man, and is at this time engaged in harvest. The inhabitants here are complete hoosiers or backwoodsmen—illiterate, unsophisticated—it does my heart good to see some unpolished human nature, after seeing nought but penny-counting, scheming mortals for some months past.
15th. Becoming more expert in managing the fly and hence more successful in taking the fish.
16th. The landlord is an excellent man, but has a most slovenly, bad mannered woman for his wife. Tom Hobbs, take heed!
17th. Today Sterling Paine left us, having become tired of the sport.
19th. Some of the neighbors came in and danced all day, while Woodruff played the fiddle for them. I kept my room, reading a few books I had luckily brought with me.
22nd. How the perch do bite! . . . I several times took two at once, as I had two hooks upon my line. These are different from the Southern perch, which are here called sunfish, they are longer and more slim. We feast on fresh fish and make a dessert of whortleberries—not easy to beat.
23rd. We concluded to return to Philadelphia on tomorrow. . . . the landlord had been so much taken with us that he proposed to board us for nothing if we would stay another week with him. On the whole our stay in Henryville was very pleasant, and would have been much more so if the hostess had been more lady like.
25th. Was awakened this morning at 5 o'clock in order to be ready for the Phila. stage. . . . gave the servant 12 cents for blacking my boots. . . . Reached the city about 2½ o'clock.
26th. Heard a splendid sermon from Prof. McClintock of Dickinson College. His remarks on the book of Job were the most elegant & critical I ever heard. Ashley and I also heard him tonight.

John McClintock, 1814–1870, was a Methodist minister, and professor of mathematics, Greek, and Latin at Dickinson College. From 1848 to 1856 he edited the *Methodist Quarterly Review,* and wrote extensively on religious subjects. Dickinson College was founded in 1783 by the Presbyterians, and in 1833 came under the auspices of the Methodist Church.

July 28, 1846. I went to some of the music stores in Chestnut St. and was referred to several persons who might be induced to go to Ala. as music teachers. I do this at the request of the Trustees of the Institute. I called on several gentlemen and urged several to commence a correspondence with said Institute.

July 29th, 1846. I called on Mr. Porter, of the Sunday School Union, and transacted some business for Rev. Simpson Shepherd; it was in regard to his naturalization. . . . Ashley and I went to see Paine. . . . We concluded as we returned by the theatre to go in and see the performance. The play was *The Hunchback,* and was managed pretty well. Mrs. Burke in the principal female character.

Cornelia Frances Burke continued to use Burke as her stage name, although she had married Joseph Jefferson, II, many years before. Their son, Joseph Jefferson, III, was born in 1829, began his stage career at the age of three, and became one of the best known actors on the American stage. He made frequent appearances in Mobile and Montgomery, Alabama, during his earlier years.

31st. The mails about Athens have been changed. . . . I wrote to Henry Malone. . . . bought an *Omnibus,* a witty paper just started here, and sent it to him. . . . met with Thomas Wood, an old schoolfellow who is travelling for his health. . . . Thermometer in sun — 114°.

August 1st. I went to Jones Hotel and met Thos. Wood. . . . we visited West's great picture of "Christ Healing the Sick." I have never seen it before, and was so much pleased that I felt as if I could study it a day and not see all its beauties. I cannot say which of the crowd I most admire, perhaps the maniac boy.

This depiction of "Christ Healing the Sick" was the most celebrated of Benjamin West's paintings. It toured the country, came to Athens, and the *Chronicle* in February, 1845, stated that the exhibition had been met with "at least satisfaction if not delight to very respectable houses, of spectators."

Sunday, August 2nd, 1846. Heard an excellent sermon from . . . Prof. McClintock. . . . Walked after the sermon to the ruins of St. Augustine's Church, which was destroyed by a mob not long since.

St. Augustine's and St. Michael's Churches had been destroyed in the riots of 1844, during the wave of anti-Catholic feeling following the mass immigration of Irish Catholics as a result of the Potato Famine in Ireland. This situation gave rise to the "Native American" Party, whose members were incensed when Catholics objected to the reading of the King James Version of the Bible in public schools. Such anti-immigration sentiment led to the formation of the "Know-Nothing" Party of the 1850s.—Burt, 576.

4th. Called on Messers. T. & P. and got another $100, went then to Benkert's and tried on my new boots. Paid for them $4.75 as they were only footed. . . . Bought *Montagu's Letters.*
August 5th, 1846. Letter . . . from Aunt C., accepting our invitation to accompany us to Ala. . . . enjoyed a fine moonlight walk to the P. Office, and a glass of Roussel's Mineral Water.
11th. Went early to the Hotel, but meeting Tom Wood, he informed me that the expected ones had arrived. We then walked down Chestnut to the wharf, and thence to the Navy Yard where we saw the vessel *Germantown,* almost ready for launching. . . . Saw Mr. Webster, Mr. Crittenden, and Gen. Cass today, all returning from Congress — was much disappointed in the appearance of the first, expected to see a larger man.
12th. This day is particularly notable for the arrival of my long-expected relatives. . . . I conducted them to Jones' Hotel, and sat until teatime, talking about our home affairs & many other matters. . . . Received an excellent present from Miss Frances Malone.
13th. We took a stroll down Chestnut, and Third as far as Mrs. Drummonds, when Uncle, leaving the ladies in my charge, went in to see her. . . . he made arrangements to come and board with her during his stay.

Dr. Maclin had evidently boarded with Mrs. Drummonds while attending medical school in Philadelphia.

14th. Found Uncle in, we went out and did some business with the brokers and the bank.
15th. Went to Mrs. D.'s and accompanied the folks to the Jews' Synagogue, where we saw and heard service *in Hebrew.* [Mikveh Israel, one of the oldest synagogues in the United States, was established in 1740.]
August 16th, 1846. I . . . accompanied the ladies to St. Mary's Church, as it is a Catholic Church, it was ornamented with some splendid paintings, the most of them were frescos on the ceiling and sides of the building. [St. Mary's Catholic Church, was built in 1763 and enlarged in 1810.]
17th. We went to the Columbia House, where we met Mr. Vasser, who had just arrived from Athens. He brought me a letter from home.
20th. At nine this morning Uncle came to my room, and soon after-

wards Mr. Barclay. We met by agreement to hear the latter perform on the piano, as he is an applicant for the chair of Music in the Institute. He took us to a room in George St., and played some time very well. . . . This afternoon at 5, Mr. B. played for the ladies, at Mrs. D.'s, who were highly pleased at his power.

Benjamin S. Barclay was born in England in 1808. Living with him in Limestone in 1850 were Emily, 15; Ida, 14; and Edward, 8. They were all born in Tennessee, while his 5-year-old daughter, Clara, was born in New Jersey. Barclay later married Mary Swain.

August 21, 1846. After dinner Cousin M. and I accompanied Mr. Sloss to buy artificial flowers. There was a small quantity at the shop we visited, so Mr. S. did not purchase. At night—by the request of Mr. Hine, I accompanied him to the Theatre. We had two good plays, the first, *The Honeymoon,* was very good, and well played. . . . Mrs. Burke as the Duchess.

22nd. I accompanied Mr. Hine to buy goods. . . . About 12 [we went] to see the launch of the U. S. vessel—*Germantown*—we all went down in an omnibus and succeeded in getting on board the receiving ship, thro' the influence of Mrs. Captain Mercer.

25th. I went down early this morning & visited the Academy of Fine Arts. . . . we continued our excursion to the asylum for the Blind. . . . A little Chinese read a few verses of Scripture. I bought a little bead-basket made by the pupils. Tonight took leave of our folks as they start very early in the morning.

The Academy of Fine Arts was the special project of Charles Wilson Peale, the distinguished artist. He filled it with his portraits of the Revolutionary War heroes, and with stuffed animals, for which he sketched backgrounds of their natural habitats, a distinctive feature of the later museums of natural history.

29th. Received [a letter] from Ma, which was mailed on the 23rd inst., thus coming in six days, the quickest time ever made by one from Athens. . . . I enjoyed a delightful shower bath tonight (25).

Thursday, September 3, 1846. Went to Jones' to seek my relatives. While I was absent, Uncle called for me . . . left his card, informing me that he was at his old lodgings. I hastened down immediately and found Aunt Cornelia & children there also.

4th. We start tonight at 10 [for Athens] and I am now squaring my book for the last time in Phila. I bought today a pair of Berlin gloves (.75) and a bottle of excellent Cologne (.25).

ATHENS, ALABAMA 1847

Friday, January 1, 1847. Just two weeks ago, I joined Leonidas Division No. 2, Sons of Temperance. This Institution has been lately organized here, and is doing very well.

5th. I went to class-meeting, and afterwards sat some time with Aunts C[ornelia] & K[eziah] at Uncle's house. My room was carpeted today.

Keziah Fennell Hobbs was the wife of John, and mother of Eliza Hobbs Maclin. This brother of Ira Hobbs lived in Madison County, where he owned extensive lands, including the island still known as Hobbs Island. —Hobbs Family Papers.

6th. Tonight we had a "happening in" at Mr. R. Vasser's, to which the young public was generally invited. I happened to go to Mrs. R.'s [Richardson] and attend Miss Mary to the party; I enjoyed some moments of chat with Mrs. R. before starting, of course, the walk was *pleasant* tho' the road was a rough one. Most of the young folks of our village were present, and the time was sociably spent in conversation, interrupted by a lunch of delicacies about 10 o'clock. . . . we parted, Miss M. losing a curl on the way home.

Miss Mary was either Mary Richardson, daughter of John, or Mary Pleasants, 1829–1907, daughter of William and Anne Bradley Davis Richardson. William Richardson, 1797–1866, was born in Goochland County, Virginia. He married Anne Bradley Davis, 1810–1861, daughter of Nicholas. Around 1834 they built a home of a strong Georgian influence on South Clinton Street in Athens. Among other children of the Richardsons were Sallie Bettie, 1831–1856, married Dr. L. H. Binford; and Dr. Nicholas Davis, 1832–1895, who married first Sarah E. Hine, 1839–1874, and second, Ann Echols.

January 7th, 1847. The rain of last night ended in a snow, so that when Scott opened my door this morning I saw the ground covered with this beautiful "stuff." . . . Played backgammon with Aunt Cornelia after tea.

8th. The rays of an unclouded sun almost entirely dissipated the snow. I kept my room closely today, and reading Byron. . . . and inditing a letter to John Keyes. . . . Attended the meeting of the Sons of Temperance tonight, we initiated several excellent members among them Rev. B. H. Hubbard. . . . The society now numbers upwards of 40, and is advancing rapidly.

Rev. Benjamin Hubbard taught in the Female Institute, and was elected president in 1849, succeeding Dr. Richard Rivers.

10th. Mr. Hine sat with me after dinner until we smoked our cigars, and had some talk about Florida, which he has just visited. The snow is three inches deep, and a good prospect for more; fine weather for huntsmen, but hard on farmers.

January 11th, 1847. This morning early Figg and I drew on our rubber over shoes, and started rabbit hunting in the snow. . . . I traced one to a hollow tree and got him — but I shot none, neither did Figg. . . . Tonight I sat some time with Col. Jones and planned an effort to raise a volunteer corps here.

Dr. R. W. Figg was a dentist. According to John Tanner, he was a favorite with everybody, a "clever good man." He later moved to Huntsville, but at the time of the 1850 census, he was residing at the Bass Hotel.

12th. Spent the rest of the morning in getting up a paper to be carried around for the names of such as were willing to form a volunteer company. . . . got my feet wet, snowballing with the girls this evening, and stayed at home to dry them.

13th. I renewed my efforts this morning concerning the military company; and with tolerable success. Such diversity of opinion exists in regard to the kind of company we should have that it is hard to get a sufficient number of any one notion. . . . Tonight I played back-gammon with Aunt Cornelia, and was most terribly beaten. She was about 8 games ahead of me when we stopped.

14th. Today it was announced in town that there had been two deaths last night here—one, a child of Mr. William Richardson & the other, John G. Smith. . . . The new music teacher for the Institute came up in the stage today from Florence; he recognized me, and I conducted him to the hotel near by, and attended to the delivery of his baggage. I went to Richardson's tonight to sit up with the corpse of the child; found some young ladies & gentlemen there. . . . Bought some cigars of Capt. Rice.

January 15th, 1847. The weather is now uncommonly agreeable for this season of the year. . . . Attended a meeting of the Sons of Temperance . . . admitted three candidates, among whom was a notorious drunkard. . . . if he sticks, we need despair of none others, no matter how debased by drunkenness.

17th. Went to Sunday-school after breakfast and taught my class. . . . Mrs. Fenner came over, to bring her daughter—she tells us much news from the army, which she learned from her husband, who has just returned from Camargo.

18th. I received a letter from Ashley and Mims. . . . Mrs. Maclin gave me some of the nicest molasses candy for my cold.

19th. I spent the morning talking with Col. Jones, relative to the organization of a military company here. We are both anxious for one & both despair of getting up one—we mean now to endeavor to raise a horse company. I was just thinking of going to the plantation, when it commenced snowing. . . . Tonight Mr. Barclay tuned our piano and played some for us.

20th. The weather today is most singular—all day a sort of very fine snow or rather mist has been falling; every one said "twould snow or rain directly, but still the mist continued, and we have had nothing else. . . . I read some today, and drew some; Mr. Sloss says I have a military mania, so I drew military figures, patterns of uniforms, etc. I read some of a French play by Molière. I found some difficulty in some of the conversational phrases, used by the speakers, but with this exception, I translated with facility. No prospect of a thaw tomorrow. The town clock stopped last night from cold.

"I have been told that the clock in the cupola of the first courthouse was the handiwork of that mechanical genius, Samuel Crenshaw, without a model—he never even having seen a town clock," wrote Mrs. R. V. Howard on May 2, 1895.—Mason Scrapbooks, Vol. I.

January 21st, 1847. This disagreeable morning I spent in moulding bullets, as 'twas too dreary to do any thing else—melted up two pounds of lead and made about two hundred balls. The road was so bad that the stage from Florence did not come up, but the mail came on horseback.

23rd. Assisted Cousin E. to assort a large pile of newspapers, which has been collecting in her house for years. I collected most all the numbers of the *Ladies' Book* since 1838, and arranged them by the year; I strongly urge her to have them bound, as the engravings are very fine and all complete. For my trouble she gave me a large bundle of the *New Orleans Picayune,* and a good many other papers; from these I mean some day to compile a splendid scrapbook.

The magazine was probably Godey's *Lady's Book,* edited by Sarah Hale, and published from 1830 to 1870. There was, however, also in publication a magazine entitled the *Southern Ladies' Book.*

January 24th, 1847. So rainy that we could not have Sunday School. . . . Mr. Scruggs preached however to a small congregation. . . . Half past eleven — stage horn blowing.

Rev. Thomas Scruggs, of Lawrence County, was an itinerant minister of the Methodist Church.

29th. Am now reading the *Wandering Jew,* a novel of most exciting interest.
30th. We practiced some vocal music tonight, under the instruction of Mrs. Swain. Ours is an amateur club, for singing songs and hymns — and meets once a week. I was weighed today — weight 126½ pounds.
31st. Rev. Scruggs preached a plain, practical sermon at 11, also at night, but I was so much disturbed by the noise made by the blacks that I did not hear much.* Visited James Coleman in the afternoon and found his room full of company.** He is said to be improving, slowly, from his long illness.

*Recent renovations on the old Methodist Church done by the late Harvey Gilbert, and his wife, Lib, show that there was never a slave gallery in the church. The slaves were probably in the basement, the sanctuary being on the second floor.

**James, the oldest son of Judge Daniel and Elizabeth Lockhart Coleman, recovered to graduate from La Grange College and medical school in Louisville. He then became a Methodist minister, and remained active in this field from 1853 to 1897.—Owen, III, 373.

Monday, February 1st, 1847. Measured my heighth . . . shall I grow any taller?
2nd. The winter is getting the credit of even the old ones, of being very bad, and a little more of such weather will characterize it as the worst yet for roads! Worked in the Carpenter's all day, and succeeded in making a picture frame of poplar, veneered with bodark, a beautiful yellow wood.
3rd. I kept comfortable, by keeping in doors, & by resorting to that best of all things for every thing, viz., manual labour. . . . Tonight plotted a survey for Mr. McCracken, county surveyor, and thus reviewed my old rules on this subject. Bought a pair of cassinet pants.
4th. Today at dinner I learned from Mr. Hine that my old friend, Bill Wilkinson, was in town. . . . I hastened up to see him—found him at the tavern—he looks very well, and I perceived from the conversa-

tion of the evening, that he still retains his droll ways, and sayings of dry humour.

"Bill," "Wilk," "Pomp," were all names that Thomas Hobbs used for this special friend, the jovial Dr. William Wilkinson, a classmate at La Grange.

February 5th, 1847. Someone is now (it is late at night), playing on the clarinet uptown, and the music sounds very well indeed.
8th. The whole cotton growing South is running mad on account of the price of cotton—it is higher than it has been for years, and every steamer from England brings the joyful news of a rise. 10 cents a pound has been refused in this county. This high price is a God-send for the bank-debtors, who are obliged to pay up all outstanding dues, next June.
10th. Wilkinson and I visited some of our acquaintances, but I could not prevail on him to visit any of our ladies. I took leave of him tonight, as he expects to start early in the morning. "I knew him well, Horatio, a fellow of infinite jest."
11th. Took dinner with Cousin Eliza, and partook of a fine roast turkey—Uncle is absent, attending the sick at the plantation. Tonight William Richardson and I called on Mr. Barclay, the professor of music. He was communicative, and we heard many interesting things from him in regard to his past life, composition of music, etc.
13th. Tonight we made some vocal music, also had some from Tom and Scott on the bones, and me with the flute.

Tom and Scott were personal slaves of Thomas Hobbs. This provides us with some insight into their social pattern.

15th. Messrs. Hine and Sloss started for Philadelphia this morning; it made me feel anxious to return thither. . . . They go via Nashville and the Ohio River. The fine weather has set the people to gardening. The atmosphere is cloudy from the smoke of the chimneys and burnings on the farms.
February 16th, 1847. Uncle returned unexpectedly from the plantation tonight. He felt symptoms of the same disease which is now raging in the county. It is very sudden in its attack, and quick and violent in its work. Several children have died from it, with only a few hours duration.

A history of the medical profession in Limestone County appeared in the *Alabama Courier,* Athens, May 2, 1895; in which the 1847 epidemic is described. It stated that the disease was typhoid fever, a new type of fever, "and its mortality was fearful under the lines of treatment then practiced." The epidemic was so great that there would be as many as twenty cases at a time on many plantations. On one occasion Dr. McDonald sent his undergraduate, Thomas Maddin, to Luke Pryor's plantation, where there were many cases of the fever. There was a general consultation of doctors: Malone, Hussey, Sheffey, Maclin, and others. "There was a common consent that the disease was new to them, and that the old methods were not only unavailing, but harmful. Dr. Maclin, having large estates, was not offering for general practice, but looked after the sick on his several plantations, said: 'Gentlemen, I have treated 33 cases, many of them had pneumonic systems, I bled each one of them, and every one died.'" They concluded that they would stop using the old remedies of calomel and bleeding, and give proper foods and stimulants.

February 19th, 1847. The frogs joined in a vast chorus last night, sure sign of fine weather. . . . Oliver and myself rode out a little way this afternoon, my horse has been ridden so little lately that he was quite fretful.

24th. Cousin Thomas Fenner came here this evening, to bring his sister, Margaret, to school. He informed us that his father has gone to New Orleans, where his duty as commissary calls him. He was attached to the Army of Invasion, but was transferred on account of bad health. . . . I rode out this evening. Milk-and-Peaches was restive from standing so long in the stable—prancing about in the road, he kicked the bottom of my foot while it was in the stirrup!

26th. Finished my *Wandering Jew* . . . too long . . . main objection . . . strongly advocates physiognomy. . . . Assisted Pa to graft some peach trees.

27th. Henry Malone arrived in today's stage, he has cultivated a mustache, and other beard, and has thus altered his appearance very much.

28th. This has been a remarkable month; the weather has been notoriously changeable; no appointment could be made calculating on the weather of tomorrow. . . . Another remarkable thing—there has been no full moon during the month.

March 1st. I received a *Union,* in which old Ritchie bears down particularly heavy on Calhoun and other Democrats who voted for his expulsion from the Senate. This was a piece of injustice, as I believe, and the "Nestor of the Press" will make his persecutors remember the deed.

Thomas Ritchie was not known for his placid disposition! He assumed editorship of the *Washington Union* in 1845 at the request of President Polk. For forty years he had been editor of the *Richmond Enquirer,* and succeeded in making both staunch enemies and friends.

March 2nd, 1847. Left for the country—accompanying Ma and Cousin E. to see Aunt Haldane, who is sick. . . . Returned in the afternoon with Cousin E., leaving Ma with Aunt. Spent an hour with Col. Jones tonight.

Aunt Haldane was Rebecca Maclin, sister of Thomas. She married James Haldane in Brunswick County, Virginia, on September 10, 1799. After Haldane's death, Rebecca lived at Slopeside with Major Maclin, and continued to live there after his death in 1845.—Hobbs Family Papers.

3rd. After breakfast came to my office and examined Hoffman's *Legal Study,* in order to see what law book it would be most proper for me to read next—Concluded after this examination to take up Kent.

5th. Received per mail . . . a comic Valentine, representing a lawyer in the act of speaking. . . . It came from Phila. and was, I doubt not, the work of Mims and Ashley.

March 6th, 1847. Today Uncle was called again to the plantation to visit the sick negroes. Some more are very sick with the pneumonia, which has raged amongst them for about a month. He thinks some of those now sick will certainly die, and several are dangerous. At Matthews' plantation, which is in sight of ours, there has not been a case, and yet his negroes are as much, or more, exposed to the weather than any in the neighborhood.

7th. What weather! . . . all unite in saying such a spring has never been seen before—generally, a considerable part of the corn crop is planted before this date, but this season ploughing has not been commenced, so rainy has it been. . . . Every mail brings us news of the starvation in poor mis-governed Ireland. They die by the family of sheer starvation. Our generous countrymen are subscribing liberally for their relief & ships are already loading with corn and provisions to succour them. The Queen has given £1000 for their relief—Albert £500.

8th. Our circuit court commenced today, Judge Daniel Coleman presiding. . . . I intend to attend court closely this week, as I will be able to learn more law there than by studying my books—who knows but the next time Court sits here, I may be admitted to the bar. "Quien sabe?"

9th. Attended court closely today, but heard but few trials—for few came off, owing to the sickness of some of the principal lawyers and the absence of parties and witnesses caused by high water. . . . Today Pa was taken ill suddenly, and has been quite sick all the afternoon — he was bled by Dr. Sowell this evening, and has been better since.

March 10th, 1847. I spent the day in waiting on Pa, who is recovering. Today it rains as if the earth were thirsty, and the rivers dry, but *every*

body says such a spell was never seen before—when will it cease?
11th. By way of variety, it was pouring when I arose this morning, and for the sake of variety, it has kept up the same cheering process all day. I went to the Court House this morning to see how the State's business got along in the prevailing drought. . . . The Judge having nothing to hear but the cry of "Not Ready" from the lawyers. The universal plea is "The creeks are impassable, and our clients and witnesses cannot arrive."
12th. I attended Pa's sick-room closely this morning, as he had occasional paroxysms of pain which were very severe. I saw Dr. Sowell's little son, Willie, who is very low; his eye was lit up with an unnatural brilliancy. . . . his father has despaired of his life.
16th. Went to Mr. Fraser's and grafted some peaches for Cousin Martha. . . . also grafted some fine kinds in our own garden. Pa is convalescent.
18th. Having the prospect of a fair day, Major Malone and I started hunting, but failing in getting a dog, and meeting Col. Jones, who urged us to accompany him to Brown's Ferry. . . . we accordingly put down our guns & did so. Col. Cox informed us that the river is higher now than he ever knew it before, & he was brought up on its banks.* It is now more than two miles wide, runs rapidly carrying down a great deal of drift. The horse-boat became unmanageable from drift yesterday, and was carried about 3 miles down. It is a slight coincidence that the last great rise was in 1826—the year I was born, and now comes this in 1847—the year when I complete my minority!

*Col. Bartley Cox, 1792–1851, was born in North Carolina to Isham and Catharine Cox, came early to Limestone County, and kept a tavern near Brown's Ferry. It was here that White, murdered by the Thornton brothers, had his last meal. Tanner mentions having had many hospitable meals and nights' lodgings while out on cotton marking tours. Bartley Cox married Eliza Freeman, 1800–1859, of Tuscumbia, and they had Joshua, Isham, John, William, Robert, Eliza, and Thomas Jefferson. In 1966 when the Tennessee Valley Authority moved the Cox graves back from the river banks in preparation for the construction of the Brown's Ferry nuclear plant, they found a number of graves without stones. Some of these were two feet deeper than the others, indicating that they were much older than the Cox burials, which began early in the 1830s.

March 19th, 1847. Uncle went to the plantation . . . killed 22 squirrels, and says he would have got as many more, if he had had more time. . . . superintended the cleaning of my stable, and a thorough rubbing of my horse, Milk-and-Peaches. What a sweet name, and what a fine horse.

. . . Attended meeting of Sons of Temperance; we initiated several among them Rev. Jacob Lindley, a white-headed old minister, and author of *Infant Philosophy*. Pa was able to leave his room today.
March 22nd, 1847. Uncle and I went to the plantation today, expecting to remain several days and hunt upon the high waters. . . . After dinner we procured a canoe, and went to the Beaver Pond bridge . . . but we found nothing to shoot except a very large turtle.
23rd. The breed of hares in this region is, I guess, almost exterminated; as the water rose, the [*sic*] climbed upon logs, which after a time became afloat, and the poor animals were either taken by the huntsmen, or perished from hunger, or else to escape, plunged into the water and were drowned.
24th. Today's mail brought rumour of a battle, between Taylor and Santa Anna, which was terminating rather in favour of the latter, owing to his greater number of men. . . . a requisition will be immediately made on this state and others, to furnish more troops. This will, perhaps, afford an opportunity to some of our friends here, to go to Mexico, who have been anxious to volunteer for some time. . . . Received a beauitful bouquet from Miss S[allie] Malone this morning, which almost inspires my Muse. Ma is quite sick.
25th. Received today 8 newspapers, which have been delayed by the high waters.
March 26th, 1847. We heard this morning that a call was made by Gen. Taylor on some of the adjacent states and our own, to send immediately a large number of troops to his assistance; he is considered in great danger and we are all tip-toe to hear more from him.
27th. I sat up with Mr. Austin last night. . . . Several of our merchants returned today from Phila. Mrs. Swain expected her daughter today, but she is to come in a few days with her uncle.

Robert Austin, 1801–1847, succeeded his father, Robert, as clerk of the County Court in 1831. Robert, Sr., had been appointed by Judge Daniel Coleman in 1824 to the position. There are many references to the clear and concise records kept by the Austins. Robert, Jr., married a Miss Davis, of Madison County. John Tanner described the Austin house as headquarters for all the young folks, and "we used to congregate there and make love to the girls of Sunday evenings, come with them in to church, etc., and many happy hours have I spent there with O. O. Nelson, J. P. Ezell, Jim Ad Binford, and many others. . . . "—Tanner, July 21, 1876.

28th. I was startled this morning to hear of the death of Mr. Austin. . . . Mr. A. was a highly esteemed citizen, and held several public offices with great praise—he was thought to be one of the best court-clerks in the State. His place will not be easily filled. He was buried at 5 o'clock this afternoon, and his corpse was followed by a large crowd of friends and relatives.

March 29th, 1847. I was up quite early this morning, leaving my little bed-fellow and namesake in bed, as he was quite unwell.

Evidently the slave, Tom, slept with his master.

30th. I rode with Bro. Scruggs and others to La Grange. . . . went immediately to the home of my old friend, Prof. Tutwiler. . . . spent an agreeable evening in conversation with them and my quondam chum, G. P. Keyes.

31st. When we arrived in Tuscumbia, we heard the report of cannon, and on inquiry learned that it was in honor of Taylor's victory over Santa Anna, the news of which they had just received. We organized a Division of the Sons of T., called Protection Division, No. 4. . . . We intended to have gone to Leighton tonight, but we concluded to stay, and attend another meeting.

Thursday, April 1st. Rev. Scruggs and Lee and I left Tuscumbia after breakfast, and after a long, slow ride, without dinner, we arrived at Mrs. Bobo's well-known stand [at Leighton] about dark. Several large ponds turned us from the road several times. They [*sic*] way we went at Mrs. B.'s good supper was a caution to dyspepsia, and then we rested so well on her clean beds.

Leighton, in Colbert County, less than twenty miles from Tuscumbia, is located at the crossroads of the Byler and Decatur-Tuscumbia routes. The most noted stand there in early days was Gregg's Tavern, owned by Nathan Gregg. The Bobo family may have owned this tavern in 1847, for Nathan Gregg was living in Lawrence County in 1850, while the family of Clark Bobo was listed, with a clerk in the household, as living in the Sixth District of Franklin (now Colbert) County.

April 3rd, 1847. Today we received confirmation of that which first arrived, in regard to a battle between Taylor & Santa Anna, near Monterey—several officers of distinction were among our killed. I made some rods and a hoop for the game of "graces," which our young ladies are anxious to play. Mrs. Swain's daughter and brother came to our house, in today's stage. . . . had my hair trimmed today by Dr. Sowell, he cut it too close.

Mary Swain married Professor Benjamin Barclay on June 25, 1850. —Jones and Gandrud.

4th. We had no service at 11, because it was a sacramental occasion at the Union Church, and on such times the churches of the village mutually give way to each other. Rev. Donnell preached today, and a collection was taken up. I gave 25 cents. After dinner sat with Mrs. M. and Aunt Cornelia, ate some scaly barks. Heard a good sermon from Rev. Rivers tonight.

The name of Robert Donnell is synonymous with that of Cumberland Presbyterianism in Alabama, for he had come to its northern area to preach in 1809, only seven years after formation of the Cumberland division from the mother church. The Reverend Donnell, 1785–1855, was born in Guilford County, North Carolina, went to Wilson County, Tennessee in 1793, and was ordained to the ministry in 1811. In 1817 he was married to Anna Smith, and in 1832 to Clara Lindley, daughter of Rev. Jacob Lindley. Robert Donnell's massive tombstone in the Athens Cemetery, erected by the Cumberland Presbyterian Church, states that he was "one of the compilers of the Confession of Faith and Discipline of the C. P. Church, an enlightened exponent and an invincible defender of its doctrines. Self made of gigantic mind, and commanding person. Social in feelings, fervent in devotion, chaste in style, graceful in attitude, eloquent in manner, logical in reasoning, convincing in argument, urbane in deportment, uniform in piety, consecrated to his calling, his praise is in all the churches . . . " The Donnell home in Athens was added to the National Register of Historic Places in 1973, and will be restored as headquarters for the Limestone County Historical Society.

March 5th, 1847. The Sons of Temperance attended the funeral of our brother, Blackburn; he is the first of our numbers who has died.
7th. We received information today, that the boats in landing at New Orleans, were driven by the winds against the shipping, and immediately sunk, and with them our cotton. We hear that 'tis not much injured, but this is only the worse for us, as it must be damaged to a certain extent, or the insurance will not be paid.
8th. This morning I set to work to make a jointed fishing rod. I used cedar wood . . . in making two joints—shall have the others of cane.
10th. By today's mail we learned that the city and castle of Vera Cruz had surrendered to our arms. This strong castle, had it been bravely defended by the 4,000 men it contained, could have sustained a tremendous attack, but the cowardly Mexicans gave it up, almost without firing a gun. Our court house bell was long and loudly rung at this news. . . . Many think the war is now at an end, for what more can we do? I suppose the capitol will be taken.
14th. Read a few pages of Mrs. Trollope's *Paris & the Parisians.*
17th. Today we had a battalion muster in town, and this, of course, brought a great many persons in from the country. . . . I am exempt on account of an appointment I lately received in Gen. Lane's staff.

General James Lane and his brother, Judge George Washington Lane, were sons of Jonathan and Mary Colley Lane. Around 1840, General Lane built one of the most interesting houses in the state, an octagon. Until it was torn down in 1953 to make way for the First Baptist Church building, it was one of few extant octagon houses in the country. Mason Scrapbooks, Vol I.

April 18th, 1847. We heard an excellent sermon from Bro. Hubbard— it was the funeral of Ruffin Coleman, a boy of much promise, who died lately at his uncle's in Miss.

Ruffin Coleman, Jr., born in 1832, died on April 3rd, 1847, and was buried in the Ruffin Coleman cemetery on Coleman Hill, Athens.

19th. This is the anniversary of my birth-day—today I complete my 21st year, and of course, my minority. I have reflected much today and indeed, for several days past upon my past life, and my preparations for usefulness and standing hereafter. I am determined to pursue a more manly life hereafter. . . . Peck finished my Codrinton coat.

George Roland Peck, 1813–1876, was born in Boutetort County, Virginia, the son of Lewis and Mary Jones Peck; and nephew of George Peck, one of the founders of Decatur. George R. Peck married Martha Jane Thomas in 1837, and had George, William, and Margaret living at home in 1850.

April 21st, 1847. I started early for Lucas' Ferry,* where I promised to meet Uncle and Levin Foote,** to try our luck with a trout line. . . . When I arrived there I found them resting on the bank, having just taken two very large cat-fish (the two weighed 65 pounds) off the line, and also some smaller ones.

*John Lucas, 1785–1835, married Martha Hobbs, born in 1790, and came to Limestone County at an early date. At the terminus of land known for many years as Beulah Land, he established a ferry sometime before 1830. Here he built a house that has been described as one of the finest of Limestone County homes, which was torn down by the Tennessee Valley Authority. Two children of John and Martha Hobbs were: Ann Elizabeth, 1819–1897, who first married William Edward Malone, and after his death married Robert N. Malone, 1807–1884; and Edmund, who married Flora Ann Lewis. Edmund's descendant, William Lucas Keyes, has carefully preserved and shared family documents.

**Levin Powell Foote, 1822–1864, was the son of George and Sarah Powell Foote. He married Margaret Tanner, 1824–1869, and had three children recorded in the 1850 census. "Lev Foote was a man of a high sense of honor and would scorn to do a mean act," wrote John Tanner in July, 1876.

April 22nd, 1847. Pa got the *American Almanac* for this year, today. I had never examined one fully before. . . . it is a very useful work . . .

After dinner Tom Jones and I fixed up in the basement of the church, a set of gymnastic bars for exercise.

24th. I came to my office about daybreak, having set up most of the night with Mr. Mc[Cracken]. I committed another somnambulism this morning. I had scarcely got to sleep, before Scott came to make a fire; the noise of the door startled me, and impressed with the notion that the house was falling on me, I rushed out, and ran with all my speed across the walk, and to the palings on the other side, then turned towards the house, and stood for a moment under Mrs. Swain's window—in this position the cries of the terrified Scott awakened me, and I ran with equal speed back to my room.

25th. Attended the funeral of Mrs. Caine [*sic*], an estimable lady, the wife of Mr. Chappell Cain.

Mary Green Malone, 1810–1847, married Allison Chappell Cain, 1800–1862, in 1827 and had seven children. Allison Cain married Martha M. Parham on October 18th, 1848, to provide a mother for the children. Mary Green was a half-sister of Henry Booth and John Nicholas Malone, she being the daughter of George Malone and his first wife, Martha Chambliss, who died in Sussex County, Virginia in 1815.—Cain, 7.

April 27th, 1847. Recruiting is now all the rage in our village. Captain Higgins goes on briskly. . . . twice a day does our Captain draw out his men for drill on our public square. . . . Cousin E. has given me a birthday present—a beautiful embroidered vest.

28th. This morning found Ma, Cousin Eliza & myself on the road to Huntsville, on a visit to Dr. Capshaw and lady.* . . . Huntsville is a pretty town of about 2 thousand inhabitants, and contains some of the most tastefully arranged residences in North Alabama. It is known for its aristocratic spirit, a portion of its citizens make money the criterion of worth, and having this qualification, the lowest may easily gain admittance among the "upper ten."

*Dr. Preston Capshaw married Anna Eliza Maclin's sister, Amanda, in 1840.—Hobbs Family Papers.

29th. Major Coffee, who acted as aid to Gen. Taylor at the battle of Buena Vista, is in town, and the people are making quite a lion of him. Wherever he stops on the streets, he is sure to collect a crowd around him, and his details of the battle, description of General T[aylor], etc., are listened to with much interest. He is a son of Gen. Coffee, who was the friend of Gen. Jackson, and who was so serviceable in the Indian Wars of the South.

The diary statement indicates that Major Coffee was the son of Gen. John Coffee, of Lauderdale County, but available Lauderdale records do not indicate that any of the Coffee sons served in the Mexican War. An article in the *Huntsville Democrat* of July 15, 1846, mentions Col. John R. Coffey as one of the officers of the Alabama Regiment who embarked for Point Isabel. This John R. Coffey, of Jackson County, was an officer in the Mexican War, and was born near Nashville on a farm that his father had purchased from his friend, Andrew Jackson.—Owen, III. 368.

Saturday, May 1st, 1847. Left this morning for Mooresville. . . . to organize a Division of the Sons of Temperance. . . . At night we organized in the old Masonic Hall (Mr. DeWoody informed me this was the first Hall built in the county, and that my father was initiated there.)

The Limestone Lodge, No. 18, Free and Accepted Masons, was built on the site of the present Bibb-Richardson home in Mooresville. The Female Seminary held classes on the first floor. In 1863 the building was torn down by Lt. Col. Jonathan Biggs, USA. Damages were claimed after the war, but no action was taken.—Pat Jones, *Mooresville,* 43.

3rd. Strolled up town, being the first Monday of the month, many persons were present.* Pa is absent tonight—he is with Aunt Martha Lucas, who is sick. I record this, for it is so rare for him to stay away from home, unless we are with him. Judge H. C. Jones and John Key had a fight today on the Square.

*The first Monday of the month was court day in many Southern county seats. In some places it became a widespread trading day. First Monday is still observed in Scottsboro, Alabama; and devotees travel for many miles to bargain for anything from guns and dogs to trundle beds.

May 5th, 1847. Making preparations to go to Mooresville.
6th. The brethren of Mooresville would not suffer us to pay our bills at the tavern, so by way of letting off surplus steam, I gave the 'ostler a "bit."

The Mooresville Tavern was built in 1825, supposedly by Griffin Lamkin. Originally it is said to have had an ell wing, which has long since been torn away, as have the ice house and other appurtenances. The square window for the first post office in that place is still visible on the facade.—Pat Jones, *Mooresville,* 20.

8th. Today's mail brought an account of the battle of Cerro Gordo, it was another bloody affair. Among the killed was Fred Nelson, son of Judge Nelson, of this place; he was brought up in this country, and was an estimable young man. He was acting captain of a company from Memphis. His father and brother [Owen] were deeply affected by the news of his death.

9th. Unseasonable—it is so cold that fire is almost necessary. This is injuring the cotton crop. Last night Mr. McCracken, one of our oldest inhabitants, died. . . . He held, up to his death, the office of County Surveyor.

May 10, 1847. Pa, with Aunt Cornelia and her children, left this morning to visit our relatives in Marshall and Madison Counties—they went to Decatur and took a steam-boat there for Fort Deposit.

14th. News of another call for volunteers came this morning in an official proclamation from Gov. Martin. Six companies are called from our State—one of which is to be mounted.

Governor Joshua Martin, 1797–1856, began his law career in Athens. He had the distinction of never having suffered a defeat throughout his long political career. Martin was the first governor to officiate from the new capital in Montgomery. He married two daughters of Judge William Mason of Athens, Mary and Sarah. The Martin home in Athens is believed to be the oldest house extant in that place.—Owen, IV, 1166.

20th. Tonight we had the last meeting of our singing class.

22nd. I attended the Examination today. It was conducted with that fairness and thoroughness for which this Institute has been justly celebrated. . . . At night went with two friends to Mr. J. C. Malone's to visit his daughters and to eat strawberries. We assisted him to open and set up a new piano and then had some good music from it.

James Chappell Malone, 1800–1863, was the son of Thomas Chappell and Mary Chappell Malone. He married Eliza Frances Binford, moved to Limestone with his parents, where his father bought the land known as Dogwood Flat. They later lived on their plantation on the Township Road some five miles south of Athens, and at the time of the diary entry were living in Athens. Among their children were Frances Hardiman, one of two members of the first graduating class of the Female Institute, who later married Sam Henderson, of New Orleans; Susan Stith, married William Brown; Elizabeth Tucker, married Alexander Wheless; Thomas Henry, married Ellen Fall, and served for many years as dean of the Vanderbilt School of Law; James Chappell; Julia Maclin; Mary Louisa; and Lucy Burton. James C. Malone died while a refugee in Marietta, Georgia, in 1863, and is buried there.

May 24th, 1847. Attended a small party at Judge Coleman's tonight. Judge Mason was present, and was the principal guest.

25th. The examination continued, deepening in interest as the higher classes come forward. Today we heard the senior class on some subjects. . . . My room is occupied by Dr. Henkle, the assistant editor of the *Nashville Christian Advocate*, who has come down to address the school.

Cousin Isham Fennell and William Rivers are down on a visit to us now.

Isham Fennell was the brother of Keziah Fennell Hobbs, and the son of Isham Fennell, Sr., of Marshall County. The elder Fennell was one of the commissioners chosen to organize the Beard's Bluff to Elyton Railroad, approved in the 1853 session of the legislature.

May 26th, 1847. The young ladies of the graduating class have stood the thorough and impartial drilling with wonderful credit to themselves. Dr. Henkle, who was a stranger to us, was most agreeably surprised at the *depth* of their learning, expecting the usual superficial display common schools make use of to puff their doings. Mr. Barclay's class in Instrumental Music gave us a specimen of their performance after dinner.
27th. The degree of Mistress of Arts was conferred on four young ladies, and several others were graduated in particular departments. . . . Miss Sarah Ford, Miss Carmichael, Miss Keziah Brooks and Miss Mary P. Richardson were the thorough graduates.
28th. This morning Mr. Barclay left for Phila., having Aunt Cornelia and her children under his care. . . . I wrote by Mr. B. for my uniform as Assistant Adjutant General, which place I fill in Gen. Lane's staff.
29th. Capt. Higgins' company having been completed, left this morning for Mexico via Florence. . . . The Brass Band accompanied them to Edmondson's hill.* I started for Decatur about ten, with Mrs. Swain and daughter, which place I reached after a quick ride, in time to enter their names as passengers on the steamboat for Knoxville. This trip to Decatur and back (30 miles), I performed almost without getting off my horse—all were surprised to see me home tonight.

*"The welcome sound of the stage horn coming down the Cuff Edmondson hill or approach on the Huntsville road has gladdened the hearts of those expecting the return of friends and loved ones," wrote John Tanner. Covington Edmondson owned the house on west Washington Street later owned by Ernest Hine, and the little rise west of Town Creek was evidently known as Edmondson's Hill.

May 31st, 1847. This morning set out with Henry Malone for La Grange—we traveled on horseback and accompanied the young ladies from Mississippi, who have boarded at our house during this session. Miss Mary Randle was also in the company. . . . I believe . . . learned something of human nature, female humanity, during the day. We parted with them at Courtland, and went to Leighton that night.
June 1st. Every locality is unchanged [at La Grange] but I see lots of new faces among the students—two of the faculty are also strangers to

me.** I went immediately to Mr. Tutwiler's, which I consider and love as my third home, Mrs. Maclin's being my second. Mrs. T. welcomed me, and invited me to the party to be at her house tonight.

**Professor N. A. Pendland, a Presbyterian minister, had succeeded Carlos Smith, and James Ward Hardy was the replacement for Professor Tutwiler, later succeeding Dr. Wadsworth as president.

June 2nd, 1847. I slept last night with Presley Keyes at his room in "Paradise."
3rd. This is Commencement Day. . . . I thought the [speech] by Garth was perhaps the chastest piece of composition and sound reasoning among them.

Jesse Winston Garth was the younger son of General Jesse Winston and Unity Spottswood Garth, whose affluent plantation lay just west of Decatur. General Garth came from Charlottesville, Virginia, where his family had a prominent position in the history of Albermarle County. They are said to have given the land upon which the University of Virginia was built. General Garth was admitted to the bar in 1809, served in the Virginia legislature, sold the beautiful home, Birdwood, to his brother, and moved to Alabama in 1817. He served as president of the first session of the state senate, was president of the First National Bank in Decatur, and was instrumental in building the Memphis and Charleston Railroad. Mrs. Garth, granddaughter of Governor Alexander Spotswood, was closely connected with Virginia aristocracy. Others in the Garth family were William Willis, classmate of Tom's at the University of Virginia; Susan Elizabeth, married Dr. F. W. Sykes; Sarah Dandridge, married Dr. C. F. M. Dancy; and Mollie, who married General John Gregg, and was buried with military honors, the first known instance of a woman in private life being so honored.—Owen, III, 642, 704; Woods, 204.

June 4th, 1847. This morning I parted from Mr. and Mrs. Tutwiler, whom I rank among my best friends. My feelings at parting were almost as sad as when I left them at the close of my collegiate course. They leave soon to reside permanently in S. Alabama, where Prof. T. is to take a private school, and build it after his own plan, unshackled by trustees. I left Ma and Pa with them, as they came over day before yesterday, and wish to spend some time with this beloved family.
5th. Ma and others came home . . . after a most toilsome drive from La Grange. . . . They brought home many flowers and roots—among them the root of a *white* blackberry which flourishes about the mountain.
6th. Rev. [William Dawson] Phelps preached a close, sound, doctrinal sermon at night—he is said to be one of the soundest doctrinal

preachers in our Conference. . . . Ma says she has more [strawberries] now than she has had at any time before.
9th. Uncle and Cousin Eliza came to board with us. . . . are now safely fixed in the room over the parlor.
10th. Tonight I drilled my squad of the Athens Rifle Guards. . . . Col. Jones gave me some instruction.
15th. Tonight Miss Mary Gannaway was married by Squire Stanley to Mr. Gilliland, a printer of this place—for some days past it has been rumored in town that he had left a wife in Illinois—and some of our citizens spoke to Mrs. G. on the subject, but she seemed satisfied with the present arrangement. Parson Newman had so much faith in the rumors that he declined to officiate on the occasion.

Rev. Newman, minister of the Presbyterian Church, lost his life on a steamer in the Alabama River.—Tanner, July 28, 1876.

June 16th, 1847. I enveloped some newspapers for John, Pomp, and Ashley; by the late law I pay postage on these in advance. The first number of the *Democratic Herald* came out today. Our town now boasts of two newspapers, more than it ever has before. May Athens continue to increase and improve!
17th. Went up to the Court House and listened to speeches from Gov. Martin, Hon. Reuben Chapman,* and Nicholas Davis, Esq.** They are all candidates for governor. The first is an independent candidate, the second democratic and the last, a thorough Whig.

*All these candidates had close ties to Limestone County. It has been previously mentioned that Gov. Martin had been a resident of Athens. Reuben Chapman, 1799–1882, married Felicia Pickett, daughter of Steptoe, of Limestone County. Reuben followed his brother, Samuel, to Alabama from Caroline County, Virginia, in 1824. He read law in Samuel's office, practiced first in Somerville, Morgan County, and then in Huntsville.—Owen, III, 317.

**Captain Nicholas Davis, 1781–1859, was one of the most colorful of Alabama politicians. Born in Hanover County, Virginia, he came to Limestone in 1817, served in the first constitutional convention for Alabama, and represented Limestone in the first legislative session. In 1820 he was first elected senator, and served as president of that body for five sessions. He was one of the original trustees for The University of Alabama. The huge log house of the Davis family, Walnut Grove, was located some six miles east of Athens. It was not unusual for the family to host fifty house guests at a time, where they always found entertainment, from horseracing to hiking through the wide fields. Tom Hobbs was often caught up with the *joie de vivre* that remains a part of the Davis heritage. A Davis descendant once told a Hobbs heir: "We Davises have been accused of everything except stupidity!"—Pickett, 654; Conversation with Mrs. Elizabeth Hobbs, Higgins.

June 22nd, 1847. Uncle commenced framing his new house today and proceeded rapidly with it. Pa is superintendent, and is now "in his glory," as the saying is. I believe I never knew anyone so fond of seeing carpenter's work done as he.

Shortly after his marriage, Dr. Maclin (Uncle) purchased a block-and-a-half of property on Marion, across the street from the Hobbs house. When Pat Jones wrote about the Maclin home in 1936, it was still considered one of the finest of Tennessee Valley homes. During the Civil War, while Thomas Hobbs lay on his deathbed in Virginia, the Maclin home was occupied by General James Garfield, the future President. In a letter to a friend, dated July 10th, 1862, Garfield called the Maclin house the finest in town, and on the 17th, wrote that he took a shower bath every morning. The home was moved to Greenbriar in 1938 or 1939, and remains in the hands of family.—Frederick Williams, 122, 124.

June 24th, 1847. Pres left this morning for La Grange. Leonidas McCracken, an old friend, is now on a visit to this place; he has settled in Arkansas to practice his profession, physic, and is doing well.

July 3rd. I slipped to the Institute, and went over my document with some facility. . . . The procession moved at the stated hour, and was quite a long one, consisting of 116. Leonard Martin read the declaration, as Fred Tate was sick. . . . I remembered my speech far better than I expected. President Wadsworth arrived here today.

Fred Tate was the son of Dr. Waddy Tate, one of the earliest physicians in the area. Fred was practicing law in Huntsville by the time of the 1850 census.

Dr. Edward Wadsworth, a graduate of Randolph-Macon College, was described by McGregor: "In the pulpit his language was so plain and simple that even the uneducated listener could understand his preaching, and the cultivated and refined were made to feel that they were listening to one who was able to present the truths of Christianity."—McGregor, 26.

Sunday, July 4th, 1847. Listened to a splendid sermon from the President [Wadsworth]. He has the clearest, most distinct enunciation I ever heard.

5th. There was a barbecue at Mooresville today, and several of our young ladies went down, accompanied, of course, by some of our "bucks."

6th. I was persuaded to accompany a party to the Springs. . . . I had not been to these springs before in near two years, so I found them much improved, and accommodations enlarged. I took a game of fives at the battery.

Advertisements in the Huntsville papers of 1846 describe the springs developed by Dr. Thomas Moore around 1845 as being some seven miles northeast of Athens. This is the area now known as Sardis Springs. References listed in the advertisement include: Drs. J. F. Sowell, B. W. Maclin, T. S. Malone, Jonathan McDonald, J. P. Coman, Waddy Tate, the Hon. Daniel Coleman, and Colonel Robert Tinnin, of Florence.

10th. Called on Miss Lowe tonight, she is on a flying visit to our village. . . . quite an interesting young lady.

William Garrett wrote: "The writer , with his family, in April, 1848, took passage on a boat at Tuscaloosa for Mobile. Among his fellow passengers was General Lowe and his daughter, Sophie, a young lady educated and accomplished in the more solid attainments of life, in that day. . . . She brought into the social circle, during the trip, much of the means that contributed to break the tedium of steamboat traveling, and made the time pleasant by her cheerfulness, intelligent conversation, and singing, in all of which she was well gifted."—Garrett, 82.

July 12th, 1847. Went hunting today with young Jackson, who has not long since returned from Mexico. He went in one of the Mississippi companies, but was discharged at Monterey on account of ill health. . . . He saw Gen. Taylor but once, and that was as he marched by his tent; he was sitting in his shirt sleeves and had his hat off, and "looked like a plain old farmer." . . . Read the *Southern Literary Messenger.*

16th. I received a *Gazette* and *Union* this morning. . . . Several letters came to our office this morning which had been opened by the mail-robber, Carpenter, near Talladega. They were still open, and bore a little printed slip announcing the cause of their condition.

18th. Thomas Maddin and Albert Jones took dinner with me.* Tom lectured us in favour of the organization of an Anti-Tobacco Society. I consented to relinquish my cigar if he would join the Sons of Temperance—to which bargain he agreed. Our pastor preached a short sermon tonight, and I should have waited on some young lady home, had I not been monopolized by Mrs. M., who is "my everlasting beau."

*Albert was one of four sons of Judge Obadiah Jones, who was the first judge in the Alabama Territory, presiding as early as 1810; Alabama then being a part of the Mississippi Territory. "The Jones brothers, Albert, Walker, Merriwether and Crawford, who lived at the Bridgeforth place, were frequent visitors to Athens. They were all high strung young men; had plenty of money, loved fine horses, guns, dogs, etc., and were the 'beatenest' men to talk in America." Tanner further states that Albert Jones married Caroline Coman, and Merriwether married her sister, Joan.

July 19th, 1847. Last night Scott got into a row with some other negroes, and was hauled up before the Mayor and whipped—receiving 25 lashes. I investigated the case this morning, and finding him much in fault, I administered a slight castigation. An unpleasant duty, but one nevertheless which in the present state of things, must be attended to. I am satisfied that it is best for them, & their masters too, that slaves should sometimes be thus punished, disagreeable tho' it may be. I was engaged most of the day in working out a problem in surveying—at the request of Rev. Levesque, whose land it is.

The Reverend William Levesque, 1790–1865, was a native of Tennessee, and veteran of the War of 1812. He married Rachel Williams, and had four children residing at home in 1850; Margarett, married Anderson Hall; Sarah, married Urah Vincent; William; and Jane.

July 26, 1847. Learned from a Charleston paper that Joseph C. Neal, the editor of the Gazette, is dead. . . . I could have spared almost any other editor in the Union, better than him. We shall have no more life-drawn pictures, which he was pleased to call "Charcoal Sketches," and his excellent efforts in behalf of newspaper literature will now cease.

Joseph Clay Neal, born in New Hampshire in 1807, established the *Saturday Gazette* in Philadelphia soon after his "Charcoal Sketches" appeared in 1838. His death occurred on July 17th.—*Who Was Who,* 446.

27th. I went to the plantation today with Ma, Mrs. M., Pa and Uncle. . . . to eat watermelons. . . . Bradley, the overseer, has planted about half an acre in watermelons. . . . Attended a good class meeting tonight—and gave a quarter towards paying for our fires last winter.

30th. Col. Jones received quite unexpectedly this morning, his commission as Captain in the 13th regiment—infantry. I loaned him my horse, and he went out recruiting today, and secured three good men.

Sunday, August 1st. I attended Sabbath School, some of my pupils there were absent, at the Camp meeting of New Garden. . . . Mr. Rivers arrived last night, & preached a good sermon this morning in his usual warm style. He looks well, and has a fine new son. . . . Young ladies are beginning to arrive to commence school tomorrow.

New Garden was one of the earliest settlements in Limestone County. A few had settled in the area before 1810, among them the Redus, Maples, Phillips, Kyle, and Prigmore families. It has been said that the family of Thomas Redus was the only one permitted to remain when settlers were driven off in 1811 by U. S. Army forces under Return J. Meigs, in an attempt to appease the Indians. Mr. Redus operated a mill, which was invaluable to both whites and Indians. The first camp meeting was held at New Garden in 1823. The carriage of Mrs. Obadiah Jones was the only one present at that time, but in the following year her carriage was augmented by that of General Keyes.—Thomas Stith Malone, June 20, 1867.

August 2nd, 1847. Today our general election was held in this state, and I cast my vote for the first time (military votes being excepted). I voted for Tate and Lane for the Legislature, and Compton for the Senate. I was summoned by the sheriff to act as clerk of the election, so all day I was confined in the room. . . . was glad to hear that the disgraceful practice of "treating" has almost entirely been abandoned.

3rd. F. Tate and J. H. I. Wynn were elected to Legislature.

John H. J. Wynn often represented Limestone in the legislature. He was described as being "a useful legislator and popular citizen."—Brewer, 323.

4th. A considerable party of young folks went down to the plantation, in Sloane's omnibus, to eat watermelons.

5th. Went to Decatur as a delegate to the Convention which met there to organize a Grand Division for this state. I went as a proxy for James Brundidge, W. P. of our division.* Four divisions were represented in the Convention—Athens, Mooresville, Tuscumbia, and Decatur. Rev. H. H. Brown was chosen president, and I, secretary, of the convention. . . . Stayed all night in Decatur at Blain's Hotel.

*James Brundidge was "good for all purposes, bad for none," wrote John Tanner. Brundidge was interested also in the Masonic movement, and was pronounced one of the best Masons the state has produced. As the state Grand Lecturer, he is said to have instructed more Masons than any one else in the history of the state organization at that time. Brundidge superintended the brickwork on Founders Hall, Athens College, as well as many other buildings in the area.—Owen, III, 243.

August 8th, 1847. Accompanied Ma and Cousin E. to Salem Campmeeting. A good many people were there from all regions round about, and the like of negroes I believe I never saw before. I heard one pretty good sermon. . . . ate a very good dinner at the tent of Mr. William Fisher, and had several invitations to dine elsewhere.

William Fisher, oldest son of Jacob and Patsy Fisher, was following a family tradition, for Jacob Fisher had always had a tent at Old Salem and Bethel campgrounds, "and it was headquarters of most all the young people; they always fed well and consequently were never short for company,"

John Tanner wrote of the Fishers. "Aunt Patsy," as Tanner called her, never allowed young men to remain long when making evening calls, and whenever the bell was rung for prayers, "the young men in the parlor would make for the door." Among the young men who called was Elbert English, who married Julia Fisher in 1840, and took her to Arkansas to share in the important positions he held in that state.—Tanner, July 7, 1876.

August 10th, 1847. Sat up part of the night, with Mr. George Malone, who has been, and is now, quite sick. Prof. Barclay returned in today's stage.

12th. About 1 today, negro boy Henry died. As he was always a good boy, and was promising, I regret his death much. He was learning blacksmithing under Mr. Armstrong. The wagon came from the plantation today, loaded with two hundred and twenty watermelons, besides muskmelons and peaches.

13th. A letter from my old friend, Ashley . . . told me of his promotion to the office of *resident physician* of the Blockley Hospital [in] Phila.

14th. I started for Mooresville in our carriage in company with Pa and Bro. Scruggs. We went down to participate in a celebration of the Sons of Temperance—we marched in procession to the grove, where Mrs. Garrett . . . presented a Bible on behalf of the ladies of the place.

Mrs. Garrett was either Sarah, wife of Edmund Garrett, Sr., or Eliza, wife of Edmund, Jr. The Edmund Garretts came from Buckingham County, Virginia, in 1817. On the banks of Piney Creek, near Belle Mina, they built their home, Piney Bluff.—Personal interview with Mr. and Mrs. Edmund Garrett, IV, June, 1967.

August 16th, 1847. This morning we received from Nashville the instruments for our new concert Band. . . . I also received my uniform which Prof. B. obtained for me in Phila.

17th. Received a letter from Henry Kimbell, of Mooresville, requesting me to write an account of the celebration there for our newspapers.

The name is spelled "Kimble" in the 1850 census. Henry, born in North Carolina in 1814, married Ann Eliza, daughter of James Hurt Gamble, in1840. They were ancestors of the late Henry Zeitler, of Mooresville, who built a library to house his large Alabama history collection. Now the collection is in the Huntsville Public Library.

19th. We had some excellent venison for dinner today. . . . the way I pitch into venison, ham, butter beans, tomatoes, etc., is curious, to say nothing of milk and peaches as dessert. . . . Commenced reading *Rob Roy*. . . . Rode out to Crenshaw's manufactory, that is to be, the house is almost finished, & his race is completed up to the house.

James W. Crenshaw, 1805–1870, is listed in the 1850 census as a manufacturer. He was a son of Freeman, 1776–1853, and Elizabeth Crenshaw, 1778–1807; and a brother of Samuel and William. "Major James W. Crenshaw, then an officer just from the United States Navy, won the heart and hand of Narcissa Beaty, daughter of Capt. Robert Beaty . . . " John Tanner was speaking of marriages that had taken place in Limestone prior to 1830. Apparently James and Narcissa went to Missouri with Robert Beaty early in the 1830s, and Narcissa died soon after. After her death he married Elvira Winston, granddaughter of the arch patriot, Patrick Henry. Their first three children, Virginia, Elvira, and Sarah, were born in Missouri; while the younger ones, Dorothea and Patrick Henry, were born in Alabama. Living with them in 1850 was Dorothea Spottswood Henry Winston, 73, widow of Dr. George Winston, and daughter of Patrick Henry and his second wife, Dorothy Dandridge.

August 20th, 1847. We now have a line of stages thro' Athens from Elkton to Decatur; this line commenced a day or two since. Going and returning, these stages pass thro' every day.

22nd. Attended the burial, at Cambridge, of the infant child of Nicholas Malone, Esq. . . . Sat up with Mr. George Malone. . . . He is very low. . . . Albert Jones sat up, also.

The deceased infant was the second child of Nicholas and Mary Lucy Kernanchan Malone. One son, Robert Bloomfield, survived. Mary Lucy Malone died a few months after this, and John Nicholas married Rebecca Simmons in 1854, by whom he had several children.

August 24th, 1847. Received a letter from Pres Keyes. . . . I am sorry to learn from this source that the college at La Grange is so badly supported. There are not fifty students. Pres speaks very highly of Prof. Hardy, who fills Prof. Tutwiler's chair, he seems to hope that the influence of this man will build up the institution. La Grange has my sincerest and heartiest wishes for its success, tho' I fear it will not flourish again soon.

James Ward Hardy, professor of chemistry, was a graduate of Randolph-Macon College. After Dr. Wadsworth resigned in 1852 to fill the chair of Mental and Moral Science at Southern University, Greensboro, Alabama, Dr. Hardy succeeded him as president, and might have built up the institution, had he not died from complications arising from tooth extraction on August 15, 1853.—McGregor, 26.

26th. George Malone died last night—he was a man of high standing in the community, and was remarkable for his uprightness, candor and piety. . . . His funeral was preached at 1 by Pres. Rivers. . . . the goodhearted speaker could scarcely command his feelings sufficiently to deliver his sermon well.

27th. At the request of Prof. Barclay, and under his instruction, I commenced making a set of diagrams to be used at the Institute in teaching vocal music. . . . Ate part of a watermelon at Brickell's room.

August 28th, 1847. The bell for the commencement of our last Quarterly Meeting was rung today, while it was raining smartly. . . . Bro. Moody [Samuel S.], the presiding elder, came down from Huntsville, where there is a fine revival going on; already about 75 have professed at the Methodist Church alone. . . . Ma exhibited the great goodness of her heart tonight by going after preaching to the other side of town to see a poor girl said to be dying.

Wednesday, September 1st. I mean to make this a day to be remembered by myself, for a reason which I shall commit to no one; not even to this faithful record. May I as often as I remember this day, smile, and if I smile at its remembrance, there are others who will likewise smile.

6th. Mr. John Finn, most worthy Patriarch for the State of Tennessee . . . has come down to organize our Grand Division. . . . I accompanied him to New Garden to start that Division. . . . We went to the house of Mr. Thomas Redus.

Thomas Redus was born in 1801, a few years before his father came to Limestone. In 1835 he married Martha Ann Clay, niece of Henry Clay, and had Octavia, married John Grigsby; and Cornelia, married Freeman Crenshaw, son of William.

10th. Capt. E. J. Jones, having received the clothing for the soldiers . . . rigged them out today, and they present quite a martial appearance.

September 11th, 1847. By the mail today we received a note from the Post Master at Tuscumbia, stating that General Scott had captured the City of Mexico, after two battles on the way. . . . The report of cannon was heard yesterday in the direction of Huntsville, so that is rather confirmatory of our news.

13th. Owen Nelson and I called at Mr. Malone's to see Miss Lowe, who came down yesterday from Huntsville. A lawsuit has lately gone against her father, which, it is thought, will take away some property supposed heretofore to belong to his children. Miss Sophy seemed in high spirits, however.

15th. Was present at a large and brilliant party at Capt. John Mason's.

John R. Mason, 1803–1862, son of William and Rebecca Richardson Mason, freely admitted that he had fallen for Glorvinia Beaty, daughter of Robert and Sallie Parrott Beaty, when she served as a bridesmaid at his first wedding to Olivia Smith, of Courtland. After Olivia's death he married Glorvinia, in 1845, and undertook restoration of the building that

Robert Beaty had built for a school in 1826. The resulting work of art, virtually unchanged, has been the home of the Masons and is now the president's mansion for Athens College.—Pat Jones, "The Mason Home," May 5, 1935.

September 16th, 1847. The State-docket was taken up today. The principal case was against a negro belonging to Alexander Jones,* for an assault with intent to kill. It was a short trial, and he was easily acquitted. . . . His master . . . was so much overcome at the joyful verdict . . . he had almost fainted. We had a called meeting of our Division, and initiated Judge George W. Lane,** who is presiding at our Court.

*Alexander Spottswood Jones, was the son of Haywood and Sallie Collier Jones.

**George Washington Lane, born in Georgia in 1806, studied law under Judge Daniel Coleman, represented Limestone in the legislature in 1829 and 1832, and was then elected judge of the county court. After his marriage to Martha Nicholas Davis he moved to Madison County, where he made known his strong Unionist views, was appointed a Federal Judge by Abraham Lincoln, and died in Louisville in 1864.—Owen, IV, 1006.

19th. I was drawn into a debate this evening with the advocates of Mesmerism; which was quite long. I took bold grounds against it—I believe it a humbug. After church tonight, I met at the hotel, Thos. Maddin, who is going to leave for Louisville in the morning.

Hobbs was in good company in doubting the methods of Franz Anton Mesmer, for in the late 18th century a group of scientists and physicians, including Benjamin Franklin, investigated Mesmer and discredited him. The movement became quite popular, however, a few years later.

September 21st, 1847. At a Mesmeric meeting this evening, I was requested to take a seat among those who wished to be put into the magnetic sleep; I did so, and then a thought came into my head that I would endeavor to hoax the operators and the crowd. . . . in due time, I fell into a most certain magnetic sleep. The operators came to me, and closely scrutinizing my countenance . . . gently raised me to my feet and directing me to fix my eyes on 'a cour,' made me follow him around the room. The believers in the thing all shouted for joy; after making me do all the things which his pupils generally did, he proposed to awake me, when I stepped away, and very politely declined. Said I, "Sir, I am already aroused, I have never been asleep." . . . the dismayed operator opened his eyes with astonishment, and then closed them in confusion.

24th. Received . . . a letter from John Keyes . . . he has just been presented with a fine daughter, whose eyes are "heaven's own blue." "Go it while you're young!"

Ellen was the first of eleven children for John and Julia Hentz Keyes. She married James Gunter, of a prominent Montgomery family.—Owen, III, 973.

September 25th, 1847. Made some preparatory arrangements to go to Florence to wait on Richard Bass, who is to be married on next Tuesday to Miss Eliza Bigger.

Eliza was the daughter of Joseph Bigger, prominent in Lauderdale County. One of his daughters married James Withers Sloss, and another married Ferdinand Sannoner, the Italian engineer who laid out the town of Florence, and perhaps Mooresville (an early map of Mooresville bears his signature).—Jill K. Garrett, C–115.

26th. The wedding party left after dinner for Florence. Dr. Wilkinson and I went in Uncle's buggy. . . . We reached Binford's stand about sunset, where we staid all night.

This inn may have been the one supposedly built by Chief Doublehead, which stood near Elgin's Crossroads on the Florence road until recent years.

28th. Waited on my first couple this morning. About half-past eight we repaired to the house of Mr. Bigger, where we found a few friends (mostly Irish), assembled to witness the ceremony. They were married about nine.

30th. Capt. Jones' company left our village this morning for the seat of war. The parting was quite a solemn and imposing scene; the line being formed in the Court house green. Bro. Scruggs gave them a short and wholesome speech; many wept, and otherwise showed their emotions at leaving. Our Brass Band accompanied them as far as Edmonson's Hill, playing the national airs. . . . They will march to Waterloo, where they will take a boat . . . attended a pleasant party at Capt. Mason's tonight.

Waterloo, at the western edge of Lauderdale County where the Tennessee River divides Alabama from Mississippi, was at that time a thriving river town. It is now isolated, there being no bridge or ferry for some fifteen miles.

Friday, October 1st, 1847. Tonight, was installed as Financial Scribe of our Division. . . . Thomas Fenner came over today with the sad intelligence of the death of his father. Capt. Fenner died in New Orleans of intermittent fever; he was employed in the commissary department of the army.

2nd. I was seized with a violent tooth-ache.

3rd. I could quiet my tooth by holding cold water in my mouth . . . so increased after Sunday School that I was forced to have it extracted. Uncle drew it; it is my candid opinion that it did not come out as easy as the cork of a bottle of brisk beer.

9th. Alabama has not supplied the quota of troops called for about five months since. . . . Several of our best young men are anxious to go; I say nothing of my feelings on this subject, as it would be productive of no good, and would render *some* persons uneasy. Be calm, Tom!

October 12th, 1847. Lieut. Richardson and I went to Mooresville to procure the uniform of Major Woodruff, which R[ichardson] wishes to use during our tour.

Major John W. Woodroof (Hobbs' spelling incorrect), was the stepson of Major Edmund Walton, who had wisely invested the Woodroof money in farmland on Beaverdam Creek in southeast Limestone. The estate was further enlarged by the prudent investments of Miss Molly Walton, under the guidance of Major Woodroof. This was probably the same person whom Hobbs mentioned as being in the fishing party at Delaware Water Gap.—Letter from Henry Willis Hill, grandson of Major Woodroof, May 18, 1965.

15th. Commenced my military career today, as Assistant Adjutant General, in General Lane's staff. Tate, Richardson . . . and I rode out to Cambridge campground. . . . I read the Governor's proclamation, calling for more troops . . . only four or five came forward. Sat down to an excellent dinner at Mr. Malone's former residence, by the invitation of Henry.

The Malone home was bought in 1851 by Allison Chappell and Martha Malone Cain, so that the tread of Malone descendants' footsteps would continue there.—Pat Jones, "The Malone Home," June 2, 1935.

October 19th, 1847. Went in company with Gen. Lane, Major Tate, and Maj. Richardson, to the house of Jack Phillips, some miles beyond Rogersville.

20th. Took dinner at the hotel in Florence. Afterwards drove to Turnley's, which we found to be a most excellent stand.

21st. It was six miles from Turnley's to the parade ground. . . . About one we reviewed the 84th Regiment, and beat up for volunteers. Col. Sterling Wood spoke to the militia and endeavored to arouse them; several of the best young men around did volunteer.

Sterling Alexander Martin Wood was born in Florence in 1823, son of Alexander Hamilton and Mary Evans Wood. His grandfather, Basil Wood, is said to have assisted Chief Justice Marshall in writing his *Life of Washington,* and to have worked closely with Alexander Hamilton in his financial efforts. Sterling Wood practiced law with his brother, William Basil, in Florence. He represented Lauderdale in the legislature in 1857, edited the *Florence Gazette*, and was captain of the Florence Guards, the first company to leave Florence as a part of the Confederate States Army.—Owen, IV, 1799.

30th. President Wadsworth & Lady arrived at our house last evening. He is on his way to Conference. I am very much pleased with this gentleman, and consider him a great and good man.

Mrs. Wadsworth was the daughter of Mrs. Elizabeth Felton, of La Grange, described by McGregor as a most gracious lady, the sister of Gov. Swain, of North Carolina.

October 31st, 1847. Heard a sermon from Dr. Wadsworth at eleven. . . . I know no minister whose style of preaching pleases me more than this gentleman's. Out of the pulpit, too, he is so pleasant a companion, and so well-informed a gentleman, that his company is very attractive.
November 4th. Tonight an excellent supper was set by the ladies of our village, which was designed to raise funds to light up the Methodist Church with lamps. Besides the supper, there were many little plans for depriving one of his surplus change. Two post-offices showered the letters out upon you, for the enormous postage of twenty-five cents a piece. Then you must have your fortune told, by a young lady and her magic wheel. Several cakes were to be cut, and at every cut, your purse bleeds. I consider that I escaped well, at paying for the whole affair only two dollars and a half.
5th. We have a most excellent Daguerreotype artist in town now, whose name is Cook. I have not seen such pictures as he takes, this side of Philadelphia.
8th. Pa got a letter from his old friend, James Rowe, who resides in Cincinnati and who had just returned from the great fair at New York, where a silver medal was bestowed on his Crusher. This crusher he invented while residing in our family, and Pa now has the first one of them ever constructed.

James and Malinda Poff Rowe, of Cincinnati, had started one of the earliest girls' schools in the state of Alabama, the Monte Sano Female Academy, in Huntsville. Mrs. Rowe died in 1833, and the Reverend Rowe returned to the Methodist circuit ministry. He had a strong inventive mind, and other patents to his credit included: the forerunner of the modern merry-go-round, an elevating box-wheel fence, and an improvement in carriage wheels. His son, Andrew Jackson Rowe, purchased the Matthews' plantation, Cotton Hill, and the home remained in the hands of his descendants, the Hardimans, until purchased recently by Mr. and Mrs. William Summerfelt, of Michigan.—Pat Jones, "The Rowe Home," June 23, 1935.

November 9th, 1847. Today, as Pa, who is all industry, was rallying me for my mental & physical inactivity, I happened to wish that I was a student at the University of Va., to which remark he and Ma responded, "Well, why don't you go there?"

11th. I wrote to Mr. Tutwiler, asking a letter of introduction. On this, of course, paid postage, 5.

13th. Pa & I commenced packing my trunk this evening; he is equal to any one I ever saw at packing; I believe he can put half as much again in the same trunk, as I can. Bought a Bible tonight, as I do not design to carry the pocket-Bible which Ma gave with me; I had rather preserve it from the injury incidental to travel.

November 15th. Left home . . . accompanied by my kind friend, Owen O. Nelson, who accompanied me to Decatur. I believe I never left home with so much regret; for altho' I am satisfied that my present undertaking is a most worthy one, and the very thing I ought to do, yet for several reasons I should [like] to remain in Athens just now. But *duty* first then, if proper, *pleasure.* Owen made me a confidant of some of his secrets; I can but wish so clever a fellow complete success. The steamboat *News* left Decatur about 2, & puffed us up to Gunter's, where we were jammed into an uncomfortable coach. Through ticket to Charleston & other expenses amounted to $23.50.

16th. Reached Rome at a late hour . . . slept an hour or two, and were off again in the stage.

17th. Arrived at Kingston to breakfast, where we took the cars. This railroad is one of the best in the Union, and as we whizzed along, this pleasant whizzing was an eulogy on the progress of the arts, for it forced me to draw a comparison between staging and rail-roading. Met Ex-Gov. Clay at Kingston and introduced myself to him. Arrived in Atlanta to dinner . . . was so unwell I did not eat—but bought a dish of mental food in the *Life of Marion.*

Clement Comer Clay, born in Halifax County, Virginia in 1789, came to Huntsville in 1811. He had read law under Hugh L. White, founder of Knoxville, Tennessee. Clay went into politics in Alabama's infancy, serving in the first legislature, and becoming the first chief justice of the supreme court. He served in the U. S. Congress and Senate, and was elected governor in 1835. In 1846 he was appointed one of three commissioners to wind up the business of the state banks.—Owen, III, 342.

November 18th, 1847. Slept nearly all night in a car, provided with comfortable berths like a steamboat. . . . Arrived in Charleston about 2 . . . failed to meet my friends at the Hotel. . . . Embarked on boat *Wilmington,* and had a fine view of the city as we left the harbor.
20th. Arrived here [Petersburg] . . . last night. I called about eleven on Mrs. Julia Meade,* who gave us so hearty welcome last fall. I found her still very pleasant, and full of real old Virginia open-heartedness. I did not see Mr. Meade, or Miss Indiana, who is said to be a pretty girl.** I brought some presents to Cousin Julia from Ma, which she seemed delighted to receive.

*Julia was the wife of Richard Kidder Meade, U. S. Congressman, and Minister to Brazil. Diligent research has failed to uncover Julia's maiden name, and her connection with the Hobbs or Maclin family is uncertain. Neither have we been able to establish the relationship of Congressman Meade to the Richard Kidder Meade who served as aide-de-camp to General George Washington, and was the father of Bishop William Meade.

**John Herbert Claiborne, in writing of Indiana Meade, said, "a woman of great beauty and vivacity, and a great belle, but, rejecting many suitors, she gave her hand to Mr. William Pannill, a young lawyer of fine attainments and of brilliant promise, but of very limited means . . ." It is little wonder that this intelligent young lady threw Tom Hobbs into a tailspin, and provided his first serious love pangs. After Indie's marriage to William Pannill, they engaged in teaching school. They were to live only two years together before his death, and their son, Willie, also died. After teaching school for fifteen years in Petersburg, Indiana married the Episcopal rector, Dr. Platt, and moved with him to serve large churches in Louisville, San Francisco, and New York.—Claiborne, 103.

November 21st, 1847. Dressed myself and met Mr. Meade's family at the Episcopal Church. . . . After dinner received a visit from Mr. Mead [*sic*] and Mr. Field. The former stands very high at the bar of Petersburg, and has just been elected to Congress. I did not think him a very great gun, but it was, I suppose, because he thought it unnecessary to show me any of his *flashes.*
22nd. Fare from Petersburg to Richmond is $1.00 . . . from Richmond to Junction, $1.50; from Junction to Gordonsville, $2.50 . . . from Gordonsville to Charlottesville, $3.00. . . . I think more highly of Virginia since I have seen the part which lies between Gordonsville & Charlottesville. There are so many pretty country seats, arranged with so much taste, that I was much pleased. The road, however, was horrible—reached Charlottesville after dark.

THE UNIVERSITY OF VIRGINIA 1847-1849

Tuesday, November 23rd, 1847. This morning in the rain I walked out to the University, and altho' I did not see it under the most favorable circumstances, yet I am delighted with its appearance. The Proctor sent me to Dr. Harrison,* who upon a slight examination as to age, study, etc., wrote me a permit to matriculate. I also called upon Prof. Minor,** whom I found to be one of the blandest, most pleasant men I ever knew; his manner reminds me of Dr. Wadsworth. He spoke kindly to me, and upon my mentioning my acquaintance with his brother,† he cordially invited me to call & see his lady.

*Dr. Gessner Harrison, 1807–1862, was one of the first graduates of the University of Virginia, a classmate and close friend of Professor Henry Tutwiler. Harrison became professor of ancient languages at Virginia at the age of twenty-one, and later served as chairman of the faculty, a position at that time equivalent to the presidency of that insitution. In 1859, Dr. Harrison left the University to found a school for boys, and died soon after. —Garnett and Page, 349–50.

**The "ablest known to Anglo-Saxon jurisprudence," was one writer's description of Dr. John Barbee Minor, dean of the law school at the University of Virginia for some fifty years. He was born in 1813 at Minor's Folly, Louisa County, Virginia, to Lancelot and Mary Overton Tompkins Minor. It was said of Dr. Minor that his superior as a teacher of law probably never lived; but with all his brilliance, he rejected all titles except that of "Mr." The wife of whom Hobbs spoke was Martha Macon (or Bacon) Davis, who died shortly after this time. Dr. Minor then married Anne Fisher Colston, by whom he had Raleigh Colston Minor, who taught at the University of Virginia for some twenty-five years. The seat of the Minor family was Topping Castle, Caroline County. Here John Minor's first cousin, Matthew Fontaine Maury, began those experiments that would etch his name indelibly in the field of aquatic science.—*Dictionary of American Biography,* 26.

†John Minor's brother, Dr. William Tompkins Minor, 1792–1859, settled at an early date in Mooresville, Alabama. At approximately the same time, Henry Augustine Washington, close relative of the President, came to Limestone from Prince William County, Virginia, and bought extensive

lands near the Maclins. In the same year of Henry's death, 1825, his daughter, Frances Thacker, married William Minor. They built one of the most interesting of all Alabama houses in Mooresville, which stood until recently. The Minors then moved to Trinity, Morgan County. Here their grandchildren were born, among them were: William Minor Lile, professor of law at the University of Virginia for forty years; Eleanor Carson Lile, who became the wife of Beverly Dandridge Tucker, Episcopal bishop of Ohio; and the Rev. Braxton Bragg Comer Lile, rector of Christ Episcopal Church, Alexandria, Virginia for a time.—Douglass, *My Southern Families,* 306.

November 24th, 1847. I heard a lecture from Prof. Minor, he is as pleasant a lecturer as one cares to hear, perhaps, if he has any fault, it is speaking too fast, and passing too rapidly over important subjects.

26th. We eat breakfast precisely at seven, which at this season is long before sunrise; sunrise is beautiful here, with Monticello and its neighbors in the foreground. Attended the class of Senior Law, and was asked some questions about remainders, and altho' somewhat flurried, I believe I answered every one. Our present textbook is Coke upon *Littleton,* edition of Thomas—it is *not* the most interesting book I ever read, tho' we have to pore over it as if we were charmed with it.

27th. Our exercises go on today [Saturday] just as on any day of the week. Indeed, some students have more recitations on this than on any other day. . . . I went into the library this afternoon for the first time—from a slight examination of it, I do not greatly like it; there are too many forbidding folios and old quaint black-lettered volumes, and too many erudite Hebrew, German & such books. There are few late publications. I took out Jefferson's *Memoirs,* which seems to be the most readable book I saw. Went to Charlottesville tonight and heard Joe Sweeny, the banjo player.

Joel Walker Sweeney, 1813–1860, is said to have created the banjo as we know it today. He played in blackface, and his music was the forerunner of ragtime.—Howard and Bellows, 103.

November 28, 1847. Sweeny is undoubtedly a great artist on his chosen instrument; he seemed in some passages to throw his hand at random upon the strings, and yet he always struck the right ones alone. . . . This morning heard our chaplain for the first time; he is a Baptist clergyman named Scott.

Jacob R. Scott was chaplain from 1847 to 1860.—Mary Anne Fulton, Alderman Library, University of Virginia, letter, dated May 19, 1971.

29th. This is a great place for taking notes; every body takes notes on everything. . . . So much of the teaching here is by oral lectures without any textbook.

30th. This morning's mail brought me a letter from . . . Cousin Eliza . . . only another evidence of the attachment which the dear cousin . . . entertains for me. . . . I took up this morning the study of Spanish. . . . It is not so smooth & sweet a language as the French.

December 1st. Wrote to Thomas Jones, in reply to his favour of a few days since, enclosing a letter of recommendation to Garth. Rhodes & I are getting on finely in music.

Richard Rhodes was the son of Dr. Henry Rhodes, who established a ferry on the south bank of the Tennessee at the spot now known as Decatur, but for some time known as Rhodes' Ferry. In 1820 Dr. Rhodes joined with J. T. Sykes, Isaac Lane, McKinney Holderness, and George Peck to form the Decatur Land Company, from which Decatur was born. Dr. Rhodes served as the first postmaster of the town, and represented Morgan County in the legislature. He grew hemp, and established a factory to manufacture bagging and rope for the planters. The Rhodes home was described as the "handsomest house that was ever in Decatur," by Caroline Leadingham, who visited the town in 1829, and left a diary of her activities. As interest in his wide enterprises waned, Dr. Rhodes suffered financial reverses, and moved west.—Jenkins and Knox, 17, 38.

December 4, 1847. I believe I have as yet said nothing of my friends here. Most unexpectedly I found on my arrival here seven old friends, and almost all of them my schoolfellows at La Grange. These are: Greenwood, Rhodes, Cham Jones, Winter, Toney, Garth & Steele. The first two room next door, & the others are not a great ways off. We are a circle of friends, scarcely visiting any but ourselves, but among ourselves very social. . . . Received . . . from Mr. Tutwiler . . . introduction to Prof.'s Minor & Harrison. I presented these today and was most cordially invited by both to see them socially at home.

DeWitt Clinton Greenwood, born in 1826, became a planter in Okolona, Mississippi. For a time he edited the *Weekly Democrat* in Aberdeen, a city which had strong ties with north Alabama. Rice Winter was the son of William Hooe and Catharine Starke Washington Winter, who built the house, Locust Hill, in Tuscumbia in 1823. McGregor mentions that Mrs. Winter moved to La Grange in order to educate her children, then moved back to Tuscumbia. Charles Toney was a member of a pioneer family of Madison and Limestone counties. George Steele was the second son of George and Eliza Weaver Steele of Huntsville. George Steele, Sr., is credited with the design of the Leroy Pope home, built there in 1815. The present First National Bank (1835), and the 1835 courthouse were among other buildings credited to him.

December 5th, 1846. Heard a sermon from our Chaplain this morn. . . . increased my estimation of the man & the preacher. His sermons are logical and the matter well selected; he gives us short sermons, and this is an evidence of his good sense, as, also, that he understands his subjects.

6th. I studied Spanish mostly today; our text-book *Don Quijote* [*sic*], is quite hard, abounding in idioms, & these idioms out of date—I believe a Spanish idiom is the hardest thing in that line I have yet found. If any doubts this, let him evince his Quixotism by taking up our text book. . . . Recited Senior Law, and then heard a lecture on Galvanism from Prof. Rogers— He is not a good lecturer, is too verbose, and gesticulates as much as a general about to lead a charge.

Dr. William Barton Rogers may not have been a good lecturer, but he knew his science! He held the chair of natural philosophy at Virginia from 1835 to 1853, then founded the Massachusetts Institute of Technology. He chaired the first meeting of the American Association for the Advancement of Science, and was elected its first honorary member. Dr. Rogers' nephew, Robert Empie Rogers, also taught at Virginia, and was recognized as one of the finest chemists ever produced.—Garnett and Page, I, 352.

December 7, 1847. In accordance with the law of the Institution, I have sent in my name, as a candidate for graduation in Spanish; but I have great fear that I will not succeed. . . . introduced Rice H. Winter to Prof. Minor.

8th. Received . . . a ticket to Prof. Minor's party on next Tuesday eveing. Won't I go and see how Virginia beauty looks?

9th. Prof. Minor gave us today, an excellent abstract of the *Federalist,* which I mean to copy if I can do so. Few persons fully appreciate that able work.

11th. Wrote to Messrs. Ritchie and Heiss, subscribing a dollar for the *Weekly Union*; I anticipate that this will be an interesting & important session, and I wish to be advised of its doings. If the war & the Wilmot Proviso do not excite warm & important discussion, I will be much mistaken.

13th. Finished *My Prisons* [by Silvio Pelico], and returned it to the Library. . . . the second volume . . . a kind of commentary on the first, by Maroncelli, is also queer. The librarian told me that Maroncelli was once a candidate for the Chair of Modern Languages in this University; he did not say why so distinguished a man was not successful.

William Wertenbaker, librarian, was one of the last choices made by Thomas Jefferson for the University. When the first books for the library came early in 1826, the ex-President carefully scrutinized each volume, called Wertenbaker to his side and remonstrated him for accepting a certain edition because of an infinitesimal mistake. By mid-July, when the second shipment of books arrived, Mr. Jefferson was dead. Wertenbaker's grandson, Dr. T. J. Wertenbaker, taught at Princeton University, and was the author of many books on American history.—Bruce, II, 190–91.

December 14, 1847. Prof. Minor gave a large dancing party tonight. . . . The beauty of Albermarle was there, and still there was not much. . . . Prof. Minor gave me pleasure of an introduction to his lady, to whom I had some messages from Misses Malone & Ford. . . . She will not compare with Mrs. Tutwiler. . . . The supper was an elegant one; oysters, boned turkies, ice cream, confectionary, etc.
15th. Prof. Minor's party did not greatly improve the character of the recitation in Coke this morning.
17th. If any man were to ask me where he could find some of the dullest, dryest, most boring English ever written, I should, without a moment's hesitation, cite him to look upon Littleton, vol. 2, middle of the chapter on Warranty.
18th. I used on my letter today one of the new Postage Stamps. They are very nice, and are a great convenience, to postmasters and people. . . . snowballing this evening on the Lawn.
20th. Read in the French paper of the death of Chancellor Kent; a loss to the nation. . . . He was . . . 85 years of age. . . . Commenced one [letter] tonight to Mr. Tutwiler. How can I thank him sufficiently for his many disinterested favours to me!

The "American Blackstone," James Kent, 1763–1847, was a graduate of Yale, and professor of law at Columbia University, where his brilliant lectures formed the basis for his publication *Commentaries on American Law.* Chancellor Kent was a close friend of John Jay and Alexander Hamilton, who with James Madison, wrote *The Federalist.* It seems appropriate that the senior law class should be studying that work at the time, for this group of essays was considered by Jefferson to be "the best commentary on the principles of government ever written," even though Jefferson greatly disliked Hamilton.—Brooks, 30.

December 25, 1847. I was up very late last night, getting some boozy friends safely stored away in their beds.
27th. Today was very cold, they are filling the University ice-house with fine ice.
28th. Prof. Schelé having returned, we recited French and Spanish as usual. . . . Prof. M. incidentally reproved me for reclining on my seat. . . . I think the affair will keep me perpendicular hereafter.

Maximilian Schelé De Vere, 1820–1898, was born in Sweden. After receiving his Ph.D. from the University of Berlin at the age of 21, he wrote several historical novels, in addition to studies on various languages. Recommended to the University by his friend, Henry Wadsworth Longfellow, Professor Schelé lent a touch of suavity to the campus. He was first married to Eliza Rives, daughter of Alexander Rives, and later to her sister, Lucy. For 51 years did this master of languages teach at the University.—Garnett and Page, I, 355.

29th. [letter] from Ma . . . contained some unpleasant news . . . the account of the drowning of the negro Abram; and the loss by fire of the gin-house and about twenty bales of cotton. The Tennessee is almost as high as it was last spring (it was then higher than ever known before). It is therefore all over the bottoms near Decatur—the negro was riding thro' these bottoms, when he was thrown from his horse and drowned. . . . Ma writes me of the marriage of Cousin Margaret & Owen Nelson.
31st. Prof. Minor in distributing the cases for the next Court, gave a very difficult case to Garth & myself. The roads are now as bad as any I ever saw; that from here to Charlottesville is quite semi-fluid.

William Willis Garth, son of Gen. Jesse Winston Garth, spent most of his early life in Virginia, following the death of his mother. He entered La Grange College as a senior, and graduated in 1847. While he was practicing law in Decatur, W. W. Garth gave a hospital to his alma mater, which became a military school in the 1850s. He served for a time in the U. S. Congress, was defeated by W. M. Lowe, and retired into private life. William Willis Garth, in his erudition, genial nature, and fluency of speech was much like his great-grandfather, Alexander Spottswood, Colonial Governor of Virginia, who built the Governor's Palace in Williamsburg.—McGregor, 50; Owen, III, 643.

Saturday, January 1, 1848. Heavenly Father! give me I beseech Thee a just appreciation of the importance of the year I have now entered upon; so that it may not be a buried talent, but may I be able to give a good account of it when it is gone if I shall so long live. Give me . . . equanimity . . . that I may be able with steadiness of purpose . . . to prosecute my literary pursuits.
3rd. I set myself to study my case, which is not an easy one. Garth is the opposing counsel . . . both confident of success.
January 4, 1848. Prof. Schelé . . . was thrown from his horse yesterday evening, and was brought to the University in a cart. The *Union* of this morning gives the pleasant rumor (which is somewhat relied on tho') that the Mexicans have appointed commissioners, to meet those from the U. S. who may be appointed, at Havana to conclude a treaty of

peace. Gen. Cass has written a plain, common-sense, but forcible letter about the Mexican War and the Wilmot proviso.

5th. I filed my declaration in the moote [*sic*] court clerk's office, and had a writ issued summoning Garth to appear & plead. He did not expect me to declare as I did, and hence he is a little puzzled to know how to proceed. Called on Dr. Schelé this evening. . . . He informed me that he had traveled in Ala., & was much pleased with that part of the U. S.

7th. Received this morning a letter from Albert and Thomas I. Jones, who are in Charleston attending the medical lectures. They room together, and suit each other very well, I imagine.

8th. Today Charles Toney came to room with me.

9th. Pryor & I went into town; partly to see (I must confess) a Miss Rice, who is highly spoken of as a beauty and a "blue." We went to the Episcopal Church, and listened to one of the dryest sermons I ever heard, even from an Episcopalean. . . . But our chaplain gave us tonight a most excellent discourse. . . . I learned tonight that he is a Bostonian and was educated at Brown University.

Roger Atkinson Pryor, 1828–1912, was obviously taken with Miss Rice, for he married her soon after. This Virginia cousin of Alabama's Luke Pryor edited newspapers in Petersburg and Richmond after graduating from the University in law. An ardent secessionist, Pryor was offered the dubious honor of firing the first shot at Ft. Sumter, which he declined. He resigned from the U. S. Congress at the time of the secession, and was made a brigadier general in the Confederate Army; but becoming impatient with the War Department for making him a "brigadier without a brigade," resigned, and entered Fitzhugh Lee's cavalry outfit as a private. Sara Agnes Rice Pryor, daughter of Rev. Samuel Blair and Lucinda Leftwich Rice, was obviously of great help to her husband. Wiley and Milhollen state, "Smart, vivacious and articulate women like Varina Howell Davis, Mary Boykin Chestnut, . . . and Sara Agnes Pryor always took a lively interest in politics and public affairs, and what they had to say on these subjects was listened to with respect by their husbands and masculine friends." It was Sara who walked to their home outside Petersburg after the war to find dead bodies and debris at every turning. Instead of whining, she rolled up her sleeves and went to work. The impoverished Pryors then sold Sara's jewels to pay their passage to New York, where Roger wrote incognito for the *New York Daily News,* renewed his law interests, and became an associate justice of the New York Supreme Court. In 1904 Sara published *Reminiscenses of Peace and War,* based on her life in Virginia.—Tyler, 378.

January 10th, 1848. I had the pleasure of attending tonight a sort of social party at Dr. Harrison's, who is at present the chairman of the Faculty. . . . There were about 20 persons there. . . . I made the acquaintance of Miss McGuffey, who has the reputation of being a "blue," but I found her very pleasant and not disposed to do the metaphysical in the least. Mrs. Harrison and I had some talk of Mr. & Mrs. Tutwiler, whom she loves very much. Bought some chestnuts.

Mary McGuffey was the daughter of Dr. William Holmes McGuffey, professor at the University, and author of the *Eclectic Readers,* "which covered nineteenth-century America like the dew," being the basic textbooks in thirty-seven states. One social historian said that McGuffey's *Readers* probably "did more to mold American thinking than any other single influence except the Bible."—Downs, 233.

January 18, 1848. Received a *Union* this morning. Gen. Scott is to be recalled from Mexico—for what reasons it is not stated.
21st. My case came on in the Moot Court this evening, and contrary to my expectation, was decided against me. Garth pleaded the Statute of Limitations, which was available. . . . Greenwood and Garth are very much amused at my discomfiture, while I, of course, see but little cause for any sport. Attended division tonight, initiated . . . S. F. Leake, formerly a member of Congress from this district.
25th. I had quite a fall down the Rotunda steps today, as we came out of Junior Law. . . . I felt considerably hurt at first, but in a moment, I recovered & was as sound as before except a rent of the pantaloons.
26th. Today we left the memorable Coke. . . . We now take up Stephen's *Pleading,* which the Prof. informs us is a most able work. . . . Tonight I found the range illuminated by candles put on each column of the arcade; it looked very pretty. I was not able to learn why we all became suddenly so joyful; perhaps it was on our leaving Coke! Was amused tonight at some conversation with La Branche, a Louisianian.
January 27, 1848. A bill has passed the [Alabama] legislature, I believe, abolishing our county court system, & organizing courts of probate in their stead. This bill was introduced by Col. J. W. McClung of Madison. . . . I write at 11 o'clock; a kettle of some combustible has been set on fire on the lawn, which illumines with fitful glares the adjacent buildings.

Colonel James White McClung, 1798–1848, came to Huntsville three years after his graduation from the University of North Carolina in 1816. His first law partner was Clement Comer Clay. McClung had entered the legislature in 1822, and served continuously from 1835–1845. Colonel McClung's mother was a sister of Hugh Lawson White, founder of Knoxville.—Brewer, 359.

February 1st. Ma says cotton is worth nothing, literally nothing, in Alabama. It is my opinion that it must rise, & that those who hold on will be benefited by so doing.

10th. The Intermediate Examination of the class of Junior Law took place today. At half-past nine we went into the room, and found the Professor writing some very general & very hard questions upon the black-board, which touched upon almost every subject the class has studied. We wrote away until each one was satisfied with his answers, & then we certified them and handed them up. . . . Many of the questions were upon Vattel, of which I know nothing, the class having passed over that before I entered the University.

The University of Virginia was the first to employ the honors system.

20th. Received a *Herald* from home. . . . It seems that the Legislature has passed a bill to charter a Company to put the Muscle Shoals Canal into operation again. I wish the project success, but I fear the stock will not be easily obtained.

The canal that circumvented the treacherous shoals, begun in 1824, was not completed until 1836, and was closed the following year. This 1848 attempt by the legislature was not successful, and it was not until 1875 that the canal was rebuilt, and remained in operation until 1918, with alterations.—Owen, II, 1063–64.

February 23, 1848. I commenced today the study of Anglo-Saxon, by copying some notes upon it from the lectures of Dr. Schelé.

26th. I should have attended Anglo-Saxon this evening, if had not been invited to Prof. Minor's to dinner. I met there besides about half the members of the Senior Law Class, the Chaplain and Dr. McGuffey. This latter is a plain gentleman of pleasant manners, but considered by many as the ablest man in the Faculty. He remarked to some of us today that he thinks a man who studies in any profession until 25, will find himself at 30 far in advance of those who actually began their professional careers much earlier.

March 1st. [translated from Spanish] The *Union,* which came this morning, is full of the passing of John Q. Adams, who died on the 23rd of Feb. in the House of Representatives, where he has worked so much.

9th. [translated from Spanish] In my paper I learn that the price of cotton is really low, it is not more than 5 cents in Memphis.

12th. I walked with my new friend, L. M. Kean, who is very esteemed for his mind and the excellent qualities of his heart.

14th. [translated from Spanish] I received a letter from my friend Henry B. Malone, who graduated a little while ago from the medical school in Charleston. We are reading *The Cid* [in Spanish].

March 16th, 1848. I learn in letters from Ma and Mrs. Maclin that Miss Mary P. Richardson will be married soon.

Mary Pleasants Richardson was married first to Joshua Richardson, and later to Thompson Anderson.

18th. [translated from Spanish] Anglo-Saxon is not taught in the United States except in this University, that comes from the good judgement of the wise founder here, Mr. Thomas Jefferson. He appreciated the value of this language, which is the mother of our language.
23rd. [translated from Spanish] A letter from Ma states that the price of cotton is rising . . . 5½ cents. We have heard today that there might be another French Revolution. King Louis Phillipe has abdicated, and tried to put his grandson on the throne, but the people declared that they are tired of the monarchy, and tried to form a republican form of government. Now 500 men are dead, because of the conflict between soldiers and people. Long live the reform!
28th. [translated from Spanish] Have seen the peach blossoms in bloom for the first time here. I'm sure they have bloomed in Alabama earlier.
29th. [translated from Spanish] I have written some verses to Miss Meade of Petersburg, replying to the valentine which I received. My friend, Charles Toney, has been very sick today, and Doctor Cabell has been to visit him.
Saturday, April 1, 1848. We are all much amused at a thing which has just happened. Yesterday it was understood that Mrs. Ward would give her boarders ice cream for dessert. By invitation I went there, and ate heartily of cream and cake, as did all of her 30 boarders. Last night I was taken with diarrhea . . . in my many visits during the night to the privy, I met with others suffering from the same disease. Still we thought 'twas only an accidental coincidence, until this morning we learned that almost every man who ate of that dessert had been running during the night. . . . It seems that a druggist sent *salts* instead of *soda,* which was an ingredient of the cake. Many anecdotes are told of the doings of the "night errants."
4th. Amused myself some at the gymnasium, which has just been repaired & fixed with ropes, etc. . . . Charley, Mordecai and Cham have gone to Weir's Cave.

This cave, near the heart of the Blue Ridge, was discovered by Bernard Weyer (or Weir) in 1804, when he chased a deer through its entrance. It was developed some years later for tourists, because of its spectacular formations.—Pollard, 266, 269.

5th. [translated from Spanish] Mr. Astor, the richest man in the United States, has died.

John Jacob Astor came to Baltimore from Germany in 1784, with twenty-five dollars and seven flutes. From flutes to furs, Astor knew how to give the buying public what it wanted. He may have been responsible for the surge of popularity in flute playing, for almost every writer and public figure in the early nineteenth century played this instrument.—Brooks, 27.

May 17, 1848. Today Dr. Schelé reported the results of the late Examinations. I was happy enough to see my name on the list of graduates, both of Anglo-Saxon and of Spanish. . . . The study and close attention of five and a half months has been rewarded with the promise of a diploma. Only a few were thrown . . . amongst them was Charley. . . . Visited Dr. Harrison's family—and spent a pleasant evening. Miss Maria is a splendid performer on the piano. She just returned from Phila., where she went to prosecute the study of music. Dr. Schelé left for Europe this evening.

19th. May Day was celebrated by the girls of the University this evening. Having been honored by an invitation, I attended. The coronation took place on the beautiful shady hill at Fitch's. Mary Harrison . . . was the Queen.

22nd. We had strawberries for dinner today, the first of the season. . . . Commenced my review of Blackstone today. . . . Green peas also today for the first time.

May 26, 1848. Cass and Butler are the nominees of the Convention, now sitting at Baltimore. These nominations I approve at once—of Butler I know little, but he will doubtless be well known to all by the time the newspaper editors have done with him.

27th. We are now discussing with zeal the merits, claims, and prospects of the nominees. It is generally conceded by the Whigs, even, that it is a very strong ticket. Even Prof. Minor who is a warm Whig, said so tonight. . . . By invitation I met at his house tonight, his brother, Lucian, a lawyer from Louisa. He used to live in Limestone with his brother, Dr. Minor, and knew there my parents, before they were married—all my uncles, Grandpa, and all that neighborhood.

Lucian Minor, 1802–1858, spent two years in Limestone County after his graduation from the College of William and Mary in 1823. He practiced law for a time, but did not care for the practice. In 1834 he made a foot journey through New England, recording his keen observations for the *Southern Literary Messenger,* from November 1834 to April 1835. A portion of the published articles was reprinted by James Russell Lowell in the

Atlantic Monthly in 1870, entitled "A Virginian in New England Thirty-five Years Ago." It was in 1830 that Lucian Minor began the campaign which won the most acclaim for him, that of the temperance cause. Thirty thousand copies of his "Reasons for Abolishing the Liquor Traffic" were distributed in 1853, and soon after, a monument was erected in his honor in Williamsburg. Two years later he became a professor of law at the College of William and Mary, and died in 1858. He was 44 when he married Lavinia Callis Price, by whom he had four children.—*Dictionary of American Biography,* XIII, 27.

Saturday, June 3, 1848. I have lately seen a speech made in Congress, by Mr. Wick of Indiana, which has pleased me very much. It was delivered on the subject of the attempt to abduct some slaves from Washington. The matter was introduced into Congress by Mr. Hale, the rabid abolitionist, and called forth a most excited & exciting debate. In the midst of the excitement, Wick's speech was delivered, & with the happiest effect.

William Wick, 1796–1868, was said to be a "Northern man with Southern principles." Born in Philadelphia, and admitted to the bar in 1819, Wick was serving his second term in Congress at the time.—Wilson, II, 96.

John Parker Hale, 1806–1873, was the only avowed anti-slavery member in the U. S. Senate at this time, and remained so until the election of Salmon P. Chase in 1849. In 1852 Hale became the Free-Soil candidate for the presidency, and served as minister to Spain from 1865-1869.

June 4, 1848. I went to Charlottesville & attended the Presbyterian church in order to hear Dr. McGuffey as a preacher. I think the Dr. must yield the palm to our chaplain; the fact is, & the Dr. himself admits it, that he is apt to grow too metaphysical in his sermons . . . Rev. Meade, the Episcopal minister from town, officiated tonight at the chapel. His sermon was not a very good one, but he is certainly a good reader. Heard this morning that peace was made!

5th. The report that the treaty had been consented to by the Mexican Congress was confirmed this morning, but nothing more is said in them than that a dispatch by telegraph had been received from New Orleans to that effect.

6th. I received a catalogue of Harvard University from Professor Greenleaf, to whom I wrote some time since.

Simon Greenleaf, 1783–1853, resigned as Dean of the Law School at Harvard in 1848.

8th. Bought today as a present for Cousin E., Griswold's *Prose Writers of America,* a beautifully bound book . . . I hope this present will please my fair cousin.

10th. I wrote my last letter, for this session to my parents today, notifying them of my early coming, and requesting that a conveyance should be sent to Decatur on the 21st inst. The desire to be assistant, if I can be, to the recovery of Cousin E.'s health, makes me more anxious to reach home. Visited tonight Miss Juliet Gilmer, (daughter of Mr. Secretary Gilmer) who is a charming miss of sixteen. . . . She is not pretty, but has beautiful, black, sparkling eyes.

Juliet was the daughter of Thomas Walker Gilmer, 1802–1844, who was elected to the Virginia legislature in 1829, became Governor of Virginia on the Whig ticket in 1840, and in 1844 was appointed Secretary of the Navy by President Tyler, but was killed only two weeks later in an explosion on board the *Princeton.—Dictionary of American Biography*, VII, 308.

Sunday, June 11, 1848. Attended the Episcopal Church in Charlottesville and heard Bishop Johns. This minister is a reverend, venerable, and fine looking gentleman; celebrated for his oratory. If the sermon this morning and tonight are fair specimens, he is surely one of the most fluent men I ever heard. His gestures are thought by some to be a little unnatural and overwrought, but they did not so seem to me, but rather most forcible and expressive. Accompanied Miss Gilmer from church.

Bishop John Johns, "first everywhere, first in everything," as described by a classmate, Dr. Charles Hodge, was ordained in 1819, and consecrated as Virginia's fourth bishop in Richmond in 1842. He served also as president of the College of William and Mary without pay.—*Dictionary of American Biography,* X, 75.

14th. The plan is that I start one day before Steele and Rhodes, in order that I may spend one in Petersburg, where they will overtake me.
15th. Took leave of friends, and went down to Monticello House.

The Monticello House, adjoining the Stone Tavern, had succeeded the old Eagle Hotel as the stagecoach stop in Charlottesville.—Albermarle County Historical Society, 30.

16th. Arrived in Petersburg about 3. Dressed and called on Cousin Julia Meade; had the pleasure of seeing her daughters, Indiana and Julia, the former of whom I never saw before—she is quite pretty, and very interesting in conversation.
17th. Anxious as I am to reach home, I think I could have spent several days pleasantly in Petersburg. Rhodes and Steele came according to agreement.
21st. We parted from Rhodes today, at Blue Pond, he remaining to go

towards Tuscaloosa tomorrow. Steele and I enjoyed a delightful bath in the Tennessee at Gunter's.

22nd. Reached Decatur about sunrise . . . there I found Billy waiting with the carriage. We drove to the plantation where we found Pa & Ma awaiting me . . . we set out for town . . . Found Cousin Eliza looking much better than I expected to find her.

26th. The workmen are busily engaged in papering Uncle's new house. Some of the paper put on, is as pretty as I ever saw. As the workmen are inexperienced, it is necessary for Pa and Uncle constantly to superintend them. I met tonight with the Concert Band . . . was pleased to see that . . . they had made a fair progress during my absence.

Saturday, July 1, 1848. Attended a meeting today called to make arrangements to give the returning soldiers a manifestation of our pleasure at their return. Committees were appointed to raise subscriptions and procure a speaker. Upon the latter committee I was named by the president, Major Wynn.

July 2nd. I record it as my conviction that the preachers of our church are not keeping pace with the progress of the times. The same preaching will not please us which would have been popular 20 years since—for there is a continual progress in hearers, and the preachers, to be interesting, must keep up an equal & corresponding movement.

4th. Today the Sons of T. had a grand celebration at Nubbin Ridge.* I accompanied Pa thither in his new buggy. A procession consisting of more than 200 Sons marched to the arbor and there Dr. Tell Sanders,** on behalf of the Ladies of the Ridge, presented a beautiful & costly banner ($75), which was received by my old friend and classmate, Tom Maddin . . . The boys in town tonight made a great noise, and the band played some good music from the cupola of our courthouse.

*Although it was said that "Nubbin Ridge" received its name because "not even a nubbin would grow on it," some of the county's most substantial citizens lived there, the Sanders, Fletchers, and Harrisons among them.

**Dr. Tell Sanders, son of William and Sarah Fox Sanders, studied medicine under Dr. Stith Malone in Athens. His brother, Judge Benton Sanders, was long a probate judge in Limestone County.—Owen, IV, 1495; Tanner, July 7, 1876.

5th. Oliver Sowell and I left town this morning, and went to the plantation for the purpose of fishing.

7th. I dressed up & attended Leonidas Division, where Pa was installed W. P.

9th. Heard a sermon . . . tonight from Rev. James Elliott. He is a good man, but does not know when he has got through his sermon. Having no order in it, he can stop at the beginning (which he never does) as well [as] at the end.

John Tanner wrote that Rev. Elliott was instrumental in doing great good in the Presbyterian Church, but his highest words of praise were for his mother, who lived one mile out of town on the Huntsville Road, usually attending church at night, walking the distance alone and with a lantern, and was ever on errands of mercy. "Would that we all were imitators of Mother Elliott!" he exclaimed.—Tanner, July 28, 1876.

16th. Heard two excellent sermons today from Rev. Hubbard . . . Oh, for more Scotts and Hubbards in the ministry!
17th. Met with the band tonight. Prof. Barclay brought us a new piece, "Strike A Light" Waltz. Some of us were able to play it off at once, but the majority will have to practice it.
18th. Wrote to Bill Wilkinson . . . and urged him to come up to Athens this summer.
July 19th. Made an early start for Huntsville with Pa, Ma and Cousin Eliza.
20th. I room at the Caldwell House with Fred Tate. The Grand Division meets here at this time, to which he and Pa came as Delegates . . . Met today Mr. John Rather, who gave me an account of the death of Buran Keyes. Heard the Thespians play *Theresa,* it was done tolerably well.

The Caldwell House was owned by J. M. Caldwell, and stood on the north side of the Huntsville square. In May, 1844, Caldwell announced in the Huntsville papers that he was prepared to provide board with lodging at the price of $1 per day, or $12 per month. The hotel burned in 1850. It is possible that this Caldwell also built the theater in Huntsville. One James Caldwell was known as the largest theater builder in the South, having built them in New Orleans, Cincinnati, Saint Louis, Natchez, Huntsville, Nashville, and Petersburg.

John Daniel Rather, 1823–1910, was married to Tom's childhood friend, Jane Keyes, sister of Buran. J. D. Rather began his law practice in Somerville, and later moved to Decatur. He represented Morgan County first in 1849, and in 1851 he was chosen speaker, the second time in the state's history that one so young was chosen for that honor. He also served as president of the state senate. He was the president of the Memphis and Charleston Railroad. After the war the Rathers moved to Tuscumbia where they bought Locust Hill, which was built in 1828 by William Winter, and suffered under Civil War occupation. The house has remained in the family, and is now owned by a granddaughter, Miss Mary Wallace Kirk, author of

Cabins and Characters, published in 1969. She has recently written a book of reminiscences of Locust Hill.—Brewer, 191.

July 22nd, 1848. Took dinner today with my friend George Steele, who lives a short distance from Huntsville. His father is a builder of considerable note, and his beautiful grounds and well-constructed house prove him worthy of his reputation. I met his brother, John, a young gentleman of education and pleasant manners. I never saw such a collection of roses as Mr. Steele has, so beautiful, and so many. I had the pleasure of seeing his daughter, a pretty girl, and I am told, of education and many *domestic* accomplishments.

Oaks Place was the name given the imposing mansion of George Steele, which was completed around 1840. Doors, sliding back into the walls, allowed one to enter from the Greek Revival portico into the entrance hall, which was flanked on the right by the largest parlor, perhaps, in the state. The gardens at Oaks Place contained many types of flowers and trees. In 1844 they were the scene of one of the most lavish parties ever given in Alabama. Four thousand people were invited to celebrate the victory of James K. Polk. The ox, Van Buren, was barbecued and stuffed with turkeys, accompanied by roast pigs and lambs, jellies, ice cream and syllabub. A cake, standing four feet high with a figure of Polk on top, was the *pièce de résistance.* The cake was made in Nashville, and carefully drawn to Huntsville for the occasion. Oaks Place was later owned by George W. Lane, and is now the property of the Baptists.—Alabama Association of University Women, 25–26.

The Steeles had three daughters living at home in 1850: Sally, Eleanor, and Eliza.—Madison County census, 1850.

23rd. Heard a sermon from Rev. Hartwell Brown . . . I should judge that Huntsville was not a church-going place, from the congregations I saw there, they were small and inattentive.

26th. My friend and former roommate at La Grange, G. Presley Keyes, is now with us. . . . Tom Jones came from Philadelphia last night—he has graduated in medicine.

July 27, 1848. Captains Jones and Higgins returned from Mexico today, they both look very well.

28th. I received this morning a Charlottesville paper containing the mournful news of the death of my late room mate, Charles A. Toney. It seems that he died at the house of that kind man, William Wertenbaker, but of what disease, the paper does not state . . . For nearly six months we roomed together, during which time, not an unkind word or, so far as I know and believe, an unkind thought, marred our intercourse. I lament his death the more, as he was an only son of a widow.

30th. Last night I practiced somnambulism. . . . I am now impressed with the necessity of getting somebody to hold me in bed & I reckon a good strong *female* will do it best. So, look out, young Amazons!
Tuesday, August 1, 1848. Read some of "that confounded old Coke," as Jefferson calls him. We are all rejoicing that the slavery question, which has been introduced into Congress in the bill organizing a territorial government in Oregon, has been adjusted by means of a compromise committee, who, it was generally supposed, would adopt the spirit & principles of the Missouri Compromise. It is pleasant to think that this exciting question is thus peaceably settled and, as supposed, forever put to rest.

The Clayton Compromise caused this temporary joy; it was an omnibus bill to force all the territories to permit slaveholding, and extend the Missouri Compromise to the Pacific. The bills were repeatedly killed by the Senate, however, until the adoption of the Clay Compromise in 1850.

2nd. But we learned by today's mail, that the Senate does not concur in the bill as reported by the Committee. The papers we have so far received, say that this change of feeling is owing to the Whigs, who called a caucus and saw that if this compromise was adopted, it would abolish one of their main charges against Cass, viz., his leaning towards the Proviso. I am sorry that anything should have prevented the passage of this peacemaking bill. Uncle moved into his new house today. It is just finished, and is considered by judges to be, not only one of the best-framed houses in North Alabama, but also one of the best finished & arranged.
August 4, 1848. Notwithstanding the low price of cotton, the Institute has done well this week; there are about 80 pupils now in, and many more are known to be coming.
9th. Today I met my friend and late companion, Greenwood, who came up to bring a pupil to the Institute . . . I find "Governor," as we all called him at the University, the same ingenuous, open-hearted fellow which he has always shown himself to be. I assisted him to settle his niece & to make the necessary arrangements for her. He took tea with us, and staid all night with me.
11th. Rode into the country today with Mr. Sloss, who is making some money arrangements for Uncle, Pa, and myself. Owing to the great commercial depression, I anticipate some difficulty in getting funds for the next session, and so begin in time to make arrangements.
12th. Attended a public speaking at Moore's Spring. Capt. Davis, Col. Terry, & Mr. Townes . . . were the speakers. . . . Rode in Owen Nelson's

buggy, who told me . . . of some of my old friends in and about Tuscumbia.

Eggleston Dick Townes, the Whig elector from the district, moved to Texas in 1852, with his wife, Martha Cousins Betts, and their newborn son, John Charles, who later became Dean of the School of Law at the University of Texas.—Owen, IV, 1678.

13th. We had preaching in the basement, owing to the upper story being in the hands of the painter.
14th. Assisted Pa and Mr. Clark to fix some book boards upon the pews in our church. Our Church is opposed to instrumental music & even to choirs when . . . put apart from the congregation in a gallery, but surely there can be no objection to those who are able to sing by note sitting among the congregation and leading them. This is all we design to do now.

Robert L. Clark "did his share in everything calculated to promote the interest of our town, not only in business but in morals and religion," wrote John Tanner, on July 28, 1876.

15th. Went to dinner on Pea Ridge, given to our returned volunteers. . . . One thing is certain, I never saw more genuine hospitality and free-heartedness displayed on any occasion, public or private.

Pea Ridge near Pettusville is located a few miles north of New Garden. In 1830 Dr. Thomas Pettus established a large resort hotel at the chalybeate springs there.—John Knox, article in the *Decatur Daily,* date unknown.

24th. Rode out this afternoon with some young ladies to the wedding of Dr. [John H. W.] Jones and Miss [Mary C.] Reese.
26th. Cousin Eliza, who is ever ready to do me a favor, has been copying some music for me this week. . . . Sometimes she, Uncle and I have quite a little concert with our three instruments.
27th. As our church is still in the hands of the workmen, we had service in the Union Church this morning, and also tonight. The sermon tonight was by Pres. Rivers, and was a very good one. . . . Our singing class made a sort of beginning today. Mr. Hilliard came round and sang with Mrs. Swain, Ma, Mrs. M., Pa & me.
28th. I was employed this morning with Pa and Henry Malone in making some spit-boxes for our church. We have long needed them, and as the church has just been cleaned & painted, we concluded to supply these conveniences at once . . . The seats of our church are now painted for the first time.
Friday, September 1, 1848. For the first time this summer, our streets

are dusty. Continued rains have kept them muddy instead of dusty heretofore . . . Our choir, or "singing class," as Pa insists on calling it, made its debut at the sermon tonight.

10th. Judge Coleman dined with us today—he greatly prefers the Virginia system of electing Judges for life . . . to our plan of frequent elections. It certainly gives the Judge more independence when he knows that he is in for life—but then there are sometimes men sticking to the bench, when their imbecility should have taken them to the quiet fireside of a private life.

11th. [in Spanish] Heard today a speech by General L. P. Walker who is the Democratic elector for our region. Our circuit court met today—a new Judge presides, named Walker from Benton County . . . To the doings of this court I must attend, and see what law I can pick up in this . . . country. Let me see how they have improved Coke and Chitty!

Leroy Pope Walker, son of Alabama's first U. S. Senator, John Williams Walker, and grandson of Leroy Pope, known as the "father of Huntsville." Leroy Pope Walker was to serve as the first Secretary of War for the Confederacy.—Owen, IV, 1717.

Thomas A. Walker, 1811–1888, had served in both houses of the legislature before being elected judge of the judicial circuit that included Limestone County. Judge Walker built The Magnolias in Jacksonville, which later became the Forney home, and is still one of the finest homes in that region of Alabama.—Owen, IV, 1719.

When the popularity of Thomas Hart Benton was at a peak, Alabamians named a county for him, but when his repeated opposition to the policies of John C. Calhoun was known, the county was named Calhoun.—Graves, 59.

16th. There is quite a battle about our house, caused by the packing of trunks, etc., for we design making an early start on Monday morning. . . . Ma and Pa are in high spirits, and so are all, except our affectionate cousin Eliza: in her eye already an occasional tear may be seen—when our departure is mentioned.

18th. We left early this morning for Decatur, accompanied by Mr. Sloss, who goes to Charleston to look after some of his goods . . . The steamboat stopped & took us from our side of the river.

23rd. Reached Petersburg at 4 A.M. and stopped at Jarratt's. I called around after breakfast and informed the Meade's of our arrival. . . . I was glad to meet both the young ladies at home, and both in their usual gay spirits.

Monday, September 25, 1848. Went with the Hon. R. K. Meade & Pa to Dinwiddie Court House to attend the trial of the celebrated Eppes for the murder of Muir. . . . After we left, the jury brought in a quick verdict of "guilty." Eppes is a large, fine looking man—and one that you would not suspect of committing so enormous an offence.

Subsequent evidence pointed to the fact that Epes (correct spelling) not only killed Muir, but also his mother-in-law and his own son. By so doing this member of a prominent Virginia family gained clear title to a large fortune. Francis A. Muir had gone to William Dandridge Epes' house on February 2, 1846, to collect for property that he had sold the latter. Epes killed Muir and hid his body in the forest, where it lay undiscovered until July of that year. Epes was believed to have killed his mother-in-law and son, and there was also a drover who had not been seen or heard from since he had gone to Epes' house some years before to collect for some hogs. A skeleton was later found in the ice house of the farm formerly belonging to Epes.—Huntsville *Southern Advocate,* September 9, 1846.

26th. Spent the day with my charming cousins, for one of whom my *cousinish* affection is growing very strong. Bought for Cousin Eliza, "The Last Rose of Summer" with variations.

27th. At the request of Cousin Indie I carried my flute & note-book to her house, and she soon learned "Waltz No. 5" . . . says she will play it often when I am gone, and intends to call it the "Thomas" Waltz. Good.

30th. We walked out to the old Blandford Church, but had not sufficient time to examine all its interesting antiquities. I noticed one tombstone which was erected in 1750.

The earliest tombstone in the old cemetery is that of Richard Fairbrough,who died in 1702. Old Blandford Church in Bristol Parish was one of the most historic of colonial churches. Veterans of at least six wars are buried there, a fitting locale for the claim that the first Memorial Day ceremony was held there in 1866. This is by no means a unique claim, however.—American Guide Series, *Virginia,* 277.

Monday, October 2, 1848. Wright and I drove to the University and found the Proctor's office crowded with students. . . . It has been long since such a crowd of new students has been seen at the beginning of a session here. If the usual number of old students return, & the new ones continue to come in, we must reach three hundred.

3rd. Today got settled and fixed in my room, No. 41, Western Lawn—it is one of the nine single rooms. Rhodes had engaged the adjoining room, but as he is not here this morning he would have lost it, had I not borrowed $170.00 and matriculated for him. I hardly know that I am justified in this step, as I have not heard a word from Dick since we parted at Blue Pond. I have moreover heard that his father has some pecuniary embarrassment on account of the failure of his commission merchants.

Oct. 7, 1848. Have employed myself for some days past in reading the *Spectator,* a standard work which I have hitherto slighted. The inimitable style, the sound morality and good sense of these papers delight me.

9th. By consent of Dr. McGuffey, I attend his classes whenever I can, without being questioned. . . . I am well pleased with the Dr.'s style of lecturing. He speaks without notes even, and then his propositions are laid down with so much brevity and earnestness that you are satisfied that he is right. Again, he has the aptest and easiest manner of illustrating I ever heard. He is enabled to do this by his large fund of common sense, which he possesses as extensively as any great man I know.

10th. The students assembled this evening to pass resolutions in regard to the death of Toney, & the erection of a monument to him. I was called on to preside, and addressed a few remarks to the meeting.

15th. Attended Sabbath School this morning; I was informed last week that I have been appointed superintendent of the school.

16th. The money I advanced . . . for Rhodes was refunded to me by the Proctor. . . . Tonight, quite unexpectedly, Jesse Coe arrived. He is just from Florida, and reports John Keyes and his family as thriving and happy. Jesse has come for the purpose of studying law.

18th. Received a letter from Ma, from Claverack. . . . Pa had been to hear John Van Buren speak, and thereby heard himself and the South generally denounced as thieves & liars. In an adjoining county a negro was a candidate for the Legislature.

John Van Buren, son of the President, was born in New York State in 1810. Because of his wit and elegance of manner, he was called "Prince John," but not by Southerners, who objected to his strong abolitionist views, and his active participation in the Free Soil movement.—*Dictionary* of *American Biography,* XIX, 151.

22nd. Received a letter this morning from Cousin E., containing the distressing news of Miss Louisa Richardson's death. . . . Cousin's letter contains news of several marriages in Limestone, and she is moreover evidently under the impression that somebody else means to marry, from the hints she throws out. Well, Quien sabe?

October 26, 1848. Tonight met Gen. Cocke at Prof. Minor's. This gentleman is said to be very rich and he moreover has the credit of applying his riches in a charitable manner. He is a very warm Temperance man . . . has been called the "Father Matthew of Va." He is a visitor of this University and takes great interest in its success. He is a relative of Judge Coleman, and inquired of me how his relatives were getting on.

General John Hartwell Cocke was "an original. Apart from the generality of the crowd, he possessed a talent in pioneering new paths for old beliefs . . ." In his home, Bremo, designed by his friend Thomas Jefferson, in his work as the first president of the American Temperance Union, and as vice-president of the American Colonization Society, this man showed amazing qualities. He established two plantations in Greene County, Alabama, for the express purpose of teaching slaves skills so that they could be self-sufficient in preparation for African colonization. Bremo was inherited by the General's great-granddaughter, Mrs. Forney Johnston of Birmingham, Alabama, and is now in the possession of her son, Joseph Forney Johnston, Jr. Mrs. Johnston has a diary written by General Cocke. The general was a brother of Judge Daniel Coleman's mother, Martha Cocke Coleman. —Coyner, 381–90.

27th. Went to Charlottesville with our Division, to join in a procession. Broadus was absent, and so I had to act as W. P.

John Albert Broaddus, described as "one of the great men of his time," was born in Culpepper County, Virginia, in 1827. After graduation from the University, he became a tutor at Bremo for a time, then an instructor in ancient languages at the University in 1856, a year after becoming the school's chaplain. His first marriage was to Maria Harrison, daughter of Dr. Gessner Harrison. It was to her that he dedicated his *Commentary on St. Matthew's Gospel,* one of many books that he wrote, and that served as theological textbooks. J. A. Broaddus has been called the "heart" of the Southern Baptist Seminary. When he joined the faculty, the school was located in Greenville, South Carolina, but was later moved to Louisville, Kentucky.—Garnett and Page, III, 59.

October 29th. Received this morning two letters, one from Cousin E., and one from Rhodes. . . . Dick will not return here this session, but will attend the medical lectures in Louisville. . . . I shall miss Dick very much, both as a friend and as an amateur musician. To me, it is one of the worst features in this much abused world, that the circle of our friendship cannot remain unbroken.

30th. Heard today of the death of Hon. Dixon H. Lewis of our state—he died in New York.

The fact that the Hon. Dixon Hall Lewis carried 500 pounds around with him may have contributed to his untimely death at 46. "History furnishes the name of no one who united so much mental activity and depth with such physical bulk," wrote Willis Brewer of this Alabama statesman. Lewis' body lay in state in New York City Hall, and was then taken to Greenwood Cemetery in a large procession of national dignitaries.—Brewer, 331.

Wednesday, November 1, 1848. I never saw a prettier fall than this has been. . . . I asked Lyon . . . in class if a *chartered hen*house was not an *egg*-sample of a *Lay* corporation? To which he replied, "That is a *set*-tled point, see *Hen*ning's Reports." Whereupon we voted ourselves most excellent punsters.

6th. This morning we had regular old-fashion morning prayers in the University chapel! . . . This is the first time such a thing was ever attempted here, I believe, and is a great innovation upon Mr. Jefferson's plans & ideas. This matter has been principally gotten up by Richard T. Davis, youngest son, I believe, of Prof. Davis, who was killed here in 1840.

Professor A. G. Davis, 1802–1840, was acting in his capacity as chairman of the faculty to dispel a student riot on November 12, 1840, when he was shot by a young man from Georgia named Semmes. Causes for the riot were later described by Professor Minor as stemming from the fact that "regulations for boys of 16 will not apply to young men of 21," an indication of Minor's understanding of the student mind.—Garnett and Page, I, 351.

9th. We are all on tiptoe now to hear from the elections. The telegraph will enable us in a few days to learn from every state in the Union.

10th. There was a negro hung near the University today—his crime was stabbing his master. Some of the medical students attended the execution and immediately took the corpse for dissection. As I passed along the road I saw the body of the felon hanging still upon the gallows, a shudder ran thro' me, as the effect of crime was thus fearfully presented to my view. With such sights in view, one almost doubts the right of the death-penalty, and his feelings must again be aroused by the commission of some bloody crime, before he can easily say, "Let him *die* for it."

November 11, 1848. The Democrats hereabouts are beginning to wear physiognomies of extended dimensions on account of the election news. Some of the most sanguine have already given up the contest. I shall still hold on to the hope that Cass is the man, notwithstanding the reports which I don't believe, because among other things, they say Alabama has gone for the Whigs. I have too much confidence in Old Fidelity for that.

The Democratic party in Alabama was severely split over support of Cass. William Lowndes Yancey, who had a large following, refused to support the nominee, and Cass carried the state over Taylor by a mere 1000 votes. The total Democratic vote was 6000 less than it had been in 1844, although the population had increased during the ensuing period.—Albert Burton Moore, I, 264.

13th. News continues to pour in upon us that state after State has given Taylor thundering majorities, so that I hardly know any states except Virginia and Alabama that may be relied on to stick to their faith.

14th. As for me, I have not taken a great deal of interest in this election—and I don't think I shall ever manifest that party zeal which some possess. The fact is, I believe too strongly in special Providence to make much of an effort for party.

18th. We found a snow of some depth on the ground this morning . . . the first of the season. Was perfectly surprised today by the entrance into my room of Nick Davis, of Limestone. I had no idea he was on this side of Alabama, until he stepped in. . . . As he has been 2 weeks on the way, he did not bring much news. He comes to enter our Law Class, and I hope he may be studious and successful. I dined with him at Prof. Minor's today, and was the only Democrat among some five or six Whigs of the rabid sort.

November 20, 1848. Spent a part of this day in getting Nick matriculated; the great difficulty is a room, and one cannot be obtained in the University, I believe. Tho' I have only a single bed, I shall keep Nick with me until he can be comfortably settled. This day three years ago, I started for Philadelphia.

21st. Received a letter from Greenwood and one from John Keyes. The latter has come to North Alabama to transport his dying brother to the warm clime of Florida. I say that Pres is dying—and mournfully do I say it, because John says as much in his letter. . . . Got Nick established at Col. Johnson's in a single room. . . . He told me in his sleep last night, among many other things, that he loved Sophy Lowe and always did.

22nd. Today Nick came to my room in a deep fit of the blues, and having determined to return home. He asked me to accompany him to the Chairman's office to get his withdrawal. I . . . treated his difficulties in so jesting a manner, that he came to think them trifling and accordingly abandoned them. I was the better able to treat his case successfully, from the fact that just about one year ago, I was in his situation precisely. . . . Received a letter from Ma; they have concluded to remain until Christmas.

23rd. Wrote to Lieut. Colonel W. W. Garth.

24th. Went down per invitation with Lyon, Howard, Davis and Gordon to meet some young ladies at Dr. Hargrave's. We . . . met Misses Janette Sanders, Juliet Gilmer, Woodson and Poore. Mrs. and Mr. Pryor entertained us in a most hospitable and agreeable manner. Miss Gilmer kept up a continual flash of puns.

Dr. Hargrave was the brother of Martha Hargrave Davis, mother of Nick. They were children of Jesse and Mary Pleasants Hargrave of Hanover County, Virginia. The name, Mary Pleasants, has passed through this family for generations. A portrait of the colonial ancestress, Mary Pleasants, of Curles Neck, Virginia, hung in the beautiful home, Carter's Grove, but was not in evidence when the author last visited there in 1970.—Virginia records, Southern History Department, Birmingham Public Library, Birmingham, Alabama.

27th. Nick came today to me, suffering under a terrible attack of blues—so much so that his countenance was perceptibly changed, and he looked like a man to whom something serious had happened. He had made a calculation, and his figures brought him in debt at the end of the session, and this he did not like. I showed him that his mathematics was of the unaxiomatic sort, which could not be relied on, and in fine, laughed away his fears. Nick's temperament is such that he is either at the tropic equator or at the pole, and hence he seldom knows the delightful sensation of the temperate zone.
28th. We had no lecture in law today, because the Prof. is called into the county of Louisa to attend the funeral of his father. . . . Nick and I called on Mrs. Pryor, and spent a pleasant half-hour; the dog Pryor is . . . a lucky dog, in having gotten such a wife.
Monday, December 4, 1848. Received a letter from Ma this morning. They are still in Brunswick, and have not yet seen all our relatives there. This evening was unanimously elected the editor from the students . . . of a periodical which we propose to publish here. . . . Two editors are elected from each of the three literary societies, and the seventh is taken from those students who do not belong to any of these. To be thus elected the first editor of such a paper, I esteem an honor.

The University of Virginia Magazine was published from January, 1849 until April, 1958. The first issue contained 36 pages. Unfortunately, Thomas Hobbs did not sign any of the articles, and his name does not appear. The magazines are on file at the Alderman Library, University of Virginia.

5th. Received a letter from Cousin Eliza. All are straight in Alabama—she tells a good joke upon Judge Lane, who circulated, by mistake, a lot of Democratic votes on election day, with which some mischievous wag had filled his pocket.
9th. Went to town this morning and heard a speech from Dr. McGuffey on the subject of Free schools in Va.; it was addressed to a convention of the friends of the scheme in Albemarle County. . . . Attended a meeting of the editorial corps this evening—it consists of Lyon & Caskie from

the Jefferson Society, Hart and Cochran from the Washington, and Payne and Marshall from the Philomathean; I am the representative of that portion of the students (about half) who do not belong to any of these societies. At the meeting this evening I was elected Chairman; Caskie, Sect'y, & Hart Treasurer for the quarter.

10th. We will bring out early next (this) week, an address to the students, alumni, & Professors, in which the design and modus operandi is to be fully explained. We hear of some pieces which are in preparation for our magazine, and have strong hopes of easily filling our pages with good original matter. The greatest difficulty is our want of time.

December 12, 1848. I fear the editor of the *Southern Literary Messenger* does not think my poetry worthy of his columns. . . . Well, "full many a flower is born to blush unseen," I must be one of them!

13th. Wrote to Mrs. M. today. I begin to wish to see this affectionate and kind cousin of mine, and I frequently enjoy the pleasure of looking at her miniature.

14th. Lyon came to consult me today in regard to a Professorship which has been offered him in Randolph Macon College. . . . I advised him to decline the offer, to stick to his Coke, graduate, leave Virginia and set up in some of the new south western States, and I am sure, talents such as he possesses will soon not only bring him money, but distinction and honor.

15th. I penned a letter to Gen. [George] Houston . . . in regard to an application for a foreign appointment which I wish him to make for me. I desire above all things to visit Europe and study the policy of those governments which are so different from our own.

December 18th. A real Alabama winter. Here we are nearly at Christmas, and the weather not warm [cool] enough for fire!

20th. We left Charlottesville [for Petersburg] at 2 this morning, and rode 8 miles in the stage. John and Daniel Lyon, Dunn, Townes, and I were the party. . . . I took a hack in Richmond and drove to the music stores in the hope of finding a flute to suit me, but could not do so.

21st. Cousin Indie's eye beams as brightly, Julia['s] as softly, and Susan's as mischievously as when last I saw them. The girls are engaged in making evergreen decorations for the church, and [I] accompanied them there today and assisted them, tho' I begin to think there are some things I had rather see tied than strings of evergreens.

22nd. Took tea with Lyon and thus made the acquaintance of his Father and mother, who are excellent people and devoted to their sons. . . . Today Epes, the murderer of Muir, was hung; he confessed his guilt—3000 persons were present.

24th. Accompanied Cousins Indie and Julia to Sabbath School; as I left them at the door, and turned to leave, a little boy sang out to me, "Ain't Miss Indie your beau?" I left the precocious juvenile unanswered, but I thought to myself, he was "some" to guess. Went with Susie to church. *Ma says she thinks I am going over to the Episcopaleans.* Mr. Meade came home from Congress today, bringing accounts of some high-handed moves the abolitionists and freesoilers are making.

26th. Tonight I wrote on a card . . . and handed it to Indie: "Cousin, you said tonight you knew no one who was going to address you; I know one who is dying to do so, and will do it as soon as time will warrant and he can believe he has the least hope of success."

December 27th, 1848. This is but a hint to her of what are my feelings toward her. . . . We left Petersburg this morning at 5 A.M.

28th. We had a good deal of sport as we came up in the cars yesterday. . . . The fire in the stove would not burn. . . . We are all regretting that we did not stay longer in Petersburg.

29th. Received a letter from Mrs. Maclin—containing the news that President Rivers had left Athens, and moved to Louisiana. There goes one of my best friends, and also one of the main pillars of the Institute. Tonight was elected W. P. of University Division. . . . We had several propositions for membership tonight, this is the natural effect of the Christmas holidays & frolicking.

Dr. Rivers went to Centenary College, Jackson, Louisiana, thence to La Grange College, and in 1876 John Tanner mentions that Dr. Rivers was at Martin College in Pulaski, Tennessee.

30th. No one but Nick Davis knows what I have done in my "affaire de cour." . . . I have thought it most prudent to say nothing. . . . Nick gives me the benefit of his experience, and says women are the same everywhere, and that I may apply his doctrines to Virginia girls. [At the back of the ledger for 1848, Hobbs states that he spent at the University $520 for the session of 1847 and 1848.]

Monday, January 1, 1849. The first day of the New Year! How have I spent it? Why, the servant awoke me and claimed a gift; I arose and attended prayers, and then hastened to the office in hopes of receiving a letter from Ma. On this day they start for Alabama, & Ma promised to write ere she went. [Bought] a bushel of good apples (37). Was scared about my Coke this morning, as I am on every Monday morning, since

I do not study on Sunday. . . . Went to town, to carry some matter to the printer of our Magazine.

January 2nd, 1849. Have a case in Moot Court, involving the doctrine of Bills of Exchange; a subject which has always been a difficult one to me. . . . Called on Mrs. Minor & Misses McGuffey.

3rd. Drew tonight my first bill in Chancery for Nick Davis.

4th. Received this morning the expected letter from my parents, informing me that they would certainly start on Monday last, and that Susan would accompany them. They are therefore tonight at or near Augusta, & will reach home on Saturday next. . . . A sentence from Pa ran thus: "In a conversation with———last night, she told me to say to you not to love her more than you can spare to a relative who loves you as such —her heart & hand are pledged to another." Here is a mystery and a novelty, and the novelty is of man's being discarded before he proposed.

6th. Wrote a piece of poetry, which was rejected by the Editors of the Magazine—don't care—perfectly despondent—will sting myself with a bumble-bee—sure.

7th. Heard two good sermons from the Chaplain. Broadus being absent, I had to lead the Choir, and the novelty of the business was quite embarrassing—but we came out very creditably.

8th. I have . . . felt in bad spirits, for I went to lecture, as I thought, well prepared, and was corked. This, with some reflections on certain subject —make me much less gay than I usually am. . . . Sometimes I think it will be an easy matter to forget her, and then when I remember her charms, I am ready to swear that I can never cease to love her.

January 10, 1849. The weather is now very cold, and they are filling the University Ice House. . . . Attended a party at Dr. McGuffey's tonight, and had a good deal to say to that charming lady, Mrs. Pryor, and something to say to the mysterious Miss Juliet. Made the acquaintance of a belle, Miss Eliza Rives. She is a very intelligent and very pretty lady. Dr. Schelé is in love with her, and shows it just as plainly as some of [the] younger & less learned ones. Love is master of us all.

Eliza Rives was married to Dr. Schelé not long afterwards. She was a daughter of William Cabell Rives, U. S. Congressman, Senator, and minister to France. The Rives home, Castle Hill, was built in 1840, on land inherited by Mrs. Rives from her grandfather, Dr. Thomas Walker, guardian of the young Thomas Jefferson. Dr. Walker's home, built in 1764, remained on the estate. The home was later inherited by the Rives's granddaughter, Ámelie, who spent much time here with her husband, Prince Troubetzkoy. When Ámelie was young, she lived with her parents in Mobile, Alabama, and their Government Street home stood until recent years.—National League of Penwomen, 283–85.

January 14th. Was up late last night with Nick. . . . Received a letter from Gen. Houston this morning—he makes me no promises in regard to my getting an office, but says he will look out for a vacancy & get Mr. Meade to help him.
16th. Received a letter from Garth this morning—he has settled in Huntsville & commenced practice in partnership with Humphries. He says he is in love deeply—and this is not a little surprising as he had a decided aversion to ladies last session. He did not write who was the lady, but I expect she is *rich.** I slept on a pallet in Nick's room last night to give him medicine at certain periods. He rested very well, and is much better today.

*She was wealthy, if the lady in question was Eliza Fearn, whom he married in 1855. Eliza was the daughter of Dr. Thomas Fearn, one of Madison County's most prominent citizens. He was the first physician in the world to use quinine in the treatment of malaria, and he owned the first waterworks system in Huntsville, first in the state, and one of the earliest in the South. Dr. Fearn is also remembered for his attempt to connect Huntsville with the Tennessee River by means of a canal which bore his name, although it was never successful.—Owen, III, 567.

17th. Finished about 11—correcting the proof sheets of Dr. Schelé's account of his visit to Fredrika Bremer. Lyon & I have most of this work to do.

Fredrika Bremer, 1801–1865, was called the "Jane Austen" of Sweden, and became one of the first leaders for the emancipation of women in her later life. Her second book, *The H. Family,* became internationally famous after its publication in 1844.

20th. Editorial Corps met at Caskie's room, and adopted an editorial for the first no. which is to be issued in a few days. . . . We are all on tiptoe to see Mr. Calhoun's address to the Southern members of Congress. . . . We have heard it is hard & heavy up on the North.
21st. Heard a day or two since that a case of the cholera has appeared in Eastport, Miss[issippi], a passenger on a N. Orleans boat. It is decreasing in almost all the cities.
25th. Bought today *Proverbial Philosophy* and the *British Spy.* . . . The latter is getting scarce, and I thought I would secure a copy while it was to be had. Did not Wirt write also *The Bachelor,* or some such name?

William Wirt published *The Old Bachelor,* after it first appeared in thirty-three installments of the *Richmond Enquirer.* Wirt, 1772–1834, who was recognized as one of the foremost lawyers in the country, assisted in the prosecution of Aaron Burr, guided the youthful Edgar Allen Poe in his study of Blackstone, and commanded tremendous influence over the minds of Southern gentlemen. Yet he had only a grammar school education before his study of law.—Brooks, 268.

27th. Today our long expected Magazine came out. . . . The students manifest much interest, and there is some amusing guessing at the authors of the pieces.

30th. Sent a copy of our Magazine to Missess Indie and Julia Meade.

31st. I have written a piece for the Magazine . . . a description of a scrape in college and is headed "Manufacturing an Earthquake."

Sunday, February 4, 1849. Went to Charlottesville to church—attended the Episcopal—saw William C. Rives there, and also Andrew Stephenson. The latter is much the finer looking of the two, but is rather pompous in his carriage. Lyon and I thought we saw great similarity between the shape of the heads of Nick and William C. Rives.

Andrew Stevenson, 1784–1857, had served as Speaker of the House, as minister to England, and as rector of the University of Virginia.

February 5, 1849. Today I wrote a letter to Indiana Meade. I did so after the maturest reflection: that I might find out from herself, in what light I stand. . . . It was sufficient to show that I entertained an attachment to her still, and was not so direct as to be considered a proposal.

6th. In my *Yankee Blade* of this morning, I found the piece of poetry which I wrote & offered to the University Magazine—so it seems the Boston editor is less exacting in his requirements than my associates.

10th. Nick is again confined to his bed, and I engaged with him, until a late hour, tonight. He will not rest unless I am with him, and scolds me for the absence of a half-hour—even when he knows I am called away by business.

11th. The long-looked for document came this morning. . . . I put it in my pocket and went to breakfast before I read it. . . . It contained a plain & candid answer to my questions—informing me that she *is* engaged, and no mistake. This piece of information was blandified by some sayings that I was a deucedly clever fellow, was worthy of a good gal, a choice sperrit and such like, all of which I knew before, and many of which I expected she would say if she was really past reaching!

February 12th. Nick says I stand a kicking better than any man he ever saw; I am conscious of a strong necessity of throwing off all the undue influence which such an event might put upon my mind. An examination is very near. . . . I trust to my contented nature, which has often enabled me to bear difficulties.

14th. St. Valentine's Day. I have the vanity to think that I should have received a valentine this morning from Petersburg, had I not put a more serious phase upon the matter. . . . Wrote to Gilbert and Gibson to engrave a vignette for our Magazine—it is to be a view of our University. Our class mate, Paxton, came to lecture today in a gown very much torn. McRae asked, "Why is he like an Episcopal clergyman?" Ans[wer]: Because he wears a *holy* gown. I asked, "If the gent's clothes are torn much more, won't he be a 'nudum Paxtum'?"

Elisha Franklin Paxton, 1828–1863, transferred to Virginia from Yale. It was at the battle of First Manassas that this young man from Rockbridge County, Virginia, showed such unusual prowess that he was chosen by General Thomas Jackson as his aide-de-camp. This was the battle in which Jackson won his immortal name of "Stonewall." Paxton was killed at Chancellorsville on May 3, 1863, and is buried in Lexington near General Jackson, who died May 10, 1863.—Warner, 229.

18th. Did not go to Sabbath School this morning . . . because I was detained by an unusual circumstance. Young Ayres became offended yesterday with Dr. McGuffey, for something which happened in the Examination room. He called this morning . . . to ask my advice about his future course. . . . I think he is a man of vindictive feelings, and I therefore extracted a promise from him to permit me to have a conversation with Dr. M[cGuffey] before he takes any further steps in the matter.

25th. Received a letter from John Keyes, and was rejoiced to hear that Pres is completely cured.

27th. Have been thinking lately of going to Washington on the 4th. Nick & Lyon have spoken of going also. Received a letter from Mrs. Meade this morning, written from Washington . . . she will be there at the inauguration, but says nothing about her daughters—wonder if they will be there?

28th. Recited in Greenleaf. Received a letter from Rhodes. He is about to leave Louisville. His Father expects to move to Texas. Dick is delighted, but I am shocked at this.

Friday, March 2, 1849. Today the Examination in Senior Law took place—we found a lot of hard, but pretty fair, questions on the boards. . . . About 11 Tyler, LaBranche, Townes, Brown and I drove down to the Monticello, and about 12 left in the stage. We had a short and pleasant ride to the cars.

3rd. Reached Washington about 5 and drove in the greatest haste to the U. States. I left the boys in the carriage and . . . asked if he [the clerk] had a stable that four young men could occupy. He seemed pleased at the humility of my request, and told me a small room had just been vacated. . . . We found the room large enough for us to lie down in conveniently and stow our baggage. We marched immediately to the capitol—saw the lobbies filling and took seats. At six the Senate met, and I had the gratification of seeing for the first time that august body. I noticed Messrs. Calhoun, Webster, Benton, Allen, Houston of Texas, Foote, Hunter, Hale, etc.* They had up the subject of the Home Department.** Messrs. Calhoun, Hunter & Mason were opposed to it, and the latter made a long speech in opposition. They opposed it because it would increase the influence of the Fed. Government. Though my interest was kept up—my body was so badly fatigued from the enormous pressure in the galleries that at 11 I was forced to leave.

*Although John Caldwell Calhoun and Daniel Webster opposed each other throughout their long careers, it was Webster who delivered the eulogy for Calhoun upon his death in 1850. Thomas Hart Benton, chief opponent of Calhoun in the nullification issue, served in Congress from Missouri for over 30 years. William Allen entered the House in 1832 at the age of 26, and the Senate four years later. Out of loyalty to Cass, he refused nomination for the presidency in 1848. Sam Houston was serving Texas as its first senator. Henry Stuart Foote became Governor of Mississippi, was in open opposition to President Davis during the Civil War, and was appointed director of the U. S. Mint at New Orleans by President Grant. Robert Taliaferro Hunter served Virginia in the Senate until secession, then served for a time as Confederate Secretary of State.

**It was the desire of some in the Senate to establish a Home Department in order to set up a more effective system of census taking. It was upon the recommendation of Alabama's William Rufus King that the matter should be put under the Attorney General's office that the question was finally settled. The 1850 census was definitely an improvement over its predecessors, for it was the first to list household members by name.—Congressional Records.

March 4, 1849. Neither body adjourned until near 5 this morning—before which there was one fight in the Senate and several in the House, in one of which Mr. Meade & Giddings were the combatants. Saw Gen. Houston this morning, he was completely worn out with last night's proceedings. Met Mr. Hine, Vasser and Keith Phillips at the General's room.

A cartoon of "Meade Choking Giddings" was widely circulated. Joshua Reed Giddings was serving in the Congress from Ohio. His rabid antislavery speeches were highly inflammatory. In December of the same year,

Mr. Meade had another altercation; this time with William Duer, of New York, who had pointed out Mr. Meade as a disunionist.—Wilson, II, 214; Claiborne, 110.

Monday, March 5th. I was awakened by the crash of music from a band passing up the street. We dressed, breakfasted and went out—saw the streets a perfect jam. Near the hour of ten—we went to the Capitol and got a good stand near the gate thro' which the procession must pass. . . . Saw the Gen. in the carriage with Polk and some others—a plain-looking old man—smiling good-naturedly and somewhat confusedly on all around him. Did not hear a word of his address, but saw him read it, & take the oath.

6th. We arrived very late in Baltimore. . . . Went to Barnum's to supper, and afterwards to the museum—saw all the curiosities and also a little play. . . . Returned to Washington. Today visited the Patent Office, Museum, Capitol, etc. Called to see Mrs. Meade, but did not say one word about Indie.

Even Charles Dickens liked David Barnum's City Hotel, begun in 1825, and completed with an incredible seven stories, elegant interior, and perhaps the most superb food in the nation.—Beirne, 193–94.

Rembrandt Peale, son of Charles Wilson Peale, started an interest in a Baltimore museum by exhibiting the skeleton of a mastodon, dug by his father. He erected a museum building in 1813, and lighted it with gas three years later. Interest in this project led to the formation of a commercial gas company, the first in America.—Hamilton Owens, 216.

8th. Spent in all . . . about $45 for the trip.

9th. Attended Division tonight—we met in our new hall. . . . We initiated nine students, some of whom were some of the boys who were so merry in Wash.

10th. Our Feby. no. is just out and all are pleased with it.

12th. Today finished and sent by T. C. Keith, a long letter to my parents—in it I unfolded some of my plans, and prospects. . . . Some of these will be novel to them and they will smile—I know, when they read that I expect to be a "practicing lawyer all my life." This is now my determination. I may be forced by circumstances to change.

Tolbert C. Keith, Athens merchant, married Ophelia Craig, "a wild, rolicking girl, full of mischief and fun, but harmless and innocent in all her actions and motives," wrote John Tanner on July 21, 1876. The Keiths moved to Mississippi and lived the rest of their lives there.

16th. Attended the Division tonight—we are now in our new Hall, which is just above a liquor shop.

17th. Our flute quartette has been invited to play for the celebrations of the Societies which are now coming on. . . . I received a day or two since a new flute from Baltimore . . . cost me $38.

18th. Dined with Jesse Coe at Col. Kemper's . . . also visited Mrs. Minor tonight with John Washington.

Wednesday, March 21, 1849. Received a letter this morning from Ma. Mr. Vasser had just reached home, & told them of having seen me in Washington. Ma says Pa "grunted" when he heard. . . . I suppose he thought of the money I was spending. But, as I wrote him, this is my last money-spending year, and I am therefore a little more liberal. Nick and I, just on the heel of that "grunt," went down tonight thro' the mud, and got some sardines. The oyster season is past, and we must therefore put up with other less luxurious snacks.

26th. This evening, accompanied by George Gordon, visited the Misses Rives. They reside in a new and elegant mansion, right at the foot of Monticello. Near the house met Miss Eliza riding out on horseback with her cousin. She sent us on to the house, where we found her mother & sister; were entertained until she returned. . . . Miss Eliza looked charming in her riding dress. It fitted her well, and became her.

29th. I find the analysis of Greenleaf my principal care now. That author certainly writes without a correct analysis in his mind, else it would not be so hard to find it out. I received this morning a letter . . . from Carlos G. Smith, my old Professor at La Grange, requesting to be considered a subscriber for the magazine. He heard of it by means of a circular which I sent Mr. Tutwiler (with whom he is now teaching), and very much approving the enterprise, thus encourages it.

Sunday, April 1, 1849. Claiborne and I went to the Methodist Church in town.

John Herbert Claiborne was to become one of Virginia's most distinguished physicians, and most vivid portrayers of the state's historical figures through his book *Seventy-five Years in Old Virginia.* Claiborne and Hobbs shared a mutual attitude in their observations on money. Claiborne wrote, "money, with its meretrious adornments and vulgar display, was not the sesame to open any gentleman's door," which corresponds with Hobbs' statement concerning Huntsville. It was Claiborne who was greatly responsible for Thomas Hobbs' first marriage, and he served as a groomsman in the wedding.—Scott and Wyatt, 164.

April 4, 1849. We signalized this night—by holding the first meeting of our University Band. . . . Mr. Deems had arranged 4 pieces for us.

6th. Attended division & presided for the last time. . . . Launcelot Kean was installed W. P.

8th. Received a letter from Cousin E., containing, as her letters always do, a delightful quantity of love and lots of news. The town is music-mad, and she is one of the diseased. . . . LaBranche says I must record it that he has been a good boy today, for he has been twice to church.
9th. I have [been] having a good deal of fun with Susan Meade now, for we exchange a message by almost every letter from home and back there.
12th. This evening, after a long delay & much anxiety, our *March* no. of the Magazine made its appearance. The new engraving of the University improves the appearance very much. . . . I am in much doubt as to whether I ought to take the Editorship again. . . . Nick and all the rest of them urge me to take it.
13th. This evening we had the celebration of the Jefferson Society. John Lyon was the orator. . . . He began his speech in a good style . . . but soon I discovered that he was flagging. . . . After he had dragged on for a few minutes longer, he stopped and seemed very much confused. At this moment, Nick Davis saw him reeling, and cried out to the President who sat just behind the speaker, "Catch him, Mr. Broadus, he is falling." . . . the doctors of the Faculty soon restored him . . . he was forbidden by the physicians to finish his speech. . . . After the speaking, we musicians went down as invited guests to a supper in Charlottesville . . . there was a great deal of wit and humour. . . . John Lyon elicited the highest praise . . . his friends would not rest until he was brought down to the supper in a carriage. I got into bed as the clock struck 3, which was spreeing it pretty late for a Temperance man.
Monday, April 16, 1849. Got up the last of the Magazines for March (tolerable late, I should guess) and Peyton and I superintended the distribution of them. . . . Only a few persons have suspected me of writing "Vattermere," and scarcely one, the "Valentine." This latter piece is much complimented, and is frequently quoted. Some attribute it to Miss Juliet Gilmer and some to St. George Tucker.

Saint George Tucker was the son of Henry St. George Tucker, professor of law at the University; and grandson of Saint George Tucker, professor of law at the College of William and Mary, who wrote an annotated edition of Blackstone that was widely used. He was the father of Beverley Tucker, noted writer; and stepfather of the brilliant and demented John Randolph, of Roanoke.

17th. The new editorial corps have gone to work. It consists of Nick Davis & Fred Page from the Jeff. Society; Archer & Clayton from the Wash.; and Paxton & Sinclair from the Philomathean. I resigned a few evenings since. . . . George Mason (a son of Senator Mason), was elected in my stead.

George Mason was the great-grandson of George Mason, builder of Gunston Hall, Fairfax County, Virginia, and author of the Virginia Bill of Rights. He was the grandson of John Mason, of Analostan, and son of James Mason who, as a Confederate commissioner, was captured aboard the *Trent* with Slidell during the Civil War.—Information gathered in a visit to Gunston Hall, June, 1971.

18th. Tonight John Lyon returned from Petersburg, bringing me a letter, or rather a note, from Cousin Indie, and also a couple of beautiful bookmarks which she promised me when I was there at Xmas. The note was couched in the kindest terms, having not the slightest allusion to any past communication between us.

19th. My birthday—therefore to be marked with chalk and passed over as a lucky day, and of itself great enough. Yesterday it snowed. All the fruit here is killed. . . . Tonight Nick had a very severe operation performed for some disease of the neck of the bladder. I was present, and while assisting, was in an ace of fainting, & should have done so, had I not stopped and sat down. He stood it like a man.

20th. Received a letter from Sloss, containing the half of a $100 bill.

Monday, April 23, 1849. I hear that the cold spell pervaded the whole South, and killed not only the fruit, but also the cotton, which was up, and all early vegetables. It seems that they had snow in N. Ala. . . . before we had it in Va. . . . on the 15th.

25th. Received a letter from Ma . . . gives a hint of her opinion of Indie, and it is not a very favorable one. She seems to intimate that Indie will be freed from her engagement, and Ma suspects me of having an attachment there. What am I to do? Should I afterwards to discover something in my favor, how could I go forward, against Ma's will? I could not do it, Ma must approve my choice, or I'll never make one.

May 1, 1849. The accounts of the effects of the late frost in the South are distressing. All the cotton and corn that was up was killed, and there are many who can't get seed to replant. The frost extended even into Florida. There was snow at Savannah, Georgia.

3rd. Received this evening a letter from my long silent correspondent, Dr. Wilkinson. Pomp writes in his half-humorous, semi-serious style, interspersing a sprinkling of his dry wit. He says he is smitten with Miss Maria Bass, who has lately been on a visit to his region . . . Henry Malone has recently visited him, and given him some hints as to my dealings in Va., which he throws up to me in a humorous manner. Confound him! It is too serious to joke about.

8th. Heard an interesting lecture tonight by Mr. Koeppen, a man who once held a chair in the University of Greece. . . . He illustrates his lectures by beautiful diagrams—one of them of modern Athens. . . . He was compelled to leave Greece by an order of King Otho . . . all the foreign professors had to leave at the same time.

9th. Mr. Minor was called to Louisa County today to see his brother, Lucian, who was thrown from his horse a day or two since, and seriously injured. He was reading as he rode along (a favorite practice of his) when he was thrown.

10th. Was surprised today to meet . . . Charles Kathrem, formerly of Athens, and now traveling with Tatum's Sacred Pictures. . . . Bought today a beautiful little present for Cousin Eliza's center table—a solid glass paper weight with beautiful flowers blown inside it.

Tatum may have been the same person whom John Tanner describes as having boarded in Athens with Mrs. Theo Thomas, who "lived where Gov. Houston now resides" (1876). Tatum was an artist "not overstocked with brains at that time, but has since become somewhat noted in his line."—Tanner, July 21, 1876.

May 14, 1849. Received today a letter from Ma. . . . It is a most sensible and affectionate epistle, showing me that whoever may be my choice, Ma will be satisfied . . . she is studiously avoiding any interference with my choice. I wish I knew myself whether or not I was in love.

18th. We were . . . allowed to go to town to attend the session of the [Episcopal] Convention. They were discussing the propriety of allowing Bishop Johns to accept the presidency of William & Mary . . . by a large majority he was allowed to accept it.

19th. I dined with Nick at Dr. Hargrave's yesterday, where we met, of course, the agreeable Mrs. Pryor. The conversation turned upon John Randolph, whom the Dr. knew very well. He told us that R. turned Dudley, to whom he wrote a series of most affectionate letters, styling him generally "my son," penniless out of doors, and he had to seek a support in humble capacity in Tennessee.

Dr. Theodore B. Dudley, nephew of John Randolph, was one of six orphan boys cared for by John Randolph in a tender manner quite different from that in which the world came to think him capable. The letters were preserved and published by Dudley after Randolph's death under the title, *Letters to a Young Relative.* To one of the letters Dudley appended a note in which he stated: "The truth and beauty of the eastern allegory, of the man endowed with two souls, was never more forcibly exemplified than in this case."—Johnson, 173.

20th. The question discussed in convention yesterday was whether a proposed canon vs. dancing (at public halls), theatre going, etc., should be adopted. Dr. Empee, one of the most learned ministers of the diocese, took the boldest ground vs. the canon, plumply denying that the church had any right to make such restrictions upon the laity, and declaring that the conscience of the member alone must decide upon the guilt or innocence of the act. He was supported by several ministers, and also by some dandified lay delegates, among whom was B. B. Minor, formerly Editor of the *S. Lit*[*erary*] *Messenger.* Both the bishops were on the other side; Johns made an eloquent and Meade a most impressive and convincing speech in favor of the cannon [*sic*].

If "dandified," as Hobbs describes Benjamin Blake Minor, is the word for him, he was certainly unlike his kinsman, Dr. John Minor. B. B. Minor, 1818–1905, was educated at both the University of Virginia and the College of William and Mary. He studied law under Beverley Tucker, and practiced in Petersburg and Richmond. In 1842, Minor married Virginia Maury Otey, daughter of Bishop James Hervey Otey. After having owned and edited the *Messenger* for five years, Minor sold it and became principal of the Virginia Female Institute at Staunton, and later became president of the University of Missouri.—*Dictionary of American Biography,* XIII, 25.

22nd. Saw yesterday for the first time, the new gold dollar; it is a beautiful coin, and I doubt not will be found to be very convenient.

29th. Nick had two fist fights, and well-contested battles they were. I cannot here explain from what causes they arose, but he stands perfectly justified for both in the eyes of this community. The second fight, which was about 15 minutes after the first and on the same ground, was with Ayres, who is considered one of the strongest men amongst us. Nick gave him some terrible blows . . . and almost everybody rejoiced when they saw him giving the bully a good licking. . . . I could not help yelling for Nick.

30th. Today, by the timely and judicious mediation of our excellent Proctor, the affair of last evening was agreed to be dropped in status quo.

Friday, June 1, 1849. Nick has left the University, and gone to stay some days with his Uncle in Charlottesville previous to starting for home. He had withdrawn before his difficulties took place, and his leaving has nothing to do with them. . . . For the first time in my life, I have thought proper . . . to carry arms about my person. I have had some reason to expect an attack from that desperate man, Ayres, and felt it my duty to prepare myself.

2nd. Tonight we had a mass meeting of the Students to set on foot a plan of erecting a monument to Jefferson upon the Lawn . . . adjourned to the Rotunda steps to hear some speaking on the subject. Nick was the first man called for, but being in the house at the time, he did not respond. I was then called for, and without a moment's thought as to what I had to say, I made a few remarks. Nick afterwards came out and made an excellent speech, which was most enthusiastically received. Lyon, Howard, Broadus, and others spoke.

The students evidently set a precedent for the Virginia legislature, which in 1853 appropriated $10,000 for a statue of Jefferson, executed by Alexander Galt.—Bruce, IV, 190.

June 4, 1849. Went to town this evening to assist Nick in getting ready, for he has concluded to start tomorrow anyhow, cholera or not. I wrote a letter to Cousin Eliza, in which I enclosed a pair of green elastic garters, as a present to Susie, viz., a *leg*acy. . . . I fear from what Ma wrote in her last that Indie is gone—the opposition on the part of her father & mother is now so great that P. never visits the house when they are there, but Indie still remains faithful & true to her love.

5th. I hastened to Dr. Hargrave's to see Nick start. . . As the stage rattled away, I almost felt like calling to the driver to stop & take me too. . . . For one week and a half more I must toil on, and then comes the much dreaded examination.

June 8, 1849. This evening we closed the Moot Court—the new constitution which I prepared was adopted, and also a memorial to the visitors.

10th. Claiborne & I lectured John Lyon today after the sermon, by way of exhortation, for his studying on Sunday, but he insists that the nearness of the examination makes him "an ass in the ditch," which must be helped even on Sunday.

12th. Reviewed Vattel, whose insipid old axioms bore me like thunder. How much could I accomplish, if I were to study for nine months as closely as I have to do now? . . . 'Tis eleven. Good night, Vattel!

15th. Received a letter from home today, containing $120, much more money than I wrote for, and more than I need. Pa continually lectures me on economy, and yet, when I write to him, and make out a strong case of need, he supplies me lavishly.

19th. Today Lyon and Paxton "threw up," viz., announced to the Prof.

that they wished not to be considered as candidates for graduation. At this we were all surprised and grieved, for these gentlemen were almost sure of their diplomas.

20th. At 8 o'clock we went to the Examination room and found our questions written upon the board . . . every man saw them so much easier than he expected. . . . We were writing just 12 hours, which is about as much as an ordinary man can stand.

21st. When we went to the lecture room today, we found a different sort of an affair to deal with. It was a very hard examination indeed. . . . Mrs. Minor sent us a good snack about 2.

22nd. I stood my oral examination today . . . quite well. For one hour the Prof. questioned me as fast as I could answer—the subjects were chiefly remainders, executory devices, and constitutional law. The two former are the most difficult topics of the law.

25th. Spent the day at Col. Randolph's, a grandson of Mr. Jefferson. He is an agreeable and well-informed old gentleman, and has several accomplished daughters. This visit was one of the most pleasant I have ever enjoyed in my life.

Thomas Jefferson Randolph, 1792–1875, son of Thomas Mann and Martha Jefferson Randolph, was born at Monticello. In 1828 he built his home, Edgehill, just outside Charlottesville. In 1832 Randolph introduced into legislature a bill calling for the gradual abolition of slavery, but the bill suffered the same defeat as that introduced by his famous grandfather years before. Randolph's bill providing for the reform of taxes, however, passed in 1842, and served as the basis of a sound financial condition for the state. The most personally rewarding task of Randolph's was the editing of Thomas Jefferson's correspondence, which he published in 1829 under the title, *Life and Correspondence of Thomas Jefferson.*

26th. Today, very unexpectedly, Prof. Minor's report came out, & showed us that every candidate had graduated. . . . The graduates are: D.A. Wright, King & Q.[ueen;] H. B. Lewis, [King George]; W. H. Anthony, Botetourt; F. W. Holiday, Winchester; C. C. McRae, Manchester; E. F. Paxton and Cumings, Rockbridge.

27th. Commenced settling up my debts, and packing up. Helped the ladies to make garlands and wreaths to ornament the rotunda. We had an address (valedictory) tonight by William P. Dabney, of the Wash. Society. . . . Last night we had an address from that excellent fellow, Paxton. The faculty were justly offended because the committee of Arrangements had placed upon the speaker's stand some liquor instead of water. Of this the speaker partook freely at the end of his speech.

William Pope Dabney, 1827–1894, was born at Montpelier, near Powhatan Court House, the son of Robert Kelso and Lucy Ann Dabney. He became an eminent judge and historian.—Tyler, Swem, et al., XII, 252.

29th. A day or two since the Chief Marshall, P. B. Whittle, appointed me his aid[e], and this morning my duties began. . . . The procession was formed in due order at the time, and marched into the Rotunda, which was already full to overflowing. There the diplomas were conferred, and an address delivered to the Alumni Society by Prof. Dabney, of Washington college.

Professor George E. Dabney taught Greek at Washington College in Lexington, now Washington and Lee.

30th. Left the University this morning, and seldom have I parted with a circle of friends with more pain. Prof. & Mrs. Minor . . . Dr. McGuffey and Miss Mary . . . Mrs. Harrison and daughters—indeed, every friend in the University gave me many evidences of strong attachment. When I parted with La Branche, he choked with emotion and could not finish a sentence. . . . I shook his hand tenderly & left him for I, too, felt deeply.

Sunday, July 1st, 1849. We arrived in Petersburg about 8, and John Claiborne and I stopped at Powell's Hotel.

2nd. Dined today at Mr. Gholson's (Tom) with all of the University boys.* This I notch down as one of the most agreeable entertainments I was ever at. . . . I have spent yesterday and today chiefly at Mr. M's with cousins Indie & Julia (their father and mother being absent at Old Point.** . . . I am satisfied that she [Indie] is devotedly attached to another. . . . I met him once or twice at the house, where he visits during the absence of the old folks.

*"I recall very vividly my first visit to Judge Gholson's mansion. It was in the month of July, 1859 [should be 1849], when returning from the U. of Virginia, in company with Judge Gholson's son, John, afterwards the Rev. John Y. Gholson. . . . at that dinner I met a young Mr. Farrar . . . [who] had with him a banjo . . . " Claiborne explained that Farrar later became known as "Johnnie Reb." Thomas Saunders Gholson, 1808–1868, was prosecuting attorney at the Epes trial, a visitor of the College of William and Mary, and president of the Petersburg bank.—*Dictionary of American Biography,* VII, 233.

**Old Point Comfort on the Virginia coast became a resort area in the 1830s.

July 3rd, 1849. Left Petersburg last night. . . . found Winter and Bankhead on the cars.†

†Probably William S. Bankhead, great-grandson of Thomas Jefferson, who lived at Courtland, Alabama. On August 6th, 1851, he married Mary Jane, daughter of Paul Watkins. They were to have less than a year together, however, for she died in May, 1852, at the age of twenty.—Huntsville *Southern Advertiser,* May 12, 1852.

4th. In Charleston we met James Paine, two McClungs and Withers, from Huntsville. Paine has just graduated at Emory College and Withers at West Point.

Withers was evidently a relative of Jones Mitchell Withers of Huntsville, who graduated from West Point in 1835, and became a major-general in the Confederate Army.—Owen, IV, 1792.

6th. When we arrived at Gunter's Landing tonight, we took a bath in the river, & after this refreshing operation, Winter & I gave them some music, which called up all the inhabitants of the burgh. We also sat up very late on the boat, to see Paint Rock and to admire the scenery of the river, of which we had a fine view by means of the bright moonlight.
7th. As I arrived home one day sooner than I expected, I did not find any conveyance in waiting for me. I landed, therefore, in Decatur and borrowing a horse from Dr. Dancy, I rode over to the plantation. Here I met Pa on his way to Mooresville, and expecting to take me up in his buggy tomorrow. While he went to M., I sent a cart for my baggage, and we came to Athens immediately. Ma was at Uncle's, where I went immediately and met them all.

Dr. Charles Fenton Mercer Dancy was born in 1814 to William and Priscilla Dancy, pioneers in Morgan County. He was married to Sarah Dandridge Garth, daughter of Jesse Winston.—Jenkins and Knox, 64.

FAMILY CONCERT
Courtesy Robert Womack, from original drawing by Thomas Hobbs, Hobbs Family Papers

DOMESTIC YEARS AND PUBLIC SERVICE 1849-1853

Sunday, July 8, 1849. Nick Davis came down last night, tho' he had gone to bed before I arrived. He was very glad to see me and I ditto to witness him.

12th. Pa and I played several pieces today, at last I am getting him to count when he plays (he can't beat time, as both his feet are employed in holding his instrument).

13th. I think I sometimes see a look of reliance given me by some of the old citizens, which is very pleasant indeed.

14th. Attended a barbecue at Piney Bridge on the Huntsville Road. We had speeches from Hubbard & O'Neal, candidates for Congress, and from N. Davis, Rip Davis, and Sanders, who are running for the Legislature. . . . I determined from what I heard today that O'Neal shall receive my vote . . . he is acknowledged to be a man of "honesty, probity & good demeanor."

This was the first election year since 1841 in which George Houston was not running for Congress. David Hubbard of Lawrence County had been defeated by Houston before, and would again be defeated in subsequent elections for Congress. Houston "naturally had less genius and grasp of intellect than Hubbard; but he was better educated, and was more logical and systematic in his arguments. In their love for the 'dear people' they stood on an equal footing, except that Hubbard had made enemies of the planters and their friends, by the course he pursued on the land question . . . the *warm affection* of Houston embraced all classes, rich and poor."—Saunders, 97.

Edward Asbury O'Neal, 1818–1890, succeeded George Houston as solicitor of the fourth district in 1841. He was a successful lawyer in Lauderdale County, served so effectively during the Civil War as to gain the nickname of "Tige," and was elected governor of Alabama in 1882. His son, Emmett, was later elected governor, the only father and son in the history of the state to serve as governors. E. A. O'Neal married Olivia Moore, daughter of Dr. Alfred Moore, and sister of John Edmund and Syndeham Moore, both prominent in the history of the state.—Owen, IV, 1301.

Lawrence Ripley Davis, older brother of Nick, was born in Kentucky in 1819. In 1850 "Rip" married Mary A. Abercrombie, daughter of James Abercrombie of Russell County, said to have been the wealthiest man in South Alabama. In 1861 Rip married Sarah Ann McClellan, daughter of Thomas Joyce and Martha Beaty McClellan. After several bids for the legislature on the Whig ticket, Rip Davis edited the *Limestone News* in Athens, was private secretary to Governor Houston, postmaster of Athens, and editor of the *Athens Post*.

Benton Sanders, from Nubbin Ridge, Limestone County, became probate judge. He married Eliza Thach, daughter of T. H. Thach of Mooresville. When most of the citizens of Athens were forced to refugee elsewhere during the siege of Athens, the Sanders among them, they sewed their valuables into a rag doll, which escaped detection.—Mason Scrapbooks, I.

July 19, 1849. Glanced today at the subject of Banks in Wayland's *Political Economy.* The question of "Bank or no Bank" is one of the main ones of the present canvass for the Legislature.

20th. It rained nearly all day, and I amused myself by teaching Pa music. This day he will set down as one of his "working days" in music—time after time I made him play over his pieces. . . . Pa would sometimes insist on quitting, but I urged him on . . . made considerable progress in a difficult piece called the "Farewell to Glasgow Quickstep."

22nd. This morning Pa and I sent a note to the preacher requesting to be informed of the hymns to be sung in order that we might adapt tunes to them before we went to church. . . . This is the beginning of the practice of knowing the hymns before church.

The prevalent practice in the early nineteenth century was to "line out" hymns, since there were no hymnbooks, instruments, or choirs in the churches as a whole.

Friday, August 3, 1849. This day, in accordance with the proclamation of the President, was observed in our town as a day of fasting & prayer. There was a sermon from Brother [Smith W.] Moore at our Church at 11 and during this service all the stores and places of business were closed.

President Zachary Taylor designated the first Friday in August, 1849, as a day of fasting, humiliation, and prayer, because of the cholera epidemic that was sweeping the country. The proclamation is reprinted in the *Virginia Historical Register* for July, 1849, p. 177.

August 4th. Pa & Ma are still staying at the Springs, but will move down on Monday next, when Uncle & Cousin E. will go up again.

7th. The Davises were elected to the Leg. . . . This may be attributed to the strong anti-bank notions of the people. McKinney is Sheriff by a considerable majority, Compton as Senator, and Hubbard far ahead of O'Neal in this county.

August 8, 1849. Went to the Springs & carried up Cousin Sue in our buggy. There is now at the Springs a ten-pin alley, which has just been completed.

September 3rd. Went to Huntsville. . . . The trial of Tate was progressing when I arrived. He was found guilty of involuntary manslaughter and fined $315. Met my old friend, Garth. I like him so much, and my liking has an upward tendency. We had much talk about old times, and those who figured in them. We called on Miss Lowe tonight.

The man on trial was probably Abner Tate, whose name was frequently on the docket in Madison County courts at this time. He had a running feud with the much-married Elizabeth Dale Gibbons-Flannigan-Jeffries-High-Brown-Routt. The feud began in 1848, when Elizabeth's wanton livestock broke into Tate's field. After the sudden death of her sixth husband, Willis Routt, and his subsequent quick burial, Abner Tate openly accused her of murder, since the rest of her husbands had been treated in similar manner.—American Guide Series, *Alabama,* 329.

4th. Spent most of the day with Garth. . . . Returned home tonight in the stage. . . . Today after a short examination, Judge Goldthwaite signed my license. I shall get the signature of another judge at our own court next week.

Judge George Goldthwaite later became chief justice of the state supreme court.

7th. Letter from John Lyon. He gives me the particulars of Cousin Indie's marriage and speaks of the affair in the most laudatory style. So the most accomplished lady in Va. is now Mrs. Pannill.

September 10, 1849. To-day our Circuit Court commenced, Judge Samuel Chapman presiding.

11th. [Today they] tried an old case which had been 13 years on the docket! Speedy justice, that!

12th. This morning the judge signed my license and I was sworn in. . . . I was startled by the information that Ma had been thrown from the buggy and was seriously injured. Uncle and I, accompanied by Dr. Sowell, & Cousin E., started immediately for the scene of the disaster. . . . We met Pa & Ma near the crossroads; Ma was lying on a bed in Aunt's carriage, and scarcely conscious of passing events. Her pain was excruciating, though no bones were broken.

13th. I sat up last night with Ma, who was suffering a great deal. . . . Today Sam Matthews' slave, Nelson, was tried for assault, etc., with intent to kill. Nick Davis and Gen. Walker defended him. Nick's effort was a creditable one indeed. . . . The jury were divided, and did not give a verdict.

14th. Copeland's negro, Pleasant, tried today for killing his master and found guilty. The evidence vs. him was circumstantial and very slight, I thought.

27th. Had some friends to spend a social hour with me after supper. Among them Garth . . . Balentine and Carter from Pulaski, Nick & Rip Davis, and Brickell.

28th. Tonight attended a splendid party at Uncle's, where I met all the beauty and chivalry of our village. Cousin Eliza had "spread herself" on the supper tables and, of course, they were grand. Cousin Tom and Garth staid with me.

October 1st. The party being over, and Uncle at leisure, I addressed myself to a work . . . teaching him to play the violin by note . . . he has often declared that "he would never cramp his genius with notes again." Today, by half-entreaty and half-argument, he consented to begin.

2nd. My new pupil set about his work in good earnest. . . . We shall have some fine music when he, Pa and I get to playing first, second and Bass.

20th. (written later). All this week have had premonitions of "slow fever." . . . Today Uncle thought it advisable that I should take my bed. . . . From this spell I did not recover for nearly four weeks. The disease was a singular one. I suffered not the slightest pain, nor was my pulse at any time above 85, and it only reached this once. Yet I was greatly prostrated and fell away to a skeleton, almost.

Sunday, November 25, 1849. Went up to Capt. Davis' with Nick, on our way to the Rail Road Convention, which meets there tomorrow.

This was the organizational meeting for Alabama's participation in the Memphis and Charleston Railroad. Although it was finally decided to use the old tracks of the Tuscumbia to Decatur Road, none of the stockholders in that enterprise participated.—Owen, II, 973.

26th. We found Huntsville full of people, and no place vacant at the hotel. We were invited to stay at Mr. Frank Mastin's, & accepted so agreeable and kind an offer. Gov. James C. Jones, of Tenn., was the Pres. of the Convention, and gave us an excellent opening address. Large delegations are in attendance from all the counties of N. Ala. . . . Slept on a settee at the Bell, because I staid at Gen. Lowe's party until it was too late to return to Mr. Mastin's.*

*Probably Francis T. Mastin, who lived on Williams Street next to the Bradley home. Mrs. Mastin was the former Ann Elizabeth Caroline Le Vert, whose brother married Octavia Walton, generally conceded to have been the most gracious of all Alabama women.—Alabama Association of University Women, 15.

If Thomas Hobbs kept a diary in 1850, it is not now in existence, so far as his descendants are aware. A small journal for 1851 was recently discovered by the Donelson Hortons, in Greenbrier.

Thursday, April 4, 1851. Fished at Beaver Pond with Rev. Joseph Myers, Missionary to Blacks.
7th. Was engaged today to defend Mr. Charles Tucker, ind. for hanging an effigy.
8th. [translated from Spanish] The "Crochet Club" met, the members are: Mrs. Maclin (piano); Messrs. Barclay and Maclin (violinists); I. E. Hobbs (violincello); Billy Richardson and I (flutes).
9th. [translated from Spanish] I wrote to my friend, D. C. Greenwood, who is editor of the *Weekly Independent,* Aberdeen, Mississippi.
16th. Cousin Eliza and I went to Huntsville. I entered 40 acres of land lying adjacent to the Swan Pond, which seems to have escaped entry heretofore. It will be valuable if the R.R. runs as it is now contemplated.
Monday, May 5th. Uncle returned from Savannah. Recv'd a letter from John Claiborne. He urges me to court Indie B.

Indiana Elizabeth Booth lived with her widowed mother, Sarah, and brother, Dr. William Booth, at Bothwell, Amelia County, Virginia.—Amelia County census, 1850.

12th. Tom Cox was married to Miss Fanny Tyus—the latter lying at the point of death from fever. This was to allow him to nurse her, as he desired to do. Singular very.

Thomas Jefferson Cox, born in 1831, was the son of Bartley and Eliza Freeman Cox. Mary Frances was the daughter of Judge Thomas Tyus. After her death, Thomas Cox married Elizabeth, sister of Fanny.—Jones and Gandrud.

15th. Wrote to Hal Malone, Cincinnati. [Apparently Henry B. Malone is henceforth known as Hal.]
16th. Attended Division—Nick Davis re-joined.
17th. Today, on nomination of Capt. J. R. Mason, was elected a Trustee of the Female Institute, a very great compliment to a little man, no other single man is a member of the Board.
19th. Met with the Board of Trustees—we had a report on the condi-

tion of Institute—and some warmth of feeling was displayed—too much was shown by Pa, which mortified me exceedingly.
22nd. Mrs. Tom Cox died this morning.
31st. Miss Mary Richardson, one of our best singers, was prevented by . . . illness from attending [our singing class]. It is very doubtful whether she will recover.

Mary was the daughter of John Richardson.

June 3, 1851. Miss Mary died, triumphing over death. . . . Her favorite Bro. (William) is absent in Mississippi.
5th. Visited Rev. Kelly, who is supposed to be near his end . . . he spoke . . . calmly of death and its rapid approach.

The Rev. A. G. Kelly, admitted to the Tennessee Conference in 1843, boarded with Robert L. Clark. He was a brilliant young man, and John Tanner said of him, "The witnessing of the death of this good man did more to confirm me in the realities of the Christian religion than anything I had ever experienced up to that time."—Tanner, July 28, 1876.

June 26, 1851. Commencement at [the] Institute. 11 young ladies graduated in some branches and 2 in all, viz., Miss Mat Coleman and Amanda Cassity. Judge Wood delivered the address, [and] the Quartette made music.
July 2nd. Col. Jones & I started to Bailey's [Springs].

Jonathan Bailey opened these Lauderdale County Springs to the public in 1846, and their popularity soon exceeded his ability to accommodate his guests in comfort. Bailey died in 1857, and the resort was bought by A. C. Ellis, who constructed a hotel there. In the 1858 season more than 1,500 guests were registered. The springs continued in operation until 1910, and ten years later the buildings burned.—Sulzby, 27–37.

3rd. Reached B.'s Springs—found them much crowded—had to occupy a small room with 6 others. But they were very pleasant comp., for instance, Dr. and Launcelot Minor, J. C. Malone, & Brinkley of Memphis.
8th. Returned home, *cured* of Bailey's.
10th. The crops are almost ruined by drought, a few more days and the farmers say they will be ruined.
12th. Signed an anti-smoking agreement today with Capt. Mason & Wm. Richardson. Penalty $1 for every violation to be paid to the new C. P. Church.
21st. It is cool enough to make fire pleasant. . . . Received a letter from Julia Meade, inclosing [*sic*] one from I[ndie] E. B[ooth] to herself.
24th. Spent this week at Moore's Springs—elaborating the plan of a school.

July 28, 1851. Recv'd the first Bounty Land Warrant, that of Freeman Crenshaw.
29th. Excessive drought is prevailing in the county.
August 4th. Election day. I acted as a Clerk—much excitement, whereof I had little share on account of no candidate having such a political creed as I profess. . . . I am daily, as I examine the subject now, strengthening in States' rights doctrines.
5th. Nick Davis and Nat. Davis are elected to Leg., and Nick Malone to Senate.
9th. Pa & Ma went to Moore's Springs to spend a week. Dr. Maclin & lady left on yest. for Cotoosa Springs in Geo. Mr. Hine and I are left alone.

Cotoosa Springs were in the Georgia mountains, just south of Chattanooga.

22nd. A good deal of interest about the invasion of Cuba.

Narciso Lopez led an invasion of Cuba in 1850 with American adventurers, and again in 1851, when he was killed by the Spanish authorities, with more than fifty of his followers.

September 16, 1851. Pres. Rivers is visiting us—he is the same warm-hearted & noble-souled man. He offered me the Prof. of Lang. in his College.
25th. Attended Dr. Stith Malone's wedding with Nick & Clinton Davis & Bill Walker. We were waiters.

This was the second marriage for Dr. Malone. His first wife, Eliza Davis, daughter of Nicholas, bore six children before her death in 1850. The second marriage was to Harriett Bolling Pryor, sister of Luke. Thomas Stith Malone was the son of Thomas and Mary Chappell Malone, and grandson of John Malone, Revolutionary soldier. He succeeded Thomas Hobbs as president of the board of trustees at the Female Institute.—Jones and Gandrud, 184.

September 28, 1851. First frost. This releases us from anti-smoking obligation.
October 8th. [Dr. Sowell and I] arrived in Memp. about dark after a pleasant trip, barring excessive dust & an overturn near Bolivar. Stopped at Commercial Hotel.
9th. We find a good many acquaintances here, all urge us to settle.
10th. Lawrence Moore & lady, Fletcher Lane & Mother, Mr. and Mrs. Mayfield, are some of the old Limestone friends who have welcomed us to Memphis.

11th. The river is so very low that but few boats are running.
12th. At night left for home via Sommerville in order to see at that place Leroy Pope, Esq. Dr. S. will return to Holly Springs & we meet at Florence.

Sommerville, county seat of Fayette County, Tennessee, just east of Memphis, was a center of wealth and culture, and maintains an air of quiet dignity.

Leroy Pope, Jr., son of Leroy and Judith Sale Pope, of Huntsville, moved to the Memphis vicinity after his marriage to Mary E. Foote, of Shelby County, Tennessee, in 1830. Pope was one of the prime movers of the Memphis and Charleston Railroad, and an incorporator of the University of Memphis.—*West Tennessee Historical Papers,* VIII, 33.

November 16, 1851. [Alpheus] Mizell, our new station preacher, gave us two sermons today. . . . The church has been draped in crepe since Kelly's death—it was removed yesterday.

The sparse diary entries for the fall of 1851 do not mention Thomas Hobbs' serious intentions to win the hand of Miss Indiana Booth, but December, 1851, found him in Virginia with this purpose in mind.

Thursday, January 1, 1852. At Mr. Edwin Booth's in Nottoway, 30 miles from P'burg. Arrived here late last night in the rain. Found Miss Indie E. Booth & Julia Meade here.

Edwin Gilliam Booth, a leading citizen of Nottoway County, Virginia, was evidently an uncle of Indie, brother to her father, Benjamin. Edwin moved to Philadelphia in the late 1850s, and John Herbert Claiborne said of him, "To the Hon. Edwin G. Booth, of Philadelphia, formerly of Virginia, Southern prisoners, wherever they could be reached by him, were endebted for great kindness, and most liberal contributions of clothes, blankets, etc. . . . there may have been other friends in the City of Brotherly Love as kind as he, but I never heard of them."—Claiborne, 38.

2nd. Today the young ladies and I went to Mr. Wm. Irby's, about 8 miles off. Drove Julia in my buggy, & we talked long and freely about by-gones and yet-to-comes. Told her how much my flame for I. had increased since I came into her presence. . . . Mr. Irby—a true old Va. country gentleman, the first I ever saw at his own house—Proof. He shows me I am welcome, and leaves me to enjoy myself as I please—that's true hospitality. Mrs. I. was intimate with Ma when both were girls.

When William Blunt Irby died in 1896, he was believed to be the oldest alumnus of the College of William and Mary, having graduated there in 1817. He married Sarah Washington Smith, of Brunswick County, and "left with ample means, he lived the life of a Virginia farmer, with a house always open to friends, who were entertained in the old Virginia style. It might truthfully be said, that during his 58 years of married life, he and his estimable wife entertained as many people as any couple did in southside Virginia." William Irby was solicited many times to run for public office, but he was not interested in any candidacy, although he was always well informed.—Richard Irby, writing in the *William and Mary College Quarterly*, Vol. V, Series I, 140.

January 9, 1852. Still at Mr. B.'s—having a glorious time, because the family do all they can to give two courting gents time & opportunities. Dr. Sam Gholson, of Cin., Ohio, son of Yates G., is the other gent—he is pleased with my sweet cousin, J. Indie and I are skirmishing—she acting with great tact on the defensive, while I am trying to find out the position of the enemy. Sometimes I reconnoitre so near as almost to make an engagement necessary.

William Yates Gholson, 1807–1870, graduated from Nassau Hall (later Princeton), studied law under Chancellor Taylor in Virginia, and married the chancellor's niece. After her death he moved to Pontotoc, Mississippi, helped to establish the University of Mississippi, and married Elvira Wright, daughter of Mississippi supreme court justice, Daniel Wright. In 1844 Gholson freed his slaves, and moved to Cincinnati, where he was soon elected to the superior court of that city. The brilliance of Gholson and his colleagues is said to have never been equaled in the history of that court. He was later appointed to the Ohio supreme court. Evidently Dr. Gholson was not successful in his suit for Julia Meade.—*Dictionary of American Biography*, VII, 232.

14th. In P'burg visiting friends, spend the days mostly at the office of Drs. Claiborne and Madison, two Univ. friends, and first rate fellows.

Dr. R. L. Madison, great-nephew of the President, was born in Orange County, Virginia. After his father's death, Madison moved to his mother's home in Petersburg. In 1853, Dr. Madison left his partnership with Claiborne and moved to Philadelphia. Still later he became a professor at the Virginia Military Institute.—Claiborne, 37.

January 16, 1852. Went by buggy to Mrs. Booth's, 33 miles in Amelia —was expected, because had made appointment with I.—found her at home—cordially received, but nothing more to encourage me particularly. More skirmishing.

18th. Looking love awfully plain—and hinting it very strong—think I see a smile of approval sometimes when very near the point.

19th. Oh, glorious day! For altho' the thermometer is lower than I ever saw it (4°), yet it was a day of great warmth to me. Had a long and

serious talk with her in the afternoon. . . . Got some unmistakable evidence that she regards me favorably. . . . I asked permission . . . to inform them [my parents] that I "had strong hopes of success." She hesitated a second and then gave that permission.
20th. Slept little last night—too much excited—nitrous oxide *nothing* to this.
21st. Returned to P'burg—cold day—streams [are] frozen hard enough to bear horse & buggy, still I was comfortable. I. gave me some of her hair, which, with some of J[ulia]'s, I have had set in a neat scarf breast-pin.
27th. Presented my sweet coz, J. with a purple velvet cloak (cost $34), at which she was much pleased . . . Played whist 'til eleven with Prof. Blanche, Benj. Harrison, and J. H. C.

Although there were many Benjamin Harrisons in Dinwiddie County, it is quite possible that this was a member of the Berkley Harrisons, since the Presidential family was closely connected with the Meades.

31st. Left P'burg . . . Arrived [Richmond] about dark. After tea went to I[ndie]'s . . . on Fifth, bet. Grace & Franklin . . . Saw Mr. and Mrs. Eggleston, pleasant people & kind to me . . . Met Munford and Archer to-night.

Mrs. William Eggleston was Indie's sister. Before moving to Richmond, the Egglestons owned Evenholm in Amelia County, which they sold to Jane and Leander Masters.—Jefferson, 72.

Monday, February 2, 1852. Walked to river this aft . . . Saw a little negro who, proud of a pair of old boots, was swaggering along *like a man,* and saying to himself, *"There's hell in these boots!"*
4th. The biographer of E. A. Poe says his Tales "are more thrilling than those of any other Amer. writer save Charles Brockden Brown." Have often tried in the Bookstores to get these latter, and hitherto in vain—but today found his *Weiland.* The bookseller did not know its value, & sold it to me for 50 cts. . . . He knew the value of *George Balcombe,* a novel by Bev. Tucker, wh. Poe says would be highly appreciated if its author lived north of 36° 30′, and asked so high a price I did not purchase it . . . Spent morn. with *her,* had it all to ourselves—glorious.

Charles Brockden Brown, 1771–1810, was the first serious novelist in America. He published *Weiland* in 1798, and some of his Gothic tales served as the basis for Mary Shelley's *Frankenstein.* Van Wyck Brooks gives a good analysis of Brown in his *World of Washington Irving.* Beverly Tucker, 1784–1851, son of Saint George Tucker, published *George Balcombe* in 1836.

7th. Accom. I. to a concert . . . Parodi not equal to Jenny Lind . . . [Indie] confessed that she expected to marry me next fall.

Madame Parodi gave a concert in Montgomery, Alabama, in 1856, according to the chronological history of that city by Blue.

8th. With a heavy heart, I left for P'burg . . . slept with Claiborne, I am forbidden by I. to tell any of my friends here, even Julia, of how matters stand between us. Very unpleasant arrangement to me.
9th. Left this evening at 7 o'clock.
11th. Arrived early in Charleston. Bought a melodion (70) for Mrs. Maclin.
13th. Met Nick Davis & Nick Malone and several members of the late Leg. at Atlanta—was glad to see them, and happy of such pleasant company home.
14th. Arrived in Chattanooga, and took a boat immediately. Miss Molly Garth was a passenger.
15th. Arrived in Decatur about 10 P.M., and stayed all night at Brown's Hotel. Nick Malone and I hired two horse wagons after breakfast and went to plantation, dined, & came to Athens in Aunt's carriage.
16th. We opened the melodion . . . and after some difficulty set it in playing order . . . Took tea at Judge Coleman's with Misses Sue Lowe & Mary Spottswood.
24th. Went around to his store and started Wm. Hine to learning the clarinet. Hope to make him a good member of our "Crotchet Club." Judge W. H. Walker & I took tea . . . at Mr. James C. Malone's.
26th. Pa returned from Huntsville—bringing information that the R. Road section which lies on our farm, is a heavy one. On calculation we ascertain that there is more work than could probably be performed by the force we could put on it, in the time required. Concluded not to make a bid, therefore, but to wait for the bridge contracts across the Slough & Swan Ponds.
29th. I came down here [to the plantation] to have a day of quiet, a day of reflection undisturbed even by the exercises of the sanctuary. There are times when I am impressed with the opinion that devotion will be more promoted by uninterrupted self-communion & reflection than by any other means.
Monday, March 1, 1852. Today attended to the issuing of my first writ . . . in a suit by Mr. John M. Richardson against Charles Hardy . . . While our club was playing [tonight] at Uncle's, in came a company of maskers, who amused us for some time by their antics . . . they were all

young men of the town. I accompanied Miss Emma B. home, and disclosed . . . a plan for the building up the departments of vocal music, drawing and . . . needlework. I shall urge it further on the notice of the friends of the Institute. Something must be done to aid these departments, or they will expire.

2nd. I am reading . . . Brown's *Jane Talbot* . . . his tales . . . are devoid of all digressions . . . I have a new music pupil, and a most promising one—Sam Tanner on the Double Bass—never was there greater contrast between the sizes of the performer & the instrument!

3rd. Ma and Mrs. M. returned from the plantation—while there they visited old Aunt Anachy—speaking of her age, she told them "she was a good stout gal in the *resolute War.*" Not a bad word for the times which "tried men's souls." This was almost equal to the mistake of a negro who, seeking an apothecary shop in Petersburg, inquired for a *"Shottecary pop."*

March 4, 1852. Visited the Institute, and spent the aft. in hearing the classes recite. Some of the trustees go now every week, and more interest is manifested in its operations than at any prior time.

6th. The best thing I have done is to get a long letter from Indie. . . . Bless thee, my dearest, for thy first letter.

16th. Mr. Wm. Richardson overheard a negro woman soliloquizing today. She had been sent to the Post Office by her mistress, an old maid, for the *Ladies' Companion.* As she was walking along she muttered, "Ladies' Companion! Never knowed missus had one before, *allays* knowed *she wanted one though.*"

20th. Left town this morn, to organize a division over Elk River on Sugar Creek. Went to Maj. Hancock's to dinner . . . We crossed the river and supped with Mr. John Arledge. . . . How pleasant it is, occasionally, to get out among the industrious yeomen and see how they manage their affairs. Life wears a very different aspect on this & that side of Elk River.

Major Josiah Hancock was one of few native Alabamians to be born in the territory as early as 1809. He married Milly Caroline Arledge, daughter of Cyrus, in 1842, and had one daughter, Lucy Ann, listed in the 1850 census.

John Arledge, son of Cyrus, was listed as 31 in the 1850 census, living with his wife, Harriett, and five children.

22nd. Wrote to Mr. Jno. A. Broadus, asking his assistance in procuring a teacher for Dr. Alfred Moore. I am frequently applied to to procure teachers, complimentary but troublesome!

When Dr. Alfred Moore's youngest son, Alfred, was born in 1848, the doctor had several grown children, including Olivia Moore O'Neal, Judge John Edmund, and Sydenham Moore. The young Alfred Moore enlisted in the Confederate Army at the age of 16, and spent much of the time as a prisoner of war. Afterwards he returned to Huntsville and worked at the First National Bank until his election as mayor of the city in 1899.—Owen, IV, 1221.

Wednesday, March 24, 1852. Scott has run away. I had determined to send him to the plantation, to work in the crop, rather than be troubled by his laziness and rascality. This mortified him exceedingly, and he tried to induce several persons to buy him, failing in which, he decamped.
30th. Scott returned yesterday very sick; being accustomed to comfortable lodgings at home, he contracted from exposure a violent cold which terminated in pneumonia. Ma has been much concerned about him, for her big heart (the biggest I ever knew), and love of human kind, make her sad at every direliction of duty.
31st. Went this morning to see the men at work on the railroad. They are felling the timber in a track 120 ft. wide between Swan Pond & Slough, and from the former to the high ground it runs upon our land.
April 2, 1852. Heard a good instance of the efficacy of patent medicines. Cousin Ann Malone applied in the night some "Mustang Liniment" to the throat & face of a fretful child. It gave *immediate relief,* but what was her surprise in the morning to find that she had in the dark gotten hold of the wrong vial, and applied *ink* instead of *liniment.*

Ann Lucas Malone, the widow of William Edward Malone, was a daughter of John and Martha Hobbs Lucas.—Hobbs Family Papers.

6th. Dr. B. W. M[aclin] frequently says good things . . . the other day he remarked that he would do something or other "when he had leisure." 'Why,' said some friend, 'you have nothing to do now.' "Having nothing to do, *I can't tell when I'm done,* and so I am still busy."
9th. Went with Nick, Clinton, and Ripley Davis to their father's . . . the main object of my visit is to get a *Richmond Whig,* containing an account of the meeting of the Va. Colonization Society.

Interest in this organization had been revived in 1850, after the Virginia legislature appropriated $30,000 annually for five years for the purpose of encouraging the emigration of freed Negroes to the new republic of Liberia, where its first president, Joseph Roberts, was elected in 1848.—Staudenraus, 242.

April 10, 1852. The day was too cold to fish, so we started for a ride to the top of Capshaw's mountain. On the way, however, we concluded to accompany Rip to Huntsville, and so, in our fishing attire, we popped into that town after a merry ride . . . Called on Cousin Pet Echols, and was agreeably entertained for a half-hour. Bob Brickell returned with us.

Mary Echols, daughter of William Holding and Mary Hobbs Echols, was twenty at this time. She married Col. Egbert Jones, and died a year later. One of Mary's brothers, William, graduated fourth in the West Point class of 1858. He had a brilliant career in engineering, and served for several years as president of the First National Bank in Huntsville. Another brother, John, served as Secretary of State in Mississippi during the Civil War. Others listed in the Echols household in 1850 were Larkin, 14; David, 11; James, 9; Charles, 6; Susan, Ellen, and Eliza Ann.

11th. Crisp, the actor who has taken the theatre in Huntsville, was at Capt. D.'s—he is a man of some ability, and is said to act well. He praises the Southern people.

An article in the Huntsville *Southern Advocate* for August 19, 1958, identifies Crisp. "William A. Crisp, energetic theatrical manager, has recovered his eyesight. He has just leased the Memphis theatre for five years. He also has a lease on the Nashville theatre." The Huntsville Theatre, built on land deeded by Leroy and Matilda Pope on the southwest corner of Lincoln and Clinton Streets, was the locale of the performance of the first professional actors in the state. These appeared in 1818, under the direction of Noah Miller Ludlow. The group of professionals were thereupon considered extremely brave, for not many entrepreneurs would venture into this savage country.—Hornblow, 342.

April 18, 1852. This is the first Sabbath the new pulpit has been used. . . . Today for the first time, some of our choir (ladies) sat on the gentlemen's side. A good move (my suggestion by the way) for this seat will always be kept for them, which would not be the case with a pew on their own side of the house.

19th. My birth-day. 26 years old today. How rapidly do the years pass now!

20th. Morgan's abduction occurred in 1826, and that was also the year of the death of John Adams and Jefferson. Byron died on the day & year I was born.

21st. Went to Captain Davis' with Nick & Walker, to meet a party from Huntsville. . . . We found the Misses Erskine, Sue Lowe, Ad. Pleasants, Caperton, Spotswood, & Clark—also Messrs. Carr, Erskine, Wilkinson. . . . Nothing uncommon occurred except that I slept in a bed in which there were one more than two.

Laura, daughter of Alexander and Susan C. Erskine; Adelina, daughter of James J. and Emily Bibb Pleasants; probably Eleana, daughter of Hugh and Pauline Caperton; Mary, daughter of Elliott and Sally Spotswood; Dr. Albert or Dr. Alexander Erskine; and Dr. Algernon Wilkinson, who married Laura Erskine.—Madison County census, 1850.

April 28, 1852. Pa and I went to Plantation . . . rode down to where they are at work upon the rail-road.
29th. Pa was engaged putting up a horse mill which has just been received and we did not return today. . . . The mill was started today & performed well, grinding 4 bushels an hour with four mules.
30th. We were sadly grieved to hear that during our absence Mr. James E. Mason & Caroline Turner had died. Both of these parents leave large families.

James E. Mason had served as sheriff of Limestone County. He was 41 at the time of the 1850 census, husband of Caroline Temperance Bass and father of seven children. Mrs. Caroline Turner, wife of William, had nine children.

May 3rd. Miss Ann Malone, daughter of T. Hill Malone, was buried today. Three in less than one week from our community.
5th. Old Mr. Collin Hobbs asked me yesterday if Land Warrants would not become valueless if Congress should pass the "Bedstead Law." He meant, as I found out by further conversation with him, the *Homestead Law,* now being discussed in Congress.
7th. Nick Davis and I learned to play billiards in Huntsville, choosing a time when there was no low company in the room.
16th. I am strongly urged to come to Va., and Nick Malone, who is about starting to Baltimore Convention, is anxious for me to accompany him. I can not well leave home now on account of business. . . . But there are reasons unknown to *any body* which influence me to go.
24th. Arrived in P'burg. . . . Dressed & went to Mr. Meade's. We did not find the girls at home, up at Bothwell with Indie . . . there will I be very soon.
27th. I. looked charming—much improved since last saw her.
30th. Arrived with N. in Baltimore—Took lodgings at Howard House.
June 2, 1852. Jesse Coe, Sr., and William are here. . . . Saw Booth as Richard III—disappointed.
4th. No election [as yet]. Alabama adheres to Buch[anan]. I prefer Dickinson of N. Y., but he has violent opposition in his own state.

Daniel S. Dickinson, U.S. Senator (1844–1851), preferred a middle-of-the-road position on the slavery subject. When invited to speak on that matter in Boston, he refused, because he did not wish to stir up more trouble. —*Huntsville Southern Advocate,* December 12, 1855.

5th. About noon today Va. led off for Gen. Pierce of New Hampshire, and she was immediately followed by enough states to give him the nomination. After dinner W. R. King, of Ala., was nominated without much difficulty. And a very broad platform adopted, after which Con. adjourned. Nick and I saw Owens as *Jim Baggs, the Wandering Minstrel,* first rate.

"The handsomest low comedian I had ever seen," said Joe Jefferson of John Edmond Owens, when he saw him in New Orleans in 1846.—*Dictionary of American Biography,* XIV, 121.

9th. Left Nick in Wash., and arrived in Petersburg.
11th. Julia & I went to Bothwell.
12th. Had several talks with her [Indie], but she is little inclined to a speedy consummation, and yet acknowledges that she has little good reason for delay.
13th. Accompanied I. and Mrs. B. to country preaching. House so full I could not get a seat. Mr. Coles preached a short sermon of an hour & twenty minutes, and this was followed up by the communion service!
June 17, 1852. Finished reading Jones' Defence of N[orth] Carolina. This is one of the best written American books, and as a history seems to be reliable. He certainly proves beyond a doubt that the people of Mecklenburg County adopted a Declaration of Independence on the 20 May, 1775. It is also an indisputable fact that the two Declarations bear a striking resemblance in their wording.

Defense of the Mecklenburg Treaty was the actual title of J. Seawell Jones' book, published in 1843. Jones, one of the founders of the North Carolina Historical Society, along with James Iredell, Richmond Pearson, and others, was a graduate of the Harvard School of Law in 1833. In his defense, he is very critical of Virginia, but in a later work, *Memorials of North Carolina,* he gave credit to Jefferson, Randolph, and other Virginians.—Ashe, et al., VI, 329–30.

19th. Good news today . . . Mrs. Eggleston . . . has been safely delivered. . . . I. has always given the delicacy of her sister's health as the reason why she could not think of an early consummation of my happiness. . . . I shall go at once to see my prudish dear one and insist on finishing this business at once.
21st. Wrote a long letter to Mrs. Maclin today. Unless I can reconcile her to my marriage, I fear something unpleasant will occur.

22nd. Left on S.S. Rail Road for Mr. Edwin Booth's. Arrived about 12, & found Miss I. sick.

23rd. Saw a reaping machine at work. It is not McCormick's, which took the prize at World's Fair, but Hussey's, which is here preferred.

24th. Saw much of Miss Indie, and all I saw increased my affection.

June 29, 1852. Today at 11½ A.M., Mr. Clay died in Washington, and shortly afterwards we had the news here by telegraph.

30th. All the bells were tolled today, in honor of Mr. Clay.

A description of Henry Clay's funeral appeared in the *Richmond Enquirer* on July 16, 1852. Thirty to forty thousand people were in attendance, and if the horses and carriages present had been placed in procession, the line would have been more than twenty-five miles long.

July 2nd. Accompanied [Indie] to Richmond.

3rd. Had a talk with Mr. Eggleston, who agrees with me . . . in regard to an early consummation. His opinion will have some weight in the consultation of the family.

5th. Not wishing to leave Richmond without seeing Indie privately, I arose at 5 this morn. & called on her at 6! . . . of course she had to be awakened, and came down complaining from loss of sleep.

9th. Went to Old Point. When I arrived Dromgoole escorted me to a room he had secured for us.

Identity of this Dromgoole has not been determined, but he was undoubtedly a descendant of the Rev. Edward Dromgoole, of Brunswick County, who died in 1835, leaving three sons and at least one daughter. The sons were Thomas, Edward, and George Coke Dromgoole. A grandson of the Rev. Dromgoole, Edward Dromgoole Sims, taught at La Grange and at The University of Alabama.—Sweet, IV, 124.

10th. Col. Erwin, of Greene Co., is the only Alabamian here, and we frequently meet in conversation.

Colonel John Erwin, 1799–1860, of Greensboro, Alabama, had been chairman of the Democratic Convention in Baltimore, in which Pierce and King were nominated. He was later president of the convention in which Breckenridge and Lane were the nominees. The Erwin home, Glencairn, is still one of the fine landmarks of Greensboro.—Owen, III, 547.

July 12, 1852. Mrs., Miss, and young Fillmore are here. They conduct themselves with the greatest propriety—no airs, no pretensions. The Miss dresses more plainly than almost any lady here, but with the most exquisite taste.

This entry refers to the Presidential family. Millard Fillmore succeeded Zachary Taylor as President in 1850.

13th. Found a letter from Ma & another from Mrs. Maclin here. . . . There is much to sadden me in the latter.
15th. Pleasants, Roy, Johnson, Walker, are some of my Univ. friends who are here. . . . This is a son of John H. Pleasants, whom Ritchie killed in a duel.

James Pleasants was the only son of John Hampden Pleasants, whose rivalry with Thomas Ritchie was of long standing, and came to culmination when Ritchie placed a card in his *Richmond Enquirer* denouncing Pleasants as a "rank coward." More than one lethal weapon was used in the duel, and although both had fired several shots, it was with a sword that Ritchie delivered the mortal wound.—*Huntsville Democrat,* February 26, 1846.

18th. I have been totally indifferent to the charms of the ladies here. . . . The magician whose spell has wrought this indifference is in Richmond, & thither I go tomorrow.
19th. A most shocking murder in Richmond—wife, child, & husband attacked in bed with a hatchet—first two killed & last one left for dead, but still alive. . . . This community excited to its center and almost at the mob-law point.

The murder of Mrs. Joseph Winston and child, and the stabbing of Mr. Winston, created much indignation in Richmond. John and Jane Williams, black servants, were charged; but in her confession, Jane cleared John of any guilt.—*Richmond Enquirer,* July 23, 1852.

July 20, 1852. The day of our marriage is fixed for the 4th of August.
21st. Bought the wedding ring, & had this motto engraved in it: *Endless, like our love.* This is original, I believe.
22nd. I asked Mrs. B.'s consent—she said she w'd give her daughter as willingly to me as to any body who w'd carry her so far off.
26th. This day was celebrated in honor of Mr. Clay. Business was suspended, & the shops and residences draped in mourning.
27th. I met last night the Rev. Jno. Early at Mr. Eggleston's . . . he inquired whose son I was.* He knew my grandfather Hobbs and his sons well. . . . Mr. E[arly] is a vigorous old man, and knows as many people as almost any body else. Mention was made during the evening of Gov. Roberts of Liberia,** & some one jestingly asked, "And do you know him too, Mr. Early?" 'Oh, certainly,' said he, 'I baptized his wife.' He is to marry us, Indie long since promised him that he should perform that duty for her.

*The Reverend John Early, 1786–1873, was born in Bedford County, Virginia. His first ministerial work was among the slaves of Thomas Jefferson. President Tyler wished to make Early comptroller of the Treasury, but the minister declined. Excerpts from his diaries, showing the vast amount of his work, are recorded in the *Virginia Historical Magazine,* vols. 33–38. At the age of 68 he was made a bishop in the Methodist Episcopal Church, South, joining Soule, Andrew, Paine, Pierce, and Kavanaugh.

**Governor Joseph Jenkins Roberts, 1809–1876, was the first President of Liberia. Born of free blacks in Petersburg, Virginia, he went to Liberia in 1829, where he became a merchant, and valued assistant to Gov. Thomas Buchanan, white appointee of the American Colonization Society. After Buchanan's death, Roberts was appointed governor, and when the Republic of Liberia was formed in 1847, he was made president. Roberts was married to Jane Waring, a highly educated woman.—*Who Was Who,* 447.

29th. Miss Indie wrote to [Miss Ellen Irby], urging her to come to R. to our wedding, and accompany us to Baltimore. She has consented to do so. Expected a letter from home & another from Mr. Scruggs in Charleston containing money. Received neither.
30th. Whew! Here's a go! About to get married & no money to carry my wife home! On hearing this, John Lyon kindly offered me the sum I wrote for.
Monday, August 2, 1852. Cousin Sue, Miss Mary Jane Booth, Miss Ellen Irby, Dr. B. & myself arrived in Richmond this night. We went straight to Mr. E.'s, where we found Julia and Indie, & formed a gay party.
4th. Lyon & Claiborne came this morning, Madison detained by prof. business. We were married at 8½ P.M. at Centenary Church by Rev. John Early, with the following attendants: Wm. Booth & Mary Jane; Lyon & Ellen; Claiborne & Julia Meade; Archer & Sue. I felt as calm during the ceremony as if it had been another's marriage, and Indie surprised herself by her calmness. Immediately from the church we went to the Balt. cars, while the company went to Mr. E.'s to partake of refreshments. . . . Mr. Early, who dearly loves Indie, would go to the cars with us, & could scarcely say "good-bye."

The Centenary Methodist Church, on Grace and Fifth Streets in Richmond, was dedicated on June 4, 1843. The dedicatory sermon was preached by the Rev. Edward Wadsworth, who succeeded Bishop Paine at La Grange College. The church was extensively repaired in 1855.—Christian, 147.

August 5, 1852. Arrived in Balt. to breakfast, took rooms at Barnum's. How my heart jumped as I registered our names, "T. H. Hobbs and *Lady.*"
10th Arrived at O[ld] P[oint].
12th. Arrived safely in P'burg, remained two or three hours, saw most of our intimate friends, & left at 6 P.M.

19th. There are not 100 persons here [Catoosa Springs] altho' the accommodations are suff. for 500. . . . Indie sang "Old Folks at Home" for them today, and everybody was taken with it; so much so that she had to sing it many times over.

This classic was a new hit at the time, only one year old. Its composer, Stephen Foster, and Hobbs were born in the same year.

20th. We reached the *Molly Garth*, and started down the river.
21st. Reached the landing opp. Decatur about 3 P.M.—there we found Pa, Ma and Mr. Bradley waiting for us. They were delighted to see Indie, & she rejoiced to meet them.
23rd. Our house being in the carpenter's hands, we stopped at Uncle's.
24th. Our friends are beginning to call to see the bride, and congratulations come thick upon me. Well, I deserve to be congratulated!
Wednesday, September 1, 1852. Today we parted with our sweet cousin Pet [Echols], who returned home with Uncle and Cousin E. She has endeared herself to me as well by a better aquaintance as by her kindness to I[ndie]. . . . Pa has *"advanced backwards"* in music.
3rd. Uncle returned from H'ville bringing Ann Eliza Echols with him. The Institute (which some punster called "the Belle Factory") opens on Monday under the care of Mr. [Smith W.] Moore.

The Bell Cotton Factory, near Huntsville, was one of the first cotton mills in the state. The pun is an obvious reference to it.

4th. Mr. Hayes gave us a complimentary party tonight, at which all the young folks of the town were present. . . . Pa says he received many congratulations on account of his beautiful daughter.

William Duke Hayes was a successful commission merchant.

6th. The Institute opened today with 47 pupils, which is a smaller number than usual.
9th. We had an uncommonly hard rain today and during it, two very severe strokes of lightning. One of them struck the cupola of our courthouse and, running down the rod and guttering, reached the ground at 3 different places. . . . The house was not much injured, and only lost some shingles and a part of the cornices. Mr. Benj. Roberts was sitting in the S.E. corner room, and one part of the stroke passed in three feet of him. He felt the jar, but was not otherwise affected. . . . Tonight. . . . Mr. William Avery died.
11th. At a meeting of the Div. tonight, Nick Davis rejoined for the 3rd time. . . . Mr. Hayes has just returned from Lawrence Co., and reports

a great deal of sickness there, especially in the neighborhood of Moulton.
September 15, 1852. This morning about 2 o'clock, Robert H. Clark, eldest son of Mr. R. L. Clark, of this place, died. . . . Party at Judge Coleman's to-night to which we were invited, but I preferred that we should not tempt disease by irregular hours at this time.
25th. Tonight, as I was talking to Big Moses at planta. about the short crop of cotton, he said it was not their fault, for they had worked it faithfully. "Whose fault is it, then?" said I. 'Why, Marse Tom, it must *be the Lord's!'*
27th. William J. Richardson is very sick. I feel great concern for him. . . . He is the main stay of his devoted parents, who, having lost several grown children in the last few years, are the more attached to him on that account.
28th. William still very sick—the whole continent is sick, so far as we can hear. The other day Mrs. Spottswood Jones died in Mooresville,* and while the messenger who went for her coffin in Huntsville was in the shop, five other measures for coffins were brought in. Mrs. Dr. Hussey died in Mooresville yesterday,** and Maj. Woodroof is now very sick there. . . . Jonathan did not more ardently desire David's life than I do Billy's. How *can* his family and his friends do here without him? Today the workmen commenced setting up the new Court House fence.

*Eliza Anne Haywood Jones, born in North Carolina in 1807, was the daughter of Judge John Haywood, noted jurist and author. She married John Nelson Spotswood Jones in 1821, and lived on their plantation at Greenbriar.—Jones and Gandrud.

**Dr. Elijah Hussey had married Mary Ann Thach, who was the daughter of Thomas Henry Thach, and was born in Mooresville in 1827.—Jones and Gandrud.

September 30, 1852. Today was called on to write William's will. . . . How sad I felt when he told me to write that his flute & his violin he gave to his brother John! That flute which has so often sounded with mine & cheered me with its sweetness. But alas! that is mute now, and mine knows no note but that of sadness.

"The harp that once thro' Tara's halls . . . "

October 1st. Billy died last night about 11. . . . This is the fourth grown child in four years [the other children of John Richardson buried in the old Athens cemetery within the period are: Dr. George, Margaret, and Louisa.] The Masons buried him this afternoon, his funeral being preached by Rev. S. W. Moore. He was not buried by his brothers and sisters because there was no room for his grave. The old burying ground is so full that they seldom try to dig a grave without striking another.

William was buried in the new Athens cemetery, which was opened in 1849 with the interment of James Henry Allen, son of the Reverend James Wilburn Allen.—Tanner, July 28, 1876.

4th. Today got the trustees of the M. E. Church together and made a contract with them for the use of the unoccupied half of the Basement, to be fitted up as a Division room and town hall. They agreed to give us the use of it for 20 years, one night in each week.

10th. The new Cumberland Pres. Church was dedicated today. Mr. Rob't Donnell preached an appropriate sermon. . . . He gave some interesting notices of the progress of this region since he first visited it. "Then," said he, "But one solitary path led thro' your town." He closed by laying down his charge as pastor and introducing his successor, a very young man named Criseman.

Rev. M. Criseman, just out of college, did not remain long; Rev. George W. Mitchell was called in December, 1852.—Tanner, July 28, 1876.

October 11, 1852. As for me, the part I took in the dedication was to pitch the tunes at the special request of Mr. Donnell. Today we moved over to our own house. . . . Things were not altogether pleasant at Uncle's.

12th. I wrote the report of the Board [of] Trustees of the Institute to Conference. It was short if not sweet, but we do not expect any favor from them and, indeed, they seem to care very little for us. There are so many Conference schools that this, which was the first, seems to have almost grown out of the memory of the reverend gentlemen.

14th. The no. of pupils in the Institute is only about 70, a smaller number than has matriculated for many years. The Faculty are discouraged and as their pay is small, they manifest a disposition to avoid as many expenses as possible. A contest arose a few days since as to who should pay for the fires of the Music Depart. The matter was presented to the Board of Trustees for judgement—and we decided that the matriculation fee which the President receives was designed to cover this expense.

15th. Today Columbia Synod of the Cumberland Presbyterian Church met here. . . . Our house is in so unfinished a condition that we can not entertain any of these strangers. . . . Mr. Donnell is treated with the very greatest respect & is literally the father of the church.

19th. Received a letter from my old room-mate, Presley Keyes, inquiring what he must do, and when he must begin. Like myself he is anxious for employment and like myself, he has difficulty in finding it. . . . Our preacher is Crittendon, Mizell goes to Florence.

October 25, 1852. Pres Keyes came . . . he and I have been very busy examining into the affairs of the *Herald* office. He seems willing to become interested in the purchase of it—and I am inclined that way.

28th. Mr. Thomas Bibb Bradley, having challenged all democrats, & Gen. Houston in particular, to meet him in debate here today, there was a political discussion. Mr. B. first addressed us, he speaks fluently and has some imagination, but was opposed to one more than a match for him in Houston. The Gen. made a firm, dignified defence of the Dem. Party and of its candidate, Gen. Pierce.

Thomas Bibb Bradley was the son of Major James and Adeline Bibb Bradley, and grandson of Governor Thomas Bibb, builder of the mansion, Belle Mina, in 1826.

20th. Division met. I was installed R.S. of it. Somehow it always happens that I get the office of scribe, secretary, etc., of every association which I enter. The fact is, I am very fond of book-keeping and the fact that I have so long kept a diary is another proof of it.

Tuesday, November 2, 1852. This is the day of the Presidential election —the Whigs manifest but little interest in the matter, for many of them are hesitating to vote for Scott. The Democrats are in fine spirits, cheered by the news of the late elections in Penn., Ohio & Indiana.

3rd. Concluded the trade with the Johnson's. . . . We are to take possession in about a week.

4th. Accompanied Nick Malone to Decatur . . . to see Pres and communicate the progress of our business. . . . Saw many other friends: Willis Garth, Dr. Kimble, Lucian Minor, Bill Cook, Mrs. Rather, etc. Decatur has much more the appearance of a business town than Athens. The Steam whistle's thrilling music is there heard, and signs of progress are visible. The bridge across the river is rapidly progressing, 3 piers already built.

Construction of the Decatur railroad bridge began in 1852, and the first train crossed it in 1855. The bridge was of prime strategic importance during the Civil War.—Jenkins and Knox, 97.

November 6, 1852. Only 4 states have probably gone for Scott: Tenn., Kent., Vermont & Mass.

10th. Took a turkey hunt with Mr. Ben Peete.

Benjamin and Darthula English Peete lived near Swan Creek, north of the Hobbs and west of the present Luke Pryor IV plantation. One of their daughters, Judith, married Luke Matthews, and another, Mary, married Peter Francisco Garrett. Three other daughters and five sons were still at home in 1850.

18th. Today our first paper was issued, and so far as I can judge, it is well received.

28th. Today, Pres. Moore preached the funeral of Mrs. Matilda Allen, wife of Rev. Wilburn Allen.

December 5, 1852. My diary is sadly neglected, owing to the pressure of business. Fact is, I never before had my hands full of matters of a pecuniary character. No service at our church—because [of] sacramental occasion at Cumberland P. Church. Heard a sermon there from Rev. Mitchell, who has succeeded the young Criseman in that charge.

The Cumberland Presbyterian Church grew rapidly under the pastorate of Rev. George W. Mitchell, and "no man ever worked with more zeal and honesty of purpose for the advancement of the cause of religion and moral influence" in Athens, wrote John Tanner. Mitchell was interested in history, also, and wrote an account of the life of Rev. Robert Donnell, and one of Rev. Constantine Sanders, known as "The Sleeping Preacher," nineteenth-century clairvoyant. During the Civil War, Mr. Mitchell kept all the Sabbath Schools together, and a few years later was called to Nashville to serve on the church's Board of Education.

Saturday, January 1, 1853. I was awaked this morning by a "Happy New Year" from Indie, and I immediately gave her a kiss. . . . The new printing office took fire on the roof today, from the stove-pipe which passes thro' it. Fortunately, it was discovered in time, & with the kindly assistance of many friends, it was easily extinguished. I exerted myself fiercely on the roof.

4th. I am preparing for the next paper, an article on the literary domination of the North and a defence of Southern Literature.

6th. The *Herald* came out as usual. . . . R. H. Rivers, Pres't of Centenary College, La., ordered a paper the other day.

7th. We can but expel him [Nick Davis] from the division. . . . Poor fellow! He shows how much he is devoted to me when he is drunk, and declared that "it is a part of his religion, and the chief part of it [is] to love me."

10th. All is bustle here, preparing for a party which we are to give on next Friday night. Indie is still [sick], but Mrs. Bass, Richardson, & other kind friends are working hard for her. . . . Little Bob Malone has been complaining of not being invited to the parties lately. He says he means when he is a man to give a large party and not invite *any body to it!*

13th. Pres says that Rollston, editor of the *North Alabamian,* says the *Herald* is the best paper published in N.A. He is a judge.

William Rollston bought the *North Alabamian* in Tuscumbia in the 1840s. This was the same newspaper owned by Arthur Keller, father of Helen. Mr. Keller published the paper for over thirty years.—Leftwich, 116.

Friday, January 14, 1853. The Party company began to assemble early, and we soon had most of our fellow citizens of both sexes and all ages, with us.* The handsomest young ladies present, were M. A. Binford and Rebecca Mason—but there were many good-looking enough.** Miss Mattie Coleman, Bettie Malone, and Cousin Pet Echols were perhaps most interesting. Every body seemed to bring their best spirits with them.

*In Henry Malone's diary for January 9, 1853, he stated that he had been informed that Mrs. Tom Hobbs intended to give him a complimentary party before his returning to Cincinnati. Strange that Hobbs does not mention it.

**Mary Ann Binford, daughter of Addison, married Thomas L. H. Maclin in 1854. Rebecca Mason, daughter of William, married Dr. Richard Fletcher, of Nubbin Ridge, lived at Birnam Wood, and bore nine of their ten children there.—Frazier, 1.

20th. Uncle's cotton, amounting to 90 bales, was sold yesterday at 7½¢ per pound. I went to the river today to receive the money, and was paid $3,330. . . . Sold our corp at same price, but it is not ready for delivery. . . . I sent to Peter Garrett to go [hunting] with me tomorrow.

Peter Francisco Garrett, son of Edmund, was born in Virginia in 1810. Shortly after his marriage to Mary Peete in 1858, Garrett built The Cedars, one of the loveliest of Tennessee Valley homes. Peter's descendant, Edmond Peter Garrett, continues to mantain extensive farm operations on this land, and the Garrett family has won many awards for their progressive techniques. A trip to the Orient was awarded to this family for the excellence of their 1973 soybean crop. Peter Francisco Garrett was named for the Portuguese giant, Peter Francisco, known as the strongest man in America, and the "Hercules of the American Revolution." Francisco was the special ward of the Winston family of Virginia and Alabama, and had a son living in Courtland as early as 1825. See Saunders, 198, for an amusing account of Francisco.

January 24th, 1853. Large sale of negroes today—this brought many people to town. . . . I wrote the piece in last paper . . . purporting to come from an old man and being a native of N. Carolina, is very anxious that the world should remember the fact of the Mecklenburg Declaration. I intend to reply and quote Mr. Jefferson's letter on the subject; this will cause the old man to bring forward his proofs.

25th. Last night the Crotchet Club had a meeting. Poor little club! . . . John Richardson removed, then Billy died, then Mrs. Maclin's health became too delicate for her to assist; and now lately, and worst of all, Prof. Barclay has moved out of town.

26th. Dr. Hal Malone brought me from Cin'i a long German pipe, the mouthpiece of which is horn, and gives precisely the right note for a turkey-caller.

27th. Peter Garrett, Schuyler Harris, & I made a long and faithful hunt for turkies [*sic*], but found none.

Schuyler Harris, son of John and Frances Rowzee Harris, was born in 1823. In 1845 he married Anne DeWoody, daughter of William, and in 1857 he built the home known as Flower Hill Farm. One of his daughters, Ida, married Richard Pryor, and a sister of Schuyler, Isabella Virginia, married Luke Pryor. The plantation has been in possession of the Pryor family for many years, the present owner being Luke Pryor, IV. Henry Augustine Washington, who first owned the property, was buried here in 1825. The land was inherited by the Harris family.

January 28th, 1853. Went to Decatur and received from J. Collier $5,438.62 for our cotton crop, (150 bales).

February 1st. The Examination at the Institute is going on. I attended this afternoon as a Trustee and a reporter for that excellent paper, the *Athens Herald.*

2nd. Misses Coleman, Echols & Sally Malone staid with us tonight, and of course, with 3 such lively girls, and Indie as girlish as any, we had a gay time of it.

3rd. Indie & I attended an oyster party at T. A. Nelson's.

4th. A cold, rainy, gloomy day. But I found pleasant employment in doors at home. Who wouldn't be married?

18th. The subject of a R. Road to Decatur is now exciting general interest. It is proposed to lay a tax on the county, in order to build it, but this is violently opposed by some—Capt. Mason is among the most talkative.

February 22nd, 1853. Rev. Randolph Finley, D. D., is staying with us. He is willing to take charge of our Institute, and is being introduced by Pa (to whom he brought letters) to the Trustees and leading citizens of our Town. He seems to be well-informed; has traveled in S. America, and been at the head of several Institutions. He is a man of agreeable manners.

24th. A new pupil on the violin has presented himself in Thomas Hanserd, one of my Sabbath School scholars. . . . The Board of Trustees elected Dr. Finley President of the Institute today. It is supposed Pres. Moore is anxious to leave at once, as he has been elected to a Professorship at La Grange. [The Reverend Isham Randolph Finley served for two years as president.]

25th. Indie has gone tonight to stay at J. C. Malone's, as several ladies were of the party and no gentlemen, I was politely requested to allow the ladies to have a "hen party." They are no doubt cackling away now, but I would like for Mrs. H. to come home to *roost.*

Thursday, March 3, 1853. We staid at Judge Coleman's—found the Basses, and Miss Betty Malone there. The Judge, who is generally an austere man, was very companionable, and contributed no little to our entertainment. I disclosed to him my plan of a school for the trades and arts, and of a contemporaneous chart of biography. He was much pleased with both.

7th. Poor Archie Johnson died this morning. . . . When we bought out the printing office, I urged him to spend the winter in Florida, but he did not think it necessary for his restoration.

18th. Today Mrs. Nick Davis died very suddenly. She walked into the garden and attended to the sowing of some seeds; said she felt better than usual . . . she died sitting in her chair.

19th. Attended Mrs. D's funeral. . . . She was buried in a metallic burial case—the first I ever saw in use. . . . Pres't Moore preached an excellent funeral sermon. Never saw the roads worse; Ma & Mrs. Hayes & I went up in carriage, had to walk over several bad places in the road.

March 24, 1853. All this week preparing to start to Va.

28th. Took the *Lookout* about sunset.

The "boss of all boats" was the *Lookout,* built by J. M. Todd at Pittsburgh in 1852. Rebuilt in Bridgeport in 1860, the *Lookout* was used by the Confederate Government until Chattanooga was captured, and then used by the Federals until it sank in 1865.—Davidson, 294.

April 18th. Getting ready to start to N.Y. on tomorrow. . . . Met Dr. E. B. Wilkinson, of Tuscumbia, who is also going on the boat tomorrow.

21st. As we passed Sandy Hook the view was more magnificent than anything I ever conceived. . . . My only regret was that my dear one was not with me to enjoy it, too. Wishing to try a hotel on the European side, we drove to Delmonico's near the Battery, and at night went to hear and see Christy's Minstrels.

Edwin P. Christy, 1815–1862, organized the original Christy's Minstrels in Buffalo, New York, in 1842. For a time he had exclusive rights to perform the songs of Stephen Foster, and had a phenomenal success.—*Who Was Who*, 106.

April 24, 1853. Heard Rev. Chapin, an eloquent Universalist preacher, at night. So popular is he that even the gallery pews are rented, & it is a difficult matter to get a seat.

Edwin Hubbell Chapin, 1814–1880, was at the Fourth Universalist Church in New York, having gone there in 1848. The church had to be enlarged twice during his ministry there.

29th. Arrived in Richmond.
30th. Indie in country.
May 2nd. Arrived at Amelia C. H. about 9 A.M.
3rd. Indie and I went to Mr. Masters'. His wife great friend of Indie. He is a sensible gent—a lawyer in fine practice.

Leander and Jane Eggleston Masters bought Evenholm from William Eggleston in 1849. General Lee stopped at Evenholm on his way to Appomattox, but declined Mrs. Masters' invitation to spend the night, in order to sleep outside with his dejected men.—Jefferson, 72.

7th. In the afternoon, went with Mr. E. and the ladies to Mr. Edwin Booth's in Nottoway. Here the visitor always receives the real Virginia welcome, for Mr. B. is a man of wealth, and able to entertain at such expense as the warm hearts of himself and wife may dictate. He is an enthusiastic farmer, and a very successful one, too, having reclaimed many of his paternal acres that were considered worn out when he was born. He says all he wants to make a crop is "guano and surface."
12th. Spent some time in the State Library. Wm. Mumford, an old University fellow student, is Librarian.
13th. Making some examination of records to see at what time Grandpa Maclin was a member of Va. Legislature. I think he was member of Senate . . . before the War of 1812. . . . A Mr. Frederick Maclin was a member of the Convention which in 1775 & '6 established the constitution of Va. Who was he? My great-grandfather? I wish I knew.

Frederick Maclin was a brother of Thomas Hobbs' great-grandmother, Elizabeth Maclin Maclin. Thomas Maclin, "Grandpa," served in the Virginia House of Delegates from 1803–1805, and in the Senate from 1806–1811. —Hobbs Family Papers.

23rd. Left Petersburg . . . for home.
24th. We have for travelling companions Rev. W. C. Buck and Dr. Burton, of Murphreesboro, Tenn. The latter has just returned from China where, in the employ of the Baptist Miss. Society, he practiced

medicine on the Chinese gratuitously. He gave me much information in regard to that country and its inhabitants. The wages of a clerk in a store is about 75 cents a month and 3 bowls of rice a day!
28th. Reached landing opp. Decatur about 3.
June 2, 1853. My name announced in *Herald* as candidate for legislature. Canvass regularly opened today. We had an appointment to speak at Piney Bridge on Huntsville road. The lot to speak first fell on me. I did it briefly, plainly, candidly. Allen is against Liquor bill & the people's voting on the tax for a R.R. Wynn in favor of the former, but against the latter. Rip—ditto. I in favor of both.

A newspaper clipping is attached on August 1, showing that Winston led substantially in Limestone for governor; that Hobbs was defeated by Allen and Hanserd for representatives; and Ezell for tax collector. Limestone County voting places listed are: Athens, Pea Ridge, Woolley's, Shoal Ford, Mooresville, Jones', Phillips', Horton's, Pleasant Grove, Wickham's, and Tindall's.

September 8th. Mother Elliott died.
September 27, 1853. Aunt Haldane died today about 12. One week ago we left her in better health than usual, but the next day she visited Mr. Ben Peete's and took a chill while there. . . . Pa and Ma were with her, but I stayed at home with Indie, who is sick in bed from chills. Aunt was in a stupor during her illness and gave no expression of her prospects beyond the grave. She was born in Greensville Co., Va., January 8, 1773.

It is probable that Thomas Hobbs kept no diary in 1854. The year was one of great emotional tribulation, as he explains in the opening sentences of 1855.

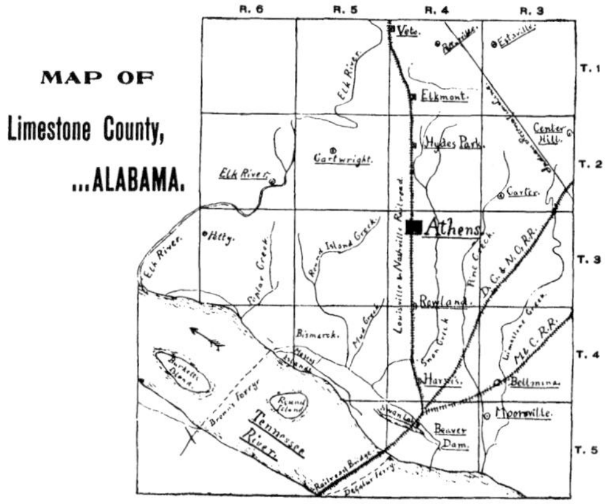

MAP OF LIMESTONE COUNTY
SHOWING RAILROAD LINES
CIRCA 1870
Courtesy Henrietta Hine,
Athens, Alabama

RAILROAD SURVEY 1855

Monday, January 1, 1855. Far from home, & among semi-civilized strangers, I began this New Year. I was glad to take leave of the last one—it had brought me so much grief; its latter months seemed oppressive to me, and to be moving slowly. . . . Oh! Memorable year! Disasters by sea & land, such as were never before witnessed—diseases raging with unprecedented violence & extent—a most bloody war convulsing Europe—are but some of the memorabilia of that ill-starred year. Surely I can never forget it, for its merriest month robbed me of my darling wife, showed me a dead child and plunged me into insupportable grief. . . . I buried in my darling's grave many well-matured plans for future action and many strong hopes of future success. These were not plans for personal aggrandizement, nor hopes of ambitious advancement. They were far nobler than these; for they had been formed by two big unselfish hearts who found their chief pleasure in loving each other, and their next greatest in serving and increasing the happiness of all others. In one moment these plans were all blasted, and I became a homeless wretch, without a plan, without a hope. In vain I attempted to find some cause for this dispensation of Providence. The impossibility of discovering even the shadow of a reason for it made me often doubt the superintending care of God. In my calmer moments I experienced a sort of submission, & endeavored to cultivate it; but very often my heart was defiant. . . . At length this feeling took poss^{n} of me; since God has marred all the plans I had formed, I will wait and see what work He will give me to do. . . . Few can be brilliant or eminent, but all can be useful in one way or other. This is the one talent wh. the parable teaches us is given to all men. And so various are the methods of exercising this talent that we ought indeed to be punished if we buried it in the earth.

It suddenly occurred to me . . . that it w'd be possible to raise from the educated young men of N. Ala., a Corps of Assistant Engineers who w'd without pay—survey the mountains wh. separate N. and S. Ala., and ascertain if there was a practicable route for a R.R. thro' them. At a meeting of the Corporators of the Ala & Tenn Central R.R., held in Decatur, I proposed to them to employ a chief Eng. and I w'd raise a sufficient no. of competent assistants who wd. work for nothing. But they seemed to think I w'd not be able to do this, and the proposition received no encouragement. I made enquiry thro' Nick Davis, Esq., of Mr. John F. Steele, for what his services could be had to take charge of the party. But he, when he learned that all the corps were to be young gentlemen & volunteers, nobly expressed his readiness also to volunteer in the cause of his native State.

Accordingly, at the next meeting of the B'd one month after their last, I again appeared before them & informed them that nothing was now lacking to their survey, except the necessary equipment and money enough to defray the travelling expenses of the survey. It was agreed that Limestone County shd. furnish the money and Morgan the equipment, and I was authorized to organize a Corps at once. This was easily done, and we met in Decatur on the 10th day of October, and forthwith commenced operations. Our volunteers were: John F. Steele, chief Eng.; Robert Armstrong, an Irishman of Decatur; William B. Wilkinson, of La Grange, Tenn; William D. Hollowell, of Huntsville; Harry F. Christian, of Huntsville; Joseph B. McDonald, of Limestone, and myself.

William D. Hollowell, son of William Dean and Mary Elizabeth Echols Hollowell, was a graduate of the University of Virginia. Joseph Bibb McDonald, son of Dr. Jonathan and Mary Briggs Malone McDonald, was born in 1833.—Jones and Gandrud.

My friend, W. B. Wilkinson, happened to be visiting me, and being very fond of camp life, readily consented to be one of our Corps. All of us, save the two first named above were unacquainted with the work, but in a few days we learned to manage all of the instruments. Under the impression that almost our only difficulty was at the mountains wh. form the So. boundary of Morgan, we did not try a line from Decatur, but moved at once to their northern foot and tried lines over all the gaps from Vaughn's to Gandy's Cove. This last mentioned line we continued to Elyton.

I was chiefly employed with the level, either managing that, or acting as rodman to it. It was hard work, but very pleasant. We rose early, breakfasted, and then to work, at which we continued without dinner generally until after sunset. Supper was ready when we reached camp and . . . I never before ate so heartily or digested so well. After supper around our huge camp fires we made ourselves merry with our pipes, anecdotes, cards, etc. Wilk was at all times the life of the party, and is one of the greatest wags and best fellows I ever saw. And thus we battled on for about four months, enduring some hardships from want of provisions, but learning much of human nature, as well as engineering. The greatest advantage I derived was that "surcease from sorrow," wh. constant mental employment brought me. Col. Steele says he never saw a more efficient Corps in the field, and certainly they were very pleasant fellows. . . . Once or twice we were out of meat, and as often out of sugar, but these little privations only served to give a little variety to our life. We saw abundance of game, but as all were employed in the work, we had little chance to hunt. We killed 2 fine bucks, however, and caught a great many hares, opossums, & raccoons. I carried my terriers and 2 old hounds, & they gave us great amusement.

January 16, 1855. Today, about 3 P.M., we ran our line into Elyton and united it with that of the N.E. & S.W.R.R. We were taken immediately by a Committee of citizens to a hotel where they had prepared a dinner for us.* Afterwards, [we were] employed in laying in supplies for [our] homeward trip. At night we met the city & the Corps of the other Road at a supper given us in Court House. W. S. Mudd made an appropriate reception speech, wh. was answered by our chief in a creditable manner.** Then supper—turkey, cakes, coffee, etc.—wh. were rapidly consumed by men who for months had subsisted on victuals cooked by men. After sup. Stovall (chief of the other party) & I [were] called on, & made short speeches.

*Of the hotels in Elyton, the jovial Colonel James Powell remarked: "They are like the roads in Arkansas, whichever one you take, you wish to h—— you had taken the other!"—Hornaday, 10.

**William Swearingen Mudd, 1816–1884, was born in Jefferson County, Kentucky, and made his indelible mark in Jefferson County, Alabama. The Mudds had first come to America with Lord Baltimore. W. S. Mudd read law under Walker Baylor in Elyton, represented Jefferson in the Legislature, was judge of the circuit court, and was one of the founders of the Elyton Land Company. He helped to found the Citizen's Bank, which merged with the First National at a later date. In 1841 he married Florence Jane Earle, daughter of Dr. Samuel Earle, prominent Jefferson County physician. Hobbs does not record it, but there is a tradition in his family that the party stayed at the Mudd home, the present Arlington, on the night of the survey completion.—Owen, IV, 1256.

22nd. Wilk and I reached my house this morning . . . Mr. Yearwood having moved out to oversee for Captain Gamble, and Mr. Napthali Lynch is here in his place.

Captain James Hurt Gamble, 1791–1855, was born near Nashville, Tennessee. He married Hulda J. Dillard, of Virginia. They were parents of several children, among them Ruffin Coleman Gamble, who was called to the tent of Lt. Colonel Jonathan Biggs, commander of occupying Federal forces during the Civil War, and was told that Ruffin's father had once done the officer a favor. He made a list of all the property that had been taken from the Gamble plantation during the occupation, and restitution was quickly made.—Pat Jones, *Mooresville,* 40.

23rd. Pa came down [to the plantation] this morn'g and carried us to Athens, where we found all who are dear to me in this world. . . . Pryor, Nick Malone, Sowell, etc., soon came in. And my dear friend, Henry Malone, of Cincinnati, now on a visit to his family here, lost no time in calling on us. He is much beloved by both Wilk and I, and deserves it all.

Luke Pryor, 1820–1900, was the son of Luke and Anne Batte Pryor, of Virginia. The elder Luke Pryor had first married Martha Scott, sister of General Winfield Scott, in Petersburg, Virginia. Luke, Jr., studied law under Judge Daniel Coleman, was admitted to the bar in 1841, and was in partnership at varying times with Robert Brickell, Egbert Jones, and George S. Houston. After the Civil War, Pryor was appointed to fill the unexpired term of George S. Houston in the U. S. Senate, and in 1883 was elected to Congress by conscription. He married Isabella Virginia Harris. The Pryor home, Acacia Grove, stands in Athens at the corner of North Jefferson and Pryor streets.—Owen, IV, 1396.

January 25, 1855. Subscribed for the *Montgomery Mail,* the only paper at our seat of Gov. wh. favors our Central Road. I now take *National Intelligence, Country Gentleman,* and the *Athens Herald.*

The *Montgomery Mail* had been established in 1852 as a Whig newspaper by Johnson Jones Hooper, the witty author of *Simon Suggs.* Hooper continued editing the *Mail* until 1861, when he was elected secretary of the provisional Confederate Congress. He moved to Richmond, but died not long after.—Owen, III, 839.

Feb. 1, 1855. Started to Nashville; the chief objects for going are to buy profile & other paper for the Report, and some agricultural implements.

3rd. At breakfast, met Tom Maddin, who boards at this hotel [City Hotel]; he showed us around the city.

5th. Arrived safely in H'ville.

6th. Dined at Oak Place, the elegant mansion of Mr. George Steele. He was confined to room . . . John, by previous agreement, packed up and came down with us.

12th. Pa, Ma, Miss Octavia Bass, and Cousin Julia came down today . . . to spend some days with us, for which I am greatly obliged to them. Housekeeping is very unpleasant to me, chiefly because it calls up such sad recollections.

21st. Engaged in transplanting some fruit trees, sent down from town by Pa. Many of them I had budded & grafted during last year. . . . A good orchard I am resolved to have. I believe N. Ala. can beat the world in growing fine peaches, & to this fruit I especially direct my attention.

Thursday, February 22, 1855. This call was published by the *Herald* of today. It is the first instance in my knowledge of man being called out by the ladies.

> Mr. Keyes: We are conscious that our duties do not lead us into the bustle and noise of the busy world. Our place and our pleasures lie in the cool and quiet shades of life. Nor have we a single wish that it should be otherwise. . . . Yet we confess that oftentimes, around our peaceful firesides, we await with anxious hearts the result of popular movements. And never before have we felt so great an interest in any movement as in the proposed project of a railroad through our county. Our love for our homes, our families and our friends, has excited our interest and enlisted our sympathies for its success. We therefore trust that no other apology is necessary for thus expressing the hope that Mr. Luke Pryor and Maj. Thomas H. Hobbs, able advocates of the road, will become candidates for seats in the next Legislature. If they will consent to yield to our earnest wish we promise them our influence and our prayers.
>
> MANY LADIES

March 2, 1855. Engaged with the Commissioners app. to assess the damages caused by M. & C. R. Road. They estimated them at one thousand dollars.

5th. A great many people are soliciting me to run for Leg. The whole State Aid party in county seemed to have settled down upon Mr. Pryor & me as their candidates. I do not wish to run, I greatly prefer to remain at home in peace and quiet—attending to my own affairs, wh. so much need it. . . . The contest is likely to be an exciting one, more so perhaps, than any wh. has taken place in Limestone for years.

8th. Ma came down bringing Mattie & Leila Coleman, Rebecca Mason and Cousin Julia. We now have a lively time . . . but alas! I am always thinking how much she w'd have contributed to their enjoyment.

9th. The little plum tree overhanging the front fence of yard bloomed today.

10th. My mare, Nelly Bly, dropped a female foal. . . . Steele and Wilk suggested she sho^{d} be named "Julia Meade," & accordingly she is.

16th. We are now and have been for several days very busy upon the work. Steele drafting the Report, Wilk making the estimates, and I on the map, profiles, etc.

21st. Miss Bettie Malone married to Mr. Alexander Wheless of Nashville, also Miss Jane Brundidge to Mr. Edward Kimbell, of Morgan. But Death also visited the town and bore away little Bettie Sowell, a sweet, interesting child of Dr. S.

22nd. This morning Wilk left us. . . . He leaves me sad; for nearly five months his delightful company has cheered me, and his inimitable drollery has exerted a most beneficial influence on my spirits. . . . His future life is somewhat undecided. . . . I think he will move westward, for he is anxious to be settled, and does not feel able to purchase land at such high prices as it commands in the older states. Nicholas the Czar is dead.

24th. At eleven Report was read in C. H. to B'd. of Corps, & a good many others. . . . ordered to be printed.

26th. Steele is unquestionably a genius—learns by intuition apparently, knows something about everything, and some things thoroughly.

27th. Staid with John at his father's last night.

30th. The *Herald* of yesterday contained [articles on the railroad meetings at Pettusville and at Gilbertsboro, both of which adopted resolutions in favor of Pryor and Hobbs for the legislature]. It is curious to observe the change in public opinion. Two years since, (nearly) almost every name signed to the Gilbertsboro document was violently opposed to me. My position on the Liquor question was the main cause of this; but they also disagreed . . . with my views in regard to the Mud Tavern R. R. I took the ground that the people had the right to decide whether they w'd be taxed for that road, and that I w'd vote for a bill allowing them to do so. In their opposition to the little road, they forgot the principle involved, but now that it is proposed to extend the road in their direction, they suddenly see the importance of the principle they once denied.

No information can be obtained on this proposed road, but it is known that the Hobbs family owned a tavern that was set up to accommodate crews working on government boats on the Tennessee River. It was known as Mud Tavern and was probably on Mud Creek. There may have been a proposal for a spur to the tavern, running from the Memphis and Charleston Railroad.—Information on tavern from Mrs. John Higgins, granddaughter of Thomas Hobbs.

April 1, 1855. Tonight sat up with the sick children of Mrs. Pleas Richardson. For two or three hours they tho't the oldest was dying, and the grief of the mother and grandmother was very great. . . . Mrs. J. C. Malone sat up with me, and how sadly I thought of the last time we met in the sick room! Poor Indie tho't Mrs. M. found a cure for her pains when all the others failed.

April 2, 1855. It is now pretty well agreed by Mr. Pryor and myself that we will run.

7th. Uncle returned from H'ville, bringing the sad intelligence of Cousin Pet's [Jones] death. . . . She was a sweet-spirited woman, and a dear friend of my Indie.

14th. Planted my little patch of experimental corn.

20th. This day, one year ago, we moved to the country . . . with a pleasant hope of soon having another member in our little family.

21st. Went with Pete Garrett to his sawmill—on the way saw cotton up, the first I've seen. Dined at Ed Garrett's.

April 24th, 1855. My corn is up well. That which was soaked in copperas water coming up best. Mrs. Finley [the Methodist minister's wife] died.

27th. The *Herald* of yesterday brought . . . proceedings at Wickham's [endorsing Pryor and Hobbs]. Strange! At this precinct two years ago, Allen got 94 or 5 out of 99 votes.

May 7th. Mr. Pryor and I declared ourselves candidates today, and had an interview with Allen & Rip Davis in wh. times and places for speaking were agreed upon.

8th. John Spottswood killed young Bradford in Huntsville this day.

In the Huntsville *Southern Advocate* of May 16, 1855, the editor, William B. Figures wrote: "It is with deep regret we are called upon to state that on the morning of the 8th inst. in this place, William C. Bradford, son of Capt. David Bradford of this vicinity, was killed by a pistol shot fired by John E. Spotswood, son of Dr. John C. Spotswood. It is improper to state in a newspaper at this time the circumstances connected with this sad affair. Mr. Spotswood was immediately arrested, and an investigation was had before magistrates on the 9th and 10th inst., which resulted in his committal for trial. Messrs. D. C. Humphreys, Luke Pryor and Nick Davis, Jr., represented the state, and Messrs. C. C. Clay, Sr., L. P. Walker, John Robinson, and William Acklen the defendant. Most able, ingenious, and effective speeches were made by Messrs. Pryor and Humphreys, and by Messrs. Walker and Clay." The same paper, on September 16, 1858, stated that the trial of Spotswood took place in that month, that he was convicted of murder in the second degree, and sentenced to spend ten years in the penitentiary. During the trial two additional defense lawyers were employed: Egbert Jones and Bob Brickell.

May 17th, 1855. One year ago . . . my darling drew her last breath. . . . Without a fear, without a doubt, she looked Death calmly in the face and triumphed over him.

18th. Dr. Finley was selected by Mrs. Booth to preach the funeral, which he did on the 18th at 8 A.M. . . . We buried her at home with her baby by her side. . . . Rev. Joseph White reading the burial service.
19th. All this week. . . . have been engaged in studying the finances of Ala., and what the State has done for int. improvements. . . . I don't believe any body understands the condition of 2 & 3 percent funds.
21st. Left town . . . to visit the regions over Elk. . . . Saw the Lentzes.
22nd. Stayed with Simpson Flannagan.

Benjamin Lentz, born in North Carolina in 1804, was the son of Henry, a Revolutionary soldier. Simpson Flannagan served as a road commissioner for Limestone. He married Martha Strange, daughter of Abner, a Revolutionary soldier who settled on the Elk River.

23rd. Stayed with this fine old man at night. The first train of cars crossed the Decatur Bridge. Visited Wickham's and Squire Ridgeway, thence up into the extreme N. W. of county. Here the people are nearly all right on R. R. question. Stayed with Rev. James Shelton, an old Baptist minister.

Samuel Wickham, born in Virginia in 1803, married Louisa Ellis in 1838, and had Elbert, Malissa Ann, and Louisa in 1850. David Ridgeway was born in Tennessee in 1800, and had seven children at home in 1850.

According to the 1850 census, the Reverend James Shelton (born in Tennessee in 1801) had ten children living at home.

May 24, 1855. Accompanied by Mr. Shelton, visited Gilbertsboro, calling on several as we went along. All right up here. Dined with Major Gilbert, and [came] home after dinner. Rev. Robert Donnell, one of the oldest of our citizens, died today. . . . James Brundidge lost a son with scarlet fever.

Major David Gilbert, born in South Carolina in 1796, lost two wives in that state, before coming to Alabama, where he was to marry five more times. Apparently, he was married to his sixth wife, Hannah, at the time of Hobbs' visit, not long before she fell to her death. The stairway that caused this tragedy leads abruptly to the second floor of the house through the central door leading off the front porch. The Gilbert house stands less than a mile south of the Tennessee line. The name, Gilbertsboro, was a short-lived one for this community, which now bears its original name of Gourdsville. —See Pat Jones, "The Gilbert Home," July 14, 1935.

May 25th, 1855. We now have excessively hot weather, which is favorable to the wheat, but death to the oats. Such wheat crops have never before been seen in Ala. Corn is now worth $4 per bhl., and hard to get.
27th. Mr. Donnell's funeral preached by Rev. G. W. Mitchell—congre-

gation as large as the church w'd hold. He was born in Ap., 1784, [1785 on his tombstone] and was perhaps the first preacher who labored in this part of the country.

29th. Visited a good many of the cit[izens] of upper Limestone. There is more sign of improvements in this part of the county than any other. A great many people are settling in here and reclaiming the old fields. Had an interview with Gatlin, Jones, Tillery, etc.

30th. Met the trustees and some of the patrons of the School at Piney Grove Church. . . . Dined with Squire Bays & thence home. Paper from Claiborne announcing his election to rep. Petersburg in next Leg.

31st. Dromgoole is elected in Brunswick.

Friday, June 1st. Judge Joe Walker . . . remarked to Pryor and me, that if we could get the State to build a Central Road we deserved to be called the "De Witt Clintons of Ala." He thinks there is too much fogyism and rivalry of sections to carry the thing yet awhile.

June 2nd, 1855. The weather is so cool that . . . fires are absolutely necessary for comfort. Stayed all day and tonight with [William] Crenshaw. He had heard of my plan for a working School, and was delighted with it when I explained it in full. He urges me to undertake it, and enters his oldest son, Freeman, who is a mechanical genius, whenever I begin.

Freeman inherited his mechanical genius. The work of Samuel and J. W. Crenshaw has been cited. Around 1830 Samuel had also begun to make cotton mill machinery in partnership with Ira and Hubbard Hobbs. Samuel's son, Cyrus, invented a machine that would make a horseshoe during the Civil War, thus speeding this vital operation greatly. The Crenshaws lived near the present Elk River Mills bridge, where the waters of Big Creek converged with the Elk.

8th. Went to Mr. Pryor's plantation, and spent the night with him and Ben Allen.

9th. While Pryor fights the trashy arguments . . . of our opponents, I play the figures on them. The coal and Iron resources of our State are indeed wonderful, and when effectively unfolded in a proper manner, the most ignorant are astonished.

15th. Rip and I stayed tonight at William Legg's—one of the most hospitable men I ever saw and one of the biggest hearted and most public spirited.

William Legg, 1783–1865, was the son of Edward and Sarah Garrett Legg, of Virginia. He married Nancy Coffman in Jefferson County, Tennessee, where her father, David, was one of the earliest settlers. The Leggs moved to

Alabama soon after William's returning from service in the War of 1812. William was appointed to lay out the seat of Jackson County by the state's first legislature. He settled on the Elk River in 1824 near the site of the present Leggtown, and served as commissioner of roads in Limestone for twenty-eight years.—*Memorial Record of Alabama*, 408.

16th. Spoke at Gilbertsboro to a very large crowd wh. was nearly unanimous for the R.R.

20th. Crops look unusually well. . . . My experimental corn is keeping pace with that of the plantation, and in my opinion, the yield will outweigh the other.

22nd. Stayed this night with Capt. Tom Phillips—a fine, open-hearted, public-spirited old Virginian.

Thomas Phillips, son of Anthony, was born in Virginia in 1789, and was also a veteran of the War of 1812. He married a Murrah, member of another pioneer family in the area near the Alabama-Tennessee border line. According to the 1850 census, there were sixteen members of Thomas Phillips' household living there at the time, among them Warren, often mentioned in the diaries.

23rd. Spoke at Pettusville to a large crowd. . . . The debate, so far as Ben and I were concerned, was much more pleasant than I expected.

28th. Went to Huntsville to attend a Concert of Bascom Institute.* I wanted to get clear of thinking about this abominable canvass. . . . I am heartily sick of such work. . . . Saw Steele, Christian, and many other friends. Stayed all night with Nick Davis and his sweet wife.**

*In the meeting of the Methodist Conference of 1851, two important items were passed. A permanent Missionary Fund was established, headed by an initial gift of $500 from J. C. Malone, of Athens; and the Bascom Female Institute in Huntsville, later called the Huntsville Female College, was accepted by the conference.—Lazenby, 308.

**Nick Davis and Sophia Lowe were married on October 4, 1854.—Madison County Records.

July 5, 1855. Today I parted with 2 of my best friends—Cousin Julia Meade and Pres Keyes. The former, who is one of the sweetest ladies I ever knew, goes with Mr. Hine to Petersburg, having been with us more than a year. . . . Everyone here is attached to her, as they were to Indie. Surely I can never cease to love her, for but for her influence & assistance, I should never have been married. Pres has been app. Register and Master in chancery in Montgomery Co. by his brother Wade. Altho' he writes a bad hand, I hope he will discharge his duties well—salary about $1000 a year. I offered to sign and did sign his official bond for $10,000. He is a fine, clever fellow.

Wade Keyes became chancellor of the southern division of Alabama in 1853, following publication of two volumes he had written on legal subjects, one being on chancery practice. During the Civil War, Wade Keyes served as assistant attorney general of the Confederate States of America, and later lived in Florence, Alabama. Except for a period of war service, Pres Keyes continued as register in chancery until he was ousted by the Reconstruction officials. He was later associate editor of the *Montgomery Advertiser,* and was a founder of Sheffield, Alabama, building both the first frame dwelling and the first brick residence there. Pres was married three times—to Fannie Gayle, to a daughter of Dr. R. H. Rivers, and to Jennie S. Rainey.—Owen, III, 973, 974.

7th.—Spoke today at George Isom's barbecue.

The Isom family came into Limestone County from Virginia before 1820. There are two George Isoms listed in the census of that year, probably father and son. The name is spelled Isham in the 1850 census, in which George is listed as 64, living with his wife Agnes, and with five children at home. Among them was George J., who married Eleanor Harrison on April 15, 1850. The Isom land lay east of Athens along the Huntsville Road.

11th. Dink Thach & I went to spend the night with Mr. John James Fletcher on Nubbin Ridge. Had a pleasant visit.

"Dink" was probably Robert Henry Thach, a lawyer in Athens, who married Eliza Lockhart Coleman in 1859. They were parents of Charles Coleman Thach, president of the Alabama Polytechnic Institute (now Auburn University).—Owen, IV, 1658.

John James Fletcher, brother of James Nicholas, Matthew, and Sarah Fletcher Bass, was born in Brunswick County, Virginia. He had six children living at home in 1850, and no wife is listed.

July 12, 1855. Appointment at Shoal Ford.

14th. Spoke in Mooresville to large crowd. 25 from Decatur (who came over on the cars now running out beyond Bibb's Lane). . . . Saw the M. & C. cars in motion in Limestone for the first time, and felt a thrill of pride and strong hope at the sight.

16th. Last Saturday morn'g, Samuel, the second son of Mr. William Richardson, died.

17th. Called to see Mrs. Richardson. . . . She loved my Indie dearly and nursed her tenderly.

20th. John Anthony Winston and George D. Shortridge, the Dem. & Know-Nothing candidates for Governor, spoke in our town today. They are poor speakers, but they seem free from demagoguism and avow their opinions clearly and boldly. They are both opposed to the State's issuing bonds to build a Central R.R., and, ergo, neither of them is progressive enough for me. I say it w'd be good policy for the State to contract a debt suff. to build a road centrally thro' the State, and develop her immense iron and other mineral resources.

John Anthony Winston was seeking reelection to the governor's chair. At the time of his first victory, he was the first native Alabamian to achieve that position. George David Shortridge, 1814–1870, was born in Mt. Sterling, Kentucky, and died in Montevallo, Alabama. After serving as mayor of Montgomery and director of the State Bank, he moved to Montevallo, served as circuit judge, and married Elizabeth King, daughter of Edmund and Nancy Reagan King. In 1823 Edmund King built the first brick house and the first to have glass window panes in the central portion of the state. It is on the campus of the University of Montevallo.—American Guide Series, *Alabama*, 264.

26th. Considerable excitement is now getting up in regard to Know-Nothingism in our midst. So far we have been able to keep it down, but it seems now to be getting almost unmanageable. Some hot R.R. men go so far as to say that they will not support Pryor because he is a member of the Order. . . . All three of my competitors are supposed to be members of that party.

The "Know Nothing" Party first made its appearance in 1852, as a result of American reaction to the great wave of immigration occurring between 1825 and 1850. In the 1855 Congress there was a large number of Know Nothings.

July 28, 1855. Today was our last appointment . . . how glad am I!
30th. Mr. Wm. F. Perry, the Superintendent of Education in Ala., visited us today, and addressed the people in the C. H. He is a plain, unpretending man, very fluent in conversation and speaking—and seems to be devoted to the cause of Education. . . . Dr. Stith [Malone], Judge Tyus, & I called on him early this morn'g. He said the educational interests of Limestone had been as well attended to as any other county in State. He took a family dinner with us, as did Nick & Stith Malone. . . . went with Dr. Malone to Capt. Davis', where I stayed all night.
August 2nd. Dr. Dick Fletcher & Rebecca Mason married.
3rd. With a glad heart I turned towards home, this being the last visit of the canvass. When opposite Tom Black's, I met a young man who . . . said, "Ben Allen is dead." . . . This news was so unexpected that it shocked me greatly.
4th. Ben's burial . . . at ten o'clock. Mr. Wilson read the burial service. Peace to his ashes! The anti-R. R. men at once nominated Capt. Nathaniel Davis in Ben's stead.
6th. Long before the votes in Athens were counted out we had the re-

turns from so many of the other boxes as to make the election of Pryor & Hobbs certain.
9th. [An unidentified newspaper article, attached at this date, states that Limestone went for Winston for governor, A. L. McKinney for sheriff, G. Wood for circuit clerk, and G. R. Anderson, tax collector. Winston had a large majority for governor in the state.]
10th. Went to Mooresville [to a dinner given by friends]. Was called on for a speech . . .thanked them for their support. . . . Pryor followed. [I] am getting to be a strong anti-K. N. The way to put down Catholicism is not by intolerance and proscription.
August 11th, 1855. Judge Walker and I drove to Wooley Springs. Heard Rev. Wm. Levesque preach at a church near the Springs.

Joel Wooley, born in North Carolina in 1783, bought the tract of land upon which the mineral springs were located in 1820 from a Mr. Tilman. Benjamin Peete was one of the first to camp there after Wooley opened the springs to the public. A hotel was built at the springs after the Civil War. One person is recorded as saying that in those pre-hotel days, "Wooley was more wooley."—Mason Scrapbooks, Vol. 1.

13th. Col. J. N. Fletcher, Mr. Wm. Richardson, & Dr. Beasley are tenting here, and their families constitute the chief company of the Springs. We have no amusements, and this is a dull place for pleasure seekers, I imagine. The water is excellent, and has already given me a fine appetite.
16th. Read in Putnam's Mag. . . . good poetry . . . credited to one Emerson or Ellsworth, a modern American poet.

Although Ralph Waldo Emerson had published his essays and a volume of poetry in the 1840s, he received little recognition until much later.

18th. Went to a Hard Shell Baptist meeting. Messrs. Millhouse and Crutcher preached. . . . After 2 sermons we had the communion and the washing of feet. It was the first time I ever saw this latter exercise. Crutcher took off his coat, girded himself with apron and washed Millh's feet from a large pewter basin; then his own were washed by M. and then the laity participated. The ladies were engaged in another part of the house to themselves. Queen Victoria and her spouse went to visit Louis Napoleon.

John Milhous (or Millhouse) was born in South Carolina in 1808. He was the son of John, 1767–1835, and Anna Stewart Milhous, who were among the county's earliest settlers. In 1839 Rev. Milhous married Tabitha Burk Powell, who was born in Tennessee in 1815. John was from a Quaker family, but adopted a religion more congruous to the early frontier. Reuben

Crutcher, 1792–1869, and his wife Eliza McCargo, 1798–1838, were active in the early development of the Primitive Baptist Church in Limestone, particularly that area around Wooly Springs.

August 29th, 1855. Have moved down home again. . . . This old desolated place is dearer to me than all the world beside.

30th. Went to Decatur and sold some wheat, about 200 bush. at 75 cts. This wheat is intended for the New York market! Now is not this an item to be noted? And how can any Anti-State-Aid man avail himself of this opportunity to get his wheat into market, when but for the Aid of Georgia to R. R., we never could have had such a chance. The same gent I sold my wheat to said he had an order to purchase 100,000 bush. corn; could give $1 a barrel—and this, he said, was intended, he supposed, for the Crimea, as he got the order from an Eng. house.

September 5, 1855. Called on my bachelor friend, Peter Garrett, and urged him to go with me to the Fair.

6th. Wilk came . . . preparatory to starting for Geo. tomorrow.

8th. Arrived in Atlanta . . . and took lodgings at the Trout House. Sebastapol taken by the Allies.

11th. The Fair opened today.

12th. Bought some cotton seed. One of the stalks of this cotton on exhibition had 528 balls. . . . We visited Mr. Thurmond's nursery, and here I . . . first saw the Scuppernong Grape, which is evidently a sort of muscadine. A Mr. Axt, a Frenchman, is trying to introduce the grape culture in Ga., he had some bunches at the fair that exceeded anything I ever saw.

14th. Arrived at Decatur.

27th. Wilk left me today. He returns to W. Tenn. . . . He is determined to be married during the coming year. I know no girl who is too good for him.

October 1st. Received today 1230 lbs. of bacon, for which I paid $150 in Chattanooga. . . . We had previously had to buy about $90 worth. This is farming with a vengeance!

7th. First killing frost—hope it will help Norfolk and Portsmouth. [Yellow fever was raging in these cities.]

12th. Pa and Ma are preparing to go to Virginia.

October 13, 1855. M. & C. cars first reached Huntsville.

14th. Dr. Finley preached for us the last time perhaps. . . . He and his family will accompany my parents to Va. The Dr. joins the Va. conference, and goes into the regular ministry. . . . He seems satisfied with his experience as a teacher.

15th. The anti-R. R. men held a convention today. Major Harris presides and Rev. Wilburn Allen drew up the memorial to Leg. This prays that a tax may not be levied, but if levied, upon such conditions as would make it sure that the road will be built. The conditions are the same as those proposed by Pryor and myself, save one which says the tax [is] not to be levied until ⅔ of stock taken to build the road from *Decatur* to *Montevallo.* This, of course, would postpone the completion of our road until the State gets into an internal improvement spirit, and that may be a long time off.
18th. Took the cars from Huntsville. Found Mrs. Sophy Davis & sisters, Miss Corrine Acklen,* etc., on board, going back from Miss *Babe* Watkins' wedding.** . . . She [Sophy] & Miss A. at once began to electioneer with me, the first for her husband (cand. for Solicitor), and the other for her brother, candidate for (Secty of State). We had a pleasant ride—going from the Madison Depot to H'ville on the construction train, as the Passenger train does not run to H'ville.

*Corrine Acklen was the daughter of William Acklen, long prominent in state politics.

**"Babe" Watkins was christened Mary Elizabeth, youngest daughter of Paul and Elizabeth Watkins, whose home Flower Hill, in Lawrence County, was a great favorite with many people. "Babe," a "great beauty and pet of her family," married James Branch, of the old Virginia family, on October 16, 1855.—Saunders, 239.

October 21, 1855. Mr. Geo. Steele, father of John, died suddenly of disease of the heart at his residence near Huntsville. He was the leading architect in this part of the country, and to his taste and skill, Huntsville owes much of its reputation for beauty.
23rd. Went down to river to meet Cousin Ed Lucas. He and Lev. Foote had just caught a catfish which weighed 69 pounds.
25th. Sam Peete stayed with me last night.
27th. Took dinner with Sloss, and tea with Mrs. Richardson. Received a letter from Ma, stating her safe arrival in Petersburg.
November 2nd. Tonight we worked on the bill, Sloss helping me a good deal about it.
3rd. Sloss told me on the way [to town] he regarded me as an industrious man. He is one of the few persons who knows this trait of my character.
4th. Our new pastor preached his first sermon to us today. His name is Gabberd. Took tea with Cousin Martha Fraser, she remarked, "I believe you have the cause of education more at heart than anybody I ever knew."

"In her system of popular education, Alabama owed more to Thomas Hobbs than to any other man."—Richard H. Rivers, obituary written for Hobbs, 1862.

5th. Meeting of the B'd of Trustees. James Donnell elected vice [president]. Hayes resigned.

Major James W. S. Donnell was the son of Rev. Robert Donnell. At nineteen Major Donnell married the fourteen-year-old Maria Jones, daughter of J. N. S. Jones. Tanner described them thus: "a man of wealth, great energy and industry, was highly educated, and perhaps no man in the county was fonder of reading, and certainly was not surpassed by any one for princely hospitality. . . . Mrs. Donnell is as near perfection in all things as is possible for human beings to attain. . . .They have a large family of children . . . "—Tanner, July 28, 1876.

THE LEGISLATURE 1855-1858

"His name is embalmed in the history of his state. It is for *her* that he has labored and made his hours that might have been hours of leisure, hours of toil."—Daniel Coleman, Athens *Herald,* March 8, 1861.

Thursday, November 6, 1855. Left home in a hard rain which continued all day. On the boat we were joined by Walker & Smith of Lauderdale; Thornton, Thorn, and Smith, of Franklin; and Sykes and Galloway [or Gallaway], of Lawrence.

Richard Wilde Walker, son of John Williams and Matilda Pope Walker, was born in Huntsville in 1823. He married Mary Simpson, daughter of John Simpson, of Florence. Henry D. Smith came to Lauderdale in 1828 from North Carolina, and became a planter. He served in the house for twelve years. Lewis Bedford Thornton was born in Virginia, graduated from the University of Virginia, and settled in Tuscumbia, where he taught school and practiced law. Francis Winfield Sykes, 1816–1883, son of James Turner and Sarah Dancy Sykes, graduated from La Grange, the University of Nashville, and Transylvania University Medical School. He served in both houses of the legislature. In 1844 Dr. Sykes married Susan Elizabeth Garth, daughter of Jesse Winston Garth. William M. Gallaway was born in 1823, the son of Wiley, fifth clerk of the circuit court. William, a judge of the circuit court, moved to Arkansas in 1859, and served in the legislature in that state. —Owen, IV, 1718, 1582, 1670, 1639.

8th. Breakfasted in Chattanooga, where we overtook Nick Davis & lady, Mr. Acklen & daughter (Corrine). . . . Stayed all night in Atlanta. . . . Reached Montgomery . . . stopped at the Exchange Hotel kept by Lanier. There we found a great many members, and almost as many candidates.

Clifford Anderson Lanier, "the boy clerk," was only eleven at this time. Nephew of the owner, Abe Watts, Clifford was joined at the hotel after the war by his frail brother, Sidney Clopton Lanier, who played his flute, devoured Swinburne, and worked on his first novel, *Tiger Lilies,* while clerking there.—Abernathy, 5–9.

10th. There is a great deal of electioneering, caucusing and wire-working. Walker of Lauderdale, Jackson of Autauga, Rice of Morgan, are candidates for Speaker; and Malone, Acklen, and Powell for the Presidency of Senate. Walker is my choice, altho' he is and has been, a Whig —he is a most courteous, dignified, and able gent.

Crawford Motley Jackson, 1820–1860, who represented Autauga in the legislature from 1843, was elected Speaker in 1857.—Owen, III, 888.

Green Pryor Rice, 1795–1857, was serving his last term in this year. He had served as president of the state senate in 1839.—Owen, IV, 1432.

James Robert Powell, afterwards known as the "Duke of Birmingham," played a colorful role in Alabama history. Born in Brunswick County, Virginia, in 1814, he ran hotels in Lowndesboro and Montgomery, Alabama. In 1836 he began running mail contracts and stagecoach lines, as a prime competitor of the Tuscaloosa tycoon, Robert Jemison. The two companies later merged to become Jemison, Powell, Ficklen and Company. Colonel Powell was first elected to the senate in 1853. During the Civil War, he furnished horses for an entire company, and gave ice to the Confederacy, for which he had been offered $40,000 by another concern. This ice, gathered on the Alabama River, was used in treatment of the wounded. The boundless enthusiasm of Powell for the development of Birmingham is well known. He left Birmingham to live on his plantation on the Yazoo River in Mississippi, and was shot to death in a tavern near there in 1883.—Hornaday, 23.

November 11, 1855. Heard Rev. Blue preach a very fine sermon.

The Reverend Oliver Rufus Blue, 1822–1893, was one of the most eminent of Methodist ministers in Alabama. He was the son of Neil Blue, who came from North Carolina to the present Montgomery in 1819, and was the second teacher at that place. He moved to Rocky Mount, Autauga County, where among his students were Bolling Hall and Albert Pickett. The church in which Reverend Blue preached was the same which had been saved from financial disaster by his father some years before. Matthew Powers Blue, author of the celebrated history of Montgomery, was a grandson of Oliver. —Owen, III, 166, 167.

12th. Went into an Anti-K.N. caucus this morn'g to nominate the officers of the House. After some discussion, Chapman of Mad., Rice. of Morg., and Cochran of [Barbour] withdrew, not being willing to abide the action of caucus.* Dick Walker was nominated on the first ballot and we soon got thro' with the selections. The Senate was similarly engaged at same time, Malone & Acklen were both beaten by Yancey, of Cherokee.** John Johnson was a candidate for doorkeeper of Senate, but just lost it in caucus. . . . The 2 houses were sworn in at 12 today by Judge Shorter.†

*John Cochran came to Benton County (now Calhoun) from Tennessee in 1835, first represented that county in 1839, and was returned twice before moving to Barbour County.

**Benjamin Cudworth Yancey, Jr., 1817–1891, was born in South Carolina, where his father was at one time a law partner of John C. Calhoun. After graduating from Yale in 1837, Benjamin came to Wetumpka, where he published the *Gazette* with his brother, William Lowndes Yancey. This was Yancey's first time to serve in the Alabama senate, although he had been a senator in South Carolina.—Owen, IV, 1819.

†Judge John Gill Shorter was born in Monticello, Georgia, in 1818, the son of General Clarke and Mary Butler Gill Shorter. He settled in Eufaula, and was admitted to the bar in 1838. After representing Barbour in both houses, he was appointed to succeed Judge Goldthwaite on the circuit bench, and served as Alabama's wartime governor.—Ibid., 1552.

November 13, 1855. Nick Davis is busily engaged in electioneering for the Solicitorship of the Huntsville circuit. I regard his election as of the utmost importance to him; being on a favorable turn of life, and anxious to do well, if he should now receive this office, it will be such encouragement as will probably complete his success, and render his good resolutions firm. So much interest do we feel in this matter, & so well satisfied that he is the best qualified candidate for the place, that we have given him permission to swap our votes in those elections where we are indifferent to all the candidates.

14th. It occurred to me that the Leg. ought to be opened each day with prayer; upon inquiry of the old members, they said the proposition had been often voted down, altho' all seemed to think well enough of it. After feeling the pulse of a good many, and failing to induce them to offer the matter again to the House, I offered a resolution today that the various ministers of the city should be invited in turn to open the caucus of the House. Smith, of Lauderdale, moved to lay on table, but the motion did not prevail, and my resolut. adopted by an overwhelming majority. Withers, of Mo[bile], Clanton, of Montg., and I were app. a committee to wait on them.

Jones Mitchell Withers, member of the prominent family of Madison and Limestone counties, was born in Huntsville in 1814. He moved to Mobile in 1841, where he practiced law and was a commission merchant. He resigned before completion of this legislative session, to become mayor of Mobile.—Brewer, 417.

James Holt Clanton, 1827–1871, of Georgia, was admitted to the bar in 1850, and settled in Montgomery. He became a brigadier general during the war, and afterwards served as the state attorney. It was in this capacity that he went to Knoxville in 1871, with the Alabama and Chattanooga Railroad case, and was shot down in the street by an angered participant. The town of Clanton in Chilton County was named for him.—Brewer, 466; American Guide Series, *Alabama,* 265.

November 15, 1855. The Speaker announced the standing Com's this mor'g. I was assured some days since that I should be at the head of Education Committee. The Speaker considers this second only to the Judiciary, and my appointment is very complimentary. Clanton & I, as a com'tee app. yesterday, called on the various ministers of [the] Gospel, all of whom cheerfully cooperated with the plan of saying prayers, except the Roman Cath. priest, who declined because, as he said, it was a part of their creed, to have as little to do with public matters as possible.
November 16, 1855. This mor'g the Rev. Mr. Blue (Meth. Ep.), attended in the House and said prayers—and thus is the system inaugurated, and for the first time the Leg. of Ala. has a sort of chaplaincy. . . . We generally meet at 10 A.M., and adjourn about 1 P.M.; but now we have our committees, and they will soon give us work enough to keep us employed all the time.
17th. House engaged with Senate in counting the official vote for Governor, which shows Winston elected by about 12,000 majority over Shortridge. . . . After the house adjourned, Pryor & I engaged upon our county bill, which we are anxious to bring forward as soon as possible. Judge G. P. Rice, of Morgan, informed P. today that he should oppose it hard & strong. But we do not fear that it will not pass. Senate passed a Reslu. to have prayer, too.
19th. Today we had the election for U. S. Senator. As I had been a member of the caucus wh. nominated him, I was obliged to vote for Fitzpatrick, altho' I did so very reluctantly. He is considered a man of political and personal integrity, and hence has some influence at Washington, but . . . I preferred either Yancey or Cochran. He [Fitzpatrick] was elected by a large majority today. The K. N.'s cast their vote for my colleague, Pryor, for the purpose of complimenting him. I would have gladly voted for him, but for the caucus. Fitz. received 79 votes, & Luke, 45.

Benjamin Fitzpatrick had served two terms as governor, and had been appointed to the U. S. Senate twice, to complete the unexpired terms of Dixon Hall Lewis and William Rufus King. In the thirty-fifth and thirty-sixth congresses, he served as president pro tempore of the U. S. Senate, and was president of Alabama's constitutional convention in 1865.—Owen, III, 582.

November 20, 1855. Pryor & I completed the draught of our bill—which we submitted to Judge Sam Rice, and received his approval.

Samuel Farrow Rice was elected to the supreme court in 1853, and in the following year became chief justice. His home stands on Monroe Street in Montgomery, and has subsequently been the home of the Semples, real estate office of John Hall Haardt (brother-in-law of the satirical sage of Baltimore, H. L. Mencken), and is now headquarters for the Alabama Historical Commission.

November 21st. Attended the [State Agricultural] Fair in procession. Gov. Winston opened it with a short and appropriate speech. . . . More plows were exhibited than at the Geo. Fair, and a very ingenious piece of furniture, which in a moment is converted from a wardrobe standing up, into a bedstead and washstand. It is manufactured of chestnut wood at Prattville.

A similar piece of furniture is illustrated in an 1855 Montgomery newspaper and called "Plimpton's Patent Secretary Bedstead."

23rd. Engaged on Committee in counting the money in the Treasury. As much of it consists of old mutilated notes of the State Bank, it is a slow and troublesome business.

26th. Today our Bill came into the House with the recommendation of the Judiciary that the bill do pass. We expected a fight upon it, and accordingly Pryor led off in a short speech, but expecting the unconstitutionality of the measure to be made the main point of attack, he was holding up his heavy fire for a reply. Manasco of Walker, made one of his scattering talks against us, and then I put in for about 20 minutes. The Speaker congratulated me upon my effort. The bill was ordered to a 3rd reading by 56 to 30.

November 27, 1855. We are caucusing every night—and what is worse, for judicial offices. Now this is against my principles, for the judiciary ought not to be selected for their politics. Nothing but my great anxiety for the election of Nick Davis would carry me where I cannot carry my principles.

29th. The bill came up . . . and was near being lost. Whereupon Pryor made a long and strong argument. . . . Rice, of Morgan, replied, but his speech had little force.

30th. So strong seems the opposition that it was tho't best that I should make some remarks. My sole object was to conciliate our opponents, and to keep down those who might otherwise speak against this. I spoke about 20 minutes, and succeeded pretty well. But W. P. Davis, of Benton, followed, and altho' a friend to the bill . . . he aroused a violent tempest by his abuse of those who held opposite opinions. In a few minutes he totally nullified whatever influence my remarks had had, and called upon Menasco, Smith of Lauderdale, etc. Cochran came to our

help, but altogether we were worsted by the course of events, and all from Davis' ill-conceived speech.
December 1st. Lynch, of Wilcox, spoke against us this mor'g, and immediately the vote was taken. It resulted much to our satisfaction—Ayes 61, Nays 26. A large party of us went out to spend the night with Dr. Chas. Lucas, and a jolly crowd it was.

Dr. Charles Lucas, brother of John Lucas, of Limestone, was one of the most prominent physicians of Montgomery County. He lived at Mt. Meigs, just east of the city. Letters written to his family in Limestone have been preserved, and are in the possession of William Lucas Keyes, descendant of John and Martha Hobbs Lucas. One of these, written after the Civil War, states that he had lost his home and lands, which were extensive, and was living in a little dependency to the rear of the big house.

December 2, 1855. Accompanied Mrs. Davis to Episcopal Church (St. John's), which was opened this day for the first time.
4th. Nick received a very large vote.
6th. Our bill has passed into the Gov.'s hands—We have some fears for it there, as he is known to be opposed to such.
7th. A bill to loan $500,000 to the M. & C. R. R. has come to us from the Senate. An animated discussion has sprung up, all the Anti-State Aid men are rallied against it, and it seems that they are determined to make this the test question on the subject of loans. There are in the Treasury about $800,000 of the bills of the State B'k & Branches—the Antis wish these to be burned, and we think by lending them to R. R.'s we get the interest upon them and make that much clear.
8th. Debate continues. . . . Today loan cut down to $400,000. . . . Nick Davis and party left. I presented Mrs. D. with a white japonica.
9th. Attended the new Ep. Church wh. was dedicated today. Bishop Elliott, of Ga., officiated.

Stephen Elliott, consecrated in 1841, was the first bishop of Georgia. In Blue's history, he does not mention the presence of Bishop Elliott, but stated: "The present St. John's Episcopal Church was consecrated by the Right Rev. N. H. Cobbs, the venerable and beloved bishop of the diocese, who was still acting, in addition, as rector of this parish. The Rev. H. S. Lay, happening to be in Montgomery at that time, upon invitation of the bishop, preached the dedicatory sermon. The original cost of the edifice was $27,000."

December 10, 1855. A rumor is afloat the Gov. will veto our bill.
12th. Today the Gov.'s veto of the Synodical College of Florence was received in our House and acted upon. The result was the bill incorporating the same; was passed over the veto by a large majority.

After Richard Rivers became president of La Grange College in 1854, he accepted the invitation of the city of Florence to locate the college in that place. There were several valid reasons for relocating the college, for it had steadily declined in effectiveness. Many staunch supporters of the college fought the move, and refused to allow transfer of the name. The new school in Florence was known as the Synodical Institute, which was incorporated as Wesleyan University, and was forerunner of the present University of North Alabama at Florence. Thomas Hobbs and Benjamin Maclin were among the trustees.—Owen, I, 600.

13th. Today . . . the Gov.'s private Secretary appeared and announced the veto of our Bill. . . . Before we could make any disposition of it, the House adjourned. Luke and I went to the Capitol and gave the message an attentive perusal. . . . Pres Keyes and I called on Miss Sallie Taylor.

Sallie was the daughter of William Henry Taylor, descendant of Thomas Taylor, who gave the land upon which the city of Columbia, South Carolina, was first laid out. They were related to the Wyches, of Brunswick County, as was the Hobbs family. The Taylors lived on McDonough Street in Montgomery. In 1860 Sallie married Col. W. A. Sanford, who served as the state's attorney general.—Owen, IV, 1653.

14th. Having made a faithful and successful effort to have all our friends present this morning, we took up the bill and I made a few remarks upon it and the vote was taken. We had 62, one more than we had on the passage. So the bill was carried and a few moments afterwards was again passed by the Senate. So the bill is a law in spite of the Veto. This is the 3rd Veto of his Excellency which has been nullified—and the disposition is increasing to oppose them.

During his two terms as governor John Anthony Winston vetoed more than thirty measures, and became known as the "veto governor."—Owen, IV, 1790.

December 15, 1855. Bob Brickell came to room with us. I suspect he came down to run for a place on the Sup. Court Bench, should there be a vacancy.

16th. Tonight we had some sacred music in the parlor—Pfister playing on a singular instrument like a melodion, only he blew it up with his elbow as he played.

Armand P. Pfister was a popular bookseller and musician in Montgomery.—Owen, IV, 1355.

17th. Today the house agreed to Senate Resolution to adjourn from 21st inst. to 7th Jan'y. . . . Luke and Nick are going home. . . . I have no business to take me there, or impatient wife who urges my return.—Alone! Alone!

18th. Tonight I met by appointment Col. Jos. Taylor, Chm'n of Ed. in the Senate, and Mr. Perry, Supt. of Ed. We canvassed the amendments proposed in the School System. At a previous meeting of the two Com's, some trouble grew up from the opposition of certain members of Senate Com. . . . we agreed to many changes proposed by the Supt. After Taylor left the room, I revealed to Perry my plan of a working school. He was greatly pleased—said it not only reflected credit on my head & heart but would accomplish the greatest benefits. He has promised to hear more and all about it.

December 20, 1855. Gov. Winston was inaugurated today at 12 in the Hall of the House. The seats of the members were given up to the ladies and we stood in the aisles. . . . Luke and Nick Malone started home tonight. . . . Attended the Inaugural Ball tonight. It was a gay affair.

21st. Scarcely a quorum present, and they indisposed to work. Received a letter from Ma, saying she would leave P'burg on next Monday, and that I must meet them in Atlanta. . . . Visited Miss Fannie Gayle with Pres Keyes.

Fannie, daughter of Matthew Gayle, Jr., and niece of Governor John Gayle, became the first wife of Pres Keyes.—Owen, III, 973.

Attached to the diary is this article from the Decatur *Journal*:

At a meeting called by the citizens of Decatur, on the 18th inst., C. F. M. Dancy was called to the Chair, and Wm. R. White, appointed Secretary. On motioned [*sic*] the Chair appointed E. W. Parker, Esq., Maj. R. N. Walden; Capt. M. Mahan, J. Fisher, C. J. Eden, W. G. Locke, and Dr. A. A. Burleson,* a Committee to express by Preamble and Resolutions the object of the meeting. The Committee presented the following Preamble and Resolutions, which were unanimously adopted:

Whereas—We have heard of the final passage of the Tax Bill of Limestone County, appropriating the sum of $200,000 for the Alabama and Tennessee Central Rail Road, in despite of the veto power of the Governor—and, inasmuch as the Bill expressed the sentiments of the majority of the voters of Limestone, a matter of Legislation violating no principle of the Constitution, and whose expediency should be determined alone by the Local Authorities, seeking its passage. Now, inasmuch as this veto power exercised in this instance, betrays an inconsistency reconcileable alone with the fogy spirit in which he brandishes this veto fire-brand, with a recklessness that becomes the days in which arbitrary rules governed and not wise principles, and as expressive of the debt of gratitude which we owe those members of the Legislature, who gallantly contended for its passage, and showed by their acts that they had rights to defend, and a will to exercise them—men who showed no fawning sycophancy to power in high places . . . who, resolute, self-willed and erect, displayed a firmness of purpose that will claim our most endearing regard as long as memory cherishes the proud trophies of the past. Therefore, be it *Resolved,* 1st. That we hereby tender to our Senator, Mr. Malone, and Messrs. Hobbs and Pryor, Representatives from Limestone County, whose efficient co-operation contributed to the passage of the Bill, and who have signally performed their duty to their constituents, and the onward progress of the age, our highest considerations of admiration and esteem. *Resolved,*

2nd. That the only panegyric we can bestow upon John Anthony Winston, may be found in the action of the Legislature, disregarding this monstrous veto power. *Resolved,* 3rd. To our representaive, Hon. G. P. Rice, who took so bold a position against our sister County, so nearly allied in interest with us, we will do for him, in charity, what the Painter of Iphigenia did in skill, throw a mantle over the features of the victim. *Resolved,* 4th. That ih[*sic*] this we are vindicating the Republican Principle of the people, that majorities should govern in all matters not unconstitutional, and that the exercise of the Veto Power, save in the defence of constitutional rights, or to prevent hasty Legislation, is a usurpation too intolerable to be borne, where the popular voice is the highest political privilege. *Resolved,* 5th. That we will cordially welcome Messrs. Malone, Pryor, & Hobbs, to the hospitalities of our Town, on their return home from the Legislature. . . . On motion, the meeting adjourned to the firing of 99 rounds, in honor to the 99 supporters of the Bill in the Legislature . . .

*Dr. Aaron A. Burleson was said to have been the first white child born in Morgan County, the Burleson family being among the very first to settle in the area. For an account of the family in Alabama and their prominence in Texas, see Saunders, 72.

December 22, 1855. The chief object of my remaining here is to prepare the new School law to be proposed by the Committee on Education. There will be a great rush to get thro' when the Leg. reassembles and we wish to have the bill ready to introduce at once. Our Committee is behindhand, owing to the pressure of other business. I do not believe it was right for the Leg. to adjourn, and I will work ahead during the recess.

The most significant portion of this school bill was the proposal to set up county superintendents of education, rather than having only the state superintendent.

25th. Arrived in Atlanta about 7 A.M. (fare $7), and stopped at the Atlanta Hotel. It is the most gloomy Christmas I ever saw—raining incessantly and cold. Staid in house all day, reading *Harper's* Mag.
26th. At 3 this aft. they [Pa and Ma] arrived. . . . walked out to Thurmond's Nurseries, where I purchased one hundred apple, peach, and grape trees to be set out next spring, when I get home. Ma bro't me a nice present from Cousin Julia Meade—a shaving case, with nail & tooth brush, etc.
27th. Left Atlanta at 3:30 this mor'g and arrived in Montg. about 4 P.M. Atlanta in 1845 contained but one house, and now it has a population of 10,000 souls, with extensive workshops, and factories, and is a beautiful instance of the development of a country by railroads. Cochran & Howard are the only members of the House left in the city, so far as I know.

William B. Howard, 1816–1876, graduated from Princeton in 1839, and represented Mobile in this session of the legislature. "A nobler spirit never breathed in the legislative halls . . ."—William Garrett, 361–64.

December 29, 1855. It rains incessantly. The river is very high, and the boats are taking out large loads of cotton.

30th. Bishop Andrew preached at the Methodist Church.

31st. And now comes the close of another year. . . . Were I not attached to my country home, this city would possess some charms, perhaps—if I had political aspiration, my present position might be a fortunate stepping-stone to a higher place. . . . I am frequently thrown into the company of ladies, and do not hesitate to inform all who might think otherwise, that I have no desire to marry. With what different eyes do I now regard the sex! Involuntarily, I compare them with a standard which none equal.

Tuesday, January 1, 1856. All families here keep open house on New Year's, and expect their friends to call. I called at Mrs. Shorter's where Miss Susan Norriss is staying, and at Mr. Ware's.

Mrs. John Gill Shorter was wife of the wartime Governor. Mr. Ware was probably Robert J. Ware, who represented Montgomery in the legislature for several years.

3rd. I have spoken to Mr. Antrobus, an artist of this city, to sketch a design I gave him for a state seal. The present seal was adopted when this was a territory and is totally meaningless.

5th. Went to the depot to meet the returning members.

An appended newspaper article, unidentified, is attache d at this date. It was written after presentation of an inkstand to the speaker of the house. Mr. Cochran presented it, and ended his speech with these words:

> All good men everywhere pray that a nationality of our rights and of fraternal feeling may speedily bind us as equals to the government. . . . But, sir, should this prayer not be vouchsafed to us, let us stand shoulder to shoulder in resisting oppression and insult—and all unite in the prayer that our future historian may dip from this stand the ink which records our triumph under the banner, "*Equality in the Union, or Independence out of it!*"

9th. This morning I was nominated by the delegation from our Congressional District as one of the delegates to the Cincinnati Convention —Henry D. Smith, of Lauderdale, as the other. . . . Resolutions commendative of Gov. Winston's policy in regard to the loans to R. Roads were introduced by Geo. Gayle, of Dallas, and after producing the utmost confusion, were withdrawn.

George Washington Gayle, of Selma, was such an ardent secessionist that he was arrested after the Civil War by Federal authorities "for conspiracy in the assassination of President Lincoln," but was discharged without a trial.—Owen, III, 646.

January 10, 1856. Gov. vetoed the loan to the M. & C. R. R., don't know on what grounds, as the message was sent to Senate.* Sam Tate, the pres't of the Road, is here with the Security required by the bill, $224,000 of which is personal.** It is now tho't to be very doubtful whether we can pass it in the Senate, as Taylor, of Greene, who was a warm advocate of it before, comes back after the recess, violently opposed to it.

*A portion of Gov. Winston's message in vetoing the bill to make a loan to the Memphis and Charleston Railroad on January 9, 1856, stated: "Experiment teaches us that any departure from the legitimate and simple purposes of government brings, as inevitably as a departure from physical law, a speedy punishment, and admonishes those who have fixed ideas of public policy of the danger of any abandonment of principle in legislation and matters of government. The experience of Alabama is fruitful of the bitter consequences of making expediency paramount to principle."—Brewer, 59.

**Colonel Sam Tate was still engaged in the reworking and building of the Alabama portion of the M. & C. R. R. at the outbreak of the war. In 1869, he agreed to furnish all the material for the construction of the South and North Railroad from Decatur to Montgomery. He was ordered to build the road as cheaply as humanly possible, and was forced to run it with "more curves, more curves, more steep grades," as John T. Milner expressed it. This railroad became a part of the Louisville and Nashville system.—Armes, 218.

January 11, 1856. Veto of the loan (extension) to the Mobile and Ohio R.R.

15th. Began my argument in favor of the Central Rail Road. The original bill proposed Commissioners should be appointed who should employ engineers to survey all the routes proposed to connect N. & S. Ala., and appropriated $400,000 per annum until the Road selected was completed. Belser offered a substitute, simply appropriating $20,000 out of the per cent for the survey. I spoke about half hour, when the time came for the election of Supreme [Court] Judge. Of course, I have the floor tomorrow.

16th. Special order did not come up. I wish it had done so, for as this day one year ago we finished the survey at Elyton, it would have been a pleasant coincidence that in the Leg., I should on the anniversary have been advocating that project.

17th. Continued and concluded my argument. I am not myself well pleased with the effort—have made better speeches on the stumps of Limestone. The excitement in regard to the M. & C. R. R. and Bob Brickell's election has made my room the headquarters of these advocates. No time was allowed me for preparation. The subjoined extracts show the reporters' views of the efforts. Many persons congratulated me on my success, and Benj. Gardner, reporter to the *Journal,* declared it the best speech of the session.

The question pending, when the bill was last under consideration, was the substitute offered by Mr. Staton, appropriating $25,000 out of the two and three per cent fund, for a survey of the several routes, and that the report of the engineers be submitted to the next Legislature. Mr. Hobbs, being entitled to the floor, resumed and concluded his very eloquent and able argument in support of the bill. Taking bold ground in favor of State aid, and urging the importance of the great work proposed by the bill. His remarks were listened to with great attention, and when he resumed his seat, was applauded by the House and lobby. Mr. Menasco offered an amendment, by adding: And one survey to commence on the South side of the Tennessee river near the mouth of Bean Creek, thence in the direction of Montevallo, and may extend to the city of Montgomery, via Wetumpka. . . . Mr. Cochran addressed the house in favor of the measure, and intimated an intention when in order, to strike out all that refers to the survey of the particular routes, and leave it to the Engineers to select the best and most practicable route, for a first class Rail Road, connecting the waters of the Tennessee valley with the waters of the Mobile bay, and report the same to the next Legislature. . . . The hour arrived for the election of a Supreme Court Judge, and the Senate appeared within the Hall of the House, and entered upon the balloting—Messrs. Stone, Brickell, and Clopton, still being in nomination. [Stone won by only two votes over Brickell, 61 to 59.]

George Washington Stone, 1811–1894, was born in Bedford County, Virginia. He was the grandson of Jabez Leftwich, who moved from there to Madison County, Alabama. Stone was admitted to the bar in 1834, was a partner of William P. Chilton, elected associate justice in this election, and chief justice in 1884.—Owen, IV, 1628.

David Clopton, 1820–1892, graduated with first honors from Randolph-Macon College in 1840, came to Alabama in 1844, and entered into law practice with his brother-in-law, Robert F. Ligon. He was elected to the Confederate Congress, and became a supreme court justice in 1884. He was married three times: to Martha Ligon, Mary Chambers, and Virginia Tunstall Clay.—Owen, III, 352.

18th. Received a request in writing today from a number of members of the House to allow my speech to be printed—think I shall do so.
19th. Today the M.& C. loan passed in senate over the veto. . . . We worked upon the Central Road and made some progress.

Appended to the diary is the following article from the Montgomery *Advertiser and Gazette:*

Thursday, January 17, 1856. The House met pursuant to adjournment. Prayer by Rev. Bishop Cobbs. The call of the counties having been suspended, Mr. Sykes offered a resolution providing for evening sessions on those days when no such sessions are held. . . . the House proceeded to the consideration of the special order, which was the substitute to the bill to build the proposed Central Rail Road. . . . Mr. Hobbs, of Limestone, continued the remarks he had commenced on Tuesday last in favor of the substitute, and which were cut off by the . . . hour of adjournment. . . . He stated that George Washington was the father of the internal improvement system in the United States, having presented the first definite plan of connecting the Ohio valley with the ocean. He showed that the Appalachian range of mountains had never been penetrated except by State aid, and that in every instance the investment had been profitable and judicious. He examined the finances of the various states which have engaged in Internal Improvements. Taking up our own State he showed how many efforts had been made by chartering companies, to connect North and South Alabama, and how all had failed. He argued that Alabama had more reasons for a rail road connection with the Ohio valley than the other seaboard states, because the difficulties in the way are less; that we have a large territory yet in the hands of the General Government; that our population is annually decreasing; that our mineral resources equal any other State, and from their geographical position, will have the monopoly of supplying the Gulf trade, which will be inconceivably great when the Amazon and Pacific markets are fairly opened. He urged the immediate survey of the mountains because the fund set apart for the purpose is now on hand, and all parts of the State are equally interested in expending it for this purpose . . . he drew a picture of Alabama as she should be, and described in detail the immensity of her resources, and the grandeur of her natural advantages . . .

January 23rd, 1856. Luke left for home, the delicate condition of Mrs. P. requiring his presence.* Senator Malone now comes to room with me. This afternoon in a thin House the bill came up unexpectedly for survey of Central Road. . . . lost—41 ayes, 42 nays. We were struck dumb.

*Apparently Luke Pryor was not aware that his daughter, Frances Snow, was born two days before his leaving for home.

24th. I got hold of Brown, of Marion, and never let him loose til he agreed to move a reconsideration. This he did, and a motion was made to postpone until Monday—this was made a test vote, and we were again beaten, ayes 48, noes 44. I now felt badly whipt. Attended the Ball (masked) of the Young Americans.

25th. This morn. in Committee of Whole took up the School law, examined some of the sections when Com. rose to take up special order. The clerk announced this morg. that he mistook the vote of yesterday, postponing the bill of Central Road; it should have been ayes 43, nays 44. We drummed up our men immediately and reconsidered *and passed the bill*—ayes 47, nays 40. I feel better now—decidedly.

January 26, 1856. Today we had quite an excitement in the House upon the reading of the message of the Gov., vetoing the Wesleyan University at Florence. It is the most indecorous State paper I ever read.

Sunday, January 27, 1856. Rev. and Hon. H. W. Hilliard preached a fine sermon.

Henry Washington Hilliard, 1802–1892, was generally recognized as being second only to William Lowndes Yancey as the leading orator of the state. He taught, preached occasionally in the Methodist Church, was a U. S. Congressman, and minister to Brazil. After his first Congressional speech, former President John Quincy Adams crossed the room to congratulate him.—Owen, III, 814.

31st. Hooper's paper of today very unexpectedly contained the subjoined notice:

> Survey of the Central Road—This, *the great measure of the session*, is now understood to be safe, unless a Veto shall throw it back and cause it to be lost for want of time. The Bill passed the House two or three days since, and may at this writing have gone through the Senate, though we have not yet learned the fact. As our readers generally know, it appropriates a fund ($25,000) for the ascertainment of a railway line to connect North and South Alabama; and provides for the election of three Commissioners to have surveys made with a view to the selection of that route which . . . is best. *Mr. Hobbes*, of Limestone, a gentleman who, it is agreed on all hands, is truly one of the sons of Alabama of whom she may well be proud, and who, we trust, is destined to a long career of usefulness to our people and of distinguished honor to himself, will very certainly be named as one of the commissioners. . . . He is a Democrat and a North Alabamian, and being one of his political opponents, it affords us real pleasure to state *the fact*, that men of all parties have the most unbounded confidence in his capacity, his thorough enlightenment, and his elevated State pride. It is lucky for Alabama that just at this particular juncture, and for this particular work, a man is found possessing the qualifications and position of Mr. Hobbes. It seems to be yielded, that East Alabama is entitled to a representation in the commission, and Montgomery is looked to, to supply them. Three gentlemen have been spoken of in that connection, in our presence—Col. Charles T. Pollard, F. M. Gilmer, Esq., and Col. F. Bugbee.* The selection of any of these would be satisfactory, in our opinion. Of Col. Pollard, we do not hesitate to say, that we believe him to possess, in regard to railroad construction and management, a higher ability, *by a very great deal*, than any other Southern man connected with works of improvements. We question if his superior is to be found in the Union—we mean as to the peculiar endowments which fit a man to comprehend great plans and to administer their affairs. Mr. Gilmer has given much attention to the subject of the North and South Alabama connection and would bring into the commission a vast deal of accurate information, a fine business experience and a reliable judgement. Col. Bugbee has, for years, studied the whole subject and was one of the earliest advocates of the work . . ."

[*31st.*] Unexpectedly called on to urge the prosecution of the Geological survey—I mean called on, by the fewness of its advocates.

*Charles Teed Pollard became one of the most important railroad builders in the South. Among roads to his credit were the Atlanta and West Point, Montgomery and Selma, and Alabama and Florida, all of which he served as president. His wife's father, John Scott, gave the land upon which St. John's Episcopal Church was built, as well as the free burial grounds in Oakwood Cemetery, Montgomery.—Owen, IV, 1373.

As a young man, Franklin Meriwether Gilmer crosed the mountains near Elyton on his way from Kentucky to South Alabama. The red ore which he saw there became an obsession to him. He founded the Red Mountain Iron and Coal Company, the Oxmoor furnace, and worked against tremendous odds after the Civil War to get the railroad built from Montgomery to Decatur.

Colonel Francis Bugbee, 1794–1877, came from Ashford, Connecticut, and Yale University to Jefferson County in 1821, and to Montgomery five years later. He was a trustee at the University of Alabama, a member of the legislature, and a Whig.—Owen, III, 252, 658.

Friday, February 1, 1856. The School law came up this morning. As soon as the amendments proposed and adopted in Com. of Whole were adopted by the House, Curry moved the previous question.* This made quite a sputter among the opponents. The strongest speech made against it was by Woolsey, of Dallas, and the Com. on Ed. insisted that I should reply.** This I did, answering his objections, but not fluently and smoothly. However, the House and lobby applauded when I sat down. The Bill was ordered to a 3rd reading. . . . Attended at night a party given by the Blues. My speech is in the printer's hands.

*Jabez Lamar Monroe Curry, 1825–1903, is credited with having made more speeches on the subject of public education than any other man in the state. "You tell me you are too poor to educate our boys and girls. I tell you you are too poor not to educate them," he told the legislative members. Dr. Curry was chosen as one of the two representatives from Alabama in the National Hall of Fame, Washington, D.C.—National League of Penwomen, 139.

**Benjamin Minthorne Woosley, 1823–1886, served as state salt commissioner during the Civil War, and returned to Selma after its termination. Woolsey's mother was married to Bishop J. O. Andrew in 1844, the same year in which the issue of his owning slaves developed, and caused the division of the Methodist Church.—Owen, IV, 1807.

February 2, 1856. Gov.'s veto of the Lunatic Asylum came in—the special friends of the bill tho't they were strong enough to pass it, but upon a trial, failed. Motion to reconsider made and undecided when we adjourned.

4th. Luke was elected tonight one of the electors of the K[now] N[othing] Party now assembled in Convention here—Elector for our district. Hilliard and Clemens for the State at large.

Jeremiah Clemens, 1814–1865, of Huntsville, was a brilliant lawyer, and a most personable man. Virginia Clay-Clopton described the impression that Clemens made on her when she was fifteen, as "the personification of manly beauty. His head was as shapely as Tasso's . . . and in his eyes there burned a romantic fire that enslaved me from the moment their gaze rested on me." Although Clemens signed the secession ordinance in 1861, he was a staunch Unionist during the Civil War. His home in Huntsville will soon be restored, and used as offices.—Brewer, 362; Clay-Clopton, 13.

5th. Central Survey taken up in the Senate and amended . . . just what we dreaded. . . . In the House we passed the Insane Asylum Bill over the veto. . . . Attended the K. N. meeting tonight at Capitol and heard two speeches, from Judge Hopkins and H. W. Hilliard.

Arthur Francis Hopkins, 1794–1866, began practice in Huntsville in 1816, moved to Lawrence County in 1819, and represented that county in the first constitutional convention. He left the supreme court bench to go into the U. S. Senate, and was temporary president of the Whig convention of 1844, in which Henry Clay was nominated. He became president of the Mobile and Ohio Railroad. Hopkins' second wife, Julia Opie Gordon, was buried in Arlington Cemetery because of her outstanding nursing service during the Civil War, through which she was known as the "Florence Nightingale of the Confederacy."—Owen, III, 843.

February 7, 1856. Heard a part of a speech by W. L. Yancey tonight. He is a very fine speaker, but not equal in my opinion to Pope Walker, whom I regard the best in Ala.
8th. Senate sent back our School Law with several amendments. One is giving the election of the Co. Sup't to the people instead of the court of county commissioners. The question now is, shall we adopt their amendments, or endanger the passage of the bill by insisting on our version? Tonight there was a misunderstanding in the Senate between the President, Yancey, and Jamieson and Baker. President resigned his office, and altho' he was unanimously re-elected, he had not accepted when the Senate adjourned.

Although Hobbs clearly says "Jamieson," he is referring to Robert Jemison, senator from Tuscaloosa, who moved from Georgia to Pickens County early in the nineteenth century, and built one of the finest plantation complexes in the state, The Gardens. In 1836 he moved to Tuscaloosa County, and built a plantation home, Cherokee. In the year 1856 he was completing a town house on the Greensboro Road in Tuscaloosa, which now serves as that city's public library. It was he who joined forces with Colonel James Powell to form the leading stagecoach line in the state. Robert Jemison was not known for his docile nature; few empire builders are!—Owen, III, 902; National League of Penwomen, 87–95.

Benjamin H. Baker, 1811–1863, was representing Russell County in the legislature.—Brewer, 516.

February 9, 1856. Senate took up the Bill to burn the Bank bills. As all the loans to the R. R.'s were made upon the supposition that they would be used for that purpose, of course, the greatest excitement prevails—increased by the fact that a small majority of the Senate is in favor of burning. The Senate did not adjourn tonight until 12 o'clock, nor for dinner or supper. We had the same excitement this mor'g in the House and spent several hours of maneuvering to prevent a vote. A majority here, too, is in favor of burning. The majority in the Senate is caused by Wilson, of Jackson, and Yancey refusing to vote for the loan to the Ala. & Miss. R. R. They ought to have done so, as Cocke had voted for all the other loans. There is no telling where or when this excitement will end.

Jack Fleming Cocke, 1812–1897, was serving in the Senate from Perry County, which was on the proposed route of the Alabama and Mississippi Railroad.—Owen, III, 365.

11th. The excitement still up—the morning and afternoon passed in skirmishing. We had no night session—because everybody wanted to hear Miss Logan as Julia in *The Hunchback.* Her acting is so much tamer than Mrs. Farrin's that we scarcely appreciated it.

Olive Logan, 1839–1909, was a fledgling in the theater, having made her debut at Wallack's Theatre in 1854. Maria Ann Russell Farrin was a veteran actress and had been in the theater since 1824. Her largest audiences were in Mobile, New Orleans, and St. Louis.—Gabriel, XIV, 170, 230.

February 12th, 1856. We beat them today. A motion was made and carried to postpone the bill-burning Bill until Thursday. . . . We carried it by 3.
13th. Saw Miss Logan as *Adrienne the Actress*, and liked her much better. . . . she sang the Marseilles Hymn, which brought down the house.
14th. The apportionment bill of the Senate does not change the Senatorial districts, while the House Bill grouped Limestone and Lawrence. I was therefore glad today when the House agreed to Senate Bill.
15th. Our resolution to adjourn at 12 today was rescinded, and we remained in session until 6 P.M. to allow the Governor to sign the bills. He pocketed the bill for annual sessions, altho' he had recommended it in his annual message. . . . left in company with a large no. of members per R. R. The Central Survey was not reached in the Senate, and this is the only Bill in which I felt much interest which was not past [*sic*].
16th. Reached Atlanta to breakfast, and Chatnga to supper, where we lay over for the night.
February 17th, 1856. Reached Bridgeport safely and took S. B. *Fanny Malone*, which brought us safely to Decatur. . . . Mrs. Sallie Bettie Binford died at her father's today after a protracted illness.

Sallie Bettie was born Sarah Elizabeth Richardson, daughter of William and Anne Davis Richardson, in 1831. She married Dr. Littleberry Binford, 1826–1891, son of Addison.

March 1, 1856. Today, altho' it was raining, I set out about 500 ft. of osage orange hedge. . . . Some body must try this thing of hedging, and I can as well bear the sneer of those who are always ready to laugh at a failure because they never attempt anything, as anybody else.
5th. Steele returned [from Huntsville] with me. My object is now to

have the line of road across this county surveyed as soon as possible, and that John should be employed to do it. He has been successfully engaged in teaching [at] Greene [*sic*] Academy.

Green Academy, Huntsville, was chartered by the Mississippi Territorial Legislature in 1812, the first such institution established in the Territory. Until the founding of La Grange College, Green Academy was the only school in North Alabama offering higher education for boys.—Betts, 38–40.

6th. We drove to Cousin Edmund Lucas' and brought home Pet and her 3 puppies. . . . We named the young ones "Jack Steele," "Nick Davis," and "Dick Walker." . . . Black cow Dinah took the Devon bull "Mac" which I got from Pryor.

10th. We visited some of our acquaintances & dined with Mrs. Maclin. Uncle started for a trip of pleasure to Louisville and Cin. on Saturday. Court is in Session. Judge Sydenham Moore, appointee of Winston, presiding. This is in consequence of the law passed by our Leg., requiring the Judges to rotate throughout the state.

Sydenham Moore, 1817–1862, son of Dr. Alfred Moore of Limestone, was married to Amanda Hobson of Greensboro, and practiced law in that place. He was a U. S. Congressman at the time of secession, was wounded in the knee at the battle of Seven Pines, and died soon after.—Owen, IV, 1235.

March 19, 1856. Went to town today to see if I could not get somebody to consent to run for County Superintendent instead of myself. Tried Messrs. Mendum and Stith Malone, but they declined. I am so anxious that the new law should have a fair trial that, if no one else will undertake it, I shall.

24th. Easter Monday, negroes all taking holiday.

25th. Planted a paper of White Lupines sent out from Patent office . . . used as a fertilizer to be ploughed when green. . . . Pa, Ma and Mrs. Childs came from H'ville. I waited breakfast for them—the train now reaching our depot at 7½ A.M.

Mrs. Jane Hamilton Childs, known as "Madam Childs," came to Huntsville from Maryland in 1842, and opened a girls' school. She then became vice-president of the Bascom Institute there, before coming to Athens as president of the Female Institute. She brought her own furniture to the school in Athens, giving "the interior a grace equal to its classic exterior, and made Athens College comparable with the finest in the East." Since it was not then the practice for a college to furnish anything other than the building, she leased Founder's Hall for a five-year period, paying $300 annually, furnished it for both boarding and teaching facilities, and was to keep it in repair. In 1869 she sold all her furnishings at public auction in Athens, after having protected the girls in her charge through the trying days of siege and occupation by Federal forces during the Civil War.—Griffin, 13.

26th. Mr. John Antrobus, an artist whom I engaged in Montg. to paint my parents' portraits, arrived this mor'g.

27th. This afternoon he made the first sketch of Pa, Ma, and myself.

March 28, 1856. Mr. A. is the most rapid workman I ever saw in his art, seeming to do with a few quick strokes of the brush what most artists take a long time to perform. He says he can paint 7 portraits in a week.

31st. Mrs. Luke Pryor and Miss Mary Pryor are sitting to Mr. Antrobus.

April 1st. He finished our portraits today. I like them very much, and think them good likenesses. Mrs. Childs likes the pictures and the artist. Came down to depot with Mrs. Muse and Ann Eliza Echols.

7th. Meeting of the corporators of the Tenn. & Ala. Central R. R. I was elected one. McDonald elected President. Mason resigned. The Board of Corps. authorized the President to employ engineers, etc. He immediately employed Steele, and the survey is to be commenced as soon as instruments can be obtained. R. R. dinner at Huntsville, couldn't attend on account of our own R. R. meeting.

9th. Procured the consent of the M. & C. Company that their agent at the Mooresville depot should act as P. M. A P. O. has been established there, and called "Fertilis"—a name which I suggested to Gen. Houston, and which he has done me the honor to accept. It has this recommendation at least, that there is no other office in the Union of the same name.

10th. Arranged my claim for damages against the M. & C. Company. . . . I have accordingly received certificate 889 for 40 shares ($1000) of their stock.

11th. Today's *Herald* contained the subjoined communications. The address was written hurriedly by myself.

The article is a bid for the support of the people for the proposed calling of a constitutional convention. One of the principal areas for needed change was in legislative elections and sessions. It stated that "in the present threatening condition of national affairs," it was deemed necessary to return to an annual, rather than a biennial, system. The article was signed by John N. Malone, Luke Pryor, and Thomas Hobbs.

April 13, 1856. Attended church in Mooresville—and dined with Ruff Gamble and his bride—a pleasant, pretty woman. Ed & Peter Garrett & Sam Peete were there—they expressed warmly their thanks to me for the new P. office.

Ruffin Gamble married Helen, daughter of James M. and Susan Dunbar Girault, of Natchez, Mississippi. They were close relatives of Sir William Dunbar, heir to a Scottish title, who came to America, was a brilliant agriculturist and scientist, and built The Forest, near Natchez.—Kane, 43; Gamble mss.; personal interviews with Mrs. John Girault Gamble, 1964.

19th. My birthday. 30 today, and what have I accomplished in these 30 years which has benefitted any body?

25th. Busily engaged in making preparations for the setting out of the party of engineers. Steele has gone to Phila. to purchase instruments, and is daily expected back; so soon as he returns the work will be begun. Townsend, Levin Foote, and I are the Executive Committee to fit out the party. I have not yet decided whether I shall make one of the party; business at home requires my attention, but Steele says I must go.

27th. Mrs. Gen. Houston's remains were buried today. She died of pneumonia in Washington a few days since. Gen. H. seems much smitten, and says he doesn't know when he will return.

General George Houston had married Mary Beaty, daughter of Robert Beaty, in 1835. In 1861 Houston married Ellen Irvine, daughter of Florence attorney James Irvine.—Owen, III, 848.

May 2, 1856. Steele arrived this mor'g, accompanied by Mr. Schmitt, a German who will assist him. . . . We went to town to dinner, and afterwards on horseback to the house of W. W. Phillips where we stayed all night. Our object is to reconnoitre the Elk hills.

Warren Phillips, 1817–1890, son of Thomas, was a successful merchant, and a most personable one. "He was always a favorite, and deservedly so, and if his body was as big as his soul, he would be as big as New Garden Camp Ground. . . . W. W. Phillips was married to the beautiful Miss Bridgeforth of Giles County, Tennessee. Quite a troop of his friends from town attended. . . . We had a big house warming that night for sure; big roaring fires, table loaded with good things, plenty of darkies to wait on the crowd; boys and girls playing 'thimble,' 'grind the bottle,' 'Old Uncle Jake grinned at me,' etc. Everybody was big happy, especially Warren and his lovely young bride."—Tanner, July 7, 1876.

3rd. Phillips went with us down to "Smith's Hollow," to where the Tenn. Company ended their line—thence to dinner with Squire Billy Brown, and thence up the Hughey Hollow and home to Athens.

May 4th. Came down home to meet the Echols boys, who come down tomorrow from Huntsville.

Larkin and David Echols were sons of William Holding and Mary Hobbs Echols of Huntsville. Both Larkin and David were deceased by 1882, when the lands of William Echols were sold; the widows of each were mentioned in Madison County records.

May 5, 1856. The Corps of Engineers set out for the Elk River hills.
6th. The party consists of Steele and Schmitt . . . Larkin and David Echols, Jim Coman, Tyus, Murrah & Grigsby, & 2 hired hands. . . . We stopped at Bryant Holmes' and slept in his barn.
19th. This afternoon left the party, in order to make preparations for my trip to Cincinnati.
24th. Took the cars this morning—arrived at Tuscumbia landing about 1 P.M. The S. B. *R. M. Patton No. 2* soon came down from Florence, bringing Dick Walker, Patton, Kennedy. Our party was afterwards increased by the addition of Hon. G. S. Houston & 2 sisters, H. D. Smith & daughter, William Cooper, Bunch, etc.
26th. Arrived at Paducah about 5 P.M., where we heard of the violent caneing [*sic*] given to Chas. Sumner by Brooks, of S. C. This, I fear, will produce no good, happening as it does just at a time when it seems so important that [there be] as much kind feeling as possible.

This incident "crystallized sentiment" against slavery more, perhaps, than any other single event to that time. Charles Sumner of Massachusetts, culminated his scathing attacks on slavery in May, 1856, when he made vituperative speeches against Senator Butler of South Carolina. Preston Brooks, a relative of Butler, entered Sumner's office and struck him so very forcefully that the latter slumped to the floor. A sequel to the Sumner caning took place on July 16th, 1856, when B. W. Vicks of South Carolina beat Jacob Stanwood of Massachusetts for stating that the attack on Sumner was a "brutal and cowardly" act.—Montgomery *Daily Journal,* July 30, 1856.

June 6, 1856. We [Alabama] voted first for Pierce, & then for Douglas, because we wished the next contest to be decided on the sole issue of the Kansas bill, and as these men were completely identified with it, it could not have been otherwise had they been selected. We are satisfied with Buch[anan]. I was so much afraid that Quitman w'd be nominated for V. P., that I was highly gratified at the selection of Breckenridge.

John A. Quitman, son of a Lutheran minister in New York, went to Natchez with well-formulated plans for his personal advancement; including his marriage to the daughter of a judge, fighting creditably in the Mexican War, becoming governor of Mississippi—but watching his popular bubbles burst rapidly as he became more involved with Lopez and Walker in their territorial power schemes.—Kane, 220.

7th. Left for Buffalo in company with Burns Moore, Clitherall, Jim Henry Malone, Dr. Yarbrough, etc.

Alexander Barron Clitherall served as private secretary to Jefferson

Davis for a time in 1861. This native of Brunswick County, Virginia, moved to Greene County, Alabama, in 1837, served as probate judge there, and represented the county in both houses of the legislature.—Owen, III, 352.

"A better man than Jim Henry never lived. Peace to his ashes," wrote John Tanner. The son of William Malone, Jim Henry married Elizabeth Yarbrough, daughter of Henry. Jim Henry was a young clerk for Keyes, Richardson and Company when the courthouse was completed in 1835, and to celebrate its completion, he climbed to the top of the spire, 110 feet from the ground, and "patted juber," much to the anguish of the onlookers below. In the 1840s the Malones built The Cedars just north of Athens. The fine old home has been gone several years.

June 10th, 1856. Visited all the sights about Niagara, including the celebrated Lundy's Lane.

Lundy's Lane was the scene of the most bitterly contested battle ever fought on the North American continent. It took place between British and American forces on July 23, 1814, and gained fame for the victorious American officer, Winfield Scott.

11th. Left for Albany—passing along by the Central Road, the route of the great Canal. The valley of the Mohawk is the most beautiful scenery I ever saw. Land is here worth $150 per acre. Arrived in Albany about dark, & stopped at the Delaware House, where the servants at the table are all girls.

June 13, 1856. Arrived in New York & stopped at St. Nicholas, wh. is the most splendid establishment I ever saw. Here I met Misses May & Sue Spence of Murphreesboro.

The Lynchburg *Daily Republican* carried advertisements for the St. Nicholas Hotel, Broadway, New York in 1856, stating: "When completed six years ago, the St. Nicholas was universally pronounced the most magnificent, convenient, and thoroughly organized establishment of the kind on this continent." When the builders of Birmingham erected their first rude shack from which to begin their work, they dubbed it the "St. Nicholas," perhaps because no greater comparison could come to their minds.—Hornaday, 9.

June 15, 1856. Went to Brooklyn and heard Henry Ward Beecher, tho' I had to stand up the whole time of the sermon. He is a smart man, but owes much of his popularity to his boldness of declaration & his great acting in the pulpit. He went into politics largely.

18th. Left N. Y. in morning boat and arrived at 11 in Phila. The black Rep. convention in session.* Today they adopted the subjoined platform, & nominated Fremont for President.

Hon. David Wilmot, on behalf of the Committee on Resolutions, read the following: This convention of Delegates, assembled in pursuance of a call addressed to the people of the United States, without regard to past political differences or divisions, who are opposed to the repeal of the Missouri Compromise; to the policy of the present administration; to the extension of slavery into free territory; in favor of the admission of Kansas as a free State; of restoring the action of the federal government to the principles of Washington and Jefferson; and for the purpose of presenting candidates for the offices of President and Vice-President . . .

*This convention was the first for the new Republican Party, called "Black Republican" by many Southerners. John Fremont and William L. Dayton were the first candidates chosen. At the next election, the party candidate, Abraham Lincoln, was successful.

June 20, 1856. Arrived in Washington.
21st. In the House this mor'g heard Burlingame, of Mass., deliver a scathing invective against the South, S. C. particularly.
22nd. Richmond. . . . Walked up past the house where I used to meet my dear during our engagement. . . . Thence I walked to Centenary Church and, entering it before service, stood at the spot where we were married. As I then reviewed our whole wedded life, I could not remember any vow she took at that spot which was not completely performed.
23rd. Petersburg. Arrived here yesterday aft., and took tea with the Meades.
24th. Am staying with Claiborne, whose wife is absent.
25th. Saw two reaping machines at work.
27th. Came to University—this is commencement day. . . . Prof. Minor instantly recognized me and met me most cordially, and would take no denial that I sh'd make his house my home. So my baggage was bro't up, and I occupied . . . the dormitory next door to his study, and which used in my day to be occupied by Willis Garth and Geo. Steele.
28th. Prof. Minor is more changed than any man I ever saw. He was not a Christian when I was a student, but now he is the most zealous I ever saw. . . . No field of usefulness which is open to him is left untried. He gave me a most touching account of the death of his son, which was the immediate cause of leading him to repentance. Visited Miss Juliet Gilmer, where I met Miss Caroline Thompson.
30th. Left University . . . for Staunton. Found Miss Thompson in the cars on the way to their home in Staunton. We crossed the Blue Ridge at the Rockfish Gap, and at such grades as I never before saw. . . . Called on Miss Thompson tonight, was kindly received by her father, Hon. L. P. Thompson, one of the circuit Judges of Va. He was a member of that celebrated convention wh. met 1829-30 to revise the constitution of Va., and which was perhaps the ablest body of men ever assembled in U.S.
July 1, 1856. Miss Caroline Thompson is very fine looking . . . glossy

yellow hair, classic face, very rosy lips, an unusually fine set of teeth. She is tall and has a graceful carriage. She wants color, being very blonde, and there is a good deal wanting in her calm grey eye. She is very placid, almost cold, she is so calm. She either disliked me, or she is distressingly prudish.

2nd. Reached Lexington by stage.

3rd. Today a statue of Washington was inaugurated in front of the Va. Military Institute. This is a copy of Houdon's in the capitol at Richmond—being cast from that & donated by Va. to the institution. Gov. Wise delivered the address.

5th. Breakfasted at Buchanan, and thence to Buford's Depot on Va. & Tenn. R. R.

6th. About sunrise started for Mr. Eggleston's Springs, called the "New River W. S. Springs." . . . Met Mrs. Booth and Mrs. Eg—the latter quite sick. We did little more than weep in this first interview. Accompanied E. G. B. to his mountain home this evening.

There is a town of Eggleston at the present time on the New River near the West Virginia border. Since Hobbs later mentions the sulphur water at Greenbrier, this long famous resort in the corner of West Virginia must have also been included in the development.

7th. Mr. Booth has purchased, in company with 2 or 3 others, more than 100,000 acres of wild land in the mountains, which is rapidly selling off at a great advance. We passed yest. the Salt Pond, a beautiful sheet of water on the top of the mountain, which in 1804 rose 25 ft. . . . Went upon the Bald Knob, one of the highest points of the Allegheny range. It commands a view of all West Va.

10th. Left the Springs in a hack for the Christiansburg Depot, where I arrived in time for the western train.

11th. Breakfasted in Abingdon, and then travelled all day in the stage.

12th. Took the cars at Morristown, and arrived in Knoxville.

14th. Reached Chattanooga to breakfast, Huntsville to dinner, and Fertilis an hour afterwards. . . . went to Athens, and was seated at supper at Pa's precisely 24 hours after leaving Knoxville.

15th. Since I left home, Mr. John Richardson, W. B. Elliott, and a little son of W. D. Hayes have died.

18th. While I was away Steele concluded his survey, & on the 4th inst. made his report to an immense meeting in Athens. About $52,000 of stock were taken on that occasion, of the $181,000 which are to be raised before the county tax can be levied. Today we had a barbecue at

Antioch Church where I spoke, followed by Dr. McDonald, Captain Bingham, and Luke. About $7,500 were subscribed.

Captain Bingham is probably D. H. Bingham, who had been induced by the oft-married Elizabeth Dale Gibbons-Flannigan-High-Brown-Routt of Hazel Green to bring charges against her neighbor, Abner Tate. Then Tate countercharged her with the murder of her husbands, in a publication entitled *Defense of Abner Tate Against Charges Preferred by D. H. Bingham.* Mr. Bingham, who had apparently considered marrying Elizabeth himself, was saved, perhaps, from a like fate, when the lady moved to Mississippi in 1855. David H. Bingham married Sarah C. Moyers in Limestone County on May 22, 1858.—American Guide Series, *Alabama,* 329.

July 22, 1856. Attended a R.R. barbecue in Decatur—not a very large crowd out, yet we raised between $24,000 and $25,000, and they say they will yet raise the amount of $38,000, which they ought to get, that being the difference in the cost of the two routes.
24th. Today I received and set up the marble monument for Indie's grave, wh. I purchased of Chas. Rule in Cin. It is of Italian marble, plain, but I think very neat and proper. It cost in Cin. $225, freight, $36.32. It will not last as long as my recollection & love for the pure woman who lies beneath it.

In his diary entry for July 13, 1856, Henry B. Malone states that he had called at Charles Rule's marble works and paid for a monument for Thomas Hobbs.—H. B. Malone, Diaries.

26th. R. R. barbecue at Gilbertsboro—large crowd—as many women as men. McDonald led off, I followed. . . . We got $13,400, all of it sound.
28th. My parents, accompanied by Roswell Hine and daughter, left for the Va. Springs. They go direct to Mr. Eggleston's.
August 1st. We put up the mud-mill today.
2nd. We moulded a few bricks this afternoon just to make a commencement. Jere Clemens spoke in Athens, and made a great deal of sport of the Cin. Convention and platform.
10th. Cambridge Camp meeting. Hamner and Rivers are in attendance. I went up today [Sunday] to see Dr. Rivers to ask him to deliver a free school address at a celebration wh. I hope will come off soon.
August 18, 1856. This aft. went to Ezell's by promise to commence my visitations of the schools in the N. W. township.
19th. Visited Hayney's and Chapman's Schools.
21st. Visited Jones Coleman's school. At all these places I have sounded the people and the children on the subject of a free school celebration to

come off the 3rd day of October. I find them much more anxious than I expected.

29th. [My parents] were delayed in P'burg, owing to the death of Mrs. Pannill's little son, William. They leave for home next Monday, and Cousin Julia is not coming with them.

September 1st. Commenced picking cotton. The corn and cotton of this co. will both be very short.

2nd. Henry and I at work upon the privy, wh. I have moved nearer the house.

8th. A discussion took place today between Yancey and Clemens. Yancey spoke first, and made a most clear, comprehensive and telling speech. I never heard any man speak so distinctly and so fast. Clemens' style is the reverse of Y.'s, slow and very tame. The Dem's claim a victory, and I am disposed to think they attained it.

9th. Clemens, Yancey, Dick Walker and Cooper dined with me today on their way to the depot. On the way, Yancey expressed gratification at seeing a Bible on a table, and at my asking a blessing at dinner. He is a Presbyterian, I think.

11th. Sulzner Pinquely & Co. gave a very fine concert in the Institute wh. was listened to by about 40 people.

12th. My horse, Badger, never having been much frightened at the cars, I left him harnessed to buggy. He took fright when the cars were leaving, and ran off despite my vigorous pulls, and smashed my buggy.

29th. Began to make preparations for the School Celebration on Thursday. Have all the work to do myself.

30th. Making seats of fence rails.

October 2, 1856. Made two stands—one for the speaker & invited guests, and the other for musicians.

3rd. Beautiful day—Children began to come in early. . . . We formed procession and moved precisely at 12—took Messrs. Mendum's, Naff's and Wilson's academies into our procession at Bass' Hotel, and thence to the grove (Pryor's). We numbered in all *336,* and made a fine show. There was a much smaller turn-out of children of free schools than I expected—and from the township which promised most, I received fewest. Mr. Rivers arrived. . . . He gave us an address which was plain, and therefore very popular with those I was most anxious to please. Dinner was served immediately.

October 6, 1856. In Pulaski, where Dr. McDonald & Luke came with me yesterday. We spoke . . . to a restless crowd, the most of whom felt no interest in our operations. My throat very sore—made the meanest speech I have made. . . . Luke followed and also fell very short. Maj. Buford and Thos. Martin also addressed the crowd, and the handsome subscription of about $13,000 wh. we got was attributable far more to their influence than to our speeches. Stayed all night at Squire Brown's.

11th. Reorganized Cecilian Society under the head of Sulzner, who like Mayer, teaches it for nothing.

13th. Started to Nashville to raise R. R. stock. . . . met Luke, Walden & Fennell, and we were joined by McDonald in H'ville. . . . Slept at Stevenson.

14th. The State Fair is going on, and the city very full. . . . there was the healthiest set of women in attendance that I ever saw, their faces not unusually pretty, but they were above the usual size of females and looked *substantial.* Elections in Penn. and Indiana yesterday.

15th. Today we were circulating among the merchants & grocers, but there is so much excitement about politics that we do not receive the attention wh. we ought. Bob Gardner, of Morgan Co., is working with and for us. Every few moments telegraphic dispatches are received from Penn., and the party most pleased by them immediately starts a drum & fife around with a placard detailing the news. Around these a crowd soon collects which cheers at every corner. But the next moment the news may be favorable to the other side; they pursue the same plan & the result is a continual ferment.

October 23, 1856. Rode to town to attend the first meeting of the "Crotchet Club," wh. we have reorganized under the leadership of Prof. Sulzner. Its members now are—Tom Tyus and Wm. Sartin (violins), Sam Tanner & myself (flutes), Milton Irvin (cornet), Pa and Dr. Malone (Basses).

31st. Left home this morning in company of McDonald & Pryor to attend the meeting at Oakville, a little place in Lawrence Co., near the Morgan line. We went to Harry Fennell's to dinner.

November 1st. We soon saw that the occasion was mainly intended to be political and that nobody was thinking of the railroad. In fact, it was a Fillmore barbecue, and the crowd most enthusiastic in his behalf —so much so, that it was openly avowed by some of them that the R. R. was an intrusion. Luke spoke. I w'd not. About $1000 was subscribed.

8th. Our R. R. meeting—day bleak and unpromising—crowd very small, prospect of getting money very slim. Dr. McD. opened the meeting. Luke followed, drawing a gloomy picture of the state of the R'd— then came I, in a ditto strain, for we all felt it; Nick Davis & Gen. Houston followed with good speeches. . . . $10,200 were subscribed—I raising mine $500, making in all 2500 for me. . . . This completes the required amount of $381,000. . . . Fennell came over this mor'g bringing news of $10,000 from Morgan.

10th. One of the strangest events of the meeting last Saturday was that Capt. Jack Mason subscribed $1000 of stock. He has been one of the bitterest and most influential of our opponents. He was brought in by good management—for some time past Luke (who is uncommonly well versed in human nature) has been soothing him and at a meeting held last Friday night it was agreed that Uncle, who has his confidence, should make an effort to induce him to subscribe. . . . He agreed to come to the meeting, and when he came he subscribed, and [so] did Squire Tanner, who was also an anti-tax man.

12th. Sowing the 10 acre lot in front of the house with grass seeds, intending to make a permanent pasture of it.

November 13, 1856. Meeting of the C. Club—full attendance save Pa, who with Ma, has gone to Florence to visit Mr. & Mrs. Rivers. Uncle joined the party tonight.

22nd. The organization of the [stockholding] Company was completed by the election of the Directors. . . . I received the highest vote, save Tom Martin of Giles. Luke was voted against . . . because he had been a K. N., which is nothing less than ingratitude—for he has made greater sacrifices for the R. R. than anybody else. The B'd of Directors met after supper and elected McDonald Pres't, (Mason nominated me, but I declined running), John Tanner, Treasurer, and Steele Engineer.—he accepted and . . . [will] begin operation on Weds. mor'g next.

26th. B'd met at my house. The salary of Pres't fixed at $1000 and Treasurer same. . . . B'd accepted proposal of Schmitt to serve us at $1200 per ann.

Friday, December 5. Hooper of the *Mail,* in calling attention to the advertisement of our letting, inserts:

. . . The *Mail* is not now the advocate of any system of State aid. . . . But while we say this . . . in the consideration of very many (perhaps most) of the Anti-State-Aid party, such a road as the Alabama Central—intended to connect the two distinct and perfectly severed sections of the State—presents altogether an exceptional aspect. It is argued, that it is emphatically the duty of the State to bring these two separated sections into social and commercial communication with each other; and the more so, because the natural obstacles in the way of the enterprise prevent its being accomplished by individual exertion. . . . The upper end of the Alabama Central, reaching from Decatur, Ala., into a most productive portion of Middle Tennessee, is soon to be placed under contract . . . will be built within a reasonable time. From Decatur south, across the ridge of mountains dividing the two sections of the State, a line is presented which cannot be constructed, except by the State. . . . We have great faith in the success of the Central Rail Road. It is in the hands of men of intelligence, information, and energy. The President, Dr. McDonald, is represented to us as a gentleman of rare capacity and invincible industry; while of Messrs. Pryor and Hobbs we can say, on personal knowledge, that they are two of Alabama's most gifted and most practical sons. They are such men as seldom fail in any undertaking.

December 16, 1856. Miss Virginia Davis married to Mr. Harris of La. I was invited to wait on them & did so with Miss Ann Maria Fletcher. Some of the family, Nick particularly, are very much opposed to the match, & would not attend the ceremony. It was to gratify her that I consented to become a waiter. The engineers, who have been staying with me, left this mor'g to go into camp near Mr. Ben Peete's.
17th. Attended Capt. Davis' sale. The land—1200 acres—was purchased by Gen'l Lane at $30.50 per acre.
26th. The Board of Directors were invited to an oyster supper at John Tanner's. . . . business came up so fast that we determined to sit up all night, *which we did.* I went to bed at sunrise and slept until nine, when we had another meeting. Numerous contractors are in town, and the prospect for the letting of our Road is very flattering. Before I shall vote to let a foot of the Road, I must be satisfied that (1st) The bids do not exceed the Eng's estimates, and (2nd) that the contractors will take 20 per ct. in the stock of the company.
December 27, 1856. Great many people in town—Contractors swarming at the Engineer's office. At 2 P.M. we met to open bids and worked thereon, comparing them until we adjourned for supper. After supper we met and the Eng. giving it as his opinion that the bids of Broughton, Burleson & Co. were within his estimates. We accepted their bid for the whole line. Tracklaying & crossties awarded to Featherstone & McDonald. At 11 P.M. we adjourned in high spirits, but much worn down in body.

The diary for 1857 is missing. During this time Thomas Hobbs met Anne Benagh, daughter of James and Elizabeth Richardson Benagh of Lynchburg, Virginia. Major Benagh was a lawyer and clerk of the court at Lynchburg for thirty years. Mrs. Benagh was a sister of William Richardson, of Athens. Their son, George William Benagh, came to The University of Alabama in 1850 to teach mathematics, and in 1852 married Mary Collier, daughter of Governor Henry W. Collier.

The late fall of 1857 found Thomas Hobbs in the legislature again, and during the recess he went to Virginia.

Friday, January 1, 1858. I took A. B. by the hand today & led her to her father, and asked his permission to our marriage. He consented, and expressed in an agreeable manner his approbation. . . . I left tonight . . . for P'burg, but before I left she gave me a most affectionate parting. God keep her 'till I come.

January 2, 1858. Mr. E. G. Booth, with whom I had business, met me by app. today, and agreed to be my agent to receive & dispose of some negroes which I am entitled to by marriage with my dear dead wife.
3rd. Cousin Julia was much surprised when I told her what had been done in L'burg. My opinion is she expected me to address some one in P'burg. . . . Sue, poor woman, still very unwell, and I fear she will not be alive 18 months from this time. One still born infant, and then a dead mother! May Heaven avert such a sad fate for Mr. Bolling!

Susan Meade married William N. Bolling, son of Robert Buckner and Sarah Melville Bolling, of Petersburg. William Bolling's sister, Mary Tabb, married the son of Robert E. Lee, Gen. W. H. F. Lee.—*Virginia Historical Magazine,* IV, 332, 1896.

4th. Left Petersburg . . . for Montgomery via Wilmington & Augusta—fare $30.
6th. Arrived in Montgomery without accident or incident.
7th. Most of the N. Ala. members arrived this mor'g, bringing news of unprecedented hard times. No cotton selling, price down to 7 cents (season opened at 14), no money to be had, and everything depressed. Redus not yet come—he will probably bring me letters from home. Wrote to A. B.

William Redus represented Limestone in this session as Hobb's colleague.

9th. Received a letter from M[ary] P. R[ichardson], containing one from A. B., the first since our engagement. It is a sweet, comfortable document. . . . Made a speech today on the Asylum for the Blind, but was called upon unexpectedly, and made a poor speech. Indeed, have not made a good one this session.

Appended to the diary is an unidentified article:

> Special order for 11 o'clock. The Bill to establish a School for the Blind. Messrs. Hobbs and Baugh offered amendments to the Bill, which were adopted. Mr. Molton, an amendment giving the selection of the location to the Legislature, pending which Mr. Dillard moved to postpone the bill indefinitely. Mr. Brewer opposed the motion, and contended that the state ought to provide for the education of the blind, as well as those who can see. He stated that the returns showed 156 blind persons in Alabama . . .

The article states further that Messrs. Wright, Hobbs, Hale, and Clarke spoke in favor of the Bill, and that Montevallo, Opelika, and Marion were suggested as locations. In 1860 an Asylum for the Deaf and Dumb *and* Blind was opened in Talladega.—Brewer, 60.

January 11, 1858. We had quite a debate on some Resolutions on Federal affairs introduced by Hale. [Z. L.] Nabors moved that a Convention be called if Kansas is denied admission with proslavery const'n. Smith, of Laud., added "or any other territory," and I proposed, "provided such refusal is *because* of the pro-slavery const'n." . . . the original proposition of Nabors adopted. Com'tee on Education met tonight, and resolved to retain the County Superintendent as a feature of the system.

Stephen Fowler Hale, 1816–1862, served two terms in the legislature. Like Hobbs, Hale was wounded at Gaines' Mill, and died a few days later. When a new county was formed from Greene in 1867, it was named for this legislator.—Brewer, 266.

January 12, 1858. Some discussion today on Resolutions asking Pres't. to promote Lieut. Maury. I was opposed to them because I tho't we had better leave that matter to those who have charge of it.

Lt. Harry Maury had commanded a vessel in William Walker's attempt to capture Nicaragua.—Brewer, 420.

13th. Attended tonight a fine party at Dr. Baldwin's.

Dr. William Owen Baldwin, born in Montgomery County in 1818, was elected president of the American Medical Association in 1868, the first year of the South's reinstatement to that organization. He was a founder and first president of the First National Bank of Montgomery.—Owen, III, 83.

15th. I introduced today, or yesterday, some Resolutions complimenting Mr. Whiting for pledging his private credit to get a loan from the brokers of N. Y. for the State. H. D. Smith, who does not speak to me now, opposed them, as did Bulger. They were, however, referred to the appropriate Committee.

John Whiting, a Montgomery cotton factor, became president of the South and North Railroad, successor to the Tennessee and Alabama Central, in 1868.—Armes, 216.

16th. Bill-burning Bill passed. . . . I did not speak upon it, because I saw it was utterly useless. An overwhelming majority was for it, and for it *quick*. I predicted this before I left home.

January 17th, 1858. Heard Rev. Mr. Petrie. . . . Clarke & I accompanied Misses Yancey and Witherspoon from church, and also to church tonight. The Ala. river is . . . out of its banks.

Rev. George Hollingshead Whitefield Petrie came to Montgomery in 1857. He was the father of George Laurens Petrie, prominent Presbyterian minister, and the grandfather of Dean George Petrie, Alabama Polytechnic Institute.—Owen, IV, 1350.

Miss Yancey was either Caro Yancey, daughter of Benjamin C., or one of several daughters of William Lowndes Yancey. The other young lady was probably Eliza Hamilton Witherspoon, daughter of Rev. T. S. Witherspoon, Presbyterian minister in Greensboro, and granddaughter of Judge Samuel Goode, of Montgomery.—Ibid., 1795, 1820, 1825.

January 18, 1858. Wm. Walker, of Nicaragua, spoke at Capitol tonight. I heard a part of his address, but was not sufficiently interested in it to stand & heart it out.

The "gray-eyed man of destiny," William Walker, 1824–1860, was born of a distinguished family in Nashville. A handsome, brilliant adventurer, he made his first attempt to conquer Nicaragua in 1855, at which time he succeeded in having Rivas proclaimed as president, and himself as generalissimo. In June, 1856, he arranged to become president, and repealed all antislavery laws, thus gaining the support of many Southerners. After a native insurrection he was captured and taken to New Orleans for imprisonment, but was released on bail, and traveled through the South to gain approval for his cause. In January, 1858, Walker presented himself to President Pierce as a prisoner of state, but the President would not imprison him. In the same year he tried unsuccessfully to conquer Honduras. His men were shipped back to the United States, and he was shot in 1860.

19th. We ordered to 3rd reading the bills for annual sessions today. It provides for the assembling of this same body next November, provided the people at the August election vote for annual sessions. . . . Senate may not concur. Wrote home tonight, enclosing Anne's last, in wh. she speaks very affectionately of my parents. Wrote also to Mrs. Maclin. Query: How will she receive the news of my marriage? She will at all events be pleased that it is not a Meade.

22nd. Today the proposition to change the Great Seal of the state, which I had carried in the Ho., was laid on the table in Senate. . . . there was nobody there who felt any interest in the matter. . . . In Hs. we passed a Bill for annual sessions. . . . Also the bill to extend the loan to the Mobile & Ohio R. R'd.

25th. We have been trying for the last day or two to agree upon some compromise among the various R. R. interests. But the misfortune is that we have to take too many into partnership. This requires an appropriation of the entire sum due from State to 3 per cent fund, most of which is not in treasury, but would have to be put there by taxation. My opinion is that all of us will fail.

27th. Attended a meeting at Capitol, called to express our confidence in Administration. It is said that the real design was to put Yancey and those who sympathize with the fillibusters [*sic*] on the defensive—but if this was the design, it signally failed, for Yancey being called on, made war open and strong upon the *Confederation* newspaper which, it is said, has been recently established here to sustain the Fitzpatrick wing and to check Yancey's aspirations to the Senate.

28th. It was supposed that the Com. app. to draft resolutions would say something about Nicaragua—but they only allude to the Prest's conduct as to Kansas. Yancey's effort was 2 hours long, and was a fine specimen of rostrum eloquence. I think he is the best popular speaker I ever heard. I made a speech yesterday on the passage of the bill for blind school, but it failed on the passage 46–41. I procured a re-consideration today, that is, a motion to re-con. was made, and lays over. The annexed is from this morning's *Confederation:*

> Messrs. N. H. Brown and Thomas H. Hobbs—These two young Representatives—the former from Tuscaloosa, and the latter from Limestone—won enviable laurels in the House yesterday, by their able advocacy of benevolent enterprises.* Mr. Brown, in his support of the bill making an appropriation for the Insane Hospital, established for himself an honorable reputation as a forcible, ready and effective debater, as well as a gentleman of enlarged views and generous impulses. Mr. Hobbs, in a manner equally able and creditable, but with less success, advocated the bill reported by himself to establish a School for the Blind. His effort was a highly honorable and eloquent appeal to the sympathies of enlightened legislators; but a regard for economy influenced the House in turning a deaf ear to even such an appeal. Both these young gentlemen are Representatives of much present usefulness and bright promise. It is due to Mr. Powell, of Tuscaloosa, to say that he ably seconded his colleague in support of the bill making an appropriation for the Insane Hospital.**

*Newbern Hobbs Brown had represented Tuscaloosa since 1853. The Insane Asylum for Alabama had been a goal with several Alabamians since the visit of Dorothea Dix to Tuscaloosa before the capital was moved from that city. Although the Asylum was built during Governor Winston's administration, it was not opened until 1861.

**Ezekiel Abner Powell was Brown's colleague from Tuscaloosa, having represented that county from 1855–1867, with the exception of time spent in service with the Confederate States Army.—Owen, IV, 1381.

February 3, 1858. Everything is in a confusion now in the House. A general scramble not to see how much we can do, but what shall be first done. The Senate this evening added by ryder to the 2 per cent Bill an app. of $10,000 of 3 per cent for our survey—to be managed, however, by Governor instead of by commissioners. We are in a great stew in the House, for it is difficult for the R. R. men who want money to agree among themselves. Hale is the head of the N. E. men—Tom Walker of the Coosa and we of the Central are respectable enough to have the balance of power.

4th. We had a good deal of excitement on the Senate floor in regard to the 2 per cent fund. The Marshall members were dissatisfied because the town of Decatur was mentioned as a starting point on the Tenn. River. I therefore proposed the amendment as shown in the accompanying slip. [The gist of the amendment was to strike out Decatur and leave the termini of the survey to the judgment of the surveyors. The article also states that the bill was ordered to be engrossed for a third reading, and that the bill would divide the amount of the 2% fund in the treasury between the Alabama and Tennessee Rivers and the Alabama and Mississippi Rivers Railroad Companies.] There is a good deal of complaint by Hale & Co. that we have gotten ahead of them, for they had agreed to give us $20,000 out of 3 per cent and desired our help on the Bill to dispose of that fund.

5th. This morning, much to my surprise, Jackson of Franklin, moved to reconsider the vote taken on yesterday on the 2 per cent bill. His manner indicated that he was miffed about something, and I thought at me. But, he never said a word about it to me, and considering we have been on quite intimate terms, it seems strange he did not do so. The entire morning was spent in . . . fruitless business.

William Moore Jackson, 1824–1889, was the son of James Jackson, builder of the Forks of Cypress in Lauderdale County, and one of the founders of Florence. The elder Jackson had been president of the senate in 1830, the same year in which he purchased the famous horse Leviathan from the royal stables in England. In 1835 Jackson purchased Glencoe, one of the best horses known to the history of racing. William Jackson named his plantation in Franklin County Glencoe for this horse. The house was used by both armies during the Civil War, and Jackson burned three hundred bales of cotton to prevent them from falling into Federal hands. He also furnished uniforms for the Franklin Rifles, C. S. A.—Sherwood, 66.

February 6, 1858. The entire day was spent in a wrangle and tonight, in order to defeat the 2 per cent bill, its opponents left the Hall, and no quorum remained.

8th. The Senate concurred in our amend't to 2 per cent Bill, and the Gov. signed it. Thus my constituents got the bills in which they felt most interest, 2 per cent & that authorizing sale of County Bonds. The Bill consolidating the various acts incorporating Athens passed both Houses. . . . The two houses adjourned at 6, the Speaker made a feeling speech alluding to the harmony which had prevailed, and stated that he could not have been more fortunate in the selection of Chairmen of Com's.

February 9, 1858. If I did any good as Chairman of Ed., it was by not reporting any change in School System. . . . Purchased a beautiful watch & chain for Anne ($201), which the jeweller assured me was as good a timekeeper as he had in his store. I preferred this . . . to a diamond breastpin which I at one time thought of.

FAMILY LIFE 1858-1859

February 14th, 1858. On account of the snow & sleet, we did not reach Lynchburg until three hours after the time appointed. . . . Anne received me with a sweet kiss. She is looking very well, and has gained flesh since I saw her.

16th. Rev. J. E. Edwards,* who is to perform the ceremony, came up tonight and I met him at Mr. B's. We are to be married by the ring ceremony—but not the same as Episcopal Church. The young men, who are to wait on me, met me tonight, and we had an oyster supper. They are Whaling, McDonald (editor of Courier),** Cosby, Abram Warwick,† James Benagh, and Hal [Malone].

*Rev. John E. Edwards was pastor of the Fourth Street Methodist Church, which was dedicated in 1851. On the night before the departure of the first troops from Lynchburg in April, 1861, he preached a sermon of encouragement to them.—Kern, 12.

**Alexander McDonald was one of the most outstanding citizens of Lynchburg, mentioned frequently in Christian's *Lynchburg and Its People.* McDonald edited several newspapers, served as a private in the Beauregard Rifles, represented Campbell County in the state senate, and was appointed Minister to Persia by President Cleveland in 1893, only four years before his death.

†Abram Warwick's family were charter members of the Fourth Street Church, as were the Benaghs. Abram's brother, John, held the first meeting of the board of trustees in his Lynchburg office. Kern states that the first organ in the church was given by Miss Carrie Warwick, at a time when that instrument was considered an "abomination to the Lord."

February 17, 1858. Anne looked beautifully in her bridal dress and really seemed little alarmed. I was not myself much alarmed, tho' I thought the ceremony long.

18th. The waiters & bridesmaids assembled tonight to cut the wedding cake. Hal left for Cin. tonight.

22nd. This is the day for the installation of the Equestrian Statue in Richmond. But it is snowing, and the weather may prevent the magnificent display which is anticipated. Nothing prevents our starting for Ala. now but the fact that Mrs. Rucker wishes to give us a party on Weds. night.

Mrs. Ambrose Rucker was the former Susan Jane Benagh, sister of Major James Benagh. The Ruckers lived on the corner of Seventh and Clay streets, across from the Benagh home. Mr. Rucker was chairman of the board of stewards of the Fourth Street Church, a commission merchant, president of the city council and the First National Bank of Lynchburg, director of the James River and Kanawha Canal Company, and a member of the Agricultural and Mechanical Society in Lynchburg. In 1868 he became the first president of the board of directors for the Lynchburg Female Orphan Asylum.—Kern, 43; Letter from Mrs. Alvin Watson, dated June 10, 1971.

26th. We started home tonight . . . Mrs. Pleas, Anne and I.

28th. Arrived in P'burg. . . . Cousins Julia & Indie came 'round after church and took us to dinner with them.

March 3, 1858. Reached Home safely. . . . Pa met us at Depot, and at home we found Ma and Mrs. Richardson.

4th. The house has been much improved by the repairs wh. Pa has made upon it. He has added a pantry dairy and gun-closet (for me) on the north side of the dining room, which have greatly increased the convenience of the house.

March 10, 1858. Mrs. Richardson gave us a party tonight—pleasant company, good supper & agreeable time.

14th. We heard Mr. Ransom this mor'g, & Reverend W. Allen to night. The . . . latter is . . . shaken by the death of his daughter, Louisa, a sweet & pretty girl.

15th. Came home, & began to garden and fix up generally. Anne is busy learning to cook & teaching Charlotte, while I find enough to do on all sides. We had company for our first dinner—J. E. Harrison, on his way to Texas, stopped to dine with us. But notwithstanding it was Anne's first & servants untrained we got through in a creditable manner and had a fine dinner. Pa and Mary Pleas came down with us.

26th. We laid first rail of the Central Road. About 20 persons present—each one driving down a spike. We then gave 3 cheers for the T. & A. C. R. R., and dispersed. Mason, Pryor, Townsend, Nick Malone dining with us.

April 15. This mor'g we had a white frost, but strange to say, the tenderest vegetables were not killed. . . . The locomotive, *Luke Pryor,* first reached Mitchell's Springs today.

19th. My birthday—took the early train for H'ville where I went to sell the cotton—did not succeed. Returned at 3 P.M., and had scarcely reached home before a rain commenced which will be long remembered in this region. For 12 hours it rained *very hard.* . . . In Athens, where I think there was less rain than here, Dr. Sowell reports 5.6 inches of rain. . . . The streams were all put out of banks, and much damage done to R.R.'s, especially M. & C.

20th. In the grass lot N. of the house, where there was not a drop of water yesterday mor'g—there is today a pond covering 2 acres, at least.

24th. We had a white frost this mor'g. . . . Killed cotton & corn.

May 17, 1858. This sad anniversary could not be past without recalling the terrible blow which once it gave me. But how do I thank the Giver of all good gifts that the return of this day finds me so much happier than I was one year since, or indeed, any time since the death of poor Indie. My Anne is a delightful companion, and a most energetic and industrious wife, more than fulfilling the high expectations I formed of the excellence of her character. This is also the anniversary of Bunyan's liberation from imprisonment.

18th. The trains on the Tenn. & Va. R. R. ran thro' today for first time. [Subjoined newspaper clipping, unidentified: "Five cars came down from the west last night, containing in all 200 passengers, thirty nine of whom had through tickets from Memphis to New York. . . ."]

June 25, 1858. Drove Mrs. Childs to Athens—she desires to examine the Institute & its furniture before she decides to accept the Presidency of it, to which she was recently elected. While in town, Mr. Jno. T. Milner came and called for me. He is the engineer app. by Gov. to survey the mountains, & has just come up thro' them from Selma. His corps is even now in the field near Elyton. He was pleased to say that the Gov. considers me the leader of the Survey policy & requested him to come to see me on the subject. Mr. M. is a younger man than I expected to see him, and seems to be better informed on his professional matters than any other. He has correct ideas of what the design of the Survey is and, in my opinion, will do justice to all sections. He staid all night with us, and I took him to Decatur next day.

John Turner Milner was born in Pike County, Georgia, in 1826. He began working in his father's coal mines at the age of ten, and at twelve began his career of railroad construction with his father. He studied civil engineering at the University of Georgia. It was Milner who selected the exact spot for the crossing of the Alabama Central and the Northeast and Southwest Railroads, the spot from which the city of Birmingham was to grow.—Hornaday, 34.

June 28, 1858. The train began to run regularly on this day, on the Central. The mail on July 1 is to turn from its present route, and come to Pulaski & Athens from Nashville. A line of stages is to run from Thompson's Station, not far from Franklin, to Athens, & then be met by our Central.
29th. Porter Bibb's son murdered by his servant.

An adjoined, unidentified newspaper clipping begins: "It has seldom fallen to our lot to record a more shocking and barberous murder and one perpetrated under circumstances of more atrocity than the one committed upon the body of Thos. Bibb, a youth about fourteen years old, and son of D. P. Bibb, Esq., near Mooresville in this county on Tuesday week by a negro be longing to Mr. Bibb, named Larkin."

The boy's father was Porter Bibb, the fifth child of Governor Thomas and Parmelia Thompson Bibb. He married Mary Pleasants Betts, and lived at the beautiful Bibb home, Belle Mina, built by the governor in 1826.—Owen, III, 143.

June 30, 1858. Was summoned to Athens to meet B'd. of Directors. Pryor & Mason resigned, and Treasurer reported less funds on hand than estimates called for. Moreover, it was stated that the Corporation of Decatur was refusing to pay its subs. Accordingly, Sloss, Jordan & myself were sent over by B'd to confer with the citizens. We had a public meeting after supper, about 30 to 40 present. Dancy made first talk, Sloss followed—Parker . . . and then I made a little speech. There seemed to be a good feeling—no opposition manifested, and the annexed resolutions were unanimously adopted.

The gist of the resolutions was to tender an expression of confidence in the Board of Directors, stating that the money in the treasury in Decatur be turned over to the Board treasurer, and that every effort would be made to collect all money due.

July 14, 1858. We started for the Valhermoso Springs, which we reached late in the afternoon. We found about 25 persons, among whom were L. P. Walker & lady, Prof. Saroni & lady, Wiggs & lady (of Huntsville Dem.), Mr. Randolph & lady, from Greene County. The co. is very agreeable, & quite large enough to suit my taste. The water has a bitter taste at first, but gradually wears off, as you drink it.

Valhermoso Springs, located some twenty miles east of Hartselle, in Morgan County, Alabama, had been a popular resort for some thirty years before this time. The Cedar Hotel, a three-story frame building set in an abundance of cedars, was built by the Manning family in 1818. In 1855 the resort was purchased by Mr. and Mrs. Jean Joseph Giers, who brought a continental atmosphere to the locale. Mr. Giers spoke nine languages, wrote poetry, and was an accomplished musician. Mrs. Giers, from Murphreesboro, Tennessee, hid Confederate soldiers in the building during the Civil War when Federal soldiers were scouting in the area.—Sulzby, 90–92.

23rd. We returned from the Valhermoso Springs today, accompanied by Mr. Brett Randolph & lady. . . . This lady is the sister of Thos. H. Herndon, whom I knew at La Grange, and who ably represented Mobile in the last Leg. These people were married in May, and not desiring to return yet to the South, accepted our invitation to spend some time with us.

Mr. Randolph was probably the son of Brett and Lucy Beverley Randolph, members of one of Virginia's most aristocratic families. The elder Brett Randolph is recorded in the *William and Mary Quarterly* as dying in Mississippi in 1828. Only three Randolphs are listed in Snedecor's *Directory of Greene County* for 1855: Victor and Theodorick B(land), planters; and Brett, lawyer, of Eutaw.

July 26, 1858. Billy, Pa's faithful old servant, died this mor'g. During the last six months he, showing symptoms of dropsy . . . was sent to Bailey's Springs—he got no relief there, and was brought home far worse than he went. This mor'g he asked to be put on his knees to pray, and after he finished his prayer, he continued in that posture, leaning his head on a chair—and thus died so calmly that the attendant tho't him sleeping. His body was carried to Athens . . . & buried there.

The following is appended to the diary on August 5th:

Despatch from Mr. Cyrus W. Field, Trinity Bay, August 5, 1858, to the Associated Press, New York—The Atlantic Telegraph fleet sailed from Queenstown on Saturday, July 17th; met at mid-ocean on Wednesday, the 28th, and made the splice at 1 P.M. on Thursday, the 29th, and then separated—the *Agamemnon* and *Valorous* bound to Valentia, Ireland, and the *Niagara* and *Gorgon* for this place, where they arrived yesterday, and this morning the end of the cable will be landed. . . . The electrical signals sent and received through the whole cable are perfect. . . .

6th. The Randolphs left us this morning per Central train.

11th. Mr. Sloss, Walden, & I started for Hanby's Mill in Walker County to attend a R.R. barbecue.* The men of the mountains are at length awakening to the importance of the Central Road, and have themselves gotten up the demonstration. We ascended the mountain at Davis', and staid all night with Sheets at the top. We ate by the light of a lamp made by filling an egg-shell with oil and hanging the wick over the edge.**

*David Hanby, formerly a machinist for Andrew Jackson, bought land on Turkey Creek and built one of the first coal operations in the state, shipping the coal on flat-bottomed boats to Mobile. In 1840 he sent two flatboats loaded with coal, couldn't sell it, and could only *give* it away by sending a Negro along with each bucketful to show recipients how to light and burn it. Soon he was shipping several boatloads to the port city, most of them going to the gas company, which had put in one of the first commercial plants in the South.—Armes, 48.

**The overnight visit was probably in the home of William and Mary Garner Sheats, whose son Christopher was the well-known "Tory of the Hills." In his belief that the Civil War was a "rich man's war and a poor man's fight," Christopher Sheats assisted Colonel Streight to enlist over one hundred men in the Union army from the hill country in Blount, Walker, and Marion counties.—Dodd and Dodd, 94.

August 12th, 1858. We went to the Blount Springs & spent the night. This is the only Sulphur water which ever affected my head, and I think it stronger than that of Greenbriar. About 50 people at the Hotel, and 150 living around in their own houses.

The Goffe House, a colonial type inn of forty rooms, stood at Blount Springs. At this time the hotel was owned by Matthew Duffee, whose daughter Mary Gordon wrote *Sketches of Alabama.* The first cottage at the springs was built by Brett Randolph of Greensboro, Alabama, shortly after the springs were opened in 1825.—Sulzby, 61.

August 13th, 1858. We reached Hanby's Mill about 10 and found a good crowd assembled—not less than 1200. I spoke first . . . and never spoke to a more respectful crowd. Walden then followed, and after dinner Sloss and Milner. . . . The dinner was plentiful, & better conducted than any barbecue I ever saw. Milner insisted that we should spend the night with him—(which we did)—his camp being only 3 miles off.

From the Elyton *Alabamian:*

> Walker County Moving—The Barbecue at Hanby's Mill—
> We did ourself the honor of attending the barbecue given by the citizens of Walker county, near Hanby's Mill, on the 13th inst., and must say . . . that it has given us a most exalted opinion of the "free state." We arrived late upon the ground, and found already assembled hundreds of honest yeomanry of the country. . . . The absorbing topic of conversation was the Rail Road, and we were rejoiced to see that the spirit of improvement had taken such deep hold of that people. They have been "mud bound and land locked" long enough, and are anxiously inquiring what they shall do to extricate themselves from this dilemma. . . . The assembled multitude was addressed first by Major Hobbs, of Limestone, in a speech of some half hour's length, in which he portrayed in glowing colors the many and important advantages accruing from rail roads, and urged upon them the necessity of immediate and zealous action on the subject of a connection of North and South Alabama by a Central Rail Road. . . .

August 15, 1858. Sloss and I reached my house about dark.
17th. We heard of the arrival in Decatur of the Montgomery delegation consisting of Belser, Judge, Brittan, Coyne, Cloud, Linn, Gilmer, etc., and Luke, Sloss, Houston & I went over and spent the night with them.

They are much inclined to our route, & readily assented to the resolutions which we carried over, & which were drawn up by Houston.

18th. The train from Athens this mor'g—consisted of 12 cars & 600 persons. . . . The best feeling prevailed, and the R. R. men in better heart than ever before. If Mont'g really does get interested in this project, its completion is beyond question. We carried the most of the del's to Athens tonight, where we had a meeting. . . . Cloud is Editor of the *Soil of the South,* and as editor of the *Advertiser* last winter was as far from being an Int. Imp. man as any body could be. Now he even intimates that it might be proper, after all other means are tried & fail, for the State to aid the Central R'd. Menasco, whose shell used to be considered the hardest of the hard, is now a good Internal Imp. man. Altogether the signs are most favorable. The preceedings of the Decatur meeting are annexed [unidentified clipping]:

1500 People in Rail Road Convention, At Decatur. Wednesday, August 18, 1858. . . . The meeting assembled at the Blue Spring, near Town, where a Barbecue was prepared. The attendance was large, respectable, and full of the right sort of spirit. Gen. J. D. Rather called the Convention to order, and, on his motion, Dr. C. F. M. Dancy was called to the Chair, and Wm. Rollston appointed Secretary. On motion of Gen. J. D. Rather, a committee of 12 was appointed to report permanent officers, consisting of John D. Rather, A. A. Burleson, of Morgan, Luke Pryor, of Limestone, Thos. M. Peters, of Lawrence, Sam'l W. L. McCleskey, of Franklin, Mr. Hanby, of Jefferson, Mr. Gibson, of Blount, Judge Gabbert, of Walker, Thos. J. Judge, of Montgomery, Mr. Byington, of Coosa.

Thursday, September 1, 1858. Anne and I started for Va. Got a through ticket in Huntsville to L'burg for $23.50.

2nd. Reached Lynchburg at 9 P.M. James & George met us at the Depot.

October 1st. Left Lynchburg. . . . During the month we have spent here, Anne has been in bed most of the time, and can not return with me. . . she would go without a murmur, but I see her heart is almost breaking to stay with Ma during the crisis which is rapidly approaching—and stay she shall. But as it is very important for me to be at home, I am obliged to go.

October 3, 1858. Arrived at home safely this mor'g. During my absence, Rev. James W. Allen has died, of paralysis, I believe. Mr. Lynch, the overseer, has by permission left the plantation and a Mr. Dawson Mitchell is in charge.

17th. [unidentified newspaper clipping:]

List of officers for the North Alabama Agricultural Association for the year 1859—Henry Fennell, President; Thomas H. Hobbs, Vice President; Jno. T. Rather, Treasurer; Lawrence S. Banks, Secretary; M. W. Troup, W. E. Murpyev [*sic*], Morgan County; Nelson Fennell, Samu'l Elliott, Lawrence; N. J. Houston, O. O. Nelson, Franklin; H. W.

Kimbell, Porter Bibb, Limestone; Robt. Fearn, W. M. Brandon, Madison; W. H. Key, R. T. Kernahan, Lauderdale.
Also:
Married—On Wednesday last by the Rev. J. G. Wilson, Dr. N. D. Richardson, to Miss Betty Hine, both of this town.

20th. The Second Annual Fair of the North Ala. Ag. & Mechan. Association commenced today. But the day was cold and rainy, and a small turnout of visitors.
21st. Better day & more people—good crowd, in fact. "Julia Meade," my Columbus filly, was entered in the class of Broad Mares for Road, and also as best 3-year-old filly. She lost the premium, however, in both and the decision gave great dissatisfaction. Gen. Garth also exhibited a year-old-mule which the Com. thought better than mine. So I got no premium on stock, but one was awarded Anne for the best fruits in air tight cans.
22nd. Pa & Ma started for Va. At the fair, Gen. Houston made a speech and I, being called upon, simply made a proposition to be one of a hundred who would give $10 each to pay the Society's debt. By means of a rivalry which we contrived to get up between the counties of the Valley, we raised the required amount in a little while.

Appended to the diary is an unidentified clipping:

First Day. Plantations. *Morgan County*—(4 entries)—First Premium, Henry Fennel. Certificate to his Manager, Peterson Taylor. Second Premium, J. W. Garth. Certificate to his Manager, Jas. Halbrooks. *Limestone County*—(3 entries)—First Premium, Milton White. Certificate to his Manager, William Lynch. Second Premium, Haywood Jones. *Lawrence County*—First Premium, Samuel Elliott. Second Premium, Bolling Byrd. [The list continues, with many repetitive winners.]

Milton White was a brother of Addison, whose Huntsville home is now the property of Senator John Sparkman. The White family is descended from Colonel James White, who traded shiploads of salt for rich acres of valley land in the early part of the nineteenth century.—Telephone conversation with Mary White Pepper, Mooresville, February 28, 1972.

Haywood Jones, son of John Nelson Spotswood and Eliza Haywood Jones, was born in 1826. After his marriage to Sallie Collier, niece of Governor Henry B. Collier, he built the home on South Clinton Street, which was subsequently owned by the Coman, Westmoreland, and Hatchett families. It is said that Federal soldiers cut up meat on the Jones' piano during their occupation.—Pat Jones, "The Westmoreland Home," July 6, 1935.

October 28, 1858. Today, when 30 mls. from Montg., the two passenger cars were thrown from the track, and a good deal smashed. Both tracks of our car became detached and passing back under us, left us flat on the ground and threw off the car behind us. Not a single person hurt, but it was a dangerous accident, and for my happy escape, I thank God.

30th. When we assembled at the Fair grounds today [in Montgomery], there was little that promised success. There was no crowd, and no seats for those who were present. The fact is, Gilmer is the working man, and his wife is so ill that he could give it no attention. . . . The meeting adjourned to Estelle Hall.

The annexed newspaper clipping, unidentified, reports:

. . . The following delegates came forward and enrolled their names:
Limestone—J. W. Sloss, Jonathan McDonald, Thos. H. Hobbs
Morgan—J. D. Rather, L. S. Banks, R. N. Walden
Autauga—Jesse R. Jones, Jacob House, W. C. Howell, John Smith, D. C. Neal, R. Spigener, J. R. Lawson, Nathaniel Jeffries
Coosa—R. Smoot, R. C. Clarke
Shelby—Horace Ware*
Jefferson—M. B. Lancaster, Joab Bagley.
(The citizens generally of Montgomery being considered delegates, their names were not recorded.)
On motion, Messrs. T. H. Hobbs, of Limestone, Ware of Shelby, Walden of Morgan, Neal, of Autauga, Smoot, of Coosa, Lancaster, of Jefferson, and Belser, of Montgomery, were appointed a committee on resolutions. After retiring for a short time, the committee made the following report, through their chairman, Mr. Hobbs.

The resolutions were generally what they had been in the Decatur meeting, stating the need for a central railroad to connect North and South Alabama, to develop mineral resources, and to serve for travel and freight, and including the additional resolve that the people of Southeastern and Southwestern Alabama realize benefits of the road by the convention's favoring the construction of a road from Montgomery by way of Union Springs to Eufaula, and a branch road from the eligible point on the Alabama and Florida R. R. to the city of Mobile.

*The name of Horace Ware is a predominant one in this list, because of his contribution to the mineral development of the state. Born in Lynn, Massachusetts, in 1812, Ware came with his father, Jonathan, to Bibb County, Alabama, where he built a water forge for the Mahan family. In 1846 Ware built the Shelby furnace, and later established there the first rolling mill in the state. During the Civil War, he supplied more iron to the Selma arsenal than any other.—*Alabama Blast Furnaces,* 126; McKenzie, 157.

30th. The report of my speech & Sloss' is incorrect. I really gave little stress to the importance of the Central to Monty, but spoke of it more as a State work and its State necessity. Sloss is not opposed to State Aid upon principle but upon policy alone. Gilmer is resolutely opposed to it. . . . But that the State must ultimately aid in its construction, I have no doubt.

November 1, 1858. I have said that Gilmer is the working man of the enterprise—but I must not underrate the powerful efforts of Watts & Judge, who have taken hold manfully and nobly.

Thomas Hill Watts and Thomas Judge were law partners in Montgomery. Watts organized the 17th Alabama Infantry regiment, and served as its colonel until selected by Jefferson Davis as attorney general of the Confederacy. Col. Thomas Judge served with the 14th Alabama, was severely injured in a railroad accident, and appointed a judge of the military court. He was later appointed to the state supreme court.—Owen, IV, 1732 and III, 951.

November 16, 1858. The annexed sketch is from the *Limestone News*, the new paper started by John A. and Reuben W. Johnson.

In our last issue we published the proceedings of the Rail Road convention held in Montgomery on the 30th ult. We this week publish the substance of the remarks of Hon. T. H. Hobbs, made before the convention. As to Mr. Hobbs' remarks, it is only necessary for us to say and the people to know that he made them, and all who have heard him will know that what he left unsaid was not important for any one to know. Tom. Hobbs and Dr. McDonald have done as much to advance the interests of the Tenn. and Ala. Central R. R. as any other men in the county or State. And what is more, they have done it without fee or reward, save a small fee to the Dr. while acting as President. Their motive has been to serve the public and advance the interest of the whole. They, with Luke Pryor and Dr. Sowell, were the originators as well as the advocates of this great scheme to connect North and South Alabama by means of a grand central trunk road. Maj. Hobbs was a member of the *volunteer* corpse [*sic*] of engineers that made the survey through the mountains from Morgan county to Elyton, in Jefferson. He, with his colleague, Col. Pryor, introduced the bill into the Legislature, and obtained for the road a liberal charter—even succeeded in its passage over the veto of the Governor. Maj. Hobbs not only rendered efficient service to this road, but he has been engaged in the cause of internal improvements, generally, for a number of years. And not only has he been engaged in internal improvements, but he has done as much, or more, to improve the agricultural condition of the county than any other man in it—and is still lending all of his energies to its success. Mr. Hobbs is a forcible speaker, always presenting his subject in so clear and forcible a manner as to carry conviction to the minds of his hearers—and this, coupled with his sound practical sense, makes him a valuable acquisition to any cause that he may espouse. . . . we have the gratifying assurance of the present able and energetic President, J. W. Sloss, Esq., that at the completion of the road to the State line, the company will not owe one "red cent." What a compliment to the sagacity of those who put the ball in motion.

November 21st, 1858. Went down to the Central this mor'g to go to Athens, and somewhat expecting that my parents might come. . . . they did, and brought Cousin Julia Meade with them. They . . . report that Anne is pretty well and . . . daily expecting her confinement, which . . . increases my anxiety to go to her. Mr. [William G.] Hensley, the new pastor, preached for the first time (as Pastor) to his cong.

24th. Accompanied by servant, Hannah, I left home this mor'g for L'burg.

25th. Reached L'burg at 9 P.M.

28th. The Meth. preachers are at Conference at Portsmouth, so James and I went to the Pres. Church, and heard an argument against dueling, which was very strong indeed. I must confess the point made by the preacher that the duellist dies in the commission of a sin *which must be inexpiable* went home to my mind with a great deal of force—almost terror. I had never thought of the matter in that light.

November 29th, 1858. This evening about six, Anne's labor began, and continued until 8:20, when she was safely delivered of a son. . . . the boy able to squall loudly, and suck very soon after his birth. . . . Anne admitted me into the room soon after the birth, and I know I never loved her so much as at that moment.

Hobbs' son was Thomas Maclin Hobbs, who married Anne Davis Richardson, daughter of Dr. Nicholas Davis and Betty Hine Richardson. They had three daughters: Anna (Frierson-Horton), Marie Pleasants (Betts), and Elizabeth Maclin (Higgins).

December 2, 1858. Dem. Convention met in Petersburg and after several stormy and uproarious sessions, Letcher was nominated for Governor.

3rd. Anne and the boy improving rapidly. Thanks be to God!

27th. After a family consultation today, it was decided that it would be best for me to return home now rather than wait for Anne . . . it is important for me to be at home at beginning of year, as I have a new overseer to set up.

29th. Arrived safely in Athens today, and took all by surprize.

31st. Mr. Spence, the new manager, is installed, and has commenced business. His family consists of a wife and two children.

Saturday, January 1, 1859. Time, as it glides along, brings with it new cares, new pleasures, new responsibilities. This New Year finds me what no predecessor has found me—a father. And during its continuance, and for many more, if it please God, I must sustain that relation, and be charged with the responsibilities that grow out of it.

3rd. Rev. James Rowe, an original man, preached twice for us on yesterday, and today came down to my house to begin the erection of one of his crushers. Twenty years ago, when temporarily occupying the pastoral relation to our church in Athens—(P. B. Robinson, the pastor, having gone north to attend medical lectures), he boarded in our family, and invented this machine.

4th. Hal Malone came down to hunt. Today Misses Mattie Coleman, Octavia Bass, and Julia Meade came down, and we shall have a pleasant week.

Attached to the diary is this little unidentified newspaper clipping:

Verses to Tom.—The pretty little poem in this paper (taken from the Home Circle,) is understood to be from the pen of our townsman, G. P. Keyes, Esq., and "Tom" is Thomas H. Hobbs, Esq., of North Alabama.

LINES TO MY FRIEND
BY G. P. K.

We are hastening, Tom, to the tomb,
  And the lights of other days fade,
As we tread along in the gloom
  Our perishing hopes have made.
Yet the stars that shone long ago
  Are beaming above in the sky;
And the brook, with its musical flow,
  Still murmuring pleasantly by.

But changes are seen all along
  The path we have patiently trod,
And friends whom we mingled among,
  Lie buried beneath the green sod.
E'en the flowers that grow by the rill,
  Bloom scarcely so sweetly as when
We angled beside the old mill,
  And rambled along in the glen.

Then often we sighed to be free
  From the tasks we had to perform,
And dreamed that the future would be
  Unbroken by shadow or storm.
We thought when we'd grow to be men,
  No clouds would darken our way:
And the earth would be beautiful then
  As the skies at the coming of day.

But, Tom, in the world do we find
  The glories we thought were so near?
Alas! we have left them behind.
  And only their shadows are here!
They live in the dreams of the past:
  Their brightness grows dim to the eye;
And they cease to enchant us at last,
  And soon in the grave we must lie.

Yet we fear not the gloom of despair,
  Though earth and its glories decay.
For a country, so lovely and fair.
  Now smiles in the distance away.
There night never blackens the skies,
  Nor darkens the beautiful plains,
And tears are wiped from all eyes,
  By Him who eternally reigns!

January 23rd, 1859. Arrived safely in Lynchburg. . . . the baby has grown very much since I saw him.
24th. We intended to start home today, but Miss Sallie Ryan, a cousin of Anne's from Balt., is going with us and has telegraphed us to expect her on tomorrow.

Sallie Ryan was the daughter of William H. and Maria Richardson Ryan of Baltimore and Lynchburg, and niece of Mrs. Benagh and William Richardson. She married Judge William Walker of Athens.

January 25th, 1859. We met Miss R. at the Depot, and off we all went. The party consists of Mrs. Benagh, Anne, Miss R., the baby and his nurse, and myself. I had seven pieces of baggage to check; besides an armful of blankets, satchels, etc., etc., and what with getting seats for 3 ladies, a child & servant and checking baggage, I was kept pretty busy at each change of cars, for I . . . had to attend to it at every change.
January 27, 1859. We arrived at Mooresville Station about 3 A.M., and found the carriage waiting for us. We were soon at home, where Ma & Pa were waiting for us with good fires and warm smiles. It has been a trip of much uneasiness for me, and I am so thankful that it is safely over.
28th. Late this evening the crusher upon which Pa & Mr. Rowe have . . . been engaged was completed. . . . The superiority of this over any other crusher is that it grinds up the shuck as well as the corn & cob. It will also grind up bones, and I propose to grind all these which I can obtain for ag. purposes. Where are all the bones of all the horses, mules, cattle, hogs, dogs, which have been killed or died since the settlement of the country? They have scarcely decayed yet, and can many of them be gathered up; so I have offered to pay 50 cts. per 100 bls. for them, and expect the negroes will soon be bringing them in.
31st. Began this week to haul out manure & spread it on the circular hillside west of gin-house. I insisted upon its being put down in piles, and in straight rows at that, so that it might be distributed equally over the surface. The negroes, who have been accustomed to throwing it out of a waggon [*sic*] think this an unnecessary particularity—and I believe the overseer halfway agrees with them, but if there is anything upon which I am resolved, it is in *heavily* & *equally* manuring what I undertake. And I am going to undertake a good deal.
February 3, 1859. The papers tell us of the death of Prescott, the Historian, which occurred on last Friday. A correspondent of *Journal of Commerce* says his grandfather Prescott commanded the Americans at Bunker Hill, and his maternal grandfather, Linzee, commanded the British. P. S. Capt. Linzee was his wife's grandfather.
February 5, 1859. Mary Sowell, daughter of Dr. Sowell, died tonight.
7th. I am laying off the circular hill-side west of gin-house for horizontal plowing. . . . I run the guide rows with the level about ten ft. apart, and split up the middles by having the team of the plowman led a certain distance from the guide rows. These rows become the centres of the cotton beds, and are subsoiled as deep as 3 mules can draw the plow.
8th. We are also engaged in cutting down a part of the peach orchard— which part is to be added to the cotton fields. This field with its

manuring, its subsoiling and its addition of the rich peach land, ought to bring near a bale to the acre.

9th. My ever faithful friend, Pompey, is to be married tonight to Miss Maggie Locke of La Grange, Tenn., who is said to be a most charming woman. She wrote us a note of invitation to the wedding, and it was certainly as tasteful an affair as I ever saw. I care not how excellent she is—she is not too good for Wilk.

10th. Mrs. B., Anne, baby and I went to town this day. . . . I rode up Lina in order to wean her colt, (which we have named "Sallie Ryan").

11th. Staid at Mr. Richardson's last night & home this morning.

14th. Did not return home til aft.—and lost my blue blanket on the way, which has travelled many thousand miles with me—besides being an important part of my & Pomp's bedding during the survey. Hope I shall recover it.

March 2, 1859. Mr. Alex McDonald, who was one of my waiters, is now on a visit to his cousin, Gab. Jordan. He came down to our house with Sallie Ryan this aft. Attended the meeting of Ex. Com. of Ag. Society. It was well attended, and as harmonious as could be expected. We were able to control the horse men, so as to prevent that department from getting too much prominence at the fair, and what was still better, we prevented so much importance being given to *speed* as a horse quality. This was accomplished by offering premiums for the *fastest*, and for the *best* horses, so that the two classes were not necessarily competitors. I urged, & secured, 2nd premiums in almost every department of importance, which I think a movement of great importance.

April 2nd, 1859. Attended a party at Mr. Richardson's, which was to be in compliment to . . . cousin Sally Ryan. This latter lady is now understood to be engaged to Judge Walker. He has given her an elegant $300 diamond ring, significant of their engagement.

15th. [A clipping from the *Herald* is appended, written by D. H. Bingham, requesting Thomas Hobbs and W. M. Redus to run for the next legislature.]

19th. Mrs. Benagh and Sally Ryan left for Va. under charge of Judge Walker. . . . It made us all sad to give these ladies up. Anne has been with her mother since Sep. 1, and has been so tenderly nursed, and the baby so completely cared for by her mother that she must miss her very much.

26th. [An unidentified newspaper article states that John B. Gilmer had committed suicide in Washington, and that Roger Pryor had identified the body.]

I knew this young man well. He was a brother of my friend, Miss Juliet.

28th. Decided today to be a candidate for Leg.—have been hesitating for a long time. For, altho' I think the chances are all in favor of my election . . . yet I have felt all along that it would be vastly more pleasant to remain at home with my family. . . . The only candidates out now are Rip Davis and Beauchamp—tho' I have no doubt that Redus will run—and that the contest between him & Rip will be a close one.

May 2, 1859. [An unidentified newspaper clipping states that the candidates had given their positions on state aid. . . . Col. Beauchamp was for internal improvements, but thought that public works should be accomplished by private enterprise. He was in favor of the 2 and 3 percent fund being used on railroads. Rip Davis declared that as a general rule he opposed state aid, but that in certain contingencies he was induced toward aid.]

Athens today. I did not intend to do more than announce myself but was led from one idea to another until I spoke several minutes.

June 9th. Dr. Wilkinson came up today in his buggy, driving his pair of mares which he wishes to breed to Foote's horse, *Columbus.* His wife . . . will come on the train tomorrow.

11th. Spoke at Mooresville, Rip and I agreeing pretty much and Beauchamp against us.

An unidentified newspaper article describes a meeting of the Board of Directors of the Tennessee and Alabama Central Rail Road:

> Mr. Hobbs then called up the following Resolutions from the table and they were so taken up and adopted.
>
> *Resolved,* that the Stockholders in the Tennessee and Alabama Central Rail Road have heard with great pleasure of the prospects and progress of the Montgomery and Pensacola Rail Road—the Montgomery and Union Springs' Rail Road—the Mobile and Great Northern Rail Road—the N. E. and S. W. Rail Road—the North and South Alabama Rail Road and the Selma and Gulf Rail Road, and that the connection of these roads and our own Central will be the realization of the long-cherished plan of uniting North and South Alabama, of developing her agricultural and mineral resources and populating her unoccupied territory. . . . Mr. Bingham then introduced Preamble and Resolutions, in reference to the policy of establishing Blast Furnaces and Rolling Mills at or near the intersection of the North East and South West, with the Tennessee and Alabama Central Rail Road, and instructing the President of this Company to open a correspondence with the Presidents of the several Rail Road Companies of this State and with practical iron masters, with a view to elicit information as to the best means of obtaining capital and skill to carry the enterprise at once into effect. . . .
>
> JOSHUA L. COMAN, PRES.
> D. H. BINGHAM AND
> O. A. VAN HOOK, SECRETARIES.

Sunday, July 3, 1859. The Memphis & Charleston R. R. started for the first time, a double daily service of passenger cars.

4th. Early went to Mooresville where we propose to celebrate the day . . . In my talk, I proposed to organize those present into a 4th July Association to celebrate the day through all time. This was done, and we elected the following officers: H. W. Kimble, Pres't; Thomas Bibb, V.P.; Steptoe Pickett, Marshal; T. H. Hobbs, Dr. T. Thach and Dr. Bibb, the Com. of Correspondence; Wm. Martin, Charles Tucker, Wm. Hundley, John R. Harris, B. B. Peete, and James Woodroof, Executive Committee. . . . We also got the names of 32 persons, mostly young men, who were willing to organize a Cavalry Company. . . . The dinner was served near the spring and was plentiful and orderly.

An article from the *Athens Herald* describing the day, ends with these words: "We were happy to observe that social, good feeling and harmony, that always prevails among an intelligent, high-toned and chivalrous community like that surrounding Mooresville."

9th. While speaking at Siloam today high words sprang up between Beauch. and Rip.

18th. Beauchamp has not been with us . . . since Siloam.

August 1st. The annexed shows the results of our election. I did not think Rip would be ahead of me, though I thought we would be close together in our vote. The R. R. men adopted him as their candidate and the Antis still gave him to a considerable extent their support.

[Davis, 758; Hobbs, 681; Beauchamp, 445.]

August 2, 1859. Went to Memphis to attend Stockholder's Convention. Anne wished some things for a party she will give Wm. H. Walker & Lady, & I avail myself of this chance to go down & come back free.

4th. Returned home. Pa & Ma & Miss Mary Walton started for the Va. Springs and a trip north for the benefit of Miss W., who bears all the expense of the trip.

Mary Ann ("Molly") Walton was born in 1829 on the Walton plantation just east of Mooresville. She gave the large chandelier in the brick church at Mooresville, and is said to have outfitted an entire company from Limestone during the Civil War. The Walton cottage in Mooresville later became the home of the clairvoyant minister, Constantine Sanders. See *X Plus Y Equals Z,* on file at the Athens Public Library, or the articles of John Knox in the *Decatur Daily,* October 14 and October 18, 1964. The Walton cottage, last owned by the architect Allison Bailey, burned in 1964.

October 17, 1859. At this date Hobbs attached a clipping from the Montgomery *Mail:*

A friend, yesterday afternoon, expressed himself as a little surprised, that we expressed so unqualified a prefence [*sic*] for Judge Meek, for the [Speaker of] the House, says Mr. Hobbs, of Limestone, was prominently in the field for the office. We were aware that Mr. Hobbs' name had been mentioned in connection with the candidacy for the Speakership, but we really had supposed that the onerous duties which devolve on him, in the special representation of several most important interests, would prevent him from allowing himself to be nominated for a post which, to a great extent, cuts off a representative from the special business of its immediate constituents. It happens, however, that Mr. Hobbs' numerous friends are seriously determined to present his claims to the Speakership, and we learn there is a singular unanimity in his favor, in North Alabama. High as was our commendation of Judge Meek's fitness, it is nothing less than truth to say of Mr. Hobbs, that very few men in any state are so worthy or so gifted. North Alabama may well be proud of such a son. We think it very hard, not say unfair, that because a man has acquired a reputation as a working man, he should be deprived of the honors to which that work justly entitles him. Mr. Hobbs has been a faithful laborer for the interest of Alabama, and for this reason, together with his eminent fitness for the station, we would like to see him promoted.

19th. Our Fair began—very large crowd present. Lieut. Maury made the address—not very appropriate, I thought. Our calvary company consisting of 8, turned out first time in uniform.
22nd. Was elected Pres't of the Ag. Society. Fair closed. Receipts at gate about $2300.
25th. Left home about sunrise with Lina and Uncle's 3 yr old filly—for Tuscumbia. Reached there a little after dark. Stopped at O. O. Nelson's.
28th. Exhibited Lina—she came in one of the premiums but lost it again.
29th. The 3 yr old got a $15 pitcher today and we all started for home. My sulky tire broke off 5 miles beyond Courtland and I took train.
November 7, 1859. Started from home with Anne, baby, and Mrs. Walker. We reached Knoxville about 12 at night. . . . Here I parted with the ladies, who, having their baggage checked through and tickets provided, think they can get along without me.
November 9, 1859. Arrived in Montgomery about 11 at night. Miss Bettie Pollard marrying a Dr. Lee of Mobile.

Bettie Pollard, daughter of Charles Teed Pollard, was married to Dr. Paul Cornelius Lee, son of Dr. Jacob Martin and Rebecca Ballard Lee, of Carlowville, Alabama. The beautiful Pollard home in Montgomery is now occupied by an insurance company.—National League of Penwomen, 261.

12th. Today it was decided that Rather should be elected Pres't of Senate, a most unexpected move, which, of course, greatly diminishes my chances, the two officers not likely to be taken from adjoining districts.

At the 13th this article is attached:

No appointment made by the Legislative assembly with the exception of United States

Senator is of more concern to the interest of a State than that of Speaker of the House. The duties required of the chair and the powers confided to it are of deep practical importance, and fully in keeping with the distinction which the statute confers on the occupant. In one view alone this is made manifest. The business of such bodies is in the main transacted by committees and in committee rooms. Unless it be a question of general interest the report from this source usually decides the fate of a Bill. The chairman of the committee on the Judiciary is chief architect in our legislative building. To the Speaker is confided the delicate task of appointing *all the committees* and of designating the chairman of each. As the organ of the House, the presiding officer gives to it more than any other member its tone and standing, and to fill it properly he must possess talents of no ordinary character. Patience, urbanity and firmness are indispensable. The writer of this would pay no unmerrited [*sic*] compliment to Mr. Hobbs. It is not too much to say that his well known abilities mark him as peculiarly suited to the place. Educated to the profession of law Mr. Hobbs has from inclination and taste followed the occupation of a farmer, and as such is conversant with the wants of this large class of our community. To a mind well balanced and closely trained, he adds the requisites of industrious working habits, and a large experience in the conduct of Legislative affairs. When he speaks it is to the point, and to the business at hand, as any one may see by reading his published addresses. Unpretending and unambitious in style, they reflect the character of the man. More than this, and above all this, his moral character is without spot or blemish, with neither frailties of youth nor the vices of age. We commend him to the delegation from North Alabama.

Nick Davis in So. Adv.

The *Limestone News* endorsed Hobbs for speaker, and the *Montgomery Mail* announced: "True, Mr. Hobbs is a gentleman every way qualified for the position of Speaker, but he is one of those practical, working members, that could illy be spared from the floor of the House. We wish there were fifty Tom Hobbses elected to the Legislature."

November 14, 1859. A. B. Meek of Mobile, was elected Speaker, the chief argument in his favor being that No. Ala. had the President of Senate.

Alexander Beaufort Meek was a man twelve years Hobbs' senior. He had served as the state attorney general, as assistant secretary and legal advisor to the U. S. Treasury Department under President Polk, and as the first chairman of the Alabama House of Representatives' Committee on Education, whereby he established the system of free schools in the state. Thomas Hobbs succeeded him as chairman of this committee. Although Meek was the author of several works, he is best remembered for his poem, "The Red Eagle," the story of William Weatherford, courageous leader of the Creek Indians.—Owen, IV, 1183.

WAR
1861-1862

It is regrettable that the diary for 1860 is missing for, in many aspects, this year was even more eventful than the ensuing one. Those passions that severed the nation came to a climax when Southerners bolted at the Democratic Convention in an April Charleston, and the convention adjourned to meet again in Baltimore in June, at which time Stephen A. Douglas was nominated. John Bell and Edward Everett were nominees of the Constitutional Union Party, and the Republicans nominated Abraham Lincoln and Hannibal Hamlin. John C. Breckenridge was the nominee for the Democratic seceders. Soon after Lincoln's election, South Carolina seceded.

The year 1860 was the year of the Pony Express, the first repeating rifle, of emerging photography, and "Old Black Joe." Ralph Waldo Emerson's *The Conduct of Life,* John Greenleaf Whittier's *Home Ballads,* and Darwin's *Origin of Species* were first introduced to American readers.

In Alabama the legislature continued passing bills for internal improvements, reforms, and educational institutions. The bay and harbor at Mobile were to be improved; masonry, iron gates, and other fixtures of the old Muscle Shoals Canal were to be disposed of, and the money proceeding from their sale used in public schools; the insane hospital opened to its first patients in Tuscaloosa; and the plans for the Institution for the Deaf and Dumb and Blind were finalized. The Alabama and Tennessee Central Railroad received appropriation, with the stipulation that the project be completed in five years; and the Alabama and Mississippi Railroad, from West Point to Jackson, was approved. Incorporations were authorized for the East Alabama Male College, the Octavia Walton Levert Normal College at Dadeville, and academies in Pickens, Walker, Barbour, Pike, and Autauga counties were sanctioned.

Secession or cooperation became the major issue throughout the state as events congealed. Delegates pledged to one opinion or another were elected for the Secession Convention to be held in Montgomery on January 7, 1861. Again, the geographical sections showed wide political differences. Thomas Hobbs, secessionist, was in the minority in north Alabama, while the majority of those in the southern section voted for secession. The 1861 diary clearly illustrates the depth of emotional feeling between life-long friends.

There was no recourse. Men like Thomas Hobbs resolutely synchronized their private lives and public duties with the mainspring of the military, confident that victory would be theirs in a short time. But the confidence that prevailed at First Manassas faded as the battles continued, and "these men, brothers all, divided only by devotion to cause and cannon line," gave their all (quotation from film shown at Gettysburg National Military Park). In 1862, when a Charleston business man was complaining to Robert E. Lee that it was difficult for so many men to have to abandon their business for the war, Lee replied, "Believe me, sir, the business of this generation *is* the war" (Ravenel, 497).

Tuesday, January 1, 1861. The new year finds me in Lynchburg, whither I have come to be present at Anne's second accouchement. The most momentous political events are daily occurring. The Cabinet is divided, and heavy robberies of one of the Departments have just occurred. So. Carolina has dissolved her connexion with the Union of the States, and her com's are now at Washgtn to treat for an adjustment of all matters for a final and perpetual severance of the State. In a day or two the Florida convention meets and will no doubt follow suit. Ala. voted for members to her convention on 25th Dec., and the papers says [*sic*] a majority in favor of immediate secession have been elected. Limestone elected Dr. Coman and T. J. McClellan, who favor a cooperation of all the So. States. So do all the delegates from N. Ala., as I learn.

Thomas Joyce McClellan, born in Lincoln County, Tennessee, in 1811, married Martha Beattie in 1836, and had several children. Among them were: Thomas Nicholas, state attorney general and chief justice of the supreme court; Robert Anderson, who married Aurora Pryor, daughter of Luke, and had Thomas Cowan McClellan, supreme court justice, and Memory Pryor, who married Robert Henry Walker, parents of Robert Henry Walker, Limestone County historian.—Owen, IV, 1093–94.

January 4, 1861. Anne was safely delivered by Dr. John H. Patterson of a fine boy.* . . . The boy is not very large, but seems to have the use of all his organs—voice, especially. . . . This is the day appointed by the Pres't as one of national fasting, humiliation, and prayer. All the stores here (Lynchburg) were closed, and services held in all the churches. Dr. Edwards preached from "Except the Lord build the house, they labor in vain who build it," Ps. 137.

*James Benagh Hobbs, died in 1883 of measles, while attending The University of Alabama.—Hobbs Family Papers.

5th. Just about the time Baby was born yest. morning, Ft. Morgan and the U. S. Arsenal in Mobile were seized by the State troops. Georgia has also taken possession of one of the Forts near, or at, Savannah.

6th. Anne is getting on finely, and so much better than when Maclin was born that we are all greatly rejoiced. The baby too is doing pretty well—he weighs 8 pounds—has a big nose, and unmistakeably red hair. *7th.* The Ala. Convention meets today. The Va. Leg. met by call of the Gov.—in his message Letcher takes ground against calling State Convention—in favor of a Central Confederacy composed of the Border Slave & Free States—leaving N. Y. and New England out in the weather—against coercion, and in favor of secession. A great deal depends upon the action of Va., and I hope she will be able to stand up firmly for our rights.

It was because of the indecisiveness of Virginia officials that the firing on Ft. Sumter was instigated by certain Virginians to force a decision. The Ft. Sumter incident occurred on April 12, and Virginia seceded five days later.

January 9, 1861. Anne & Baby getting on finely. I left for Mont'y to attend the extra session of Leg. called by Gov. Moore, anticipating secession. On train found Col. Powell, of Mont'y, accompanied by Gen. Heningsen, the companion of Walker in his campaigns in Nicaragua. *11th.* Today a little after two o'clock the Convention passed the ordinance of secession—by a majority of 22. Clemens of Madison voted for it, but Nick Davis against it.

One of the most dramatic events concerning Alabama's secession was the death of Bishop Nicholas Hamner Cobbs, who had wished that he might die before Alabama should secede. Early on the morning of January 11, Bishop Cobbs was granted his wish.—American Guide Series, *Alabama,* 107.

13th. Convention in session—as the most stirring events are every moment transpiring it was thought best to sit today.

14th. Legislature met. House pretty full. Did not organize because the Convention has not yet prescribed the new oath to be administered to the new members. Troops are parading the streets and leaving for Pensacola, the Gov. having been requested by Gov. of Florida to send them to assist in holding Pensacola. The Federal troops there have retired to Ft. Pickens—the strongest of the works. Sloss came down, bringing news of the greatest excitement in Mad. & Limestone against the passage of the ordinance. They are offended that the question was not submitted to the vote of the people. He says they were to hold a meeting on yrst. at which he expected they would recall their delegates to Conv., and instruct members of Leg. to vote against an appropriation to raise money to maintain the present movement. If they do so, I will resign, for I will not sanction any backward step from the position of the State.

January 20, 1861. [An article from the Montgomery *Mail* is appended.]

The election of delegates to represent this State in the Congress which meets in this city next month, took place in the Convention on yesterday. This action on the part of the Convention clearly demonstrates the fact that there is a large majority of its members in favor of a prudent, deliberate, and conservative policy. Judge Chilton, Judge Shorter, Judge Lewis, Dr. Fearne, Robert H. Smith, Esq., Judge Walker, Col. Hale, are men who are conservative in their views, and although some of them approved of the policy of Separate State Action, they are nevertheless in favor of no unwise measures. The minority (Co-operationists) aided by several conservative men on the other side, voted for a majority of the successful candidates. This action of the Convention shows another fact. It is beyond dispute that there is a large majority of the Convention who are not in favor of the rash plans, and the precipitate measures of the defeated Regency. The conservative men having elected these gentlemen to such responsible positions, will look forward with eagerness to the result of their mature and serious deliberations. Were it a time now for us to laugh and be merry, we should certainly do so over the down-fall of the Regency. Subjoined may be found the vote, etc. *First District:* McRae, 57; Lyon, 28; Pettus, 13. *Second District:* Shorter, 56; Cato, 38. *Third District:* Rice, 21; Judge, 16, Chilton, 51; Yancey, 4; Cato, 5. *Fourth District:* Whitfield, 45; Cochran, 1; Yelverton, 1; Hale, 51. *Fifth District:* Lewis, 65; Moore, 11; Pryor, 6; Cato, 1; Blank 1. *Sixth District:* Fearne, 72; Harwick, 26; Walker, 1. *Seventh District:* Curry, 52; Smith, 47. *State at Large:* Walker, 86; Jemison, 3; Smith, 50; Yancey, 38; Pettus, 8; Walker, 2. Messrs. R. W. Walker and R. H. Smith were elected for the State at large, having received the highest number of votes cast.

Mr. Yancey's friends say that his repeated refusals to allow his name to be run is the cause of his failure to be elected to some of the offices, but it is thought that he has lately lessened his popularity even among his own side, by intemperate speeches. McRae was put in because he is a leading merchant in Mobile, and it was thought the interests of commerce required one of his profession to be in the Congress.

January 21, 1861. It seems the meeting in Limestone on this day week was a failure, as we have heard nothing from it. From other parts of N. Ala. we learn that the feeling of opposition is decreasing, and the people coming finely up to the support of the ordinance. Pryor, Mason, Paul Jones & co., who were going to take up arms to coerce S. C., will scarcely do so now.

22nd. Mr. Sloss, who has been here several days, left last night. Rip Davis, my colleague, left last night also. Nick says he knew Rip would bolt when he saw that resolutions endorsing the action of the Convention in seceding had been introduced in the Senate. I received a letter from home telling of the death of Wash—and the mysterious cutting the throat of a good brood mare.

An attached clipping, unidentified, states that the Alabama delegation had presented a letter of withdrawal to the Speaker of the House in Washington on the 21st.

23rd. Yest. the bill I introduced on Thursday, substituting the Mountain R. R. Contracting Co., for the Central R. R. Co. in the three per cent bill of last session, was passed. It was amended so that the road should not discriminate against connecting roads & vice versa.

An attached clipping from the *Chattanooga Advertiser* declared that the Tennessee River was then higher than at any time since 1847 and the losses were very heavy.

An article from the *Athens Democrat,* contains two letters, the first dated January 22, 1861, and the other dated January 31, 1861.

> Ed. Democrat:—Today has been a glorious day for the town of Athens, in spite of the threats of that arch traitor, Yancey to compel us, the citizens of Limestone county to submit to treason and Disunion. We have this day run up the glorious flag of our Union on the Court House, and the working men of Athens have just been out and fired one hundred guns in honor of the Union and the flag. Long may it wave! We did not forget the music for we had that same old tune played frequently, that our fathers used to keep step to the Union, and for the Union. You may depend that this town will be the first to meet any traitors on the line of North Alabama. As to the people here, I can say with confidence that there is no Disunion men here; and, as for the ladies, God bless them! they are all true blue . . . Yours respectfully, Union.

> Ed. Democrat: We, the undersigned, do state that the statement in your paper of January 25, in relation to the hoisting of the American flag, and the firing of one hundred guns, in honor of the Union of the thirty-three States, and of the flag, is correct in every particular, the *Union and American* newspaper of your city to the contrary notwithstanding.—*Their friend* is not posted, and should not use bad language to the working men and Union men of Athens. John Green, J. Hurd, Geo. B. Anderson, James L. Raney, B. H. Glaze, J. R. Green, L. F. Smith, R. S. Gray, Jo. Lacy, Jas. S. Kelly, William B. Holt, D. M. Elliott, B. R. Williams, John H. Butler, Milton J. Sloan, S. A. Hunt, John H. Elliott, S. T. Bacon, Napoleon B. Cook, J. H. Allison, F. H. Oglesby, R. H. Cartwright, Thomas Bass, Jr.; J. F. Danforth, F. Green, H. C. Murrel, W. P. Oglesby, John Jackson, C. E. Tucker, Benjamin F. Reid, Samuel B. Higgins, B. A. Dailey, W. S. McKinney, John J. Higgins, Sam Booth, Wm. P. Everett, Chas. W. Raisler, John R. Stanback, W. T. Swett, J. W. York, A. P. Reid, A. H. Williamson, C. F. York, J. B. East.

Saturday, February 2, 1861. Both branches passed the Bill legalizing suspension of the Banks. Letter from Ma announcing the death of Sue Meade. She has been declining for several years. Poor girl! . . . Peace to her ashes!

3rd. The annexed from the *Union Banner* of the 2nd inst. shows the feeling which its editor has towards the leading men of the Se. movement, also that he is insidiously trying to arouse the workingmen against others as a class. This feeling is getting up pretty strong in Athens and will result in the injury, of course, of the mechanics.

> Yancey in Pickle—On Saturday night last, Yancey, the notorious secessionist and agitator, was publicly humiliated by a portion of the populace of Athens. A large crowd assembled on the public square; the *Hon. gentleman* was rigged up *a la effigie,* escorted around town in an old fashioned stick gig, and finally consumed by a more devouring element, than that, with which Southern hearts are fired. These doings are unmistakable evidences of the feeling of a part of the public of Athens, and foreshadow a resistance to secession and its ringleaders, which we presume nothing else but a backing down from some of the recent acts of the Convention will serve to eradicate. The idea of governmental oppression very justly serves to rekindle the fire of patriotism in the work-

ingman's breast, and hence these outbursts of expression among the bone and sinew of our land. We have good cause of sympathy with the working masses, we are a working man ourself, and while we go with them heart and hand in asserting and maintaining their just rights. . . . We have not a word condemnatory to utter against effigieical demonstrations in general, yet we are not prepared to advise them, for the reason that they inflame the public mind without effecting any salutary or permanent good; they are strong expressions of hostility, and serve to convey to the victim of them malignant ill will, but that they have the least tendency to the correction of evil is very doubtful in our mind. We would rather advise the people, the bone and sinew, to meet together in formal assemblies and give expressions to their sentiments in any way they see fit, but in a spirit compatible with the dignity and independence which attaches to those who earn their bread by the sweat of their brow. Let the laboring man take a stand, let him side-by-side with the politician, make his mark, but let it be the mark of a benefactor, not of an agitator, a mark that time can not efface, or that memory cannot recall without pride and pleasure. While the spirit of secession is greatly to be deprecated, it has nevertheless become overpowering in its influence and coextensive in its sway.—Six sovereign States have thus far adopted it, and it has therefore acquired an influence that cannot be disregarded. All conservatives should look to this fact, and still further, to a reconstruction of the government and act accordingly; by this means the plans of those who will be satisfied with nothing but a devastating warfare, will be defeated, and conservatism finally prevail.

Attached newspaper article of February 7, 1861, to Mr. A. B. Hendren:

Sir: I have seen a Nashville paper to-day, reaffirming that the stars and stripes were raised here on a certain date, and guns were fired in honor of the same at night. I understand that because my name appears among others to that document; I am suspected as having something to do with the hanging or burning (for I really do not know which was done) of Col. Yancey in effigy, here recently. I cannot help what others attribute to me, but I emphatically state that my sole object was to sustain the statement about the raising of the flag, and firing of the guns, which I knew to be true. I am a man of but few words, but my voice has always been raised in disapprobation of the burning or hanging of any one in effigy. I never heard until to-day that any unkind demonstration was contemplated towards an Hon. Gentleman of this county; and if I had I should have used every means in my power to prevented [*sic*] it. He is my personal friend, and I should not be true to my nature if I stood passively by and suffered any indignity offered him. I am and always have been a Union man but have no disposition to resist the action of my State.

GEO. R. ANDERSON

We concur in the above.

JESSE LACY, B. F. REED, W. B. HOLT, THOS. BASS, JR.

The Hon. gent of this county was, I learn, myself. A knot of mechanics led on by one Green, an Irish tinner, and in my opinion an abolitionist, burned Yancey in effigy and intended to burn me also, but were dissuaded. I have not heard the reason why they wished to show dislike to me—very likely they have none.

February 8, 1861. As the Leg. has agreed to adjourn tomorrow, I left for home tonight, with Mr. Patton,* of Laud., and [Senator William] Austin, of Jackson. My object in leaving . . . was to reach home before Sabbath—but being delayed by the injuries to the . . . bridge, we got only to

Chattanooga on Saturday night and stayed thru Sunday—reaching home on Monday morning.

10th. We were overtaken at Chattanooga by Rather, Bynum & others,** who reported the election of Davis and Stephens to the Presd. & V. Presidency of the new Government, and that its name is the "Confederate States of America."

*Robert M. Patton, 1809–1885, was serving as president of the state senate at the outbreak of war. Robert Patton's father, William, was one of the founders of the Bell Cotton Factory, near Huntsville. Robert moved to Florence in 1829, married Jane, daughter of General John Brahan, and completed building Sweetwater, the mansion begun by Brahan east of Florence. Since 1832 Patton had served almost continuously in the house and senate. During the war he raised large sums of money for the Confederacy, and in 1865 was elected Governor, conducting the financial affairs of the state in such a creditable manner that the U. S. Congress suspended collection of the war tax. Some thirty thousand impoverished Alabamians were fed under his direction before he was displaced under the reconstruction acts of 1868. He then became active in inducing Eastern capitalists to invest money in railroads, helped to rebuild The University of Alabama, and served as a trustee of that institution, as well as the State Normal College at Florence, the Florence Synodical Female College, and the University of Missouri.—Owen, IV, 1328.

**Oakley Bynum, born in North Carolina in 1818, became one of Lawrence County's most influential citizens. He began his legislative career in 1839, and was first elected to the senate in 1857.—Owen, III, 276.

At the date February 15, 1861, an appended article from the *Herald* reported that the flag on the Courthouse had been taken down. An article, unidentified, attached to the 18th, stated: "The inaugural ceremonies to-day were the grandest pageant ever witnessed in the South. Davis' inaugural address was chiefly based upon propositions contained in the Declaration of the American Independence."

23rd. Received a telegram from Anne, saying she would be at home on Weds. next. This surprises me, but the prevalence of small pox in Lynchburg has hastened her return. James will accompany her.

February 28, 1861. The party came this mor'g at 3. Anne has stood the trip very well.

From the *Herald* March 8. The annexed will show the result of our meeting on Monday. Our efforts to harmonize the county and set her right before the world were not seconded by our influential men, but on the contrary they insisted on introducing matter about which we could not agree. Their object is to commit the county to the reconstruction of the Union, before the question is fairly examined by the people. Could we have voted I am sure we could have passed the report of the Com.

The wrangle between Houston and me, wh. caused an adjournment without a vote grew up as follows: He said our side bro't up the reconstruction matter—that my president and my papers had taken bold grounds against it. In reply I asked him to state what position his papers and his president took. This repartee bro't down the house. . . . When he replied he asked if I intended to insinuate that he was a follower of Lincoln, I had done what was unworthy of myself. I said, "I make no insinuation—I only ask a question." He repeated his remark, to wh. I could not take offence because it was based on a condition wh. had not occurred—viz., the making an insinuation wh. I had disavowed. All evidently expected a row and Pryor, McDonald & Malone rushed in between us as if to keep us apart. It was tho't best to adjourn, and the meeting did so on Pryor's motion. . . . During the proceedings it became evident to me that he is opposed to the whole Southern movement, and w'd put us back today under Lincoln if it lay in his power. He complained of the doings of our Gov't, but had not one word to say against the rule of Lincoln.

At a meeting of the citizens of Limestone county held at the Court House on the 4th called for the purpose of harmonizing the various political complexions of the county. On motion of Dr. Jonathan McDonald, Mat. Redus, Esq., was called to the chair, and on motion of Maj. T. H. Hobbs, Daniel Coleman, Esq., was appointed Secretary. Mr. Redus in taking the chair addressed the meeting in a few calm and appropriate remarks. He stated the object of the meeting to be to correct the impression that had gone abroad, that we were in a state of hostility to the action of our Convention, and to try and harmonize the different elements of the county. Maj. Hobbs, then made a few remarks concerning the object of the meeting, and moved that a Committee of five be appointed by the chair to draft resolutions to be presented to the meeting, and also that any resolutions that any one might have to offer, should be read for the Committee to take into consideration. While the chair was appointing the Committee, Maj. Hobbs presented the following resolutions to the meeting: viz.,

"WHEREAS incorrect impressions prevail in regard to the position of Limestone county, touching the present condition of public affairs, and whereas it is highly important that our true position should be known. Therefore *Resolved,* That whatever may have been our individual preferences as to the proper method of resisting Black Republican rule, now that the State has taken action, we acknowledge that our allegiance is due to her and that we will stand by and sustain her. *Resolved,* That in our opinion it will be proper to submit the permanent Constitution of the Confederate States of America to the ratification or rejection of the people of the States, and that our delegates in the State Convention be requested to use their influence to procure action on the part of our Convention." Maj. J. N. Malone read the following resolutions for the consideration of the Committee:

"WHEREAS, The people should be heard and their wishes obeyed, both in destroying and building up Governments, (and whereas the Ordinance of Secession by which the State of Alabama was withdrawn from the Union was not submitted to them for consideration and the great principle of self government thus ignored.) Therefore *Resolved,* That the Constitution for the Confederate States of America should be referred to the voters of this State for ratification before it becomes binding on the people, and in the event of its reference to the State Convention this day assembled in Montgomery according to its own adjournment. Our delegates are to use all proper efforts to have it referred to the people for action. *Resolved,* That while we disapproved the means used and the policy adopted in passing the Ordinance of Secession. Yet, as the State of Alabama, has by that act been made to assume a position outside of the Union of the United States. We declare our purpose to assist in her defence against force or coercion on the part of the Federal Government, sharing the responsibilities and dangers of our fellow-citizens. At the same time we avow our desire for a reconstruction of the government in the event the non-slaveholding States will give us proper and satisfactory constitutional guarantees. *Resolved,* That we approve the acts of our delegates, Coman & McClelland [*sic*], touching the Ordinance of Secession and thereby avow our confidence in them as our representatives."

The Chair appointed the following Committee on resolutions: viz., Dr. J. McDonald, Maj. T. H. Hobbs, Dr. C. J. Massenburg, E. W. Grigsby, Edward Hatchett, Esq., and on motion of Maj. T. H. Hobbs, Maj. J. N. Malone was added to the Committee. The committee retired and after some time reported unanimously through their chairman, Dr. J. McDonald, in favor of Maj. Hobbs' two resolutions and Maj. Malone's third resolution. The chairman of the committee made a few brief remarks urging the adoption of the report. Maj. Malone also sustained the report in a few plain but forcible remarks. Loud cries were then made for Gen. Houston. Gen. Houston took the stand and addressed the meeting at some length. He said he could not go for the resolutions because they did not say enough. That he wanted a resolution to the effect that in the event proper guarantees were given by the Northern States the Union should be reconstructed.—He spoke disparagingly of a Southern Confederacy and said that it could not sustain itself. . . . A man in the crowd asked the Gen. which side he was on. If you do not yet know, sir, I despair of enlightening you, and will permit you to grope on in the dark. We don't pretend to quote the speech. Gen. Houston was loudly cheered and applauded several times. . . . Mr. Pryor was then vociferously called for and spoke at considerable length. He said he objected to the resolutions. He wanted Maj. Malone's resolutions to pass without any change whatever. He spoke against the present government established at Montgomery. He said that it was a government without the consent of the governed. . . . He was very much excited, and his remarks called forth a great deal of applause. Maj. Hobbs was then called on and addressed the meeting warmly and ably in defence of the report of the committee. He said it was the highest compliment that could be paid the report, that Gen. Houston and Mr. Pryor had addressed the meeting in lengthy speeches, and had not found any objection to the report. He said that his only object was conciliation and harmony—to throw oil upon the troubled waters; that he had expressly waved his individual sentiments for the sake of harmony. He spoke in a feeling and touching manner about his attachment to this State, and his remarks elicited frequent and enthusiastic applause. . . . Gen. Houston objected seriously to the word proper in Mr. Hobbs' resolution. A very strong and unpleasant feeling was gotten up. . . .

At the date Friday, March 8, 1861, an unidentified article is attached, possibly from the *Herald,* edited by Daniel Coleman:

We cannot refrain from giving our unqualified approval of the manly, dignified and firm course pursued by Major Hobbs here on Monday. We believe that his efforts for conciliation and harmony were sincere and honest. We believe that his course was sustained by a large portion of that large assembly. But he failed in his laudable efforts. We must say that we believe that if he had been met in the same spirit which he himself manifested he would have succeeded and all would have been well, but borne down by three of the best skilled speakers that we have upon the stump he had to yield and nothing was effected.—But a want of success is not always an evidence that one is wrong. We beg leave to give our feeble support to Mr. Hobbs' efforts and to say that if we believe his sincere attempts to promote harmony here on Monday shall call down any opprobrium upon him, we ask to share it with him. . . . His name is embalmed in the history of his state. It is for *her* that he has labored and made his hours that might have been hours of leisure, hours of toil. It is true that he has not figured in the national councils. He is a young man comparatively, but he is none the less true to his state. We hope that sustained by a constituency that have ever been proud of him he may continue to reflect honor and credit not only upon his native county but upon his state.

At the date March 11, 1861, an attached unidentified newspaper article describes a meeting of the citizens of the Southwestern part of Limestone, held on March 9, at which resolutions were adopted pledging allegiance to the State, the new government at Montgomery, the defense of home and fireside, approbation of the course of Thomas Hobbs, disapproval of the indignities offered to William L. Yancey, and approval of the policy of the *Athens Herald.* Among those who signed in subscription to the resolutions was J. D. Beauchamp, opponent of Hobbs in the legislative race of 1859.

18th. We held our adjourned co. meeting today. . . . We lost a large vote, [139–69]. . . . So the meeting adopted the Malone resolutions (wh. I learned today were drawn by Houston). Houston, Luke and Malone made speeches for, and I against, the Resolutions. Through the kind offices of Sloss, Pryor & Malone, Houston and I have agreed to go with friendly relations as before. [Nathaniel Davis acted as chairman and Daniel Coleman as secretary.]

An unidentified newspaper article, attached at the 20th, reports that at a meeting held in Pettusville on March 9th, the citizens voted unanimously in favor of Hobbs' resolutions. The Rev. William Levesque was chairman, and J. W. Meisenheimer was secretary. The committee on resolutions was composed of Dr. C. W. Massenburg, Wm. M. Redus, T. J. Bailes, Jesse Atkinson, and William Andrews. Another unidentified article states:

> At a meeting of the citizens of Limestone County, residing in and near the town of Mooresville, held in said town on March 25, 1861, to take into consideration the position of Limestone County in the present political crisis. On motion, Col. [Sherley] Tisdale was unanimously elected to take the Chair and D. R. Hundley appointed Secretary. On taking his seat the venerable chairman in a few terse remarks indicated the purpose of the meeting, and appointed on motion of Col. Steptoe Pickett, the following committee to prepare resolutions expressive of the sense of the meeting, viz.: Col. Steptoe Pickett, Major Thomas H. Ashford,* D. R. Hundley,** Major T. H. Hobbs and John H. Hunt, who after retiring reported . . . [resolutions favoring the action of the state in seceding.] Before the regulations were offered to the meeting to be approved or rejected, Major Hobbs being numerously and earnestly called upon to speak on the resolutions, arose amidst profound silence and delivered one of the most chaste, eloquent, and stirring addresses ever delivered before the people of Limestone in behalf of the resolutions, in behalf of the reputation of the citizens of the county, and which has been heretofore somewhat injured by the injudicious resolves of a certain meeting held at the County seat, and in behalf of the new Constitution of the Confederate States, which he contrasted to great advantage with the old Constitution, quoting from the *New York World,* an abolition paper the concession that no better Constitution than that of the Confederate States ever was devised or framed since the origin of civil governments. He was continually greeted with applause during its delivery, and was listened to with the profoundest attention. After he had concluded, Mr. Hundley, whose residence is in Chicago, Illinois, but who is a native of Alabama, was called upon for a speech but excused himself, asserting that he approved of all that Major Hobbs had said, and did not feel that any necessity existed to add one word more to his eloquent and able address, since it was of itself sufficient to convince every son of Alabama present that his duty and honor required he should stand by his State and the Southern Confederacy . . . on motion of Col. Steptoe Pickett, the resolutions were adopted unani-

mously. . . . It was then resolved that the proceedings of the meeting be published in the Athens *Herald,* with a request that the Huntsville papers republish the same and the Nashville *Union and American.*

*Major Thomas Ashford was the son of Thomas and Jane Elgin Ashford, of Free and Easy plantation, Lawrence County. Thomas married Caroline Tate, daughter of Enos and Nancy Tate, whose home between Mooresville and Triana still stands, known as the Ashford home. It was the scene of many a gay houseparty for young society in the early twentieth century.—Mrs. Caroline Cortner Smith, Birmingham, descendant of the Ashford family.

**Daniel R. Hundley, born in Madison County in 1832, was the son of John and Malinda Robinson Hundley. After graduating from the Harvard School of Law, he practiced law in Chicago, where he wrote *Social Relations in Our Southern States,* published in 1860. This book has been highly regarded by analysts of the South, such as W. J. Cash, in *Mind of the South,* and W. R. Taylor in *Cavalier and Yankee.* When the course of the South became inevitable, Hundley left Chicago, returned to his Limestone County home, helped to organize the 31st Alabama Infantry, and served as its colonel. He was captured during the Atlanta campaign, and imprisoned. After the war he moved to Lawrence County, resumed his law practice, and wrote his prison reminiscenses, entitled *Prison Echoes.* Copies of Hundley's diaries of 1858 and 1861 are in the author's possession, telling in more implicit details some of the stirring events, particularly of the latter year. Original diaries are on file at the University of North Carolina Library, Chapel Hill.—Owen, III, 869.

At the date April 6, 1861, Hobbs appends to the diary an unidentified article describing the meeting at Centre Hill on this date, at which Reuben Crutcher was chairman, and P. H. D. Newby, secretary. They unanimously adopted the Hobbs' resolutions, and in addition, adopted a resolution reprobating the course of George W. Lane, who had accepted the judgeship for the Northern District of Alabama under Lincoln. It is to this action that the following article refers, which is printed anonymously, but upon which is the written inscription, "by T.H.H."

We understand that the administration will order the Federal Court for the Northern district of Alabama, to be held in Athens. . . . The above extract from the Washington *Star* certainly calls for a word of comment from us. It implies that the appointee of Lincoln, with a Black Republican commission in his pocket, could hold a Black Republican court in our town; that our citizens would endure the presence of such a Judge, and quietly allow the proceedings of such a court. We have done nothing to deserve such an implication as this. Dissatisfied as some of our citizens may have been with the particular manner of resistance adopted by our Convention, tardy as some of them may have been in abandoning the idea of a reconstruction of our late Union, there never was a time, not even when a foreign and hostile flag was too quietly allowed to float in our streets, that any Lincolnite official, high or low, could have safely attempted such an insult to us as to claim jurisdiction over us in any manner shape or form. We think we know the political sentiment of this county and this town, and we believe that we correctly state it, when we declare that not a single, southern-born, permanent citizen of this county would today put Alabama back into the old Union if he could; that the hope that satisfactory guaranties would be offered by the North is totally extinct, and that the expectation or desire of a reconstruction of the late Government only finds a place in the breasts of the most sanguine of the "Hope-on-hope-ever" family. Never did a political sentiment die so speedy a death as that of reconstruction has died in North Alabama.

Attached to diary at April 13, 1861, are these headlines from the semi-weekly *Banner:* "For Governor, Hon. T. H. Hobbs, of Limestone. . . . We regard it as the duty of every section and neighborhood to bring out their strongest man for Governor. By this means the people will avoid the distractions consequent on party issues. We believe the Hon. Thomas H. Hobbs to be that man, in North Alabama, and therefore place his name, permanently, at the head of our columns."

But it was a day of dire impermanence. Even as the *Banner* was reaching its readers the first shots of the war were exchanged at Ft. Sumter. On April 16th, Lincoln called for more volunteers to serve in the U. S. Army, while young rebels by the scores almost trampled each other in the eagerness to volunteer their services. Virginia seceded, blood was spilled in Baltimore, and the serious business of war was at hand. Hobbs does not resume his diary until Monday, June 3rd. He had been occupied with the organization of a company of soldiers, Company F, of the 9th Alabama Infantry.

June 3rd. Went into camp at Clem's Spring, 6½ miles N.E. of Athens. The encampment at the Fair Grounds (which we have occupied for some weeks past) was too near town, and a free pass on the R.R. afforded too great a temptation to the men to run home every day or two. We therefore moved camp to one of the finest springs in this region. The men marched out, carrying their knapsacks, and on the way some of them became convinced that it is not advantageous to a soldier to have too much baggage.

4th. Anne visited the camp today, and I returned with her to town. When the cars came in they brought me a despatch from Gen. O'Neal, of Florence, that his co. and mine were ordered to Richmond immediately. This comes like a great shock to Ma and Anne, who had a lingering hope that we might not be called for.

5th. Went to camp to breakfast, accompanied by Rev. A. F. Lawrence, who feels a great interest in the co. We took the vote and all agreed to start tomorrow. We accordingly marched back to town, and most of the men dispersed to their homes.

6th. A very sad day, and one which impressed its sadness on the most thoughtless of the company. I was very busy making the necessary preparations, in wh. I was greatly assisted by Pa & Townsend. I took leave of Ma and Anne at home—they were greatly cast down—and Anne seemed scarcely able to bear up. For myself, I feel that nothing but an imperious sense of duty could justify my leaving home at this time. But, having been connected with a military co. for nearly two years in time of peace, I thought it unbecoming me to play citizen in war. Besides, the enemy must be met promptly and heartily. We can not stand an invasion. It increases 100 fold our difficulties. Hence we must meet them at the frontier. But this is the most important year of Maclin's education, for he must now be controlled and heretofore he has not been governed as he should have been. It moreover necessitates the removal of Anne & all to town, where, of course, they are more restrained than at home. The events of the day are well described in the accompanying slip from the *Banner*:

> DEPARTURE OF THE FIRST COMPANY FROM LIMESTONE—
> Thursday the 6th of June will long be remembered by the people of Athens and the surrounding country. The news having reached the friends of the volunteers comprising Hobbs' corps, that it would leave for Richmond by the 1½ train, large numbers assembled at the depot, long before that hour, and still they continued to arrive, until the departure of the train. . . . The Rev. Mr. Lawrence, who appeared deeply impressed with a sense of the overwhelming solemnity of the occasion stepped immediately in front of the corps, and after a spirited address, which was softened and rendered doubly affecting by an occasional tear seen stealing down his cheek, being assisted by the Rev. Mr. Mitchell, presented each member with a copy of the Holy Bible. Immediately succeeding this ceremony, the Mayor presented to each of the commissioned officers and the four sergeants, a company roll and concluded the ceremonies by a speech, and an appeal for pocket change, for two or three members who were known to be without it, and without moving ten feet from the spot he occupied . . . a sum amounting to about $50, was thrown in his hat. This amount in addition to the hundreds previously given this company, by our citizens, gave each individual member everything essential to a complete outfit. At the conclusion of the ceremonies, the following resolution from Mr. Daniel Coleman, formerly Editor of the *Herald*, but now a private in the company was adopted by acclamation.
> "Resolved: That the prayers of the ministers and members of the various churches of Limestone county, be earnestly requested for the safety of our company, from the dangers of the field, and the temptations of the camp, and for the speedy and complete triumph of the cause of the South."
> [It] was a scene sublimely painful but which, alas! will too soon recur by the departure for the same seat of war, of Houston's corps. The lofty and manly bearing of Capt. T. H. Hobbs during these trying scenes, were themes of general comment and admiration. . . . the conduct of Mr. Harrison the engineer was that of a gentleman of superior sensibility. The slow movement of his train not going beyond the speed of a footman at a walk afforded a last *"fare-you-well"* and one more lingering look, and grasp, of the hand of friendship.

June 8, 1861. All day yest. we stayed in Chattanooga. Some of the men got drunk, but general good order prevailed. Reached Knoxville and stayed several hours. A few days ago a train bearing soldiers was fired into at Strawberry Plains, by the Union men who abound in this part of Tenn.

9th. All day on the Road. There are 5 to 600 troops on our train, mostly from La.—and some of them very low fellows. Some Texas men today went into a yard when the train stopped for water and commenced shooting at the fowls, all in the presence of the poor woman who dared not open her mouth.

10th. Arrived in L'burg about 11 o'clock. I had telegraphed Mr. Rucker to have some provisions for me at Depot, as those with which we started from home were long since exhausted. He sent us [in] answer an invitation to dine with him. He met us at Depot and the company was marched up to his house, where we found a most elegant meal, with coffee, etc., all ready. The men were completely carried away with his hospitality and gave three hearty cheers as they left the house. . . . James B. presented me with a Navy repeater—the very thing I needed. Tuesday we arrived in Richmond and were met by a Q. Master who conducted us to a grove back of reservoir where we [found] Caps. King and Warren and Houston of Laud. No colonel has yet been appointed for this Reg.

July 12, 1861. Our Reg. organization is now complete and is as follows:

Cadmus M. Wilcox, CSA Col.
Samuel Henry, of Marshall Co., Lt. Col.
Ed A. O'Neal, " Laud. " , Major
A. A. Burleson, Morgan " , Q. Master
Stephens, Jackson " , Commissary
Anderson, Sumter " , Surgeon
John M. Hayes, Laud. " , Ass. [Surgeon]
J. R. B. Burtwell, C. S. A., Adjutant
Capt. Fitz Ripley, of Mobile Co. A
Capt. Williams, " Marshall Co. B
Capt. Sheffield, " Marshall Co. K
Capt. Gillis, " Lauderdale Co. I
Capt. J. B. Houston, " Co. D
Capt. Horace King " Morgan Co. E
Capt. E. Y. Hill " Butler Co. G
Capt. David Houston Limestone Co. H
Capt. T. H. Hobbs " ours is Co. F

July 14, 1861. Marched from Rd. We received orders to march immediately to Winchester. Gen. Johnston being threatened by a large force under Patterson.* Our Col., who only joined us yest., has given all the proper instructions for the formation of our line and the march thro' the city. We left camp at 2 P. M. and took the cars at six. Being off-day, I have command of the guard wh. brings up the rear and picks up stragglers. We were greatly cheered along the streets and at depot, but I had a hard time of it with some drunken Irish soldiers, principally of Williams' and Ripley's co^{s}.

*Joseph Eggleston Johnston was named for the Revolutionary War soldier, Joseph Eggleston, of Amelia County, Virginia. He was the son of Judge Peter and Polly Wood Johnston, of Prince Edward County, and was a great-nephew of Patrick Henry. This gentleman, who faced both Grant and Sherman in battle repeatedly, was selected as a pallbearer for each of these Union soldiers, according to Warner in *Generals in Gray.*

General Robert Patterson, born in County Tyrone, Ireland, in 1792, served in the War of 1812, the Mexican War, and was mustered into service at the outbreak of the Civil War as a major general, U.S.A., of volunteers, training the raw recruits. In July, 1861, he was forced to retire because of criticisms of his actions, and in 1865 published a defense of them, entitled *A Narrative of the Campaign in the Valley of the Shenandoah.*

15th. Left Junction at sunrise, and arrived at Manassas Junction at 2 o'clock, overtaking the co[s] of the Regt. Our rear car was detained because train too long for Locomotive. We overtook the Regt. at Manassas. Went up a mile to the entrenchments, and saw some sandbags for the first time. No attack is expected here soon, all eyes being turned to Patterson & Johnston. Left about 2 P. M. and rode all night in a very crowded car. Men are breaking out with measles as we go, and several left behind on that account.

July 16, 1861. Arrived at Strasburg at day; breakfast and a hard march to Winchester, leaving at 11:20 and arriving at 7. Ammunition was distributed to us at this place and, as we were to make a quiet march, the knapsacks of the men were left behind to come with the baggage. We had a fine turnpike road & a pleasant day, but the men suffered much for water. It is a beautiful valley and has the appearance of great comfort & well-to-do among the people. We got to our camping ground 1½ ms. beyond Winch. at 7, and lay down upon the ground with nothing over us or under us but some wheat-straw taken from a neigh'g field. Near us the troops were drawn up in line of battle, and we were told that we might expect an attack before day.

17th. No attack last night. On the contrary, as we afterwards learned, Patterson was in retreat to H. Ferry—the movement upon Manassas being determined on, and he gone there. He was much blamed by his masters for not engaging Johnston at all hazards for it was the arrival of a part of J.'s command wh. turned the day wh. was at one time lost to us. We had our 1st dress Parade under Wilcox today, and our Brigadier, E. K. Smith, was also present.

E. Kirby Smith, 1824–1893, was called "Seminole" at West Point, since he was from St. Augustine, Florida. He had a brilliant record in the Mexican War, taught at West Point, and was commissioned brigadier in June, 1861, promoted to major general in October, after being severely wounded at First

Manassas. He became chancellor of the University of Nashville, and was later professor of mathematics at the University of the South, Sewanee, Tennessee.

July 18, 1861. Left Winchester.
19th. Crossed Shenandoah—wading. Marched on to within 1½ ms. of Piedmont Station.
21st. The great Battle of Manassas—which overthrew the finest army the U. S. can or will bring against us. Our company, on picket duty on a high hill at Piedmont Station, heard the guns occasionally, but had no idea of the warm work wh. was going on near the Junction. Late in the night a train arrived wh. told a battle had been fought, & that the 4th Ala. had been hotly engaged. We suffered here greatly for provisions, and I sent out Roden and a squad, who returned after a while [with] a good turn wh. they purchased. But from our high hill we could see soldiers shooting down the stock of the farmers.
22nd. Took the cars about 7—half the men being put on the tops of the cars, and it raining. Arrived at Junt^{n}—men swarming and every body asking & telling about yest. fight. We learned here how severely the 4th Ala. Regt. suffered; its field off^{s} all being wounded, Jones very severely in both thighs. We marched thro' rain to the battle field and then lay down without tents in a wet place. I was never in more disag. circumstances to spend a night, and yet the men slept well, & so did I. I set this down as the most disag. day of my life—nothing but the excitement of an expected attack kept us up. To make matters worse, many of the men were just out of measles.
July 23rd, 1861. Went to the battle field after breakfast. It was a horrid sight. Our dead were mostly buried, but the enemy's were not touched, and there they lay, men & horses, in all the various & ghastly shapes that death in battle leaves its victims. The hill we first visited was thickly strewn with the dead, mostly of N. Y. Five Zouaves and the 14th N. Y. from Brooklyn. This latter wore scarlet breeches and were very conspicuous. In one place five horses of an artillery carriage were lying as if one shot or shell had killed them in the harness. Near by a Capt. Brown of the N. Y. 79th was lying—his men had pillowed his head upon some of the ordnance packing and put a cup of water by his side. They left him wounded, but he was stiff in death when we saw him. Nearly every corpse had been stripped of its shoes, buttons, and the pockets rifled. Some of our boys are without serviceable shoes, and I advised them to get them from the dead, for we have no chance to get them otherwise, for love or money. I was myself willing to wear a pair, my own having given out on the march, but I could not find a pair to suit. I walked over

a part of the battle ground, all of it I thought, but afterwards learned that it was a very small part. It was several miles long, the battle moving around from east to west as the enemy tried to flank us.

28th. Went over to Sudley Church—where are a large No. of Yankee prisoners & wounded. Capt. Ripley, of our Regt., is part of the guard. In conversation, the prisoners expressed a great contempt for their officers, and blamed them for their defeat. They all deny the display of the Confed. flag, and I am inclined to doubt it myself. Still there are many credible persons who assert it. I told one of them that it was reported that Commissioners had passed on to R'd. to treat for peace. He said fervently, "Thank God, we shall be once more a united people." I answered, "That can never be—peace may come, but a re-Union never." He looked surprized, and I then proceeded to give him what he never had before, a Southern view of the question. He listened with much attention, and seemed much surprized that we never intended to re-unite with them under any circumstances.

July 31, 1861. Private T. A. Neal was left in Richmond, sick of fever. He was so far recovered as to be going about, but when news of the great battle reached R'd., the excitement was so great down town that Neal went down in the night air, took cold and relapsed, and died on this day. He was a very good young man, and tried to do all his duty as a soldier, but being of weak constitution, was not always stout enough to make an efficient soldier.

An article in an Athens paper, unidentified, states that the body of Pvt. Neal, a "Limestone Trooper," had been carried to Athens by train, and borne to his father's residence five miles in the country.

At August 5, 1861, an appended clipping, unidentified, gives election results in Limestone County, showing that Thomas Hill Watts carried over John Gill Shorter for Governor, although Shorter won statewide. J. P. Coman won over William Hundley and S. J. Ragland for the senate; Thomas McClellan and J. W. S. Donnell, representatives; A. L. McKinney, sheriff; George R. Anderson, tax collector; and Mace Gilbert, tax assessor.

8th. I was most agreeably surprized to learn that Anne & Pa had arrived in the neighborhood. Learning the difficulty of my getting away, they concluded to come to see me. Arriving at Junction, they were much puzzled to find a conveyance to our camp, 7 ms. off. But an artillery man of Latham's battery, who had an ambulance there, on learning that Anne was a L'burger, took them in & brought them to our camp. . . . I got the co. off, and started to meet them, but missed them, & they came on to our Bull Run camp, where I overtook them.

August 9, 1861. We stopped at the house of a man named Gregory, where the family was kind to us, but they gave us a dirty bedchamber and the buggiest of beds. So today I rode over to camp (the new one) and found a new boarding house, where we went this aft. in an open wagon, and were caught in one of the hardest rains. Worse than that, when nearly to the house, we were stopped by a creek, wh. was swimming, and had to turn back. We claimed lodgings at the first house we reached. Here we found no fire, but I soon cut some wood and made a big fire, by which we dried by 11 o'clock.
10th. This morning we went to the house where I engaged the room, but it was full of sick soldiers. The owner went with us to the house of a neighbor, where we got a room. Altogether the disappt. was in our favor, for we got into an excellent family . . . on the camp side of Broad Run. . . . Here we got a nice chamber with not a bed bug in it!
19th. Anne left me today. She goes alone to L'burg as Pa wishes to stay a few days longer. She leaves loathfully but thinks it her duty to go to her children. I was much tempted to go a part of the way, but it seemed inconvenient.
24th. Pa left for home. He has remained some days, thinking there might be a forward movement on Alexandria, but as there seems no present prospect of it, he has concluded to leave. He was much moved at our parting, and so was I, for we may never meet again on earth. I accompanied him to Bristoe.
31st. Col. Wilcox left us today on a mysterious mission. He said he was merely taking a few days of rest, but he is not the man to rest. He has undoubtedly gone on some military business, no doubt of importance. From his intimacy with Gen. Johnston (having served on the same staff with him in Mexico), we think that Gen. has sent him to reconnoitre the upper Potomac with a view to select a crossing place. This, of course, is surmise, but we know that he took the R. R. towards Winchester.
Monday, September 2, 1861. The gallant Jones is dead. He was wounded in both hips and never made a step afterwards. Was taken prisoner, his wounds dressed, and then retaken by us after the enemy's flight. For several weeks after the battle his recovery was considered probable, but at length it was discovered by Henry Malone, who was waiting upon him, that the bone in one leg was fractured.

Two unidentified newspaper accounts are appended:

Tribute to the late Col. Egbert J. Jones.—We are indebted to Major Geo. W. Jones, Qr. Master of the 3rd Brigade in the Army of the Potomac, for the following order of Brig. Gen. Whiting, officially announcing to the Brigade the death of Col. Jones, in terms of deserved compliment. . . . Col. James was among the first of the men of the far South

. . . to defend the soil of Virginia.—He has been one of the first to give his life in her cause. On the 21st, he led his brave troops with distinguished gallantry, and fell severely wounded, while fiercely contending against superior numbers, in the most advanced position held by our troops during the day . . .
. . . Col. Jones was a very popular citizen and distinguished lawyer, and was an experienced and most gallant officer. He had served in the Mexican war. Probably the death of no man could be more deeply regretted in North Alabama than that of this favorite and distinguished son. His home was in Huntsville, whither his remains have been carried for interment.

September 4, 1861. Our Col. returned today—and the object of his absence has transpired. Gen. Johnston was informed that a large No. of mules, wagons, etc., had been left by Gen. Banks at Frederick, Md., 18 ms. from Harper's Ferry, and our Col. was sent to ascertain if it was true, and if true, to take a cavalry force from the neighborhood of the Ferry and bring in the plunder. On reaching the Ferry he learned that he was too late, the plunder having been taken away. His escort had a skirmish with a Fed. patrol in H. Ferry, and one of ours badly wounded. The Col. dined with us by invitation today, we having a roast turkey and some tomatoes. My sensible little wife sent me a pocket compass in a box of shoes which we ordered from Lynchburg.
16th. Today Capt . . . who has been under arrest for two weeks, was restored to his command by the Secty of War, quashing the proceedings. He went to recitation one day very drunk, and after a few moments, dropped to sleep. After nodding awhile he stretched himself upon the Col's bed, and so slept the balance of the time. The Col. at once arrested him and preferred charges against him. His father came [to] help him out, and tried to get the Col. to stop the proceedings—which he refused to do. . . . [His father] then went to Richmond and brought back an official request from Secretary [Leroy Pope] Walker that the matter be dropped. . . . In the meantime, poor Capt. Ripley, under arrest for the same offense, having no friends at court, will be courtmartialed, and perhaps cashiered.
20th. Got orders to move to Centreville on Sunday morning. We have been expecting to be attached to Gen. Whiting's Brigade, which moved to the mouth of Occoquan a day or two since. . . . I now begin to believe that we intend to attack Washington, for every man hereabouts has gone to the Potomac except our Brigade, and now we move.
September 21, 1861. All the Reg. of our Brigade except ours and 38th Va. moved to Centreville today. We go tomorrow at 6 A. M.
22nd. We got off about 7:30, having one wagon to the company. All the well men had to carry their knapsacks, and thus we were able to put all our camp equipage in one wagon, tho' the load was a heavy one. We

left 15 men of our co., being those unable to march, and one or two to nurse them. Jerry Robertson is now very low of typhoid fever at the house of Michael Houk near our camp, and John Baugh is also ill in camp of same disease. The sick are in charge of our . . . assistant Surgeon, John Hayes. We took a near road across the country and before we knew it, found ourselves upon the battle field of the 21st July. A halt of a few moments allowed us to look around a little. . . . We had an elegant day for marching, cloudy and cool, and the boys stood the march very well. Arrived at Centreville about 2 P. M., and pitched camp on a high hill east of town, and at west edge of wood. All around us the troops of our Brigade and Gen. Walker's La. Brigade are encamped. The sound of drums and brass bands is incessant, and wherever we look out, we see soldiers drilling.

25th. We had our first Brigade drill today; Col. Forney, of the 10th Alabama, being in command. Col. Wilcox manifested a perfect acquaintance with the evolutions of the line.

John Horace Forney, 1829–1902, of Jacksonville, Alabama, graduated from West Point in 1852, and served as instructor of tactics there until his resignation in 1861. He was appointed colonel of the 10th Alabama in June, 1861, commissioned brigadier in March, 1862, became commander of the District of the Gulf, and was commissioned major general in October. He was taken prisoner in 1863 at Vicksburg, exchanged, and returned to active service. Douglas Southall Freeman spoke of Forney's Brigade as "Cadmus Wilcox's pride." It has been said that the Forney brothers held a record close to that of the Lee family, in the number of high ranking officers in the one family. Of the four, there were a major-general, brigadier-general, lt. colonel, and major.—Freeman, III, 750.

Tuesday, October 1, 1861. For several days we have had three days' provision cooked and on hand, as if about to move—The Washington Artillery galloped past, being sent back for their heaviest pieces—and everything indicated a speedy move forward. Prest. Davis came up yesterday to Fairfax C.H. He has not been in this region since the battle of Manassas.

3rd. We received orders to no longer keep 3 days provision cooked.

6th. By order today all our baggage not necessary for daily use was sent back to Manassas, and all men not fit for duty were sent back to our old camp at Broad Run. Those who went with baggage report that it was pouring in from all directions, and in the greatest quantity. This looks like a move in some direction, but whether forward or back, remains to be seen.

7th. Mr. Steptoe Pickett, of Limestone, who has been appointed our

Q.M., arrived yesty. Some time ago I wrote to Secty. Walker, and suggested him as a suitable person to fill the vacancy of Dr. Burleson. It seems he thought it a good nomination. . . . There was rapid cannonading towards Alexandria this morning, and the 19th Miss. was ordered off to do picket duty. It is understood that the other Regts. of this Brigade will in turn be sent on same duty. Tonight is very stormy. . . . Recvd a long letter last night from Mr. John C. Orr, of Danville, asking leave to nominate me for the Senate of the Conf. States Congress. He is a member-elect of the next Ala. Leg. I had no idea that anybody thought me fit for such a place, and nobody could convince me that I am.

John C. Orr was active in recruiting servicemen, and his name is attached to a document in December, 1861, calling for twelve-month volunteers to serve in the Confederate cause.—Saunders, 16.

October 14, 1861. Received orders to march tomorrow on outpost duty —to remain five days. Orders did not say where—perhaps on Accontink creek—where the 19th Miss. went last week, and where the 11th Ala. now is. Our boys greatly delighted at the prospect of going to the front.
15th. We moved to the Braddock ford of Accontink creek, a small stream which runs near Annandale—relieving the 11th Alabama. Arrived about 4 P. M., 3 right co[s] thrown forward as outposts about a mile. We then threw out detachments from these, still farther in advance. Our furtherest detachment under Corp. Baugh, was near the "Roundhouse." The Yankees kept up an incessant drumming from sunset until 8 o'clock, and seemed to be about two ms. off. How near their pickets were to us we could not tell . . . probably not nearer than a mile. About 1 o'clock we got orders to fall back to the Regt., which we did. It was a beautiful moonlight night, & very still.

16th. We were much surprised to receive an order to fall back at once to Langston's St. on the R. R., burning all public property wh. we could not remove, as we went. We started after an early breakfast, and heard as we went, a rapid cannonade in our rear wh. confirmed our idea that we were pursued by a large force. We halted by order of Gen. Stewart [J. E. B. Stuart] for several hours, and then going by Fairfax St. to Langster's we found that the destruction of public property had been accomplished by others. There we found 5th N. C., wh. had fallen back with such haste that they burned their tents, commissary stores, and some boxes of new clothing.

October 17, 1861. Our bivouac last night did not prevent sound sleep and we rested until 12, when we were ordered to Chantilly, five ms.

beyond Centreville. We made a rapid march. As we neared Centreville the number of troops increased. . . . Everybody seemed tending thither and several breastworks had been thrown up since we left. . . . We moved rapidly to Chantilly which is 5 ms. N. of C'ville arriving late at night.

18th. Remained at Chantilly till evening—relieved by 15 Alabama, which saw the enemy's pickets within half-mile of Ffx C. H. Came down to the Braddock ford of Cub Run. . . . Bivouacked—very clear night and looked right up at the bright moon that seemed to be smiling at us.

19th. Remained all day & night at the Ford. . . . What can all this sudden retiring of all our forces mean? I confess I do not see the wisdom of the movement, but perhaps I will hereafter. There is a rumor that the enemy is pushing a heavy column up the Potomac towards Leesburg. The people are coming in numbers from the unprotected front. It is sad to see the women and children huddled together in waggons and fleeing with their household goods.

Centreville proved to be a battleground of the Confederate generals! Joseph Johnston, who felt that he should be in supreme command, had been angered on August 31st to learn that he had been placed fourth on the list of brigadiers to be made full generals. His difficulties mounted with Judah P. Benjamin, the brilliant new Secretary of War. This fluctuation of orders possibly reflected the turmoil within himself.—Freeman, I, 111–12.

October 20, 1861. The 38th Va. relieved us and we marched down Cub Run to the place our tents had been pitched and where we found the entire Brigade, except Stannard's Battery. A great panic has prevailed at camp—momentarily expecting to be attacked, all baggage, including the men's knapsacks, sent to Manassas Junction—my trunk gone, no clean shirt—no nothing. Got a letter from Anne saying the R. R.'s forbidden to bring any more freights to Man. Junction. The boys tell amusing stories of the excitement of our Lt. Col. and Major. Bibb says the Major declared a buzzard sailing in the air to be a balloon.

22nd. Ran down to the Stone House to see 500 Yankee prisoners, taken by Col. Evans at Edward's Ferry near Leesburg. . . . Evans gained a complete victory, chasing them back into the Potomac—many drowning from the swamping of the boats.

Colonel N. P. (Shanks) Evans had engaged Federal forces on the 21st at Ball's Bluff, and had succeeded in driving them back across the Potomac.—Freeman, I, 111.

23rd. Two hundred more prisoners were sent down today by Evans.

These, as the others, sent on to Richmond without being brought to Centreville to H.Q.'s.

24th. Last night Col. recvd notice to put his Regt. in order to move at 30 minutes notice.

October 25, 1861. Col. Wilcox was today promoted Brig. General upon the recommendation of Johnston, Beauregard & Smith. . . . Gracie, majr. of the 11th Alabama, has been suggested [as replacement]. First frost.

Archibald Gracie, 1832–1864, graduated from West Point in 1854. His family had moved from New York to Mobile around 1844, and returned to New York at the outbreak of war. In 1856 Gracie married Josephine Mayo, of Richmond, niece of Gen. Winfield Scott. In 1861 he was captain of the militia that seized the Mt. Vernon arsenal just prior to Alabama's secession, recruited the 43rd Alabama, was elected brigadier in November, 1862, and was killed in the Battle of the Crater, December 2, 1864.—Warner, 113.

Friday, November 1, 1861. Our Regt. went on picket at the Frying Pan ford of Flat Lick, a tributary of Cub Run . . . it began to rain, and rained incessantly for twenty hours.

2nd. I have heretofore thought our first night at Bull Run the most disagreeable of my life, but it must yield the palm to last night.

3rd. Our co. on outpost duty.

5th. When we reached camp we found Tom Redus very ill of typhoid fever. Some of the boxes of clothing sent by our friends at home have arrived, and our ragged boys begin to look better.

6th. I telegraphed Mr. Alfred Redus of the illness of his son.

7th. Tom Redus died this morning. . . . He was a capital young man and one of our best soldiers.

8th. Col. Henry and Lieut. Col. O'Neal, having entered on the discharge of their duties, (being recently promoted), the officers of the Regt. had a consultation tonight to recommend some one for Major. My name and Capt. Williams' were put in nomination—but he received a greater number of votes. He is a clever man . . . and is one of the few officers of the Regt. who tries to do his duty. He was in the Mex. War, and this, with the fact that he, next to Ripley, is the ranking Captain, were the chief arguments used in his favor. . . . I could no doubt obtain this position now, for Gen. W. told me yest. he would recommend me, and as my friend, Wade Keyes, is the right hand man of Secty Benjamin, he would no doubt give me the place . . . but . . . "the path of duty is the path of honor."

Judah Phillip Benjamin, born in the West Indies in 1811, was the son of English Jews who were waiting to get into the United States at the time of his birth. After graduating from Yale, he began law practice in New Orleans in 1832, and was serving in the U. S. Senate at the time of Louisiana's secession. Benjamin also served as Attorney General and Secretary of State for the Confederacy. He escaped to England after the war, was there admitted to the bar, received the silk gown, and wrote legal classics in that country. Wade Keyes served as Assistant Attorney General for the Confederacy throughout the war.—Brewer, 304.

November 11, 1861. Pa & Warren Phillips arrived on last Saturday bringing with them the new uniforms of our Co. . . . We sent to Pa a part of the $21 paid by the C. S. as a clothing commutation, and he purchased the goods & the ladies of Athens made the suits. These came in good time, for some of the boys were getting very ragged.

12th. I was in charge of a party at work on the breastworks. Centreville is now surrounded by a cordon of entrenchments which frown from every hill. We are on the hill next to Rock Run.

November 16, 1861. Mr. Alfred Redus arrived today. He did not receive my second dispatch, telling him of the death of poor Tom. He did not hear it until he reached the Junction . . . was greatly moved when he met us. He would disinter and remove his remains, but is unable to do so because he cannot get a burial case. The Yankees supplied us that convenience, and now we do not get any.

Over twenty years after the last gun had been fired in the Civil War, the famed "spokesman for the new South," Henry Grady, brought this situation before the American people. In his editorial, "Pickens County Funeral," Grady stated that the deceased from that county had been buried in the midst of the marble quarry, yet the tombstone came from Vermont. Buried in the pine forest, his pine coffin was brought from Cincinnati, the nails in the coffin and the iron in the shovel that dug the grave were from Pittsburgh, even though the grave site was near an iron mine.—Nixon, 10.

At the date November 21, 1861, an unidentified newspaper article is appended and reports: "The Hon. W. L. Yancey and the Hon. C. C. Clay, Jr., were elected today Confederate Senators."

27th. This was the day I appointed for Anne to come . . . she and Maclin stopped at Bristoe. . . . I [walked there] and soon . . . had the pleasure of seeing my dear wife and sweet little boy. They were both quite well. Maclin has not grown a great deal, but has greatly improved in his speech and thought.

29th. Maclin's birthday. How times have changed since he saw the light first! His third birthday finds him an active, healthy, energetic, go-ahead, self-reliant boy, much inclined to have his opinion about things and to insist on it. If controlled and well-broken to unhesitating obedience at once, he will make a man his father may be proud of. But if not—

30th. Pa is so unwell that today he came out to stay at the house with us. He has some symptoms of typhoid fever. He exposed himself a good deal in building a chimney to my tent.

Sunday, December 1, 1861. I report to the Regt. every morning, but the balance of the day I spend with my family. Maclin is very interesting to me. He saw a pair of snuffers for the first time last night and exclaimed, "Papa took the fire out de candle with the scissors."

2nd. As I returned from camp today, I broke off some willow twigs and carried them home for Maclin's benefit. He is of very strong will, and loves to have his own way. As this visit may be the last time I ever see him, I feel it my duty to do what I can towards teaching him obedience. I regretted my absence from home more on his account than any other. He soon gave me an occasion to use them, and I did so heartily from a solemn sense of duty.

December 6, 1861. Today a Captain of Wheat's Battalion came to the house and said Gen. Johns[t]on had informed him that he had better bring in his wife, who is some miles outside the lines. This produced a considerable stir among the ladies, and some of them began to pack up forthwith. We held a family council of war and resolved that . . . Anne and Pa had better go tomorrow.

7th. We arrived safely at Bristoe—Pa was improved by the trip. Both he and Anne were greatly moved when I parted with them, and little Maclin said imploringly, "Papa, *don't* go." Ah! What would I not give if I could conscientiously obey his request! I returned to camp, arriving at night—but I did not feel merciful to the dead Yankees as I passed them on the battlefield.

8th. Went to Centreville to church and heard an excellent sermon from Col. Pendleton, of the Artillery.* We had communion, and I was glad to see Gen. E. K. Smith among those who knelt around where the altar used to be in the little Episcopal Church, which the Yankees so much disfigured the night before Manassas. They scribbled all over the walls and pulpit not only their names, but abuse of Jeff Davis and other rebels.

*"Who the devil commanded that battery on the left, that killed so many of our men?" asked prisoners after the Battle of First Manassas. "Our reply was that it was commanded by a saint, named Pendleton." William Nelson Pendleton, 1809–1883, was both a West Point graduate and an Episcopal minister. In 1839 he established the famed Episcopal High School for boys in Alexandria, Virginia. In 1862 he was promoted to brigadier general.—Freeman, I, 615.

10th. The camp rumor today is that the Lincoln Congress has adjourned for 17 days, because there is a peace party in it which will much clog its operations unless, during the recess, McClellan can do something to revive the military feeling of the North. In the report of Secty. Cameron which I read today, he says they have 600,000 men in the field, and more offered than would make 1,000,000. He intimates that the army will soon advance.

12th. Bibb's resignation accepted by War Department. He is at home on sick leave. He had a slight attack, got greatly alarmed, & was sent to Richmond, whence he was sent home and turned loose.

13th. Anne has arrived safely at home, parting with Pa at Gordonsville, who has gone to Petersburg to visit Mr. Meade.

18th. The camp excited today at the rumor that England was ablaze with excitement at the capture of Slidell & Mason, & that large and enthusiastic meetings were held to call on Govt. to demand satisfaction for the insult to the British flag. How humbling it will be to the Northern pride which has talked so big, to have to send back the men her Congressmen have thanked a naval officer for taking!

The capture of James Mason and John Slidell, commissioners from the Confederate States to France, was effected on the British steamer, the *Trent,* by the U. S. Navy under Captain Charles Wilkes. The act was retracted under pressure, and the two sailed again, procuring a large loan for the Confederacy, even though they were unsuccessful in gaining recognition for the Government of the Confederate States.

December 20, 1861. A large foraging party sent out today—4th Regt.—of which the 10th Ala. is one. Their object was to forage about Drainsville, but in the aft. the wagons came back & reported that the enemy came out in force, and that we were having a battle. Soon a courier galloped up, & our Brig. had orders to inspect arms, etc., & hold ourselves in readiness to move at a moment's notice. Soon we began to hear more definite accounts, and the affair turned up to be quite serious. Col. Forney, of the 10th, is wounded in the arm; Lt. Col. Martin (Judge J. B. Martin, of Calhoun),* is killed, and Col. Taylor, of 1st Ky. is missing. My friend, Capt. Forney,** is wounded in the leg, but not seriously.

*James Benson Martin represented Talladega County in 1857, served as judge of the 10th judicial district in 1860, and was appointed to his rank in the 10th Alabama by President Davis. Martin had a premonition of his death, for on the morning of the 20th, he knelt in prayer, and "expressed the conviction that the last day of his life had dawned, and he was prepared for it."—Brewer, 544.

**Captain William Henry Forney had served with Thomas Hobbs

in the legislature in 1859. Forney was again wounded at Gettysburg, and was commissioned a brigadier general in 1865. He returned to his home in Jacksonville, Alabama, to practice law, and served in the U. S. Congress from 1875–1893.—Owen, III, 597.

December 22, 1861. I called to see Capt. Forney. . . . He describes the fight as a blunder on the part of Gen. Stuart who was surprised by finding the enemy where he did not expect him. . . . Col. Martin . . . had obtained a leave of absence to hold his courts, & was to start in a few days.

23rd. Was summoned today to act as Judge Advocate of a Gen. Court Martial of which Judge Benning, of Geo. (Col. of 17th Geo.) is President. We met in Centreville and organized the Court. I was appointed in lieu of Capt. Caldwell, who goes home as escort for Col. Martin's body.

Henry Louis Benning, "Old Rock," was born in Columbia County, Georgia, in 1814. He served for six years as an associate justice of the Georgia supreme court, was the colonel of the 17th Georgia Infantry, and was commissioned brigadier general in 1863. After the war Benning resumed his law practice in Columbus, Georgia. The huge military base there was evidently named for him.—Warner, 25.

25th. Court did not meet as it is Christmas—and how different from any Xmas most of us ever saw before! No family reunions, no happy children, no Santa Claus, no old & long tried friends to shake your hands and wish you joy. Last night was the anniversary of my proposal to Anne, and . . . I thought much of her and those circumstances. How I would like to see her and those little boys tonight! There is a good deal of drinking in camp, altho' the soldiers have to give $5 a quart for whiskey.

December 26, 1861. Court met again, but as all of the Reg's composing it are moving to the vicinity of the Lewis House we adjourned to meet January 4th. Toomb's Brig. and ours go into winter quarters there. . . . Saw Gen. Stuart in town, and heard him say that Prince Albert was dead, & Gen. Scott had returned to U. S.

The Lewis house, Portici, was burned during the war.—Gamble mss.

Robert Toombs, 1810–1885, was a brigadier general at this time, but had almost been elected President of the Confederacy. Davis appointed Toombs Secretary of State, a position he resigned to go into active service. He became annoyed with the predominance of West Pointers, and is credited with having made the observation that the epitaph of the Confederate Army should be "Died of West Point." After being wounded at Sharpsburg, Toombs resigned his commission, and turned his interests into a peace movement, which worked against the Confederate cause. He escaped to Europe to avoid arrest, and returned to Georgia in 1867, soon amassing a fortune in his law practice.—Warner, 306.

31st. So goes out the eventful year of 1861! It began with a tumult which soon shook the nation to pieces, and its end finds us standing face to face as foes who long were friends. I see no earthly prospect for peace. . . . General Johnston persists in declaring that we shall fight here, and that soon—but it looks to me like Ky. & Missouri will most probably be the theatre of the active campaign during the winter. . . . Goodby, old '61. May your successor have a brighter history, or else,

" 'Twould take the tears of all the angels,
To blot the record out."

Friday, January 3, 1862. The papers . . . bring confirmation . . . that Slidell & Mason have been surrendered by the Yankee Government.

4th. Called to see Col. and Capt. Forney—both getting on well. Col. says that Gen. Stuart's off. account of the fight at Drainsville is generally correct, but "highly colored."

6th. I learned the Court had been ordered to meet at the Lewis House. Went over with Col. Benning, but no one else came. The Col. came back and dined with me as did also Capt[s]. Macon and Cannon.

7th. Court met & tried Stevenson of 11th Alabama.

19th. This morning we had good light rolls for breakfast, an event wh. Floyd & Wayland voted of greater importance than Bull Run or Manassas. Anne left me a few cakes of leaven with instructions for making the bread. So last night I pulled off my coat & rolled up my sleeves and made up the dough.

20th. The officers of our Co. moved into our hut today—it is a double log cabin with narrow passage between. . . . The poor horses dying every day from exposure, overwork, and no hay.

23rd. Major Gracie, of our Court, whiles away the tedium of sessions by sketches . . . which he makes with great rapidity and happiness.

24th. The morning news brings bad news from Kentucky. One of the Richmond papers told of the defeat and rumored death of Zollicoffer. After court adjourned I met Major Davis, just back from General Johnston, who stated that the General had a dispatch from the War Department, which told of Gen. Zollicoffer's death, defeat, and the death of 500 of our men, the loss of Cumberland Gap and all our cannon, etc. This is a terrible blow, for if it be true, all East Tennessee will rise up against us and destroy the railroads and give us great trouble in that quarter. We have also heard of the advance of the enemy in considerable force on Harper's Ferry.

Felix Kirk Zollicoffer had acted against the advice of General Albert Sydney Johnston in moving his forces to the Kentucky side of the Cumberland River, and forced his superior, General G. B. Crittenden, to attack in his defense at Mill Springs. Because of his subsequent defeat, Crittenden was imprisoned, and later resigned his commission.—Warner, 349.

January 31, 1862. It is now nearly 2 weeks since the battle of Somerset [Mill Springs], and yet we have no account of it by our side. . . . This silence is but another proof of how shameful an affair it was. Col. O'Neal, who has just returned from Ala., says Knoxville is full of the refugees. I annex an account from a Cincti. paper from which it seems that Wood's Regt. from N. Ala was there, and took to the swamps. This may be a mistake, as I did not know that (Reg.) was there.

The entire army that had retreated from Mill Springs starved for several days in the Cumberland Mountains. Only two horses were left in the regiment, with which soldiers foraged for food. On one day three sacks of cornbread were brought back, and Colonel W. B. Wood divided the bread among his men, saving none for himself. The men shared theirs with him. After the war, Colonel Wood was serving as a circuit judge in Lauderdale County when an old case was brought before him, in which several young men were indicted for ten pin rolling. As the docket was read, tears streamed down the judge's face, for he recognized many names as those who had fallen at Mill Springs or in other battles under his command.—McGregor, 68.

February 8, 1862. Heard tonight that the recommendation forwarded by my Lieutenants that I should be sent home on recruiting service, had been adopted. Gen. Wilcox sent me word that I had better go to see Gen. Smith in order to be excused from the Court. I don't fancy this trip. 1st, Because I don't believe I shall get any recruits, for it seems that all the men must by this time be gone from Limestone. 2nd, Because it is not agreeable as a trip home, for I shall be so busy running about that I shall get no good of my visit. It is so short (30 days), that I don't know whether Anne will be willing to go with me or not.

9th. I went to see General G. W. Smith—found him in his office at Centreville—in citizen's dress, not a brass button—with a clean, starched, standing collar—the first one I've seen for many a month. He said the J. Advocate of a C.M. should not have been detailed for recruiting service—referred the matter to Gen'l Johns[t]on, who informed him by note that our Court w'd be dissolved on tomorrow—and left the inference that after tomorrow I could go. . . . While waiting for Gen. J.'s reply—Gen. S. chatted familiarly about the war—said the enemy might penetrate up the Tenn. River into Tenn., but that was only attacking a limb, "but the army of the Potomac is the heart."

General Gustavus Woodson Smith, 1821–1896, graduated from West Point, served in the Mexican War, and at the time of secession was street commissioner of New York City, where he lived the last twenty years of his life. Pictures show him wearing a white starched collar even under his uniform.—Warner, 281.

END OF JOURNALS

General Smith was correct in his prophecy, for the next decisive engagement of the war brought the Army of the Potomac and Lee's Army of Northern Virginia face to face. Soon after Hobbs' return from his recruiting trip to Alabama, his regiment was drawn into fierce fighting for the defense of Richmond. At Gaines' Mill, on June 27, 1862, the Ninth Alabama suffered its first heavy losses.

During the battle, Thomas Hobbs was severely wounded in the leg. He lay unattended through the night, and on the 28th was taken to the Bargoman mansion in Richmond. His condition steadily worsened, despite excellent care there. Foreseeing that he would not recover, the surgeons decided that he should be moved to Lynchburg in order to be near his wife. Tom arrived there on July 18th, and died four days later. Bishop John Early was with him that morning, and listened to his prayers—which were for his wife and children, his parents in Athens, his country, and his enemies.

Funeral services were conducted by Bishop Early at the Court Street Methodist Church, where Tom and Anne were married only four years previously. The body was taken to Spring Hill Cemetery overlooking the James River for interment. Above his grave, Anne had a small stone erected, with the inscription:

"A brave and simple man who died in a brave and simple faith."

Confirmation of the death did not reach Athens until the middle of August, although Tom's parents had received a telegram earlier stating the gravity of his illness. The news compounded the burden of woe which the war had already forced upon Ira and Rebecca Hobbs. During April, 1862, Athens had suffered the first of repeated Federal raids when forces under the Russian-born General Ivan Turchinov sacked it. Atrocities were committed to the extent that federal authorities ordered a subsequent investigation under General James A. Garfield. Later in the year, the Hobbs family joined others in leaving Athens for a place of refuge. They stopped at Talladega, while many of their fellow citizens went on to Georgia.

Just after the Emancipation Proclamation was issued in January, 1863, a freedman's camp was set up on some 1800 acres of the Hobbs plantation. It was soon stripped of stock, implements, and produce. Later it was estimated that 40 head of horses and mules, 41 colts, 12 work oxen, 75 head of cattle, 225 head of fatted hogs, 250 sheep, 75 goats, 400 bushels of wheat, 20,000 bushels of corn, 80 bales of cotton, and 10,000 pounds of bacon were seized.

Both the Hobbs and Maclin homes were badly damaged during the occupation of Federal forces. While the Maclin home was occupied by General Hatch in September, 1864, bureau drawers were used as feed troughs for the horses, which were sheltered in the kitchen. An excellent description of these trying times is to be found in the diaries of Mary Fielding, who lived at the Maclin home and had supervision over it, after the illness of Eliza Hobbs Maclin prevented her from exercising these duties. Copies of these diaries are in the Athens Public Library. Eliza died in 1868, and Ira Hobbs in 1869.

Anne Benagh Hobbs brought their two sons from Virginia to the denuded plantation, and began restoration, but she died in 1872. The indomitable Rebecca then moved into the Maclin house to look after Dr. Maclin and her two orphaned grandsons, Thomas Maclin and James Benagh Hobbs. Dr. Maclin died in 1879, and James Benagh in 1883, while a student of The University of Alabama. When Rebecca died in 1888, Thomas Maclin Hobbs was the sole survivor of the family. Maclin married Anne Davis Richardson, daughter of Dr. Nicholas Davis and Bettie Hine Richardson. For a time the couple lived at the plantation home, Slopeside. Then Maclin acquired the Maclin home, which had passed out of the family briefly, and moved his family back to Athens. Slopeside eventually burned, and a portion of the plantation was sold to the Pryor family.

The eldest daughter of Maclin and Anne Richardson Hobbs, Anna, was married first to John Morgan Frierson of Columbia, Tennessee. They had one son, Maclin Hobbs Frierson, a prominent businessman in Athens. After Mr. Frierson's death, Anna married Judge James Edwin Horton and they were parents of Senator James Edwin, Jr., and Donelson Branch Horton. Judge Horton presided at the Scottsboro trials of the 1930s. His courageous stand during this emotional time has been widely heralded, particularly in Dan Carter's article, "A Reasonable Doubt," appearing in *American Heritage Magazine* in October, 1968. Judge Horton died in his 95th year in 1973.

Marie Pleasants, second daughter of Thomas Maclin Hobbs, married General Edward Chambers Betts, author of *Historic Huntsville, 1804–1870,* and judge advocate of the European theater during World War II. They had one daughter, Anne. Elizabeth Maclin was the youngest of the Hobbs daughters. She married General John David Higgins, who commanded the second largest army reserve unit in the United States. Their children are John David Higgins, III, and Elizabeth Richardson Jackson.

LIST OF SOURCES

Abernathy, Cecil. "Lanier in Alabama." *The Alabama Review*, XVII, (January, 1964).

Alabama Association of University Women, Huntsville Branch. *Glimpses into Ante-Bellum Homes*. Huntsville, Ala.: no date.

Alabama Portraits Prior to 1870. Compiled by the Historical Activities Committee for National Society of the Colonial Dames of America in the State of Alabama. Mobile, Ala.: Gill Printing and Stationery Company, Inc., 1969.

Albermarle County Historical Society. *Early Charlottesville, Recollections of James Alexander, 1828–1874*. Charlottesville, Va., 1942.

American Guide Series, Works Progress Administration.

Alabama, A Guide to the Deep South. New York: Richard R. Smith, 1941.

Pennsylvania, A Guide to the Keystone State. New York: Oxford University Press, 1940.

Philadelphia. Harrisburg, Pa.: The Telegraph Press, 1937.

Virginia, A Guide to the Old Dominion. New York: Oxford University Press, 1940.

Armes, Ethel. *The Story of Coal and Iron in Alabama*. Cambridge, U.S.A.: The University Press, 1910.

Ashe, Samuel A.; Weeks, Stephen B.; and Van Noppen, Charles L. *Biographical History of North Carolina*. Greensboro, N.C.: Edwards and Broughton, 1907.

Beirne, Francis. *The Amiable Baltimoreans*. New York: E. P. Dutton and Co., Inc., 1951.

Betts, Edward Chambers. *Early History of Huntsville, 1804–1870*. Montgomery: The Brown Printing Company, 1916.

Blue, Matthew Powers. *A Brief History of Montgomery*. Montgomery: originally published in Beale and Phelan's City Directory, 1878, copied in Birmingham Library Project 3529, W.P.A., under sponsorship of the Birmingham Library Board, 1937.

Brewer, Willis. *Alabama, Her History, Resources and Public Men*. Tuscaloosa: Willo Publishing Company, 1964 reprint.

Brooks, Van Wyck. *The World of Washington Irving.* New York: H. Wolff Book Mfg. Company, 1944.

Bruce, Philip Alexander. *History of the University of Virginia, 1819–1919.* 5 vols. New York: The MacMillan Company, 1920.

Burt, Nathaniel. *The Perennial Philadelphians, The Anatomy of an American Aristocracy.* Boston and Toronto: Little, Brown and Company, 1963.

Cain, Stith Malone. *History of Our Malone Family of Virginia, Alabama, and Tennessee.* White Water, Wisc.: privately printed, 1970.

Cathcart, William. *The Baptist Encyclopedia.* Philadelphia: Louis H. Everts, 1881.

Christian, William Asbury. *Lynchburg and Its People.* Lynchburg, Va.: J. P. Bell and Company, 1900.

———. *Richmond, Her Past and Present.* Richmond, Va.: L. H. Jenkins, 1912.

Claiborne, John Herbert. *Seventy-five Years in Old Virginia.* New York and Washington: Neale Publishing Company, 1904.

Clay-Clopton, Virginia. *A Belle of the Fifties.* Edited by Ada Sterling. New York: Da Capo Press, Inc., 1905.

Congressional Records. Periodical Room, Birmingham Public Library, Birmingham, Ala.

Coyner, M. Boyd, Jr. "John Hartwell Cocke, of Bremo." Unpublished doctoral dissertation, University of Virginia, 1961.

Davidson, Donald. *The Tennessee, the Old River, Frontier to Secession.* New York: Rinehart and Co., Inc., 1946.

Dictionary of American Biography. 21 vols. New York: Charles Scribner's Sons, 1928–1936.

Dictionary of National Biography. Edited by Leslie Stephen and Sidney Lee. 21 vols. London: Oxford University Press, 1937–38 edition.

Dodd, Donald B. and Dodd, Wynelle S. *Winston, an Antebellum and Civil War History.* vol. IV of *Annals of Northwest Alabama,* edited by Carl Elliott.

Douglass, Hiram Kennedy. *My Southern Families.* Gillingham, Dorset: Blackmore Press, 1967.

———. Taped interview by Rutland Cunningham and William L. McDonald. University of North Alabama Library, Florence, Alabama.

Downs, Robert B. *Molders of the Modern Mind, 111 Books that Shaped Western Civilization.* New York: Barnes and Noble, Inc., 1961.

Edwards, Mrs. Thomas. Limestone County Historical Society. Manuscripts.

Florange, J. *Le Conventionnel Hentz Depute De La Moselle.* France: 1911. Pamphlet sent to the author by Hal Hentz, grandson of Dr. Nicholas Hentz, Quincy, Florida.

Frazier, Octavia Fletcher. *Dr. Richard Matthew Fletcher, A Sketch of His Life and Works.* Tuscaloosa: 1964.

Freeman, Douglas Southall. *Lee's Lieutenants.* 3 vols. New York: Scribner and Company, 1942.

Fulton, Mary Anne. Alderman Library, University of Virginia. Letter, dated May 19, 1971.

Gabriel, Ralph Henry, editor. *The Pageant of America.* 15 vols. New Haven: Yale University Press, 1929.

Gamble, Robert. A compilation of Alabama and Virginia homes. Unpublished manuscripts. Copy in author's possession.

Garnett, James Mercer and Page, Rosewell. *The University of Virginia, Its History, Influence, Equipment, and Characteristics, with Biographical Sketches and Portraits.* New York: Lewis Publishing Company, 1904.

Garrett, Mr. and Mrs. Edmund, IV. Interview. June, 1967.

Garrett, Jill Knight. *A History of Florence, Alabama.* (With 1850 census of Lauderdale County). Columbia, Tennessee: 1968.

Garrett, William. *Reminiscences of Public Men in Alabama for Thirty Years.* Atlanta, Georgia: Plantation Publishing Company's Press, 1872.

Graves, John Temple, editor. *The Book of Alabama and the South.* Birmingham: Protective Life Insurance Company, 1933.

Griffin, Richard W. *Athens Academy and College.* Alexander City: Outlook Publishing, 1958.

Higgins, Elizabeth Hobbs. Interviews.

Hill, Henry Willis. Grandson of Major John Woodroof. Letter, dated May 18, 1965.

Hine Family Papers. In possession of Miss Henrietta Hine, Athens, Ala.

Hobbs Family Papers. In possession of Maclin Frierson, Donelson and Ed Horton, and the estate of Mrs. Elizabeth Hobbs Higgins.

Hornaday, John Randolph. *The Book of Birmingham.* New York: Dodd Mead and Company, 1921.

Hornblow, Arthur. *A History of the Theatre in America.* Philadelphia and London: J. B. Lippincott, 1919.

Howard, J T. and Bellows, George. *A Short History of Music in America.* New York: Crowell, 1957.

Hyde, Lemuel. *"Over Sixty," Old Settlers Around Elkmont.* Typewritten copy in the Athens Public Library, Athens, Ala.

Jefferson, Mary Armstrong. *Old Homes and Buildings of Amelia County.* Amelia, Va.: Amelia County Historical Society, 1964.

Jenkins, William H. and Knox, John. *The Story of Decatur, Alabama.* Decatur, Ala.: Decatur Printing Co., Inc., 1970.

Johnson, Gerald W. *Randolph of Roanoke.* New York: Minton, Balch and Company, 1929.

Jones, Pat. *The Story of Mooresville.* Reprinted from the *Huntsville Times* in Decatur: North Alabama Historical Association, 1968.

———. Series of articles on area homes appearing in the *Huntsville Times,* May–July, 1935.

Jones, Pauline and Gandrud, Elizabeth. Notes on the 1850 census, Limestone and Madison counties.

Kane, Harnett T. *Natchez on the Mississippi.* New York: Bonanza Books, 1947.

Kern, Alfred A. *Court Street Methodist Church.* Richmond, Va.: The Dietz Press, Inc., 1951.

Lazenby, Marion Elias. *History of Methodism in Alabama and West Florida.* Methodist Publishing House, 1960.

Leftwich, Nina. *Two Hundred Years at Muscle Shoals.* Birmingham, Ala.: Multigraphic Advertising Company, 1935.

Limestone County Records. Limestone County Courthouse, Athens, Ala.

Linscott, Robert N. *State of Mind, A Boston Reader.* Clinton, Mass.: The Colonial Press, Inc., 1948.

Maag, Howard T. Deputy Librarian, Historical Society of the Eastern Pennsylvania Conference of the United Methodist Church. Letter, dated March 25, 1971.

McClellan, Capt. R. A. "Early History of Limestone County," *Athens Post,* 1881. Reprinted by his grandson, Robert Henry Walker, in *Legendary Limestone.* Athens, Ala.: 1966.

McGregor, A. A. *History of La Grange College.* No place or publisher, 1904.

McKenzie, Robert L. "Horace Ware: Alabama Iron Pioneer." *The Alabama Review,* XXVI (July, 1973).

Madison County Records. Madison County Courthouse. Huntsville, Ala.

Malone, Henry Booth. Diaries. Athens Public Library, Athens, Ala.

Malone, Thomas Stith. "Scraps," series of articles appearing in the *Athens Post* in June, 1867.

Mason, Mary. Scrapbooks. A compilation of Limestone County history. 9 vols. Houston Memorial Library, Athens, Ala.

———. "The Octagon House," *Limestone Democrat,* July 7, 1953.

Memorial Record of Alabama. 2 vols. Madison, Wisc.: 1893.

Moore, Mary Norman. *History of Athens College.* Athens: 1916.

Moore, Albert Burton. *History of Alabama and Her People.* 3 vols. Chicago and New York: The American Historical Society, Inc., 1927.

National League of Penwomen, Alabama Branch. *Historic Homes of Alabama and Their Traditions.* Birmingham, Ala.: Birmingham Publishing Company, 1935.

Owen, Thomas McAdory. *History of Alabama and Dictionary of Alabama Biography.* 4 vols. Chicago: S. J. Clarke Publishing Company, 1921.

Owens, Hamilton. *Baltimore on the Chesapeake.* Garden City, New York: Doubleday, Doran and Co., Inc., 1941.

Parker, Price. *From Alabama to Appomattox.* Athens: Athens News Courier, Inc. No date.

Pepper, Mrs. Mary White. Telephone conversation. Information about the White family. February 28, 1972.

Pickett, Albert James. *History of Alabama.* Sheffield, Ala.: Robert C. Randolph, 1896. Republished in Birmingham by Birmingham Book and Magazine Company, 1962.

Pollard, Edward A. *The Virginia Tourist.* Philadelphia: J. B. Lippincott Co., 1870.

Posey, Walter B. "La Grange, Alabama's Earliest College," *Birmingham Southern College Bulletin,* XXVI, #6 (1933).

Ravenal, Mrs. St. Julien. *Charleston, the Place and the People.* New York: MacMillan Company, 1927.

Robotti, Frances Diane. *Key to New York, Empire City.* Fountainhead Publishers, 1964.

Royall, Anne Newport. *Letters from Alabama, 1817–1822.* Edited by Lucille Griffith. University, Ala.: The University of Alabama Press, 1969.

Saunders, James Edmonds. *Early Settlers of Alabama.* With Notes and Genealogies by his Granddaughter, Elizabeth Saunders Blair Stubbins. New Orleans, La.: L. Graham and Son., Ltd.,Printers, 1899.

Schonberg, Harold C. *The Great Pianists from Mozart to the Present.* New York: Simon and Schuster, 1963.

Scott, James G. and Wyatt, Edward A., IV. *Petersburg's Story—A History.* Petersburg, Va.: Titmus Optical Co., 1960.

Sherwood, Waring. *The Story of Sarah (Sally) Moore.* Memphis: privately printed by James Jackson, 1970.

Smith, Caroline Cortner. Birmingham, Ala. Information about the Ashford family.

Smith, Winston. *Days of Exile, the Story of the Vine and Olive Colony in Alabama.* Tuscaloosa, Ala.: W. E. Drake and Son, 1967.

Snedecor's *Directory of Greene County.* Directory of 1855–56. Edited 1957 by Franklin Shackelford Moseley, Eutaw, Ala. Off-set Press Process by the *Greene County Democrat,* 1957.

Staudenraus, P. J. *The African Colonization Movement, 1816–1865.* New York: Columbia University Press, Inc., 1961.

Sulzby, James F., Jr. *Historic Alabama Hotels and Resorts.* University, Ala.: The University of Alabama Press, 1960.

Sweet, William Warren. *Religion on the American Frontier, 1783–1840.* Chicago, Ill.: University of Chicago Press, 1946.

Tanner, John T. "Athens Fifty Years Ago." A series of articles appearing in the *Athens Post,* June–July, 1876.

Tennessee Valley Historical Society. *Historic Muscle Shoals, a Guide to Places of Historical Interest in Colbert and Lauderdale Counties, Alabama.* No place or publisher, 1962.

Thomas, Lately. *Delmonico's, A Century of Splendor.* Boston: Houghton Mifflin Company, 1967.

Tyler, Lyon Gardiner, editor. *Encyclopedia of Virginia Biography.* 5 vols. New York: Lewis Historical Publishing Company, 1915.

Tyler, Lyon Gardiner, Swem, E. G., and others. *William and Mary College Quarterly,* Williamsburg, 1892. Series I, 27; Series II, 23; Series III, 31.

Van Zandt, Roland. *Catskill Mountain House.* New Brunswick, N. J.: Rutgers University Press, 1966.

Virginia Historical Magazine; Vol. IV, (1896).

Virginal Historical Register; Vol. II; III; (July, 1849).

Walker, Robert Henry, Jr. *History of Limestone County.* 1973.

Warner, Ezra J. *Generals in Gray.* New Orleans, La.: State University Press, 1959.

Watson, Mrs. E. A. Lynchburg, Va. Letter concerning Benagh and Rucker families, dated June 10, 1971.

West Tennessee Historical Papers. Memphis: Tennessee Historical Society, 1947.

Who Was Who in America. Chicago: A. N. Marquis Company, Revised Edition, 1967.

Wiley, Bell Irvin and Milhollen, Hirst D. *Embattled Confederates—an Illustrated History of Southerners at War.* New York, Evanston, and London: Harper & Row, 1964.

Williams, Benjamin B. "Alabama Civil War Poets." *The Alabama Review,* XV, (October, 1962).

Williams, Frederick D. *The Wild Life of the Army, Civil War Letters of James A. Garfield.* Ann Arbor: Michigan State University Press, 1964.

Wilson, Henry. *Rise and Fall of the Slave Power in America.* 3 vols. Cambridge: Houghton Mifflin Company, 1874.

Woods, Edgar. *Albermarle County in Virginia.* Bridgewater, Va.: C. J. Carrier Company, 1964.

Woodward, Joseph H. *Alabama Blast Furnaces.* Woodward, Ala.: Woodward Iron Company, 1940 .

ACKNOWLEDGMENTS

The editor wishes to express a general thanks to all those who have been of assistance in this research, and specifically to a few, without whom the work would have been impossible.

The descendants of Thomas Hobbs, particularly the late Mrs. John D. Higgins of Birmingham, for allowing me the privilege of editing and annotating the diaries deserve a special note of appreciation. They have shared family records, newspaper clippings, and other related materials.

Sincere gratitude is extended to Athens College and President Sidney Sandridge for their sponsorship.

Robert Gamble, a native Alabamian, now historian on the staff of the Advisory Council on Historic Preservation in Washington, D.C., has been of invaluable assistance with his notes and comments. He is now preparing a catalog of Historic American Buildings Survey Records in the Library of Congress.

Librarians in Alabama and Virginia patiently and diligently assisted me. Among the most helpful were Mrs. Phillip Davis, Miss Mary Bess Kirksey, Mrs. Bessie Russell, Mrs. Nancy Malone Johnson, Mrs. Wilma Wilson, and Mr. James Ballew.

Mrs. Alvin Watson of Lynchburg, Virginia, answered my inquiries relating to the history of that city during the period covered by the diaries, and Mr. Willis Hill of Mooresville furnished information concerning that portion of Limestone County. Mr. Luke Pryor, IV, took me to the site of the old Maclin-Hobbs cemetery, and Robert Henry Walker showed me the old Athens cemetery and the site of the Nicholas Davis home, Walnut Grove. In his recently published book, *History of Limestone County,* Mr. Walker was able to draw much information from these diaries. Miss Elizabeth Brown of Birmingham translated the Spanish entries in the diaries.

Others to whom I am grateful are Mrs. Thomas Edwards, President of the Limestone County Historical Society, the late Harvey Gilbert of Athens, and Miss Henrietta Hine—whose home is truly a museum of papers and portraits that bear on early Limestone history. Mrs. Edwards, Mrs. Bert Hayes, and Mrs. Billy Malone are worthy of distinct recognition for the long hours they spent assisting in the preparation of the manuscript. Finally, special acknowledgment belongs to my family, who have long forgotten the pleasures derived from a clean house and decent meals!

FAYE ACTON AXFORD

INDEX